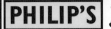

Ipsw

Felixstowe

www.philips-maps.co.uk

First published 2008 by

Philip's, a division of
Octopus Publishing Group Ltd
www.octopusbooks.co.uk
2–4 Heron Quays
London E14 4JP
An Hachette Livre UK Company

First edition 2008
First impression 2008

ISBN 978-0-540-09263-5

To the best of the Publishers' knowledge, the information in this atlas was correct at the time of going to press. No responsibility can be accepted for any errors or their consequences.

The representation in this atlas of a road, track or path is no evidence of the existence of a right of way.

Ordnance Survey and the OS symbol are registered trademarks of Ordnance Survey, the national mapping agency of Great Britain

Printed and bound in China by Toppan

Contents

II **Key to map symbols**

III **Key to map pages**

IV **Route planning**

2 **Street maps** at 2¼ inches to 1 mile

6 **Street maps** at 4½ inches to 1 mile

66 **Street maps of central Ipswich** at 7 inches to 1 mile

68 **Index**

Key to map symbols

Roads

(12)	**Motorway** with junction number
A42	**Primary route** – dual, single carriageway
A42	**A road** – dual, single carriageway
B1289	**B road** – dual, single carriageway
	Through-route – dual, single carriageway
	Minor road – dual, single carriageway
	Rural track, private road or narrow road in urban area
	Path, bridleway, byway open to all traffic, road used as a public path
	Road under construction
	Pedestrianised area
	Gate or obstruction to traffic restrictions may not apply at all times or to all vehicles
P P&R	**Parking, Park and Ride**

Railways

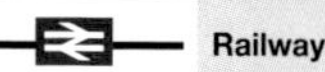

	Railway
	Miniature railway
	Metro station, private railway station

Emergency services

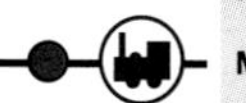

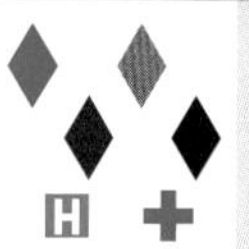

◆ ◆	**Ambulance station, coastguard station**
◆ ◆	**Fire station, police station**
H ✚	**Hospital, Accident and Emergency entrance to hospital**

General features

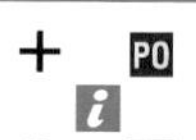

✚ PO	**Place of worship, Post Office**
i	**Information centre** (open all year)
⬛ 🛒	**Bus or coach station, shopping centre**
	Important buildings, schools, colleges, universities and hospitals
	Woods, built-up area
Tumulus FORT	**Non-Roman antiquity, Roman antiquity**

Leisure facilities

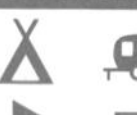

△	**Camping site, caravan site**
▶ ✕	**Golf course, picnic site**

Boundaries

• • • • • • • •	**Postcode boundaries**
— — • — —	**County and unitary authority boundaries**

Water features

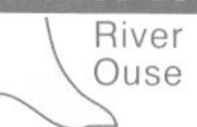

River Ouse	**Tidal water, water name**
	Non-tidal water – lake, river, canal or stream
	Lock, weir

Enlarged mapping only

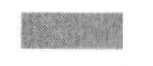

	Railway or bus station building
	Place of interest, parkland

Scales

Green pages: 2¼ inches to 1 mile 1:28 160

0   ¼ mile   ½ mile   ¾ mile   1 mile
0   250m   500m   750m   1 km

Blue pages: 4½ inches to 1 mile 1:14 080

0   220 yds   ¼ mile   660 yds   ½ mile
0   125m   250m   375m   ½ km

Red pages: 7 inches to 1 mile 1:9051

0   110 yds   220 yds   330 yds   ¼ mile
0   125m   250m   375m   ½km

 44 | **Adjoining page indicators** The colour of the arrow and the band indicates the scale of the adjoining page (see above)

Abbreviations

Acad	**Academy**	Mkt	**Market**
Allot Gdns	**Allotments**	Meml	**Memorial**
Cemy	**Cemetery**	Mon	**Monument**
C Ctr	**Civic Centre**	Mus	**Museum**
CH	**Club House**	Obsy	**Observatory**
Coll	**College**	Pal	**Royal Palace**
Crem	**Crematorium**	PH	**Public House**
Ent	**Enterprise**	Recn Gd	**Recreation Ground**
Ex H	**Exhibition Hall**	Resr	**Reservoir**
Ind Est	**Industrial Estate**	Ret Pk	**Retail Park**
IRB Sta	**Inshore Rescue Boat Station**	Sch	**School**
		Sh Ctr	**Shopping Centre**
Inst	**Institute**	TH	**Town Hall/House**
Ct	**Law Court**	Trad Est	**Trading Estate**
L Ctr	**Leisure Centre**	Univ	**University**
LC	**Level Crossing**	Wks	**Works**
Liby	**Library**	YH	**Youth Hostel**

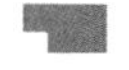

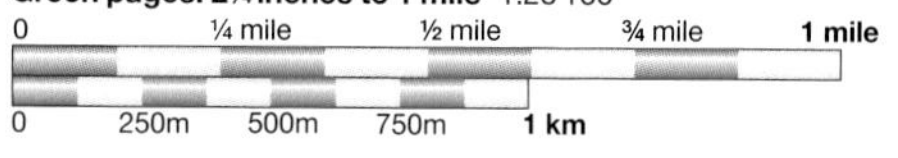

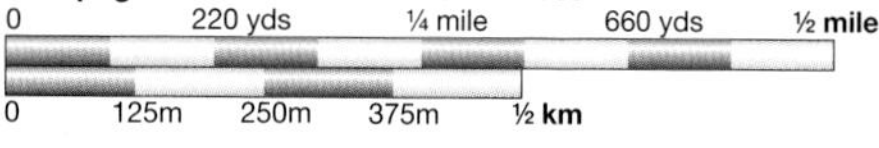

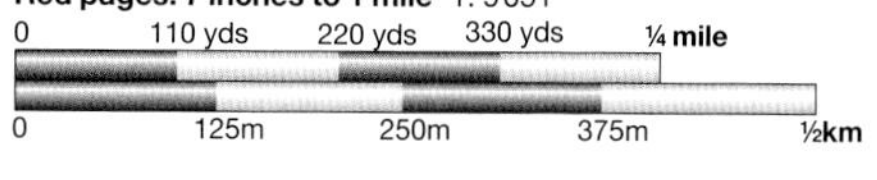

Key to map pages

Atlas pages at
7 inches to 1 mile
66

Atlas pages at
4½ inches to 1 mile
42

Atlas pages at
2¼ inches to 1 mile
5

Scale
0 1 2 3 4 5 6 km
0 1 2 3 miles

Wickham Market 53

Woodbridge
Melton 12 13
Maidensgrave 14 15

Martlesham
Martlesham Heath 4

Kirton
Trimley 5
St Martin

Trimley St Mary
58 59 Walton
Old Felixstowe 60 61
Felixstowe 63 64
62
The Port of Felixstowe 65

Harwich

Playford 24 25
Kesgrave 32 33
40 41
A1156 49
48 Nacton

Rushmere 22 23
Street
California 30 31
Warren 38 39
Heath A1156 37
46 47

Westerfield 20 21
Castle Hill
Ipswich 66
Stoke 67
Gainsborough 36
44 Wherstead
45

Henley 3
Claydon 16 17
Akenham
Whitton 18 19
Bramford
Westbourne 26 27
Sproughton 34 35
Chantry
42 43 Belstead

28 29

2

Braintham 55
Mistley 56 57
Lawford Manningtree

Capel St Mary 52

East Bergholt 54

Needham Market 10 11

Stowmarket 6 7
Combs Ford 8 9

Hadleigh 51
50

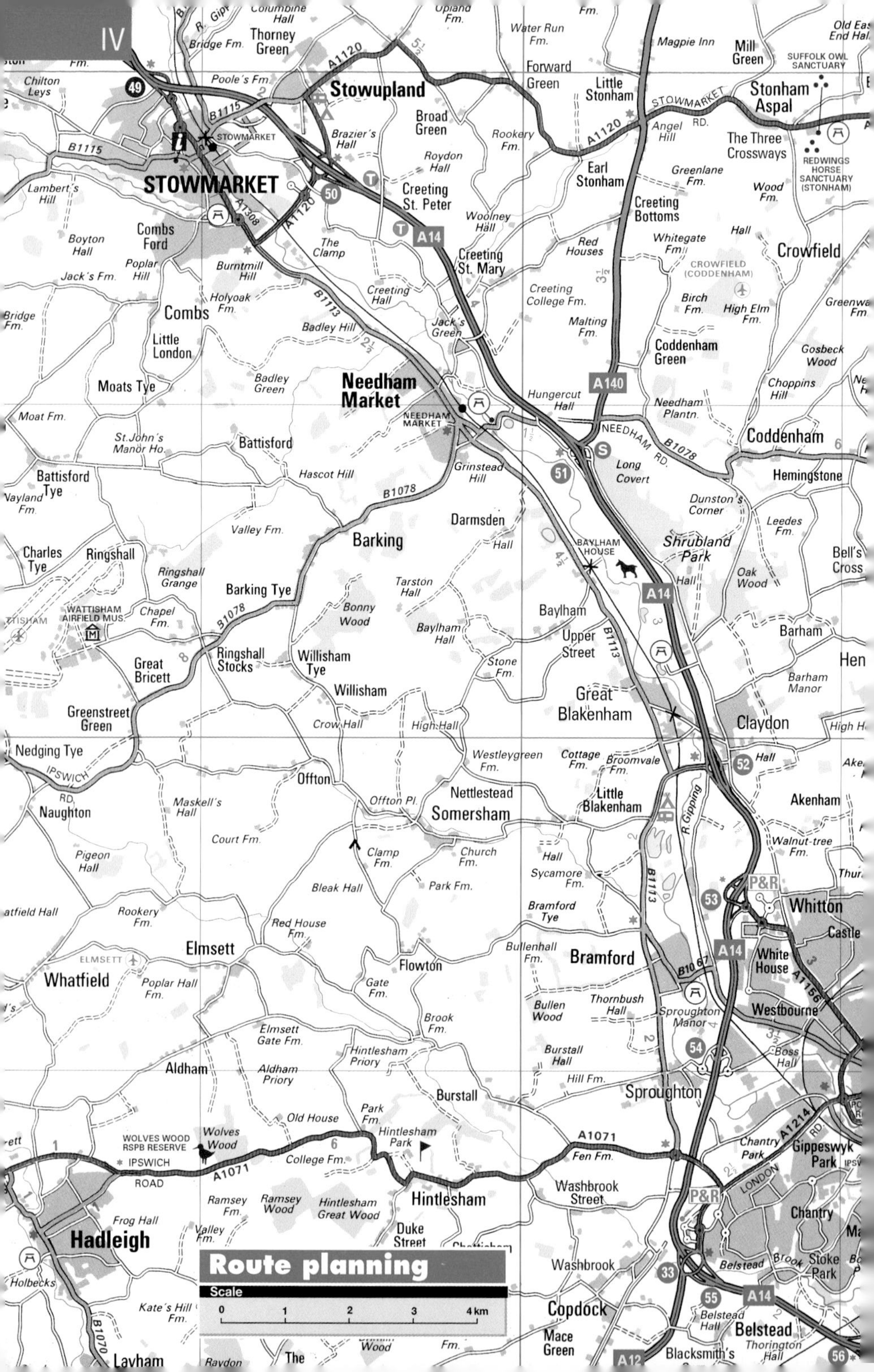
IV
Route planning
Scale
0
1
2
3
4 km
Columbine Hall
Thorney Green
Bridge Fm.
Upland Fm.
Water Run Fm.
Magpie Inn
Mill Green
Old East End Hall
SUFFOLK OWL SANCTUARY
Chilton Leys
Poole's Fm.
Stowupland
Forward Green
Little Stonham
Stonham Aspal
STOWMARKET
B1115
Broad Green
Brazier's Hall
Rookery Fm.
Angel Hill
The Three Crossways
REDWINGS HORSE SANCTUARY (STONHAM)
Roydon Hall
Earl Stonham
Greenlane Fm.
Lambert's Hill
Creeting St. Peter
Wood Fm.
Combs Ford
A1308
A1120
Woolney Hall
Creeting Bottoms
Hall
Crowfield
Boyton Hall
The Clamp
A14
Creeting St. Mary
Red Houses
Whitegate Fm.
CROWFIELD (CODDENHAM)
Jack's Fm.
Poplar Hill
Burntmill Hill
Creeting Hall
Creeting College Fm.
Birch Fm.
High Elm Fm.
Greenway Fm.
Bridge Fm.
Holyoak Fm.
Combs
B1113
Badley Hill
Jack's Green
Malting Fm.
Coddenham Green
Gosbeck Wood
Little London
Moats Tye
Badley Green
Needham Market
A140
Choppins Hill
Hungercut Hall
Needham Plantn.
Moat Fm.
NEEDHAM MARKET
NEEDHAM RD.
B1078
Coddenham
St.John's Manor Ho.
Battisford
Battisford Tye
Hascot Hill
Grinstead Hill
Long Covert
Hemingstone
Vayland Fm.
Dunston's Corner
Darmsden
Leedes Fm.
Valley Fm.
Barking
Hall
BAYLHAM HOUSE
Shrubland Park
Charles Tye
Ringshall
Bell's Cross
Ringshall Grange
Tarston Hall
Oak Wood
Barking Tye
Hall
WATTISHAM AIRFIELD MUS.
Chapel Fm.
Bonny Wood
Baylham
Baylham Hall
Upper Street
Barham
Great Bricett
Ringshall Stocks
Willisham Tye
Stone Fm.
Hen
Barham Manor
Willisham
Great Blakenham
Greenstreet Green
Crow Hall
High Hall
Claydon
High H
Nedging Tye
IPSWICH RD.
Westleygreen Fm.
Cottage Fm.
Broomvale Fm.
Hall
Offton
Nettlestead
Little Blakenham
Akenham
Naughton
Maskell's Hall
Offton Pl.
Somersham
R. Gipping
Court Fm.
Walnut-tree Fm.
Pigeon Hall
Clamp Fm.
Church Fm.
Hall
Sycamore Fm.
P&R
Bleak Hall
Park Fm.
Whitton
atfield Hall
Rookery Fm.
Red House Fm.
Bramford Tye
Castle
Elmsett
ELMSETT
Bullenhall Fm.
Bramford
White House
Whatfield
Poplar Hall Fm.
Flowton
Gate Fm.
Bullen Wood
Thornbush Hall
Sproughton Manor
Westbourne
A1156
Brook Fm.
Elmsett Gate Fm.
Hintlesham Priory
Burstall Hall
Boss Hall
Aldham
Aldham Priory
Burstall
Hill Fm.
Sproughton
Old House
Park Fm.
A1071
A1214
Wolves Wood
WOLVES WOOD RSPB RESERVE
Hintlesham Park
Chantry Park
Gippeswyk Park
IPSWICH ROAD
College Fm.
Fen Fm.
LONDON RD.
Washbrook Street
Ramsey Fm.
Ramsey Wood
Hintlesham Great Wood
Hintlesham
Chantry
Frog Hall
Valley Fm.
Duke Street
Hadleigh
Washbrook
Belstead
Brook
Stoke Park
Holbecks
A12
Kate's Hill Fm.
Copdock
Belstead Hall
Belstead
B1070
Mace Green
Thorington Hall
Layham
Raydon
The
Wood
Fm.
Blacksmith's

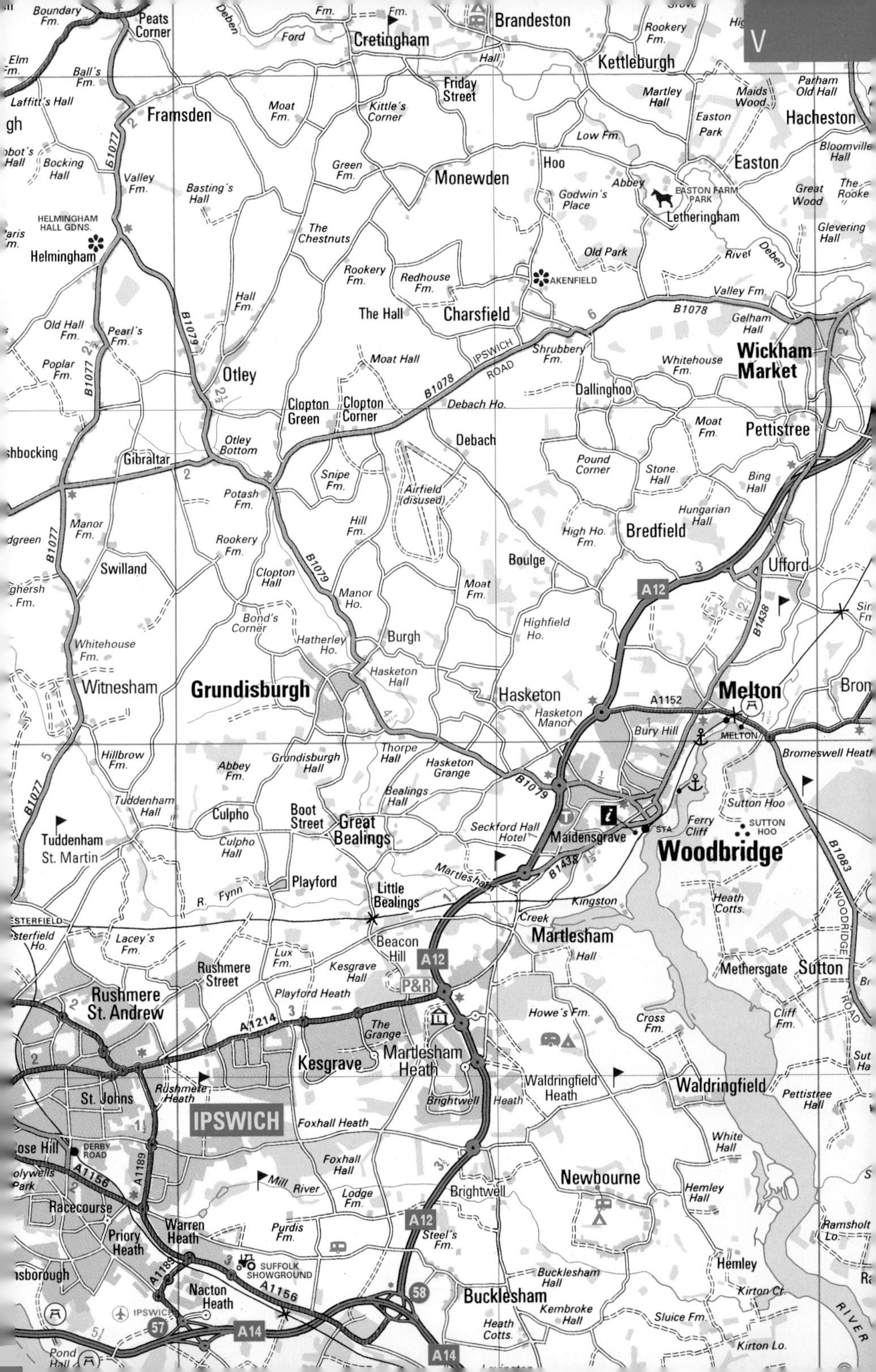
V
Boundary Fm.
Peats Corner
Deben
Ford
Cretingham
Brandeston
Rookery Fm.
Kettleburgh
Elm Fm.
Ball's Fm.
Hall
Laffitt's Hall
Framsden
Moat Fm.
Kittle's Corner
Friday Street
Martley Hall
Maids Wood
Parham Old Hall
Hacheston
Easton Park
Low Fm.
Easton
Bloomville Hall
Bocking Hall
Valley Fm.
B1077
Basting's Hall
Green Fm.
Monewden
Hoo
Abbey
EASTON FARM PARK
Great Wood
The Rooke
Godwin's Place
Letheringham
HELMINGHAM HALL GDNS.
Helmingham
The Chestnuts
Old Park
River Deben
Glevering Hall
Rookery Fm.
Redhouse Fm.
AKENFIELD
Hall Fm.
Valley Fm.
B1078
Old Hall Fm.
Pearl's Fm.
The Hall
Charsfield
Gelham Hall
B1079
IPSWICH ROAD
Shrubbery Fm.
Poplar Fm.
Moat Hall
Whitehouse Fm.
Wickham Market
Otley
Clopton Green
Clopton Corner
Debach Ho.
Dallinghoo
Moat Fm.
Pettistree
Otley Bottom
Debach
Gibraltar
Pound Corner
Stone Hall
Bing Hall
Potash Fm.
Snipe Fm.
Airfield (disused)
Hungarian Hall
Manor Fm.
Hill Fm.
High Ho. Fm.
Bredfield
Rookery Fm.
Boulge
Ufford
Swilland
Clopton Hall
A12
Moat Fm.
Manor Ho.
B1438
Bond's Corner
Highfield Ho.
Whitehouse Fm.
Hatherley Ho.
Burgh
Hasketon Hall
Witnesham
Grundisburgh
Hasketon
Melton
A1152
Hasketon Manor
Bury Hill
MELTON
Hillbrow Fm.
Abbey Fm.
Grundisburgh Hall
Thorpe Hall
Hasketon Grange
Bromeswell Heath
Tuddenham Hall
Bealings Hall
Sutton Hoo
Culpho
Boot Street
Great Bealings
Seckford Hall Hotel
Maidensgrave
STA.
Ferry Cliff
SUTTON HOO
Tuddenham St. Martin
Culpho Hall
Woodbridge
B1083
Playford
Martlesham
Little Bealings
R. Fynn
Kingston
Heath Cotts.
Creek
Lacey's Fm.
Beacon Hill
Martlesham
WOODBRIDGE ROAD
Lux Fm.
Rushmere Street
Kesgrave Hall
Hall
Methersgate
Sutton
P&R
Rushmere St. Andrew
Playford Heath
A1214
The Grange
Howe's Fm.
Cross Fm.
Cliff Fm.
Kesgrave
Martlesham Heath
Waldringfield Heath
Waldringfield
Pettistree Hall
St. Johns
Rushmere Heath
Brightwell
Heath
IPSWICH
Foxhall Heath
White Hall
Rose Hill
DERBY ROAD
Foxhall Hall
Newbourne
Holywells Park
A1156
A1189
Mill River
Lodge Fm.
Brightwell
Hemley Hall
Racecourse
Purdis Fm.
Steel's Fm.
Ramsholt Lo.
Warren Heath
Priory Heath
SUFFOLK SHOWGROUND
Hemley
Bucklesham Hall
Nacton Heath
58
Bucklesham
Kirton Cr.
IPSWICH
57
A14
Kembroke Hall
Sluice Fm.
Heath Cotts.
RIVER
Pond Hall
Kirton Lo.

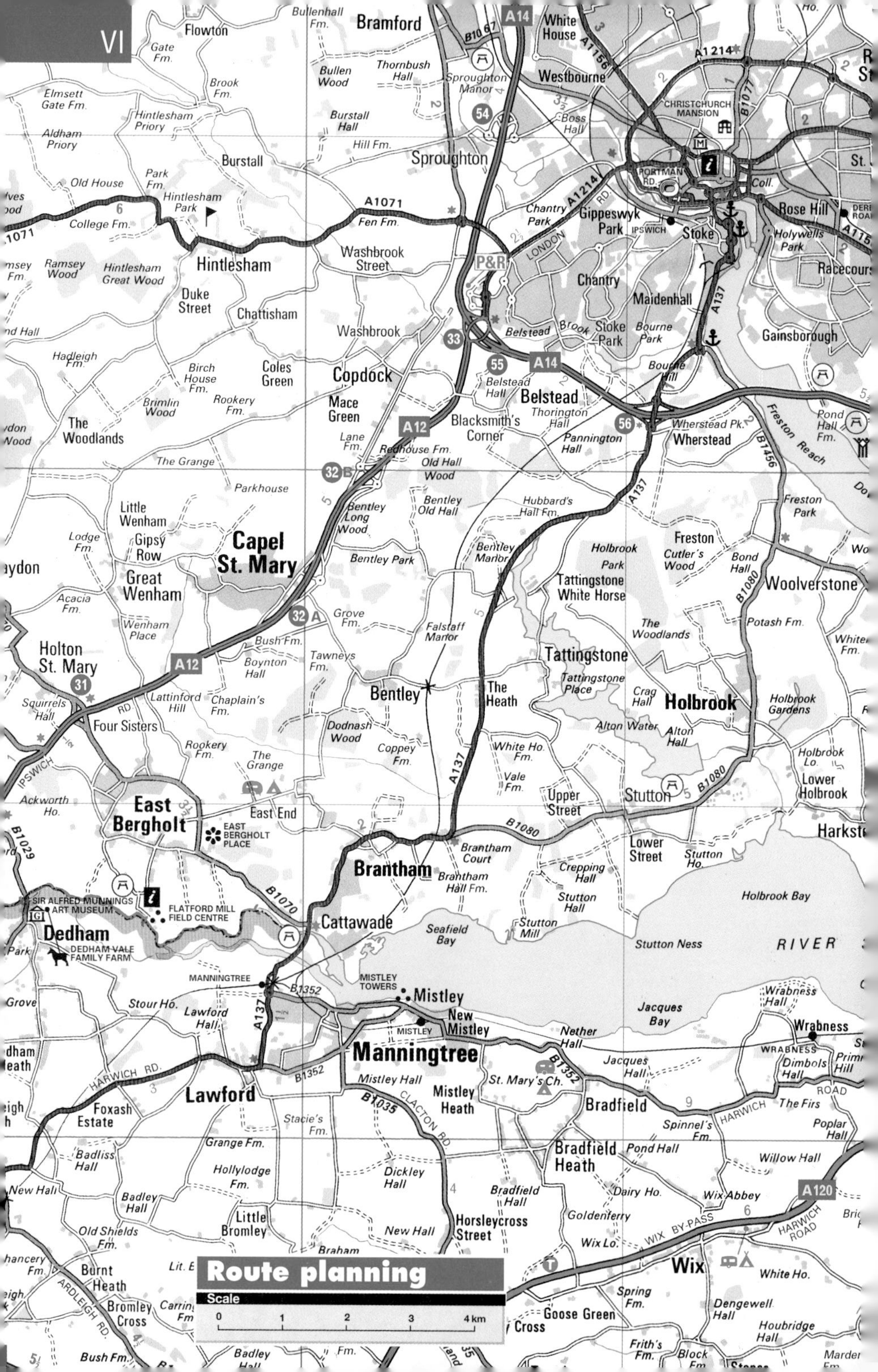
VI
Flowton
Bullenhall Fm.
Bramford
A14
White House
A1156
A1214
Gate Fm.
B10 67
Thornbush Hall
Bullen Wood
Sproughton Manor
Westbourne
B1077
Brook Fm.
Elmsett Gate Fm.
CHRISTCHURCH MANSION
Hintlesham Priory
Burstall Hall
54
Boss Hall
Aldham Priory
Hill Fm.
Sproughton
Burstall
St.
Park Fm.
PORTMAN RD.
Old House
Coll.
Hintlesham Park
A1071
Chantry Park
Gippeswyk Park
Rose Hill
College Fm.
Fen Fm.
IPSWICH
Stoke
Holywells Park
Ramsey Wood
Hintlesham Great Wood
Hintlesham
Washbrook Street
LONDON RD.
P&R
Racecourse
Duke Street
Chantry
Maidenhall
A137
Chattisham
Belstead
Brook
Stoke Park
Bourne Park
Gainsborough
Washbrook
33
Hadleigh Fm.
Birch House Fm.
Coles Green
Copdock
55
A14
Bourne Hill
Belstead Hall
Belstead
Brimlin Wood
Rookery Fm.
Mace Green
Thorington Hall
Pond Hall Fm.
The Woodlands
A12
Blacksmith's Corner
56
Wherstead Pk.
Wherstead
Freston Reach
Lane Fm.
Redhouse Fm.
Pannington Hall
B1456
The Grange
Old Hall Wood
32 B
Parkhouse
Bentley Old Hall
Hubbard's Hall Fm.
Freston Park
Little Wenham
Bentley Long Wood
Lodge Fm.
Gipsy Row
Capel St. Mary
Bentley Manor
Holbrook Park
Freston
Cutler's Wood
Bond Hall
Bentley Park
Great Wenham
Tattingstone White Horse
Woolverstone
B1080
Acacia Fm.
32 A
Grove Fm.
Potash Fm.
Wenham Place
Falstaff Manor
The Woodlands
Holton St. Mary
Bush Fm.
Tattingstone
Boynton Hall
Tawneys Fm.
31
The Heath
Tattingstone Place
Crag Hall
Holbrook
Squirrels Hall
Lattinford Hill
Chaplain's Fm.
Bentley
Holbrook Gardens
RD.
Four Sisters
Dodnash Wood
Alton Water
Alton Hall
Rookery Fm.
Coppey Fm.
White Ho. Fm.
Holbrook Lo.
IPSWICH
The Grange
Vale Fm.
Lower Holbrook
Ackworth Ho.
East Bergholt
East End
Upper Street
Stutton
East Bergholt Place
B1080
Harkstead
B1029
Brantham Court
Lower Street
Stutton Ho.
Brantham
Crepping Hall
Brantham Hall Fm.
Holbrook Bay
Sir Alfred Munnings Art Museum
Flatford Mill Field Centre
B1070
Stutton Hall
Dedham
Cattawade
Seafield Bay
Stutton Mill
Dedham Vale Family Farm
Stutton Ness
River
Manningtree
B1352
Mistley Towers
Mistley
Wrabness Hall
Stour Ho.
Jacques Bay
Lawford Hall
New Mistley
Wrabness
A137
Mistley
Nether Hall
Manningtree
Wrabness
Harwich Rd.
Jacques Hall
Dimbols Hall
B1352
Mistley Hall
St. Mary's Ch.
B1352
Lawford
Mistley Heath
Foxash Estate
B1035
Clacton Rd.
Bradfield
The Firs
Stacie's Fm.
Harwich Road
Spinnel's Fm.
Poplar Hall
Grange Fm.
Bradfield Heath
Pond Hall
Willow Hall
Badliss Hall
Hollylodge Fm.
Dickley Hall
New Hall
Bradfield Hall
Dairy Ho.
Wix Abbey
A120
Badley Hall
Little Bromley
Horsleycross Street
Goldenferry
Harwich Road
Old Shields Fm.
New Hall
Wix Lo.
Wix By-Pass
Braham
Wix
Burnt Heath
White Ho.
Ardleigh Rd.
Bromley Cross
Spring Fm.
Dengewell Hall
Goose Green
Houbridge Hall
Bush Fm.
Badley Hall
Frith's Fm.
Block Fm.
Route planning
Scale
0
1
2
3
4 km

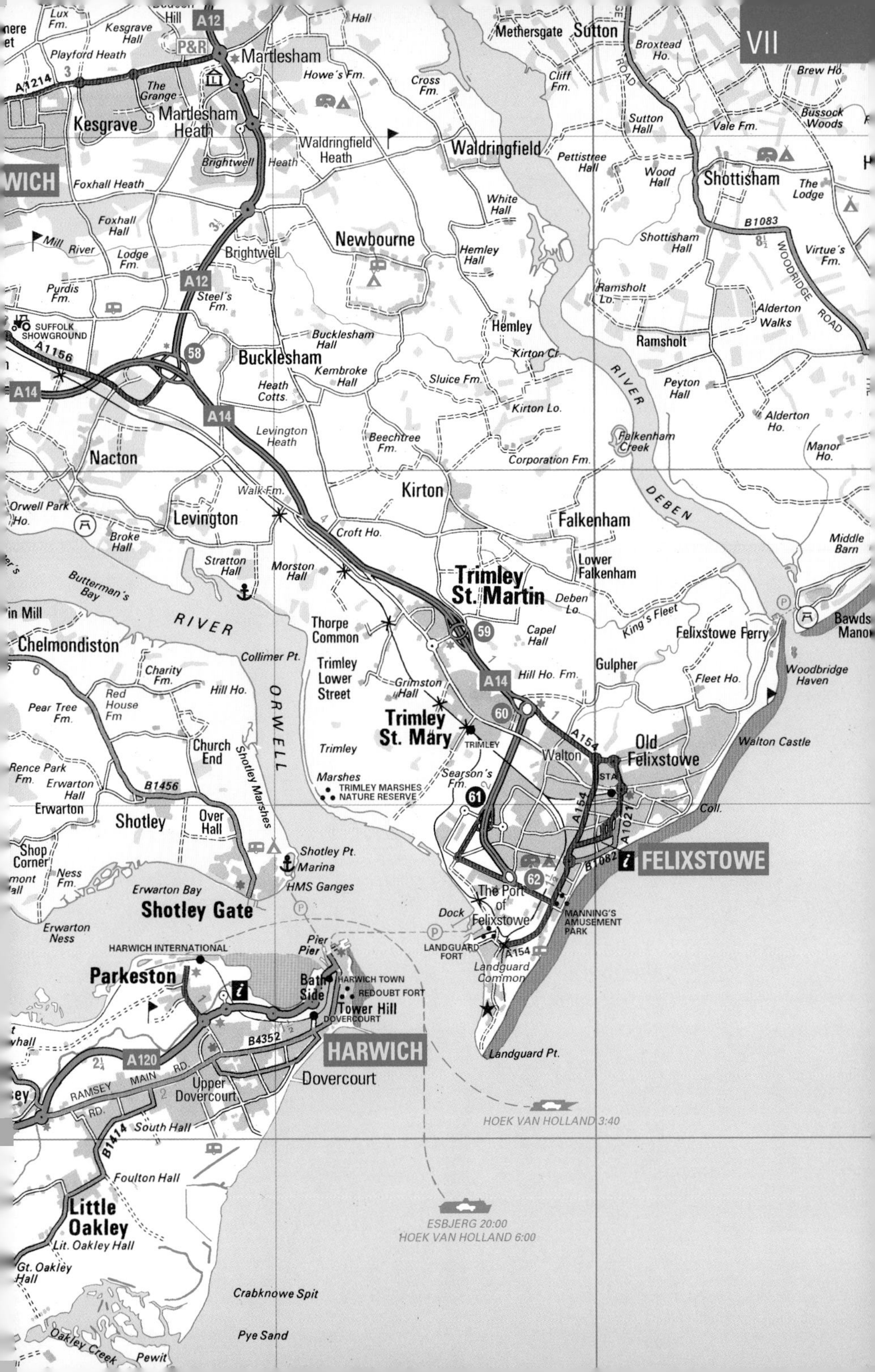
Lux Fm.
Kesgrave Hall
A12
P&R
Martlesham
Playford Heath
A1214
The Grange
Martlesham Heath
Kesgrave
Brightwell
Heath
Howe's Fm.
Hall
Methersgate
Sutton
Broxtead Ho.
Brew Ho.
Cross Fm.
Cliff Fm.
ROAD
Bussock Woods
Sutton Hall
Vale Fm.
Waldringfield Heath
Waldringfield
Pettistree Hall
Wood Hall
Shottisham
The Lodge
WICH
Foxhall Heath
Foxhall Hall
White Hall
B1083
Mill River
Lodge Fm.
Brightwell
Newbourne
Hemley Hall
Shottisham Hall
Virtue's Fm.
WOODBRIDGE ROAD
A12
Purdis Fm.
Steel's Fm.
Ramsholt Lo.
Alderton Walks
SUFFOLK SHOWGROUND
Bucklesham Hall
Hemley
Ramsholt
A1156
58
Bucklesham
Kirton Cr.
A14
Heath Cotts.
Kembroke Hall
Sluice Fm.
RIVER
Peyton Hall
A14
Kirton Lo.
Alderton Ho.
Levington Heath
Beechtree Fm.
Falkenham Creek
Nacton
Corporation Fm.
Manor Ho.
Kirton
Walk Fm.
DEBEN
Orwell Park Ho.
Levington
Falkenham
Croft Ho.
Middle Barn
Broke Hall
Stratton Hall
Morston Hall
Lower Falkenham
Trimley St. Martin
Butterman's Bay
Deben Lo.
King's Fleet
Bawdsey Manor
Mill
RIVER
Thorpe Common
59
Capel Hall
Felixstowe Ferry
Chelmondiston
Collimer Pt.
Woodbridge Haven
Charity Fm.
Trimley Lower Street
A14
Hill Ho. Fm.
Gulpher
Fleet Ho.
Red House Fm
Hill Ho.
ORWELL
Grimston Hall
Pear Tree Fm.
Trimley St. Mary
60
Church End
Trimley
TRIMLEY
A154
Old Felixstowe
Walton Castle
Walton
Shotley Marshes
Marshes
TRIMLEY MARSHES NATURE RESERVE
Searson's Fm.
Rence Park Fm.
Erwarton Hall
B1456
61
STA
Erwarton
A154
Coll.
Shotley
Over Hall
A1021
Shop Corner
Shotley Pt. Marina
B1082
FELIXSTOWE
Ness Fm.
HMS Ganges
62
Erwarton Bay
The Port of Felixstowe
Shotley Gate
Dock
MANNING'S AMUSEMENT PARK
Erwarton Ness
Pier
HARWICH INTERNATIONAL
LANDGUARD FORT
A154
Parkeston
Landguard Common
Bath Side
HARWICH TOWN
REDOUBT FORT
Tower Hill
DOVERCOURT
B4352
HARWICH
Landguard Pt.
A120
MAIN RD.
Upper Dovercourt
Dovercourt
RAMSEY
RD.
HOEK VAN HOLLAND 3:40
South Hall
B1414
Foulton Hall
Little Oakley
ESBJERG 20:00
HOEK VAN HOLLAND 6:00
Lit. Oakley Hall
Gt. Oakley Hall
Crabknowe Spit
Pye Sand
Oakley Creek
Pewit

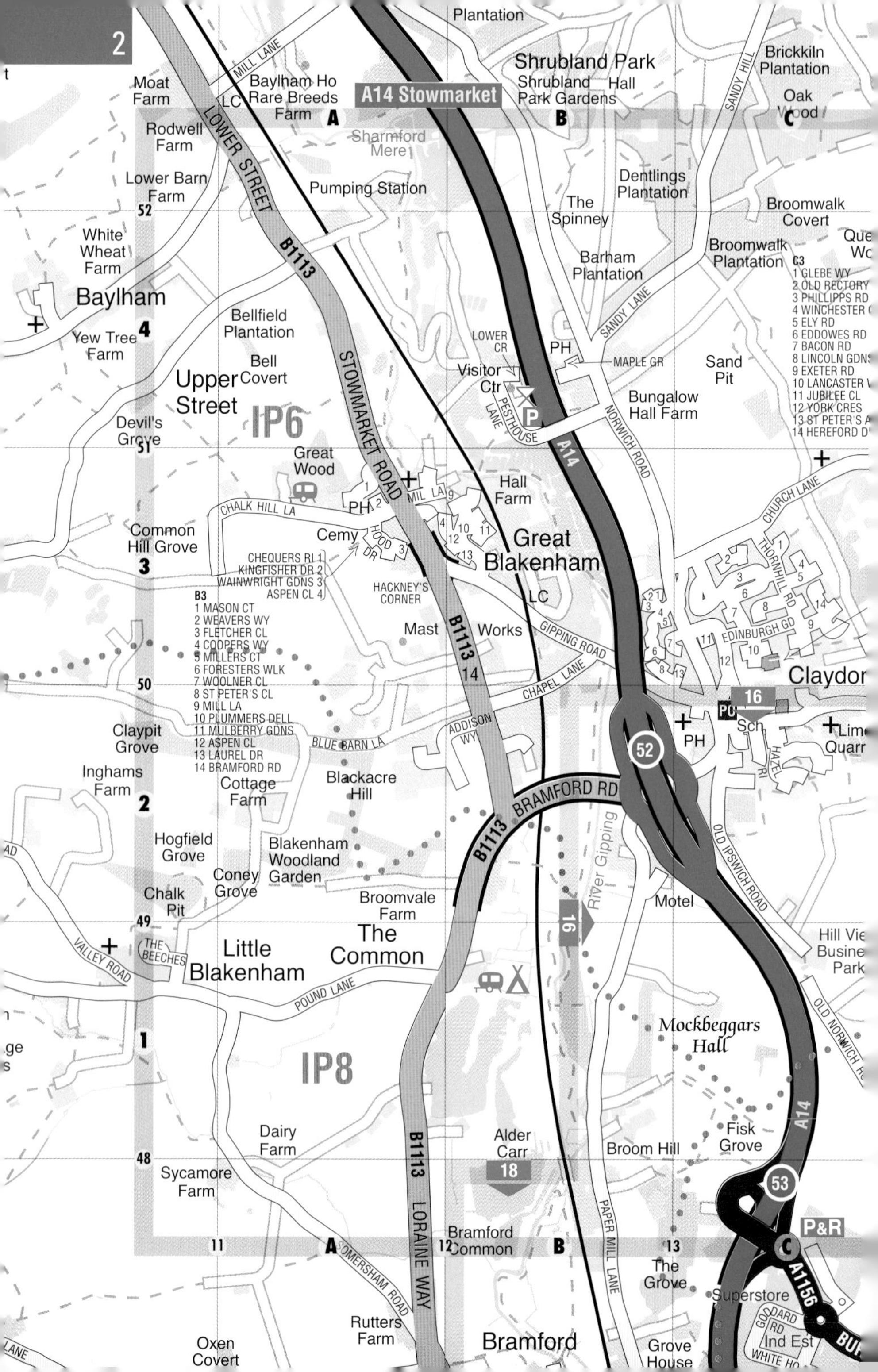

A14 Stowmarket
Plantation
Shrubland Park
Shrubland Hall
Shrubland Park Gardens
Brickkiln Plantation
Oak Wood
Moat Farm
Baylham Ho Rare Breeds Farm
LC
MILL LANE
LOWER STREET
Rodwell Farm
Sharmford Mere
Pumping Station
Lower Barn Farm
SANDY HILL
Dentlings Plantation
The Spinney
Broomwalk Covert
Broomwalk Plantation
Barham Plantation
White Wheat Farm
B1113
Baylham
Yew Tree Farm
Bellfield Plantation
SANDY LANE
C3
1 GLEBE WY
2 OLD RECTORY
3 PHILLIPPS RD
4 WINCHESTER
5 ELY RD
6 EDDOWES RD
7 BACON RD
8 LINCOLN GDNS
9 EXETER RD
10 LANCASTER
11 JUBILEE CL
12 YORK CRES
13 ST PETER'S A
14 HEREFORD D
LOWER CR
PH
MAPLE GR
Sand Pit
Visitor Ctr
Bell Covert
Upper Street
STOWMARKET ROAD
PESTHOUSE LANE
Bungalow Hall Farm
IP6
Devil's Grove
NORWICH ROAD
A14
Great Wood
MIL LA
Hall Farm
CHURCH LANE
CHALK HILL LA
Cemy
HOOD DR
Great Blakenham
THORNHILL RD
Common Hill Grove
CHEQUERS RD 1
KINGFISHER DR 2
WAINWRIGHT GDNS 3
ASPEN CL 4
HACKNEY'S CORNER
LC
B3
1 MASON CT
2 WEAVERS WY
3 FLETCHER CL
4 COOPERS WY
5 MILLERS CT
6 FORESTERS WLK
7 WOOLNER CL
8 ST PETER'S CL
9 MILL LA
10 PLUMMERS DELL
11 MULBERRY GDNS
12 ASPEN CL
13 LAUREL DR
14 BRAMFORD RD
Mast
Works
GIPPING ROAD
EDINBURGH GD
Claydon
CHAPEL LANE
PO
Sch
Claypit Grove
ADDISON WY
BLUE BARN LA
Lime Quarr
HAZEL RI
Inghams Farm
Cottage Farm
Blackacre Hill
BRAMFORD RD
Hogfield Grove
Blakenham Woodland Garden
River Gipping
OLD IPSWICH ROAD
Coney Grove
Chalk Pit
Broomvale Farm
Motel
The Common
Hill View Business Park
VALLEY ROAD
THE BEECHES
Little Blakenham
POUND LANE
OLD NORWICH R
Mockbeggars Hall
IP8
Dairy Farm
Alder Carr
Broom Hill
Fisk Grove
Sycamore Farm
LORAINE WAY
PAPER MILL LANE
P&R
Bramford Common
SOMERSHAM ROAD
The Grove
A1156
Superstore
GODDARD RD
Ind Est
WHITE HO
Rutters Farm
Oxen Covert
Bramford
Grove House
A B C
52 51 50 49 48
4 3 2 1
11 12 13
14 16 18 52 53

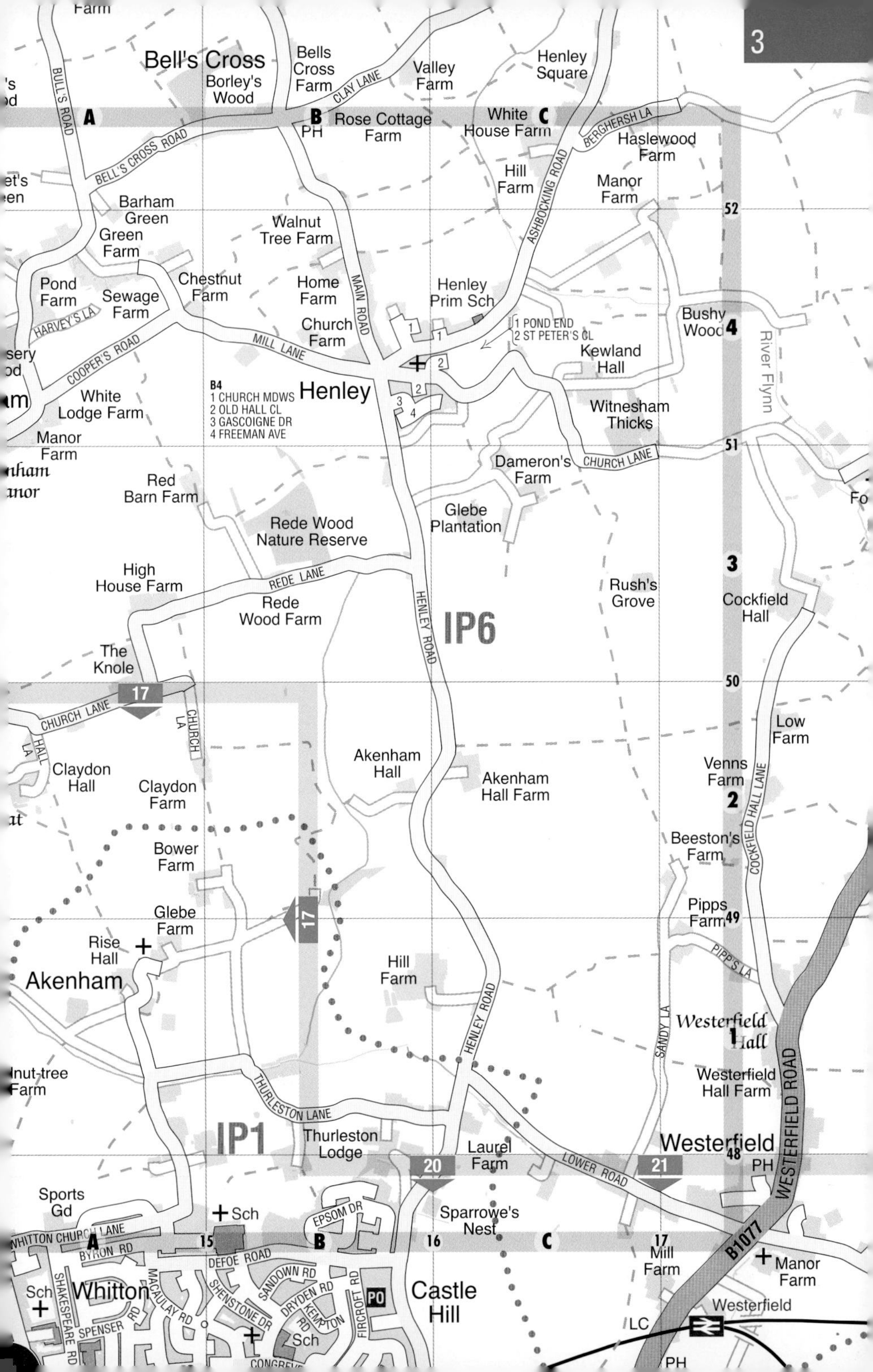
Bell's Cross
Borley's Wood
Bells Cross Farm
Valley Farm
Henley Square
CLAY LANE
BULL'S ROAD
A
B
C
PH
Rose Cottage Farm
White House Farm
BERGHERSH LA
Haslewood Farm
BELL'S CROSS ROAD
Hill Farm
Manor Farm
ASHBOCKING ROAD
52
Barham Green
Green Farm
Walnut Tree Farm
Pond Farm
Sewage Farm
Chestnut Farm
Home Farm
Henley Prim Sch
Bushy Wood
4
HARVEY'S LA
COOPER'S ROAD
MILL LANE
Church Farm
MAIN ROAD
1 POND END
2 ST PETER'S CL
Kewland Hall
River Flynn
White Lodge Farm
B4
1 CHURCH MDWS
2 OLD HALL CL
3 GASCOIGNE DR
4 FREEMAN AVE
Henley
Witnesham Thicks
Manor Farm
51
Dameron's Farm
CHURCH LANE
Red Barn Farm
Glebe Plantation
Rede Wood Nature Reserve
High House Farm
REDE LANE
Rede Wood Farm
Rush's Grove
3
Cockfield Hall
HENLEY ROAD
IP6
The Knole
17
50
CHURCH LANE
CHURCH LA
HALL LA
Claydon Hall
Claydon Farm
Akenham Hall
Akenham Hall Farm
Low Farm
Venns Farm
2
COCKFIELD HALL LANE
Bower Farm
Beeston's Farm
Glebe Farm
Pipps Farm
49
Rise Hall
Akenham
Hill Farm
PIPP'S LA
HENLEY ROAD
Westerfield Hall
1
SANDY LA
Walnut-tree Farm
THURLESTON LANE
Westerfield Hall Farm
WESTERFIELD ROAD
IP1
Thurleston Lodge
Laurel Farm
Westerfield
48
PH
LOWER ROAD
20
21
Sports Gd
Sch
EPSOM DR
Sparrowe's Nest
WHITTON CHURCH LANE
15
16
17
BYRON RD
DEFOE ROAD
B1077
Mill Farm
Manor Farm
Whitton
SANDOWN RD
DRYDEN RD
FIRCROFT RD
PO
Castle Hill
SHAKESPEARE RD
MACAULAY RD
SHENSTONE DR
KEMPTON RD
Westerfield
SPENSER RD
Sch
LC
PH
CONGREVE

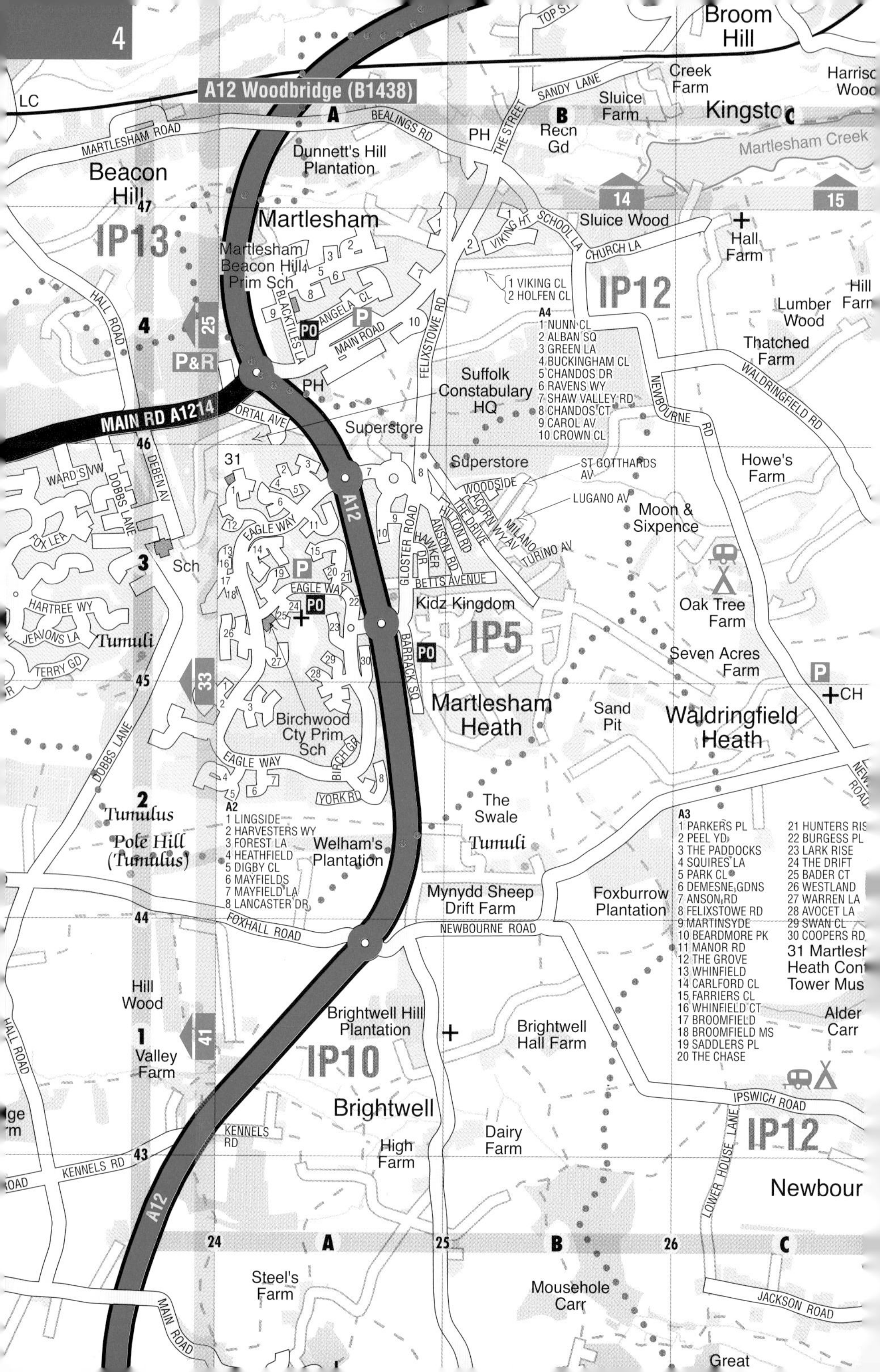
A12 Woodbridge (B1438)
Broom Hill
Creek Farm
Sluice Farm
Kingston
Martlesham Creek
MARTLESHAM ROAD
BEALINGS RD
SANDY LANE
THE STREET
Recn Gd
Beacon Hill
Dunnett's Hill Plantation
Martlesham
IP13
Martlesham Beacon Hill Prim Sch
Sluice Wood
SCHOOL LA
CHURCH LA
VIKING HT
Hall Farm
IP12
1 VIKING CL
2 HOLFEN CL
A4
1 NUNN CL
2 ALBAN SQ
3 GREEN LA
4 BUCKINGHAM CL
5 CHANDOS DR
6 RAVENS WY
7 SHAW VALLEY RD
8 CHANDOS CT
9 CAROL AV
10 CROWN CL
Lumber Wood
Thatched Farm
WALDRINGFIELD RD
NEWBOURNE RD
HALL ROAD
BLACKTILES LA
ANGELA CL
MAIN ROAD
FELIXSTOWE RD
Suffolk Constabulary HQ
P&R
MAIN RD A1214
PORTAL AVE
Superstore
Howe's Farm
ST GOTTHARDS AV
LUGANO AV
WOODSIDE
Moon & Sixpence
WARD'S VW
DOBBS LANE
DEBEN AV
EAGLE WAY
FOX LEA
HARTREE WY
JEAVONS LA
TERRY GD
Tumuli
A12
GLOSTER ROAD
HAWKER DR
ANSON RD
HILTON RD
THE DRIVE
ACORN WY
MILANO AV
TURINO AV
BETTS AVENUE
Kidz Kingdom
Oak Tree Farm
IP5
BARRACK SQ
Seven Acres Farm
Martlesham Heath
Sand Pit
Waldringfield Heath
CH
Birchwood Cty Prim Sch
BIRCH GR
YORK RD
DOBBS LANE
Tumulus
Pole Hill (Tumulus)
The Swale
Tumuli
A2
1 LINGSIDE
2 HARVESTERS WY
3 FOREST LA
4 HEATHFIELD
5 DIGBY CL
6 MAYFIELDS
7 MAYFIELD LA
8 LANCASTER DR
Welham's Plantation
Mynydd Sheep Drift Farm
Foxburrow Plantation
FOXHALL ROAD
NEWBOURNE ROAD
A3
1 PARKERS PL
2 PEEL YD
3 THE PADDOCKS
4 SQUIRES LA
5 PARK CL
6 DEMESNE GDNS
7 ANSON RD
8 FELIXSTOWE RD
9 MARTINSYDE
10 BEARDMORE PK
11 MANOR RD
12 THE GROVE
13 WHINFIELD
14 CARLFORD CL
15 FARRIERS CL
16 WHINFIELD CT
17 BROOMFIELD
18 BROOMFIELD MS
19 SADDLERS PL
20 THE CHASE
21 HUNTERS RISE
22 BURGESS PL
23 LARK RISE
24 THE DRIFT
25 BADER CT
26 WESTLAND
27 WARREN LA
28 AVOCET LA
29 SWAN CL
30 COOPERS RD
31 Martlesham Heath Control Tower Museum
Hill Wood
Valley Farm
Brightwell Hill Plantation
Brightwell Hall Farm
Alder Carr
IP10
Brightwell
IPSWICH ROAD
IP12
KENNELS RD
Dairy Farm
High Farm
LOWER HOUSE LANE
Newbourne
A12
Steel's Farm
Mousehole Carr
JACKSON ROAD
MAIN ROAD
Great

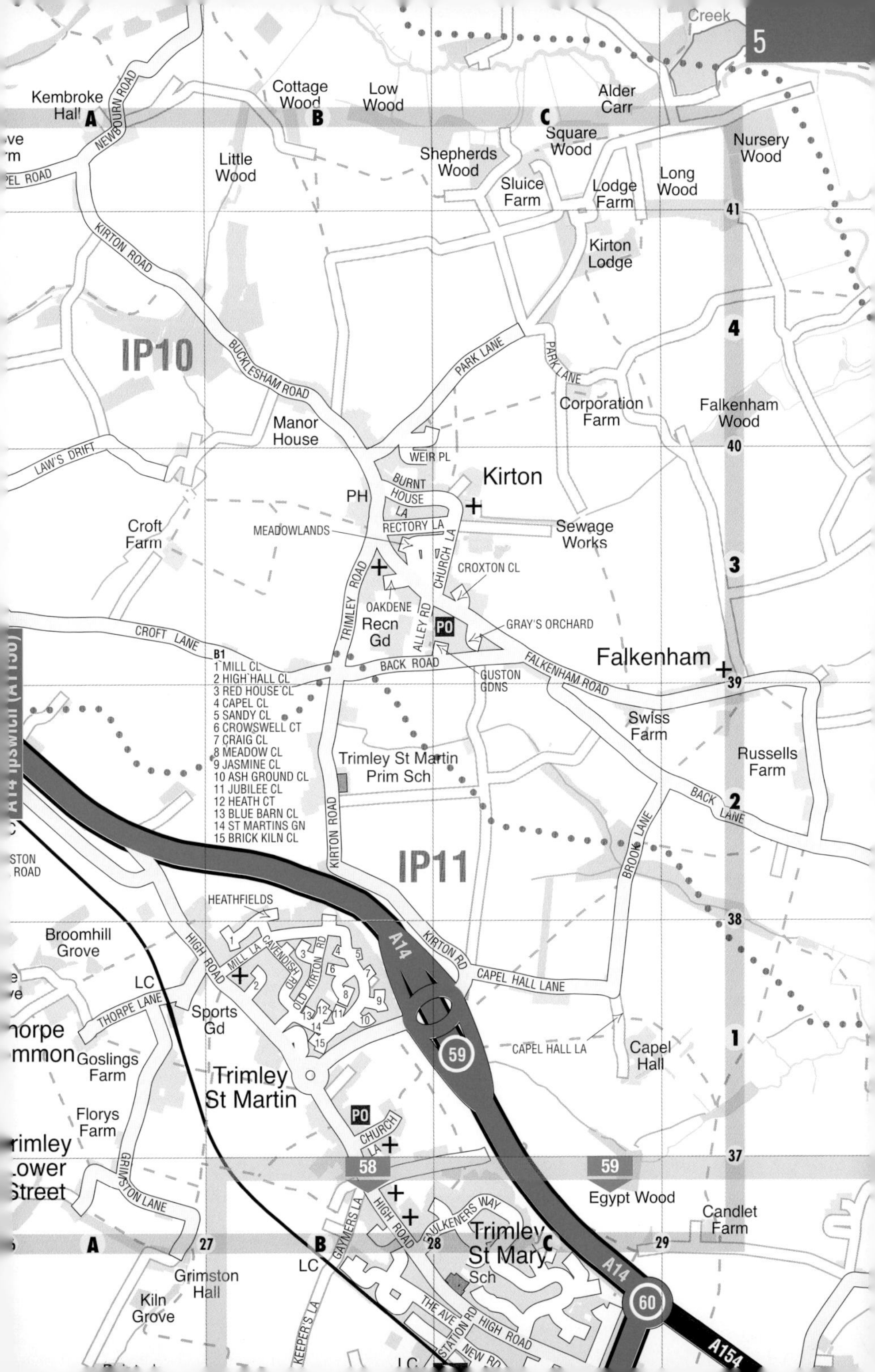
Creek
Kembroke Hall
Cottage Wood
Low Wood
Alder Carr
NEWBOURN ROAD
Little Wood
Shepherds Wood
Square Wood
Nursery Wood
Sluice Farm
Lodge Farm
Long Wood
KIRTON ROAD
Kirton Lodge
IP10
BUCKLESHAM ROAD
PARK LANE
Corporation Farm
Falkenham Wood
Manor House
LAW'S DRIFT
WEIR PL
Kirton
BURNT HOUSE LA
PH
Croft Farm
MEADOWLANDS
RECTORY LA
CHURCH LA
Sewage Works
TRIMLEY ROAD
CROXTON CL
OAKDENE
Recn Gd
ALLEY RD
PO
GRAY'S ORCHARD
CROFT LANE
B1
1 MILL CL
2 HIGH HALL CL
3 RED HOUSE CL
4 CAPEL CL
5 SANDY CL
6 CROWSWELL CT
7 CRAIG CL
8 MEADOW CL
9 JASMINE CL
10 ASH GROUND CL
11 JUBILEE CL
12 HEATH CT
13 BLUE BARN CL
14 ST MARTINS GN
15 BRICK KILN CL
BACK ROAD
GUSTON GDNS
FALKENHAM ROAD
Falkenham
Swiss Farm
Trimley St Martin Prim Sch
Russells Farm
BACK LANE
KIRTON ROAD
IP11
BROOK LANE
HEATHFIELDS
Broomhill Grove
HIGH ROAD
MILL LA
CAVENDISH RD
OLD KIRTON RD
A14
KIRTON RD
CAPEL HALL LANE
LC
THORPE LANE
Sports Gd
CAPEL HALL LA
Capel Hall
Goslings Farm
59
Trimley St Martin
Florys Farm
PO
CHURCH LA
GRIMSTON LANE
58
59
Egypt Wood
Candlet Farm
GAYMERS LA
HIGH ROAD
FULKENERS WAY
Trimley St Mary
Sch
Grimston Hall
Kiln Grove
LC
KEEPER'S LA
THE AVE
STATION RD
HIGH ROAD
NEW RD
60
A154
A
B
C
A
B
C
27
28
29
37
38
39
40
41
1
2
3
4

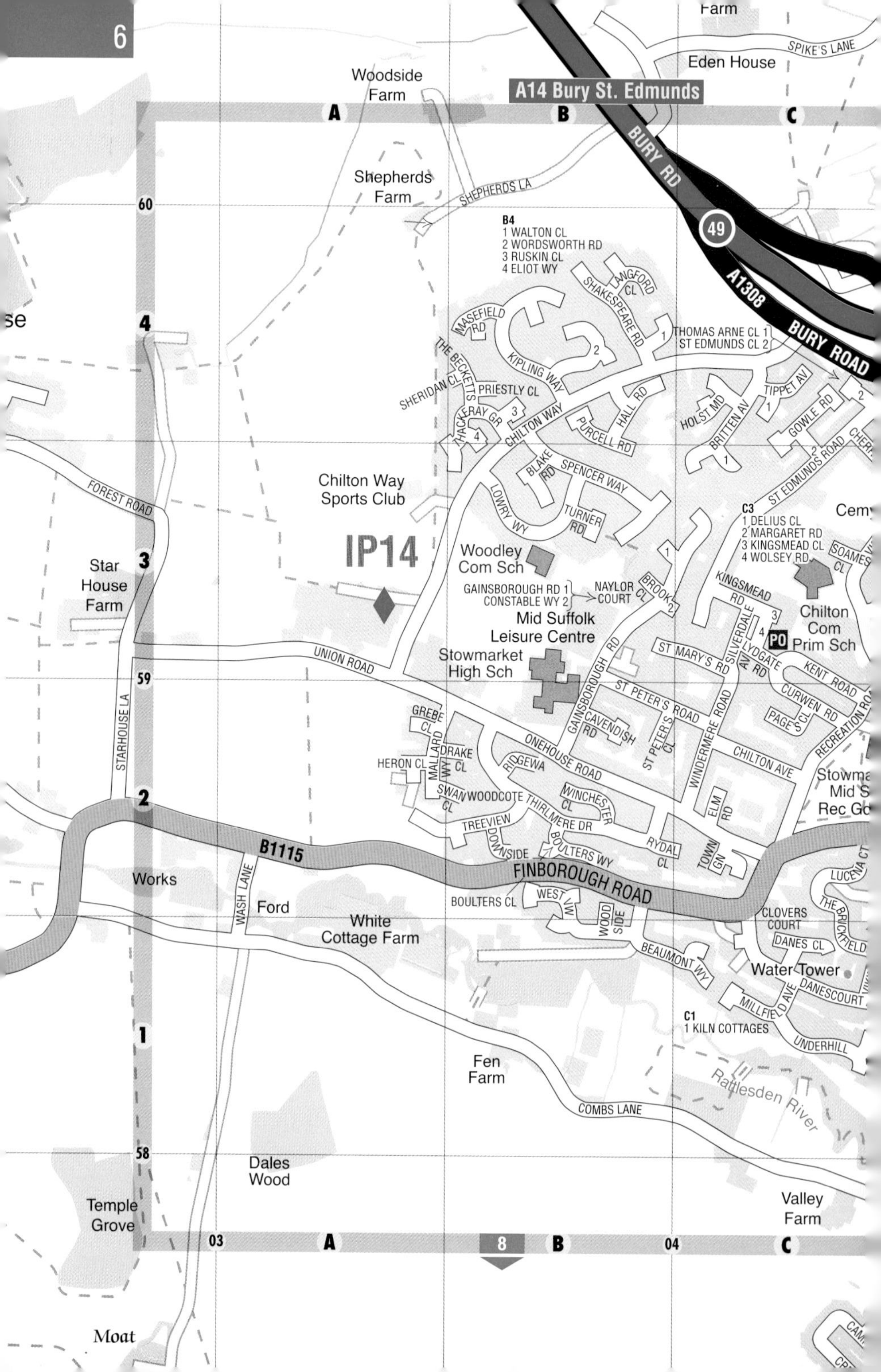

Farm
SPIKE'S LANE
Eden House
Woodside Farm
A14 Bury St. Edmunds
A
B
C
BURY RD
Shepherds Farm
SHEPHERDS LA
60
B4
1 WALTON CL
2 WORDSWORTH RD
3 RUSKIN CL
4 ELIOT WY
49
A1308
BURY ROAD
LANGFORD CL
SHAKESPEARE RD
THOMAS ARNE CL 1
ST EDMUNDS CL 2
MASEFIELD RD
KIPLING WAY
THE BECKETTS
SHERIDAN CL
PRIESTLY CL
THACKERAY GR
CHILTON WAY
HALL RD
PURCELL RD
HOLST MD
BRITTEN AV
TIPPET AV
GOWLE RD
ST EDMUNDS ROAD
BLAKE RD
SPENCER WAY
LOWRY WY
TURNER RD
Chilton Way Sports Club
FOREST ROAD
Star House Farm
IP14
Woodley Com Sch
C3
1 DELIUS CL
2 MARGARET RD
3 KINGSMEAD CL
4 WOLSEY RD
SOAMES CL
Cem
GAINSBOROUGH RD 1
CONSTABLE WY 2
NAYLOR COURT
BROOK CL
KINGSMEAD RD
Mid Suffolk Leisure Centre
Chilton Com Prim Sch
PO
SILVERDALE AV
LYDGATE RD
ST MARY'S RD
KENT ROAD
UNION ROAD
Stowmarket High Sch
59
GAINSBOROUGH RD
ST PETER'S ROAD
CURWEN RD
PAGE'S CL
RECREATION RD
STARHOUSE LA
GREBE CL
MALLARD WY
DRAKE CL
CAVENDISH RD
ST PETER'S CL
WINDERMERE ROAD
CHILTON AVE
HERON CL
RIDGEWA
ONEHOUSE ROAD
Stowma
Mid S
Rec Gd
SWAN CL
WOODCOTE
THIRLMERE DR
WINCHESTER CL
ELM RD
TREEVIEW
DOWNSIDE
BOULTERS WY
RYDAL CL
TOWN GN
B1115
FINBOROUGH ROAD
LUCENA CT
Works
WASH LANE
Ford
BOULTERS CL
WEST VW
WOOD SIDE
CLOVERS COURT
THE BRICKFIELD
White Cottage Farm
BEAUMONT WY
DANES CL
Water Tower
DANESCOURT
MILLFIELD AVE
C1
1 KILN COTTAGES
UNDERHILL
Fen Farm
Rattlesden River
COMBS LANE
58
Dales Wood
Temple Grove
Valley Farm
03
8
04
Moat

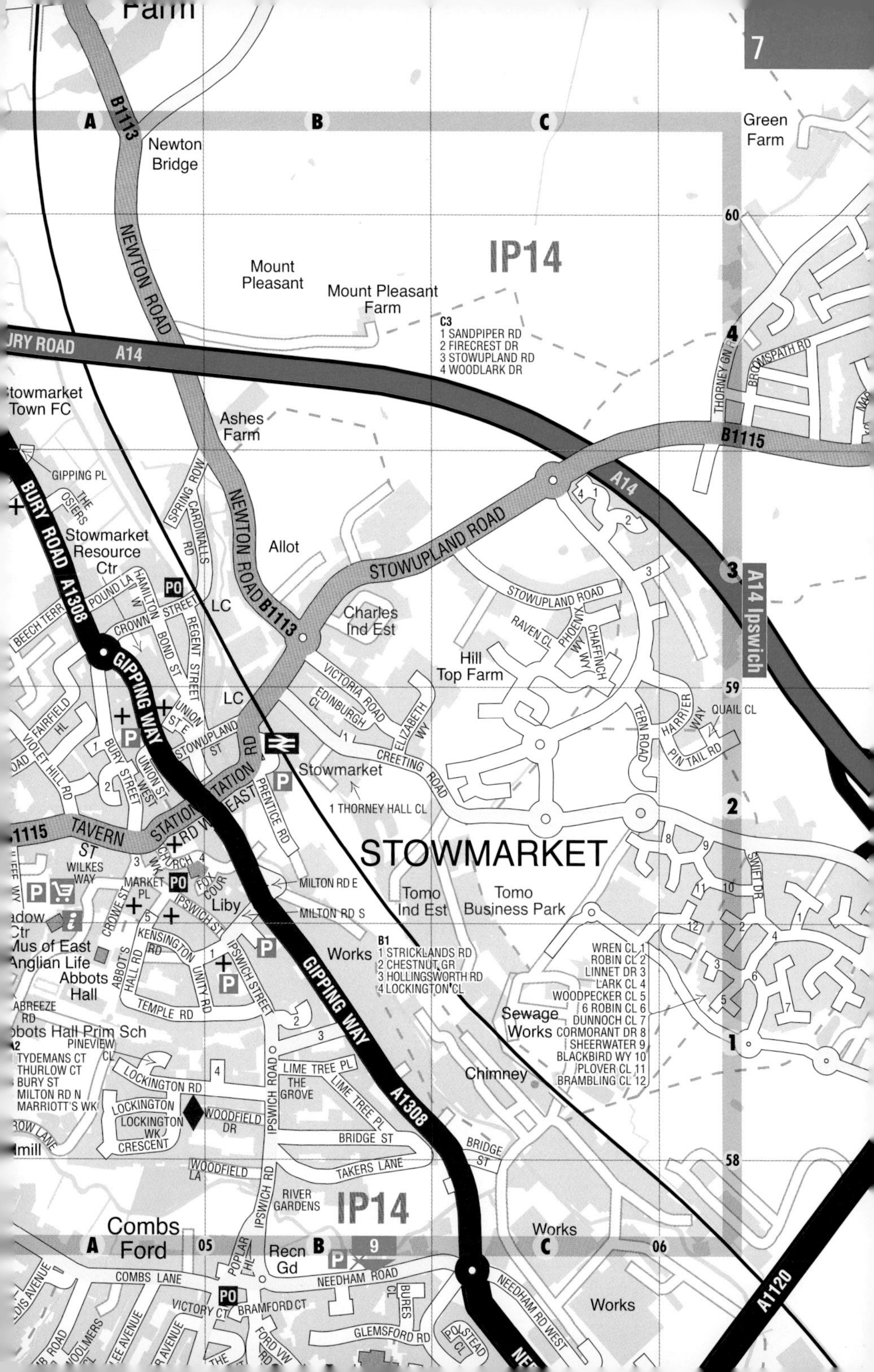
Newton Bridge
Mount Pleasant
Mount Pleasant Farm
IP14
Green Farm
C3
1 SANDPIPER RD
2 FIRECREST DR
3 STOWUPLAND RD
4 WOODLARK DR
A14
NEWTON ROAD
B1113
Ashes Farm
Allot
STOWUPLAND ROAD
B1115
A14 Ipswich
Charles Ind Est
Hill Top Farm
Stowmarket Resource Ctr
BURY ROAD A1308
GIPPING WAY
Stowmarket
1 THORNEY HALL CL
STOWMARKET
Tomo Ind Est
Tomo Business Park
Works
B1
1 STRICKLANDS RD
2 CHESTNUT GR
3 HOLLINGSWORTH RD
4 LOCKINGTON CL
WREN CL 1
ROBIN CL 2
LINNET DR 3
LARK CL 4
WOODPECKER CL 5
6 ROBIN CL 6
DUNNOCH CL 7
CORMORANT DR 8
SHEERWATER 9
BLACKBIRD WY 10
PLOVER CL 11
BRAMBLING CL 12
Sewage Works
Chimney
Liby
Abbots Hall
Abbots Hall Prim Sch
A2
TYDEMANS CT
THURLOW CT
BURY ST
MILTON RD N
MARRIOTT'S WK
IP14
Combs Ford
Recn Gd
Works
A1120
A
B
C
05
06
9
60
59
58

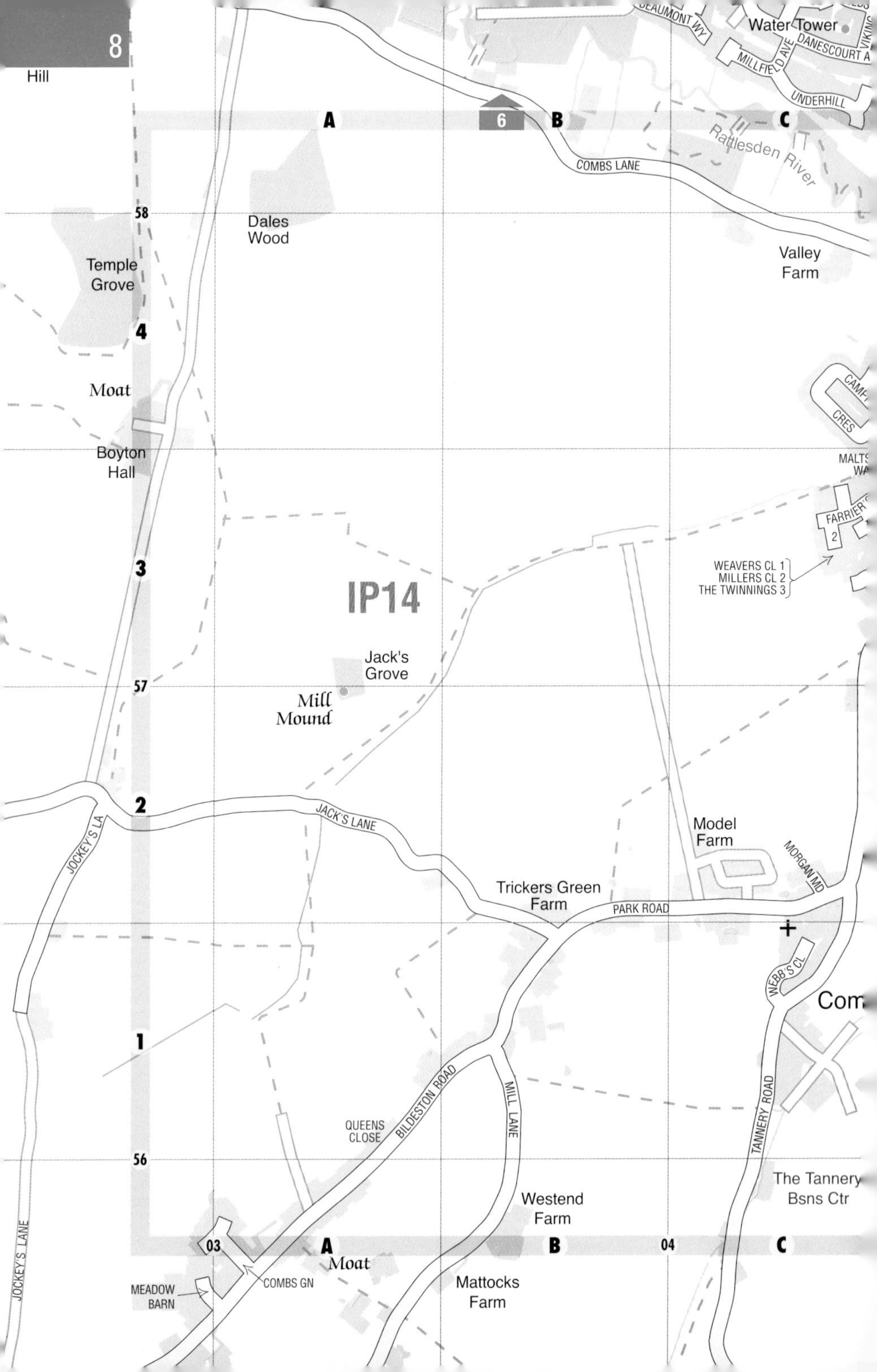

Hill

Water Tower

BEAUMONT WY

MILLFIE

CLAY LANE

DANESCOURT A

VIKING

UNDERHILL

A

6

B

Rattlesden River

C

COMBS LANE

58

Dales Wood

Valley Farm

Temple Grove

4

CAMP

CRES

Moat

MALTS
WA

Boyton Hall

FARRIER
2

WEAVERS CL 1
MILLERS CL 2
THE TWINNINGS 3

3

IP14

Jack's Grove

57

Mill Mound

2

JOCKEY'S LA

JACK'S LANE

Model Farm

MORGAN MD

Trickers Green Farm

PARK ROAD

+

Com

1

WEBB'S CL

BILDESTON ROAD

MILL LANE

QUEENS CLOSE

56

TANNERY ROAD

The Tannery Bsns Ctr

03

A

Moat

B

04

C

JOCKEY'S LANE

MEADOW BARN

COMBS GN

Westend Farm

Mattocks Farm

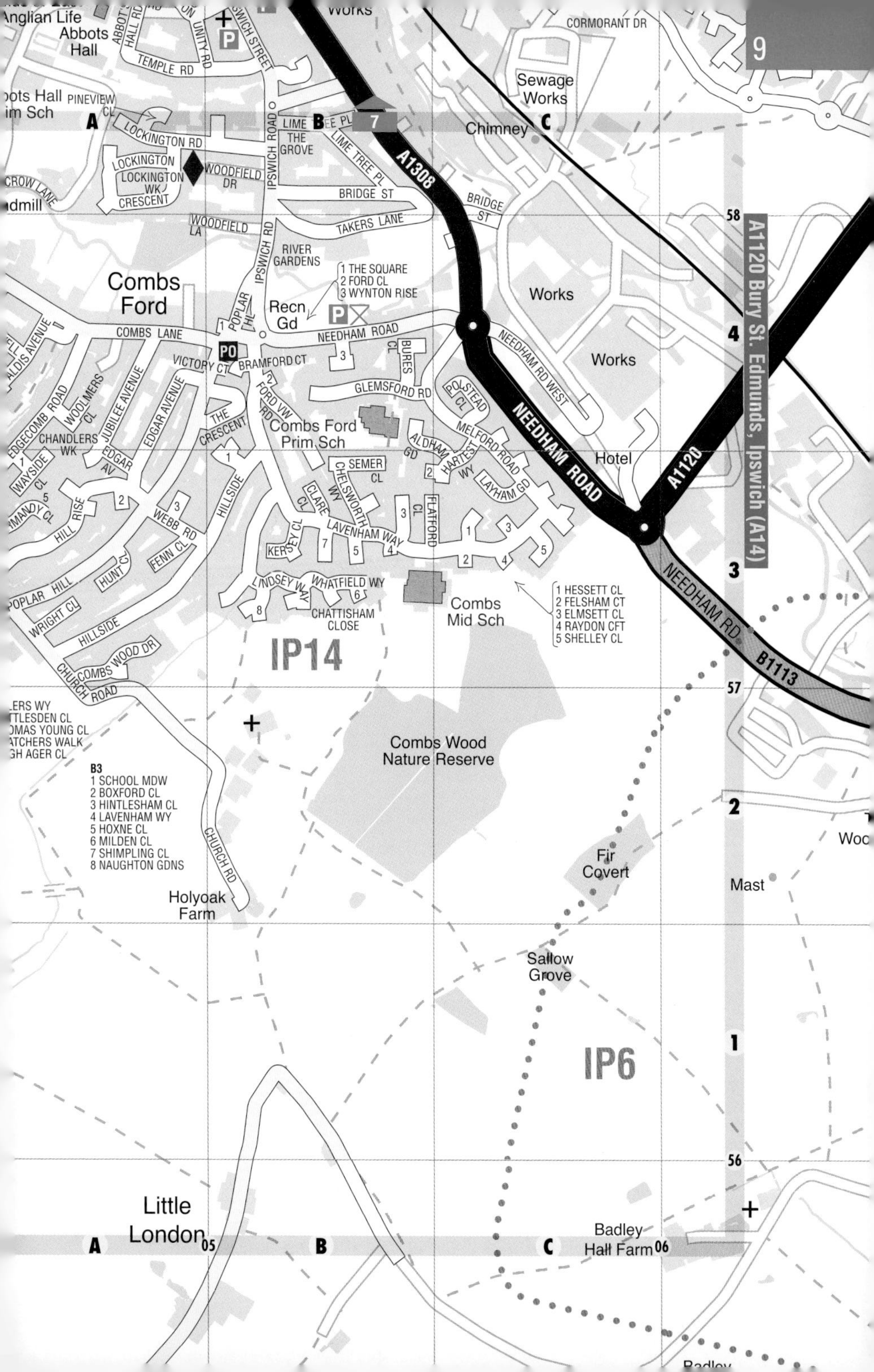
Anglian Life
Abbots Hall
Abbots Hall Prim Sch
Sewage Works
Chimney
Works
Works
Works
Hotel
CORMORANT DR
TEMPLE RD
UNITY RD
IPSWICH STREET
PINEVIEW CL
LOCKINGTON RD
LOCKINGTON
LOCKINGTON WK
CRESCENT
WOODFIELD DR
WOODFIELD LA
IPSWICH ROAD
IPSWICH RD
LIME TREE PL
THE GROVE
BRIDGE ST
TAKERS LANE
RIVER GARDENS
1 THE SQUARE
2 FORD CL
3 WYNTON RISE
Recn Gd
Combs Ford
COMBS LANE
NEEDHAM ROAD
NEEDHAM RD WEST
NEEDHAM ROAD
NEEDHAM RD
A1308
A1120
B1113
A1120 Bury St. Edmunds, Ipswich (A14)
POPLAR HL
VICTORY CT
BRAMFORD CT
BURES CL
GLEMSFORD RD
POLSTEAD CL
MELFORD ROAD
FORD VW RD
Combs Ford Prim Sch
ALDHAM GD
HARTEST WY
LAYHAM GD
SEMER CL
CHELSWORTH WY
CLARE CL
LAVENHAM WAY
FLATFORD CL
KERSEY CL
LINDSEY WAY
WHATFIELD WY
CHATTISHAM CLOSE
Combs Mid Sch
1 HESSETT CL
2 FELSHAM CT
3 ELMSETT CL
4 RAYDON CFT
5 SHELLEY CL
WOOLMERS CL
JUBILEE AVENUE
EDGAR AVENUE
EDGECOMB ROAD
CHANDLERS WK
EDGAR AV
THE CRESCENT
WAYSIDE CL
HILL RISE
WEBB RD
HILLSIDE
FENN CL
HUNT CL
POPLAR HILL
WRIGHT CL
HILLSIDE
COMBS WOOD DR
CHURCH ROAD
IP14
B3
1 SCHOOL MDW
2 BOXFORD CL
3 HINTLESHAM CL
4 LAVENHAM WY
5 HOXNE CL
6 MILDEN CL
7 SHIMPLING CL
8 NAUGHTON GDNS
Combs Wood Nature Reserve
CHURCH RD
Holyoak Farm
Fir Covert
Mast
Sallow Grove
IP6
Little London
Badley Hall Farm
A
B
C
58
57
56
05
06
4
3
2
1
7

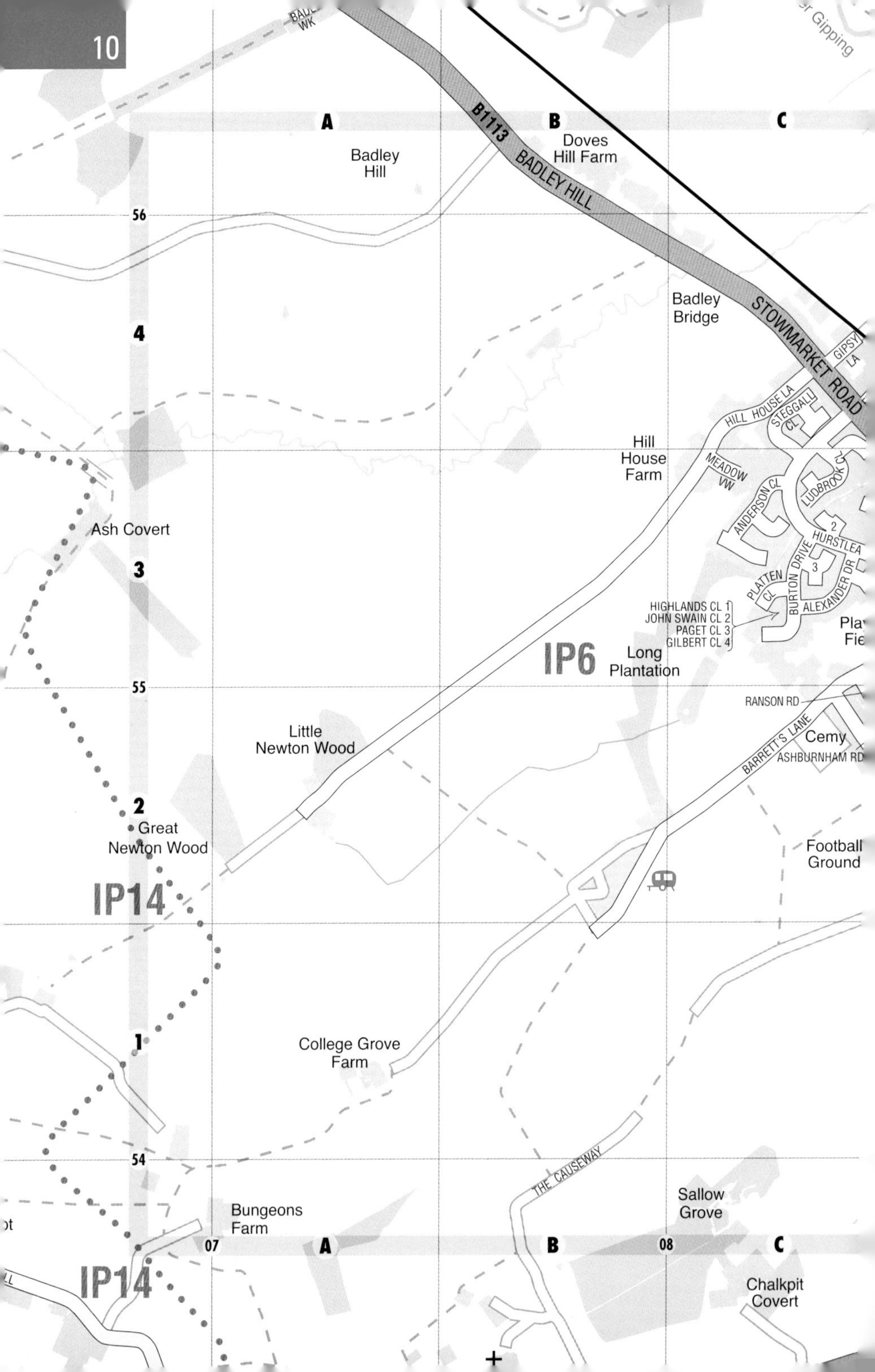

A   B   C

BAD...
WK

BT113
BADLEY HILL
Doves
Hill Farm

Badley
Hill

STOWMARKET ROAD

56

4

Badley
Bridge

GIPSY LA

HILL HOUSE LA
STEGGALL
CL

Hill
House
Farm

MEADOW
VW

ANDERSON CL

LUDBROOK CL

Ash Covert

3

HURSTLEA

2

PLATTEN
CL

BURTON DRIVE

ALEXANDER DR

3

HIGHLANDS CL 1
JOHN SWAIN CL 2
PAGET CL 3
GILBERT CL 4

Pla
Fie

IP6

Long
Plantation

RANSON RD

55

Little
Newton Wood

BARRETT'S LANE

Cemy

ASHBURNHAM RD

2

Great
Newton Wood

Football
Ground

IP14

1

College Grove
Farm

54

THE CAUSEWAY

Sallow
Grove

Bungeons
Farm

07   A   B   08   C

IP14

Chalkpit
Covert

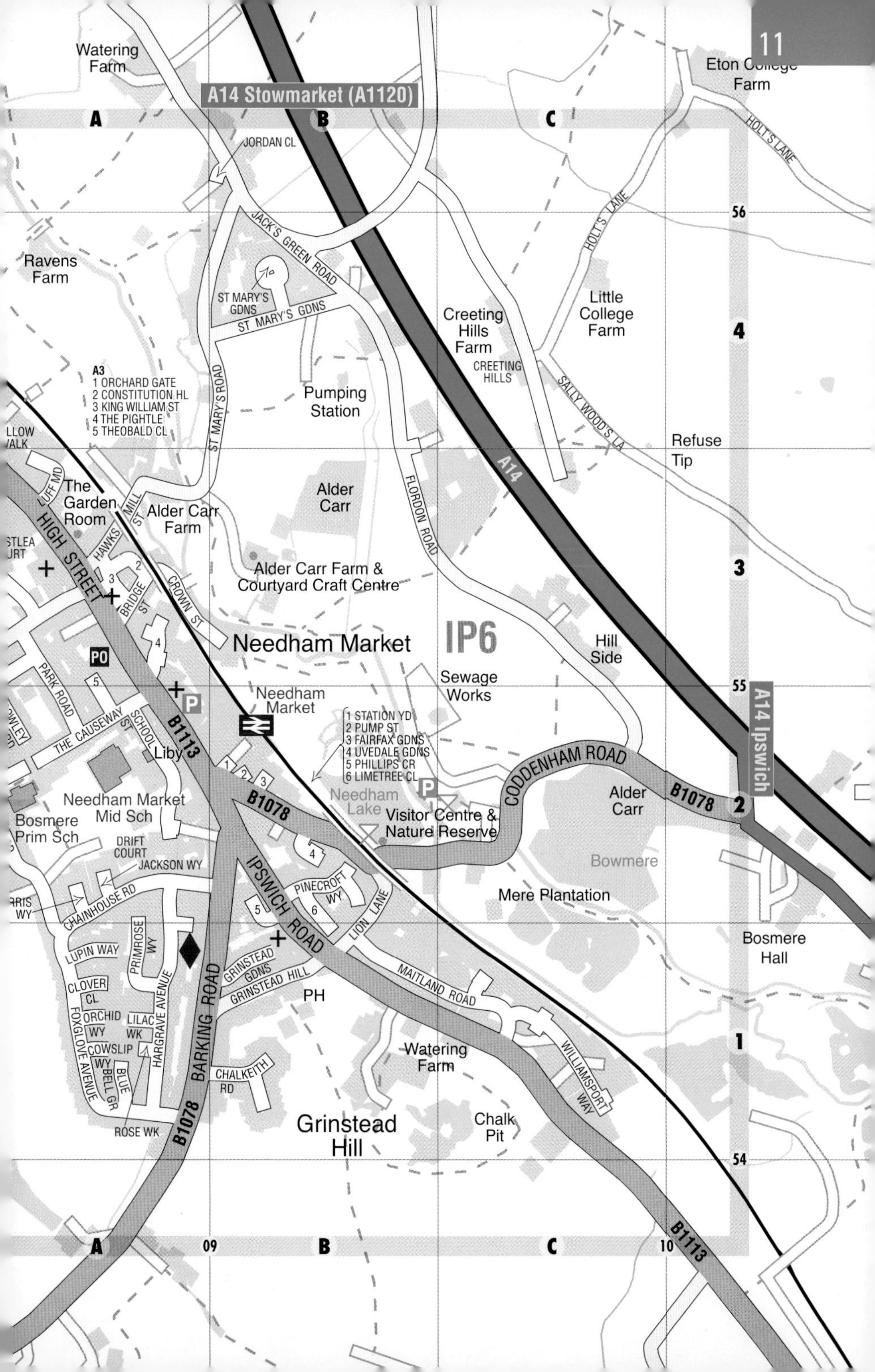

A14 Stowmarket (A1120)
A14 Ipswich
Watering Farm
Eton College Farm
HOLT'S LANE
JORDAN CL
JACK'S GREEN ROAD
Ravens Farm
ST MARY'S GDNS
ST MARY'S ROAD
A3
1 ORCHARD GATE
2 CONSTITUTION HL
3 KING WILLIAM ST
4 THE PIGHTLE
5 THEOBALD CL
Pumping Station
Creeting Hills Farm
CREETING HILLS
Little College Farm
SALLY WOOD'S LA
Refuse Tip
A14
The Garden Room
LUFF MD
HIGH STREET
HAWKS MILL ST
Alder Carr Farm
Alder Carr
FLORDON ROAD
Alder Carr Farm & Courtyard Craft Centre
BRIDGE ST
CROWN ST
Needham Market
IP6
Hill Side
Sewage Works
PO
PARK ROAD
THE CAUSEWAY
SCHOOL ST
B1113
Needham Market
Liby
1 STATION YD
2 PUMP ST
3 FAIRFAX GDNS
4 UVEDALE GDNS
5 PHILLIPS CR
6 LIMETREE CL
CODDENHAM ROAD
Alder Carr
B1078
Needham Lake
Visitor Centre & Nature Reserve
Needham Market Mid Sch
Bosmere Prim Sch
DRIFT COURT
JACKSON WY
Bowmere
Mere Plantation
CHAINHOUSE RD
PINECROFT WY
IPSWICH ROAD
LION LANE
Bosmere Hall
LUPIN WAY
PRIMROSE WY
GRINSTEAD GDNS
GRINSTEAD HILL
MAITLAND ROAD
CLOVER CL
HARGRAVE AVENUE
BARKING ROAD
PH
ORCHID WY
LILAC WK
FOXGLOVE AVENUE
COWSLIP WY
BELL GR
BLUE
Watering Farm
WILLIAMSPORT WAY
CHALKEITH RD
ROSE WK
Grinstead Hill
Chalk Pit
A
B
C
09
10
1
2
3
4
54
55
56

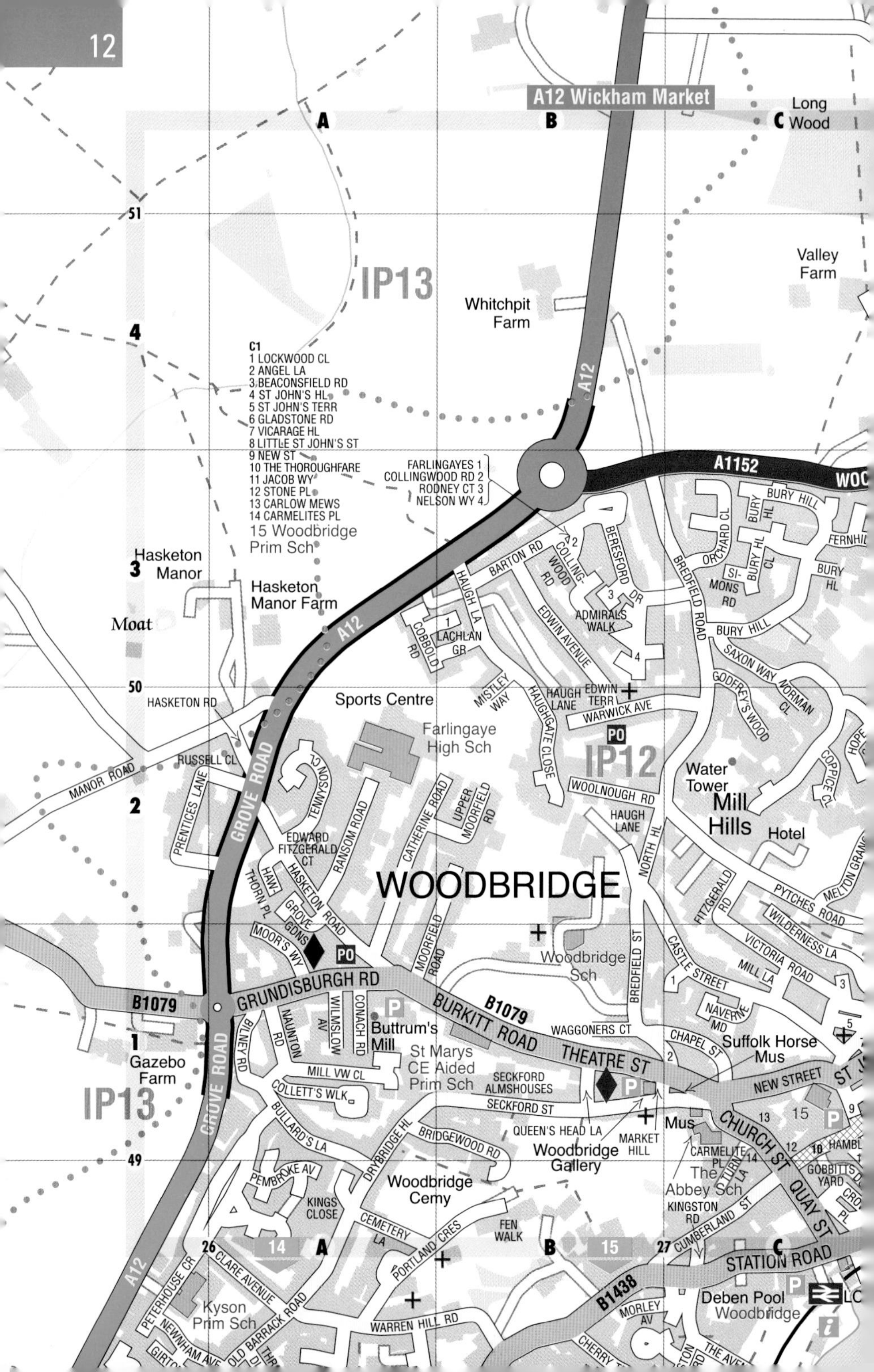
A12 Wickham Market
A
B
C
Long Wood
51
IP13
Whitchpit Farm
Valley Farm
4
C1
1 LOCKWOOD CL
2 ANGEL LA
3 BEACONSFIELD RD
4 ST JOHN'S HL
5 ST JOHN'S TERR
6 GLADSTONE RD
7 VICARAGE HL
8 LITTLE ST JOHN'S ST
9 NEW ST
10 THE THOROUGHFARE
11 JACOB WY
12 STONE PL
13 CARLOW MEWS
14 CARMELITES PL
15 Woodbridge Prim Sch
FARLINGAYES 1
COLLINGWOOD RD 2
RODNEY CT 3
NELSON WY 4
A12
A1152
BURY HILL
3
Haskéton Manor
Hasketon Manor Farm
Moat
BARTON RD
HAUGH LA
COLLINGWOOD RD
BERESFORD DR
ORCHARD CL
BREDFIELD ROAD
SIMONS RD
BURY HL CL
EDWIN AVENUE
ADMIRALS WALK
LACHLAN GR
COBBOLD RD
SAXON WAY
NORMAN CL
GODFREY'S WOOD
50
HASKETON RD
Sports Centre
MISTLEY WAY
HAUGH LANE
EDWIN TERR
WARWICK AVE
HAUGHGATE CLOSE
PO
Farlingaye High Sch
IP12
Water Tower
Mill Hills
Hotel
RUSSELL CL
MANOR ROAD
TENNYSON CL
GROVE ROAD
2
PRENTICES LANE
RANSOM ROAD
CATHERINE ROAD
UPPER MOORFIELD RD
WOOLNOUGH RD
HAUGH LANE
NORTH HL
COPPICE CL
EDWARD FITZGERALD CT
HAWTHORN PL
HASKETON ROAD
WOODBRIDGE
FITZGERALD RD
PYTCHES ROAD
MELTON GRANGE
WILDERNESS LA
GROVE GDNS
MOOR'S WAY
MOORFIELD ROAD
Woodbridge Sch
BREDFIELD ST
CASTLE STREET
VICTORIA ROAD
MILL LA
B1079
GRUNDISBURGH RD
BURKITT ROAD
NAUNTON RD
WILMSLOW AV
CONACH RD
Buttrum's Mill
St Marys CE Aided Prim Sch
WAGGONERS CT
THEATRE ST
NAVERNE MD
CHAPEL ST
Suffolk Horse Mus
1
Gazebo Farm
BILNEY RD
MILL VW CL
COLLETT'S WLK
SECKFORD ALMSHOUSES
SECKFORD ST
NEW STREET
CHURCH ST
IP13
BULLARD'S LA
DRYBRIDGE HL
BRIDGEWOOD RD
QUEEN'S HEAD LA
Woodbridge Gallery
MARKET HILL
Mus
CARMELITE PL
TURN LA
49
PEMBROKE AV
Woodbridge Cemy
KINGS CLOSE
The Abbey Sch
GOBBITTS YARD
QUAY ST
CEMETERY LA
PORTLAND CRES
FEN WALK
KINGSTON RD
CUMBERLAND ST
26
14
15
27
CLARE AVENUE
PETERHOUSE CR
STATION ROAD
B1438
Kyson Prim Sch
OLD BARRACK ROAD
WARREN HILL RD
MORLEY AV
Deben Pool
Woodbridge
NEWNHAM AVE
CHERRY

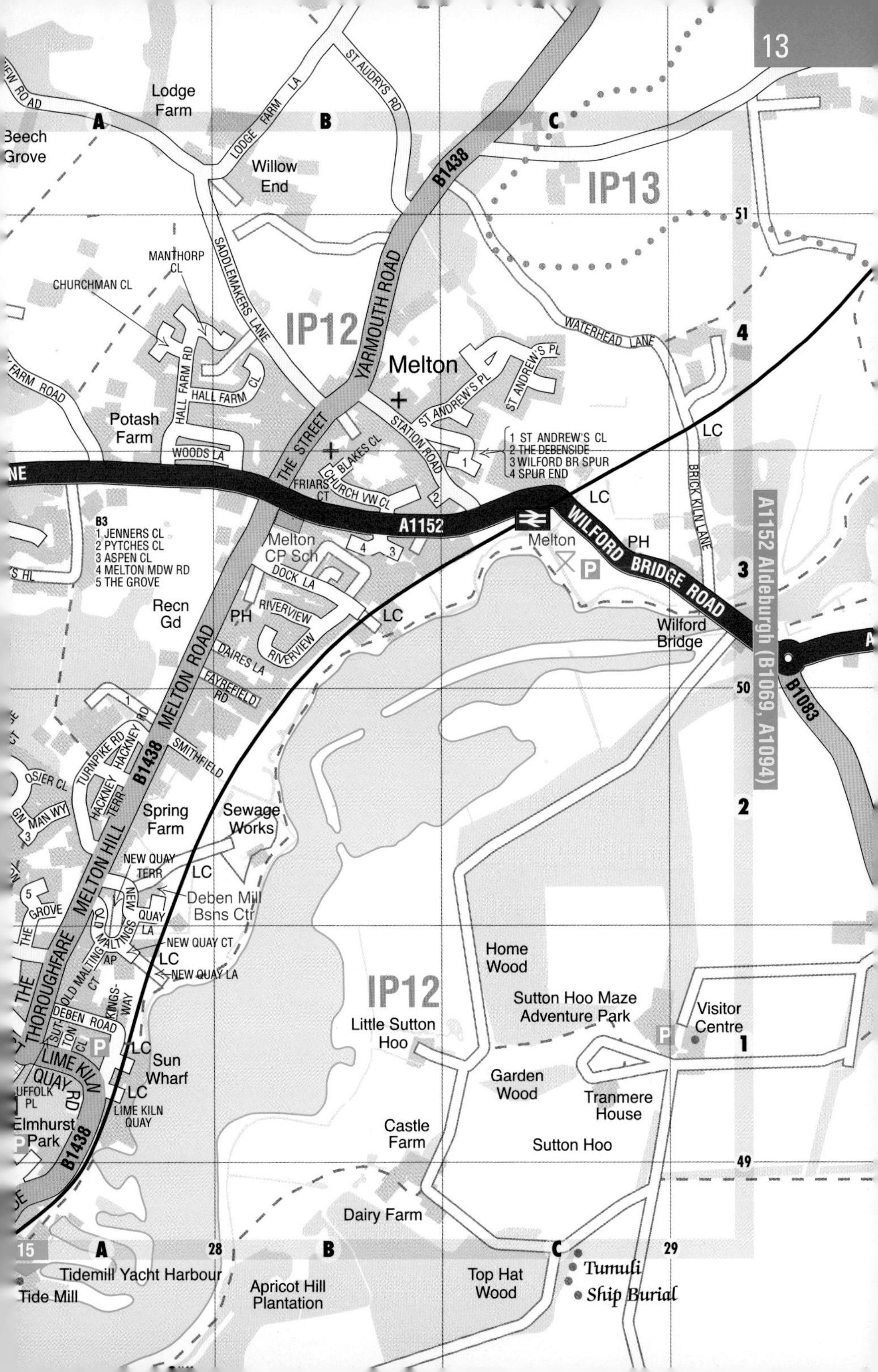

Lodge Farm
Beech Grove
Willow End
LODGE FARM LA
ST AUDRYS RD
NEW ROAD
B1438
IP13
IP12
YARMOUTH ROAD
SADDLEMAKERS LANE
MANTHORP CL
CHURCHMAN CL
HALL FARM RD
HALL FARM CL
Melton
WATERHEAD LANE
ST ANDREW'S PL
STATION ROAD
BLAKES CL
THE STREET
Potash Farm
WOODS LA
FRIARS CT
CHURCH VW CL
1 ST ANDREW'S CL
2 THE DEBENSIDE
3 WILFORD BR SPUR
4 SPUR END
LC
BRICK KILN LANE
A1152
A1152 Aldeburgh (B1069, A1094)
WILFORD BRIDGE ROAD
PH
Melton
B3
1 JENNERS CL
2 PYTCHES CL
3 ASPEN CL
4 MELTON MDW RD
5 THE GROVE
Melton CP Sch
DOCK LA
RIVERVIEW
Recn Gd
DAIRES LA
FAYREFIELD RD
MELTON ROAD
Wilford Bridge
B1083
SMITHFIELD
TURNPIKE RD
HACKNEY RD
HACKNEY TERR
OSIER CL
MAN WY
Spring Farm
Sewage Works
MELTON HILL
NEW QUAY TERR
Deben Mill Bsns Ctr
THE GROVE
NEW QUAY LA
OLD MALTINGS AP
NEW QUAY CT
THE THOROUGHFARE
OLD MALTING CT
KINGSWAY
DEBEN ROAD
SUTTON CL
LIME KILN QUAY RD
SUFFOLK PL
Elmhurst Park
Sun Wharf
LIME KILN QUAY
Home Wood
Sutton Hoo Maze Adventure Park
Little Sutton Hoo
Visitor Centre
Garden Wood
Tranmere House
Castle Farm
Sutton Hoo
Dairy Farm
Tidemill Yacht Harbour
Tide Mill
Apricot Hill Plantation
Top Hat Wood
Tumuli
Ship Burial
A B C
1 2 3 4
28 29
49 50 51
15

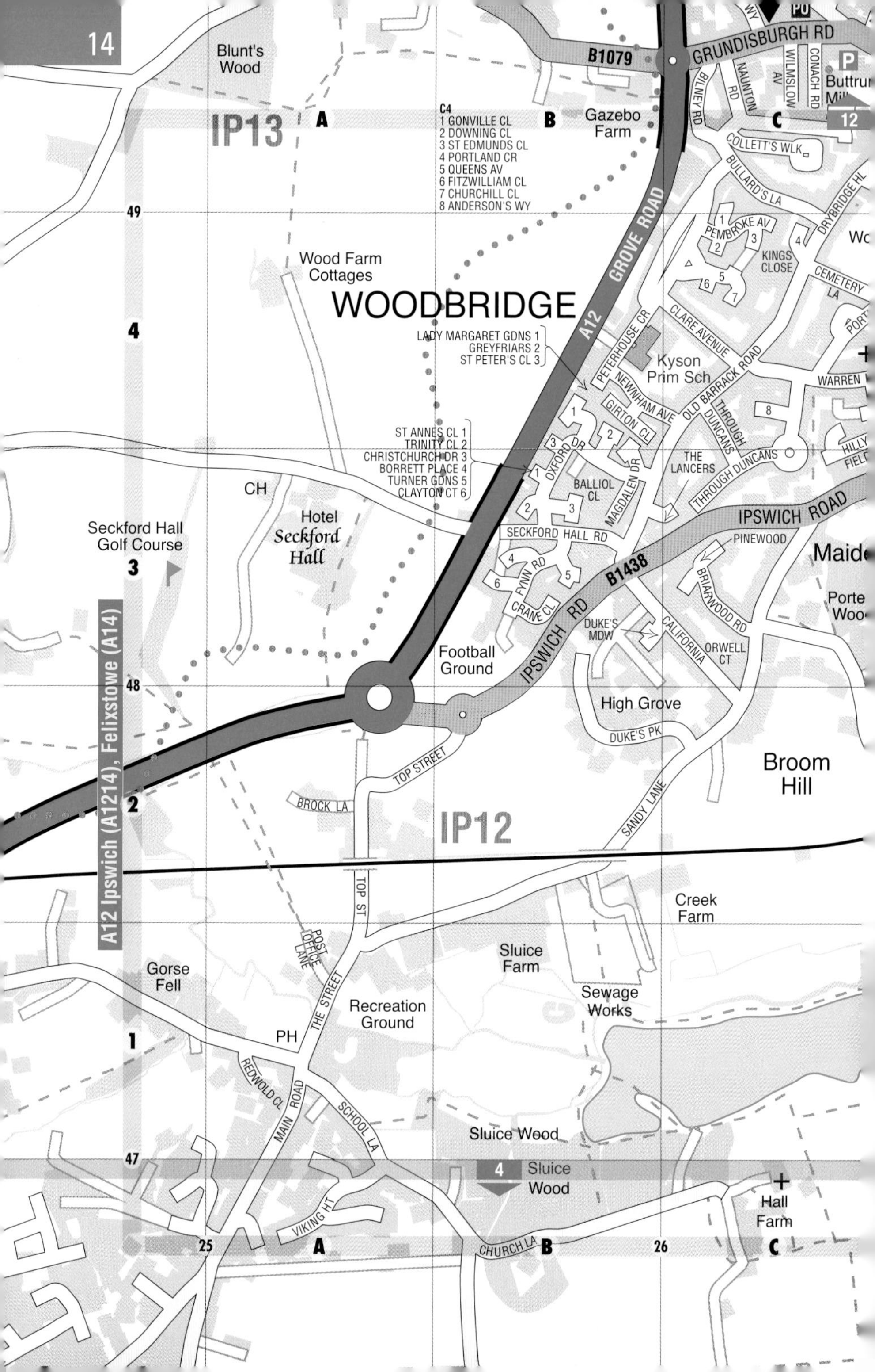
Blunt's Wood
B1079
GRUNDISBURGH RD
BILNEY RD
NAUNTON RD
WILMSLOW AV
CONACH RD
Buttrum Mill
IP13
A
C4
1 GONVILLE CL
2 DOWNING CL
3 ST EDMUNDS CL
4 PORTLAND CR
5 QUEENS AV
6 FITZWILLIAM CL
7 CHURCHILL CL
8 ANDERSON'S WY
B
Gazebo Farm
C
12
COLLETT'S WLK
BULLARD'S LA
GROVE ROAD
PEMBROKE AV
KINGS CLOSE
DRYBRIDGE HL
CEMETERY LA
49
Wood Farm Cottages
WOODBRIDGE
A12
4
LADY MARGARET GDNS 1
GREYFRIARS 2
ST PETER'S CL 3
PETERHOUSE CR
CLARE AVENUE
Kyson Prim Sch
OLD BARRACK ROAD
NEWNHAM AVE
GIRTON CL
WARREN
THROUGH DUNCANS
ST ANNES CL 1
TRINITY CL 2
CHRISTCHURCH DR 3
BORRETT PLACE 4
TURNER GDNS 5
CLAYTON CT 6
OXFORD DR
MAGDALEN DR
BALLIOL CL
THE LANCERS
CH
Hotel Seckford Hall
Seckford Hall Golf Course
SECKFORD HALL RD
IPSWICH ROAD
PINEWOOD
3
FYNN RD
CRANE CL
B1438
IPSWICH RD
DUKE'S MDW
CALIFORNIA
BRIARWOOD RD
ORWELL CT
Porter's Wood
A12 Ipswich (A1214), Felixstowe (A14)
Football Ground
48
High Grove
DUKE'S PK
TOP STREET
Broom Hill
2
BROCK LA
SANDY LANE
IP12
TOP ST
Creek Farm
POST OFFICE LANE
Sluice Farm
Gorse Fell
Sewage Works
THE STREET
Recreation Ground
1
PH
REDWOLD CL
MAIN ROAD
SCHOOL LA
Sluice Wood
47
4
Sluice Wood
Hall Farm
VIKING HT
25
A
CHURCH LA
B
26
C

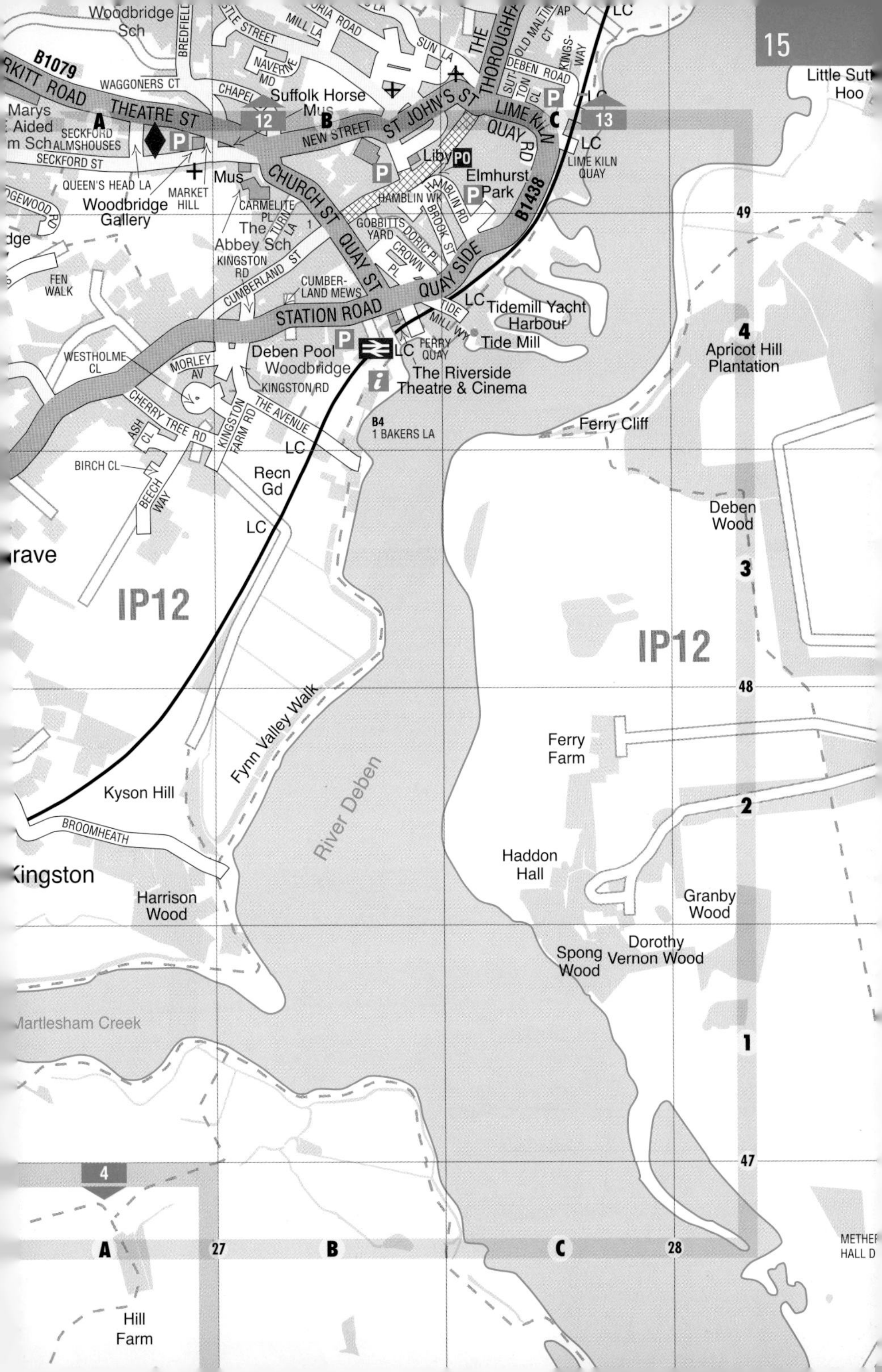
Woodbridge Sch
B1079
THEATRE ST
SECKFORD ALMSHOUSES
SECKFORD ST
QUEEN'S HEAD LA
MARKET HILL
Woodbridge Gallery
Mus
Suffolk Horse Mus
NEW STREET
ST JOHN'S ST
THE THOROUGHFARE
LIME KILN QUAY RD
LIME KILN QUAY
CHURCH ST
QUAY ST
CARMELITE PL
The Abbey Sch
KINGSTON RD
CUMBERLAND ST
CUMBER-LAND MEWS
STATION ROAD
QUAY SIDE
B1438
Liby
PO
Elmhurst Park
HAMBLIN WK
HAMBLIN RD
BROOK ST
GOBBITTS YARD
DORIC PL
CROWN PL
Tidemill Yacht Harbour
Tide Mill
TIDE MILL WY
FERRY QUAY
Deben Pool Woodbridge
The Riverside Theatre & Cinema
B4
1 BAKERS LA
WESTHOLME CL
MORLEY AV
CHERRY TREE RD
KINGSTON FARM RD
THE AVENUE
ASH CL
BIRCH CL
BEECH WAY
FEN WALK
Recn Gd
LC
IP12
Fynn Valley Walk
River Deben
Kyson Hill
BROOMHEATH
Kingston
Harrison Wood
Martlesham Creek
Hill Farm
Ferry Cliff
Apricot Hill Plantation
Deben Wood
Ferry Farm
Haddon Hall
Granby Wood
Dorothy Vernon Wood
Spong Wood
Little Sutton Hoo
A
B
C
12
13
4
27
28
49
48
47
1
2
3
4

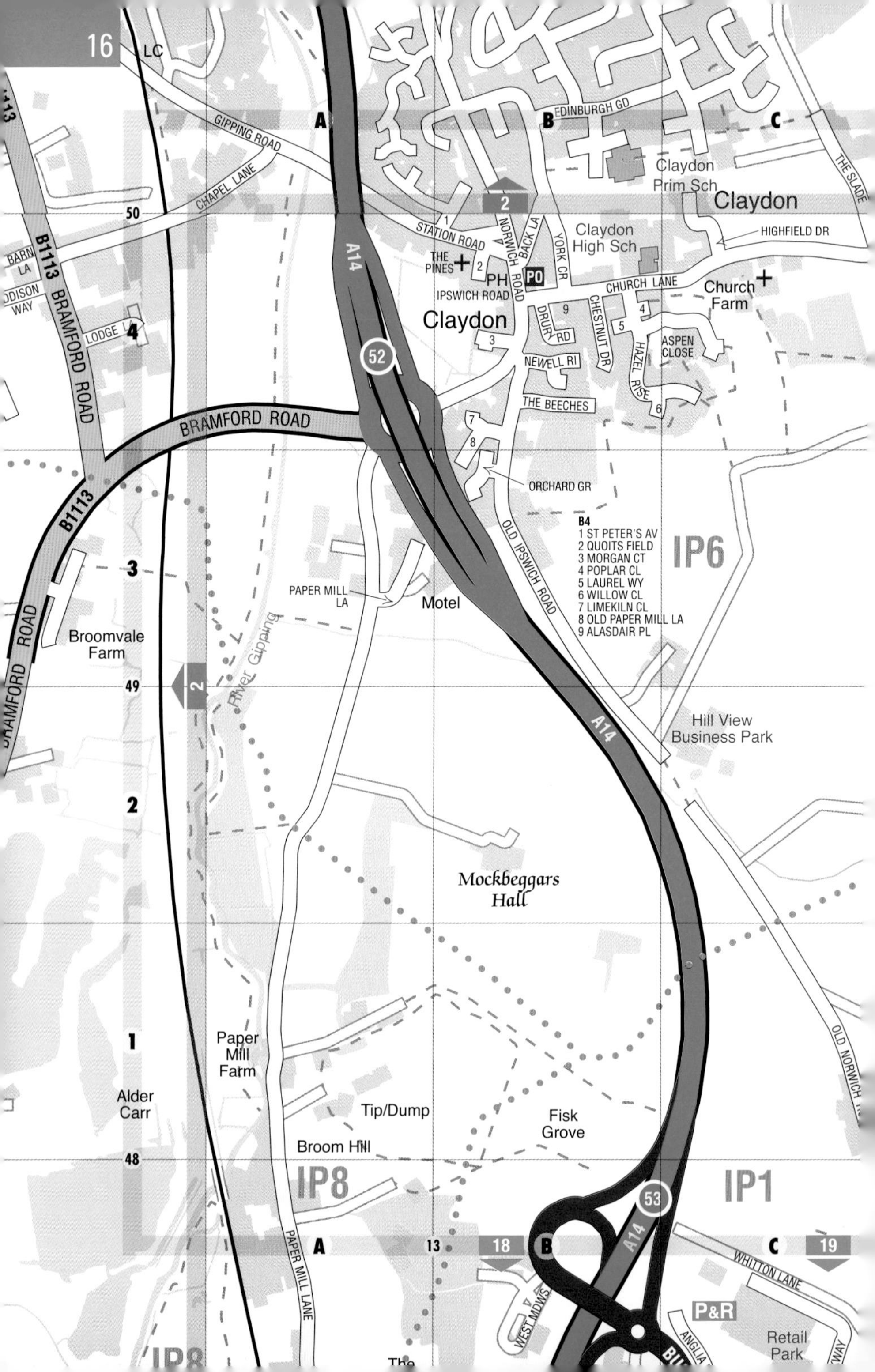

LC
GIPPING ROAD
CHAPEL LANE
EDINBURGH GD
Claydon Prim Sch
Claydon
HIGHFIELD DR
THE SLADE
STATION ROAD
NORWICH ROAD
BACK LA
YORK CR
Claydon High Sch
THE PINES
PH
PO
IPSWICH ROAD
CHURCH LANE
Church Farm
Claydon
DRURY RD
CHESTNUT DR
HAZEL RISE
ASPEN CLOSE
NEWELL RI
THE BEECHES
ORCHARD GR
A14
52
BARN LA
ODDISON WAY
B1113 BRAMFORD ROAD
LODGE LA
BRAMFORD ROAD
B1113
OLD IPSWICH ROAD
B4
1 ST PETER'S AV
2 QUOITS FIELD
3 MORGAN CT
4 POPLAR CL
5 LAUREL WY
6 WILLOW CL
7 LIMEKILN CL
8 OLD PAPER MILL LA
9 ALASDAIR PL
IP6
PAPER MILL LA
Motel
BRAMFORD ROAD
Broomvale Farm
River Gipping
Hill View Business Park
Mockbeggars Hall
OLD NORWICH
Paper Mill Farm
Alder Carr
Tip/Dump
Fisk Grove
Broom Hill
IP8
IP1
53
PAPER MILL LANE
18
19
WHITTON LANE
P&R
WEST MDWS
ANGLIA
Retail Park

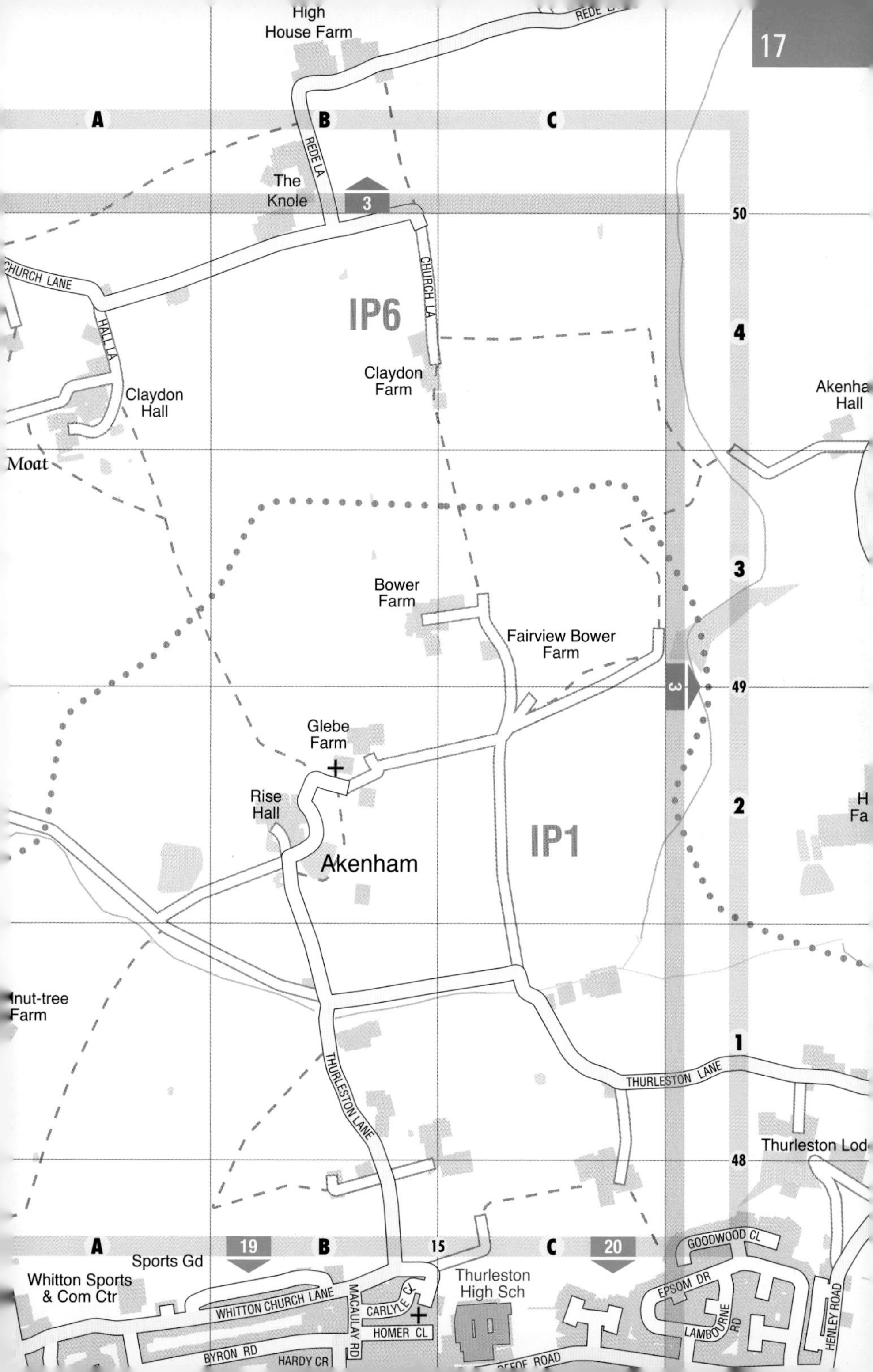
High House Farm
REDE LA
A
B
C
The Knole
3
50
CHURCH LANE
CHURCH LA
IP6
HALL LA
4
Claydon Farm
Claydon Hall
Akenham Hall
Moat
3
Bower Farm
Fairview Bower Farm
3
49
Glebe Farm
Rise Hall
2
IP1
Akenham
nut-tree Farm
1
THURLESTON LANE
THURLESTON LANE
Thurleston Lod
48
A
19
B
15
C
20
GOODWOOD CL
Sports Gd
Whitton Sports & Com Ctr
Thurleston High Sch
EPSOM DR
WHITTON CHURCH LANE
MACAULAY RD
CARLYLE CL
HOMER CL
LAMBOURNE RD
HENLEY ROAD
BYRON RD
HARDY CR

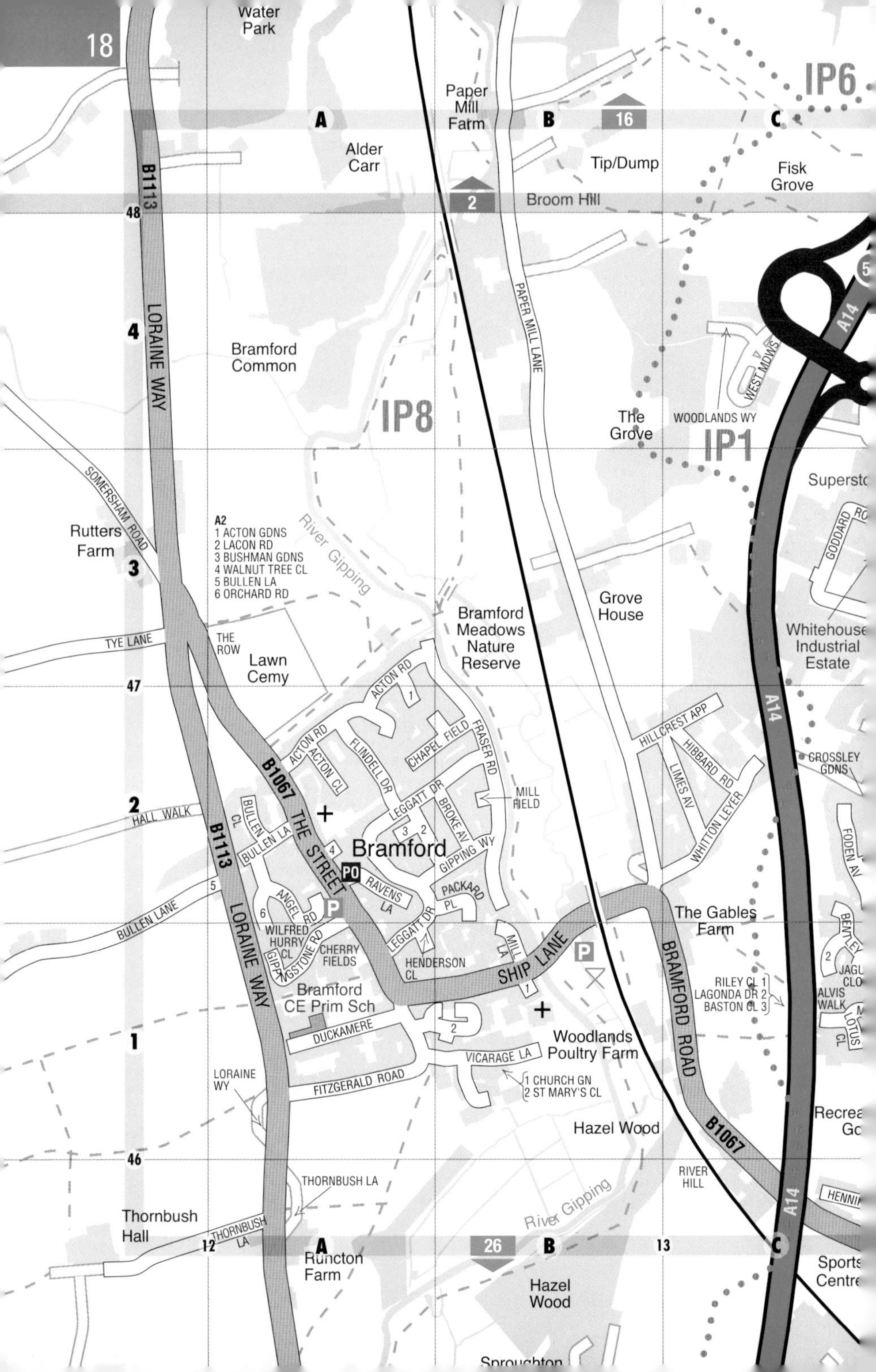

Water Park

18

Paper Mill Farm

A

Alder Carr

B

16

C

Tip/Dump

Fisk Grove

IP6

B1113

48

2

Broom Hill

4

Bramford Common

PAPER MILL LANE

IP8

The Grove

WOODLANDS WY

WESTMEADOW

IP1

Supersto

A14

5

Somersham Road

Rutters Farm

3

River Gipping

Grove House

Whitehouse Industrial Estate

GODDARD

RO

A2
1 ACTON GDNS
2 LACON RD
3 BUSHMAN GDNS
4 WALNUT TREE CL
5 BULLEN LA
6 ORCHARD RD

Bramford Meadows Nature Reserve

TYE LANE

THE ROW

Lawn Cemy

47

ACTON RD

HILLCREST APP

HIBBARD RD

LIMES AV

CROSSLEY GDNS

WHITTON LEYER

A14

FODEN AV

HALL WALK

2

B1067

THE STREET

BULLEN LA

ACTON RD

FLUNDELL DR

ACTON CL

CHAPEL FIELD

FRASER RD

LEGGATT DR

BROKE AV

MILL FIELD

GIPPING WY

B1113

LORAINE WAY

BULLEN CL

5

BULLEN LANE

Bramford

PO

RAVENS LA

PACKARD PL

The Gables Farm

BENTLEY

JAGU CLO

2

6

ANGEL RD

BAGSTONE RD

WILFRED HURRY CL

CHERRY FIELDS

LEGGATT DR

HENDERSON CL

SHIP LANE

MILL

P

BRAMFORD ROAD

RILEY CL 1
LAGONDA DR 2
BASTON CL 3

ALVIS WALK

LOTUS CL

Bramford CE Prim Sch

DUCKAMERE

2

VICARAGE LA

Woodlands Poultry Farm

LORAINE WY

FITZGERALD ROAD

1 CHURCH GN
2 ST MARY'S CL

Hazel Wood

B1067

46

THORNBUSH LA

RIVER HILL

A14

HENNI

Thornbush Hall

12

THORNBUSH LA

A

Runction Farm

26

B

Hazel Wood

13

River Gipping

C

Sports Centre

Sproughton

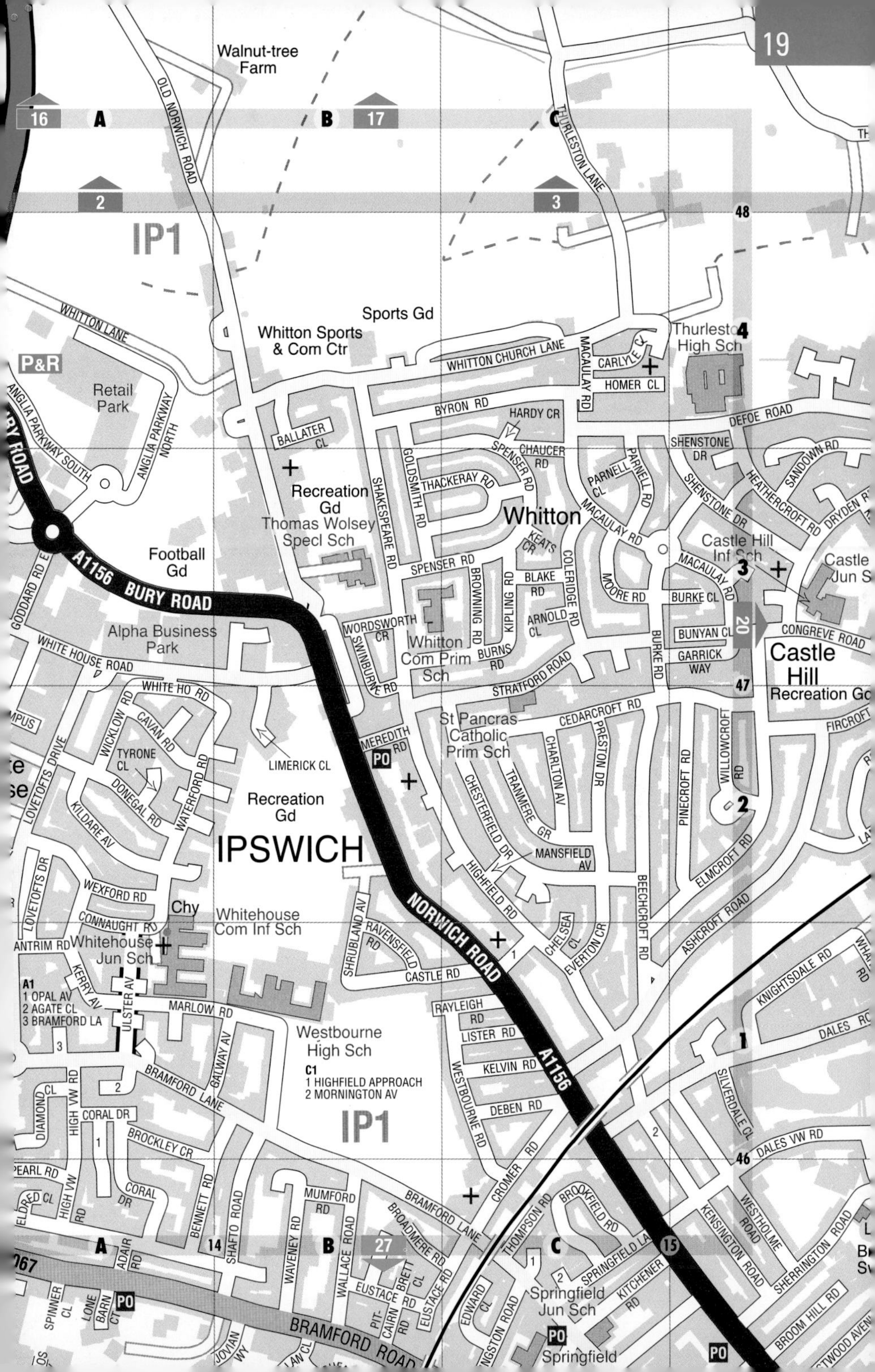
Walnut-tree Farm
OLD NORWICH ROAD
THURLESTON LANE
IP1
WHITTON LANE
Sports Gd
Whitton Sports & Com Ctr
P&R
Retail Park
ANGLIA PARKWAY SOUTH
ANGLIA PARKWAY NORTH
WHITTON CHURCH LANE
MACAULAY RD
CARLYLE CL
HOMER CL
Thurleston High Sch
BYRON RD
HARDY CR
DEFOE ROAD
BALLATER CL
SHENSTONE DR
SANDOWN RD
CHAUCER RD
SPENSER RD
THACKERAY RD
GOLDSMITH RD
SHAKESPEARE RD
PARNELL CL
PARNELL RD
HEATHERCROFT RD
DRYDEN RD
Recreation Gd
Thomas Wolsey Specl Sch
Whitton
KEATS CR
Castle Hill Inf Sch
Castle Jun S
Football Gd
A1156 BURY ROAD
BROWNING RD
KIPLING RD
BLAKE RD
COLERIDGE RD
MOORE RD
BURKE CL
ARNOLD CL
Alpha Business Park
WORDSWORTH CR
SWINBURNE RD
Whitton Com Prim Sch
BURNS RD
BUNYAN CL
CONGREVE ROAD
GARRICK WAY
Castle Hill
Recreation Gd
WHITE HOUSE ROAD
WHITE HO RD
STRATFORD ROAD
BURKE RD
WICKLOW RD
CAVAN RD
MEREDITH RD
St Pancras Catholic Prim Sch
CEDARCROFT RD
FIRCROFT
TYRONE CL
LOVETOFTS DRIVE
DONEGAL RD
WATERFORD RD
LIMERICK CL
PO
CHARLTON AV
PRESTON DR
PINECROFT RD
WILLOWCROFT RD
KILDARE AV
Recreation Gd
IPSWICH
CHESTERFIELD DR
TRANMERE GR
ELMCROFT RD
MANSFIELD AV
LOVETOFTS DR
WEXFORD RD
HIGHFIELD RD
BEECHCROFT RD
Chy
CONNAUGHT RD
Whitehouse Com Inf Sch
NORWICH ROAD
SHRUBLAND AV
RAVENSFIELD RD
ASHCROFT ROAD
ANTRIM RD
Whitehouse Jun Sch
CHELSEA CL
EVERTON CR
KNIGHTSDALE RD
KERRY AV
CASTLE RD
A1
1 OPAL AV
2 AGATE CL
3 BRAMFORD LA
ULSTER AV
MARLOW RD
RAYLEIGH RD
LISTER RD
DALES RD
Westbourne High Sch
A1156
KELVIN RD
C1
1 HIGHFIELD APPROACH
2 MORNINGTON AV
BRAMFORD LANE
GALWAY AV
WESTBOURNE RD
SILVERDALE CL
DIAMOND CL
HIGH VW RD
CORAL DR
DEBEN RD
IP1
DALES VW RD
BROCKLEY CR
CROMER RD
PEARL RD
CORAL DR
BENNETT RD
MUMFORD RD
BROOKFIELD RD
WESTHOLME ROAD
KENSINGTON ROAD
SHERRINGTON ROAD
SHAFTO ROAD
WAVENEY RD
WALLACE ROAD
BROADMERE RD
THOMPSON RD
SPRINGFIELD LA
ADAIR RD
BRETT CL
EUSTACE RD
KITCHENER RD
BROOM HILL RD
SPINNER CL
LONE BARN CT
PIT-CAIRN RD
EDWARD CL
Springfield Jun Sch
BRAMFORD ROAD
JOVIAN WY
Springfield

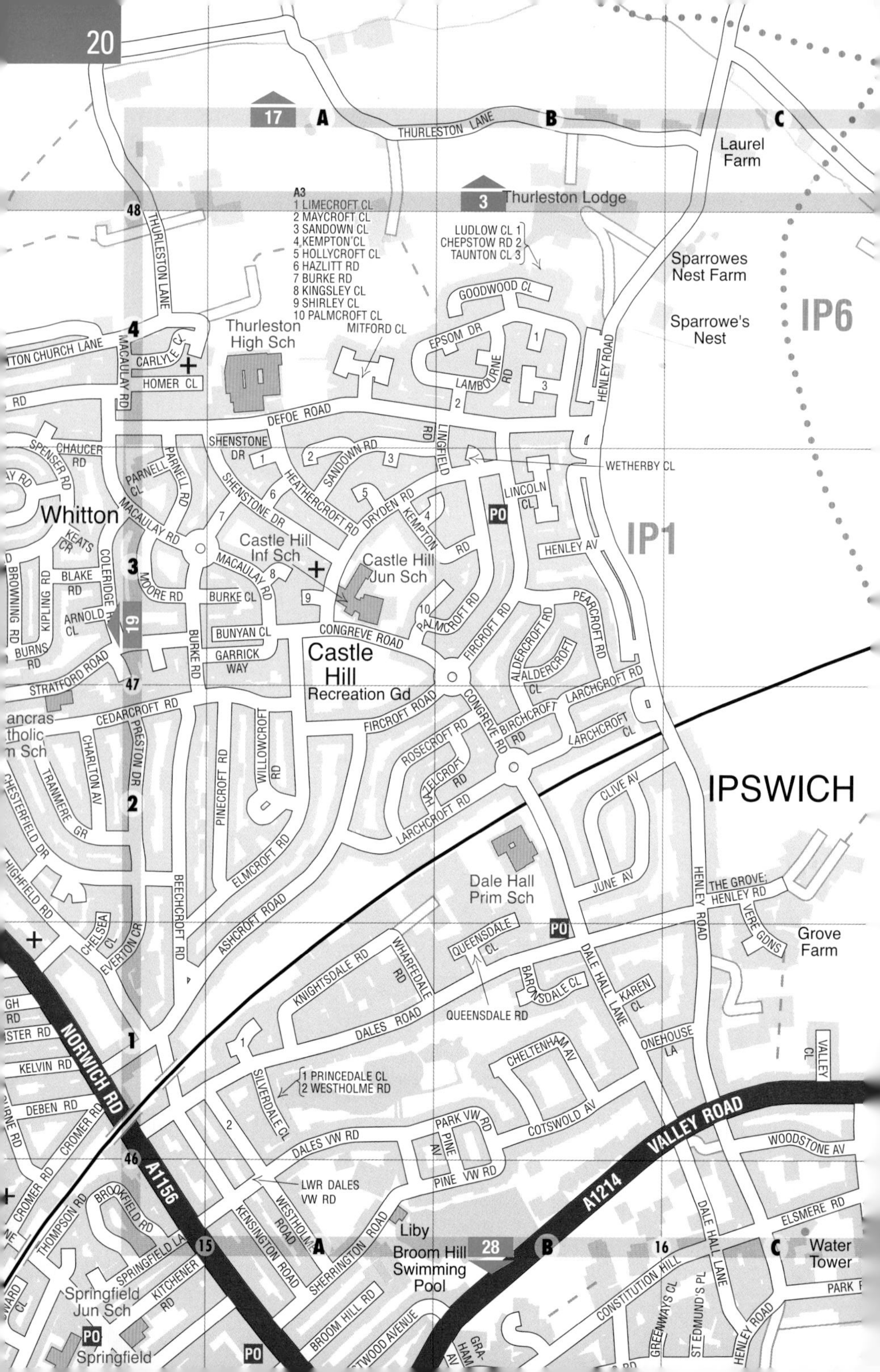

17
A
B
C
THURLESTON LANE
Laurel Farm
3
Thurleston Lodge
48
THURLESTON LANE
A3
1 LIMECROFT CL
2 MAYCROFT CL
3 SANDOWN CL
4 KEMPTON CL
5 HOLLYCROFT CL
6 HAZLITT RD
7 BURKE RD
8 KINGSLEY CL
9 SHIRLEY CL
10 PALMCROFT CL
LUDLOW CL 1
CHEPSTOW RD 2
TAUNTON CL 3
Sparrowes Nest Farm
GOODWOOD CL
Sparrowe's Nest
IP6
4
TON CHURCH LANE
MACAULAY RD
CARLYLE CL
Thurleston High Sch
MITFORD CL
EPSOM DR
LAMBOURNE RD
HENLEY ROAD
HOMER CL
RD
DEFOE ROAD
SHENSTONE DR
SANDOWN RD
LINGFIELD RD
WETHERBY CL
CHAUCER RD
SPENSER RD
PARNELL CL
PARNELL RD
SHENSTONE DR
HEATHERCROFT RD
DRYDEN RD
KEMPTON RD
LINCOLN CL
PO
Whitton
MACAULAY RD
Castle Hill Inf Sch
Castle Hill Jun Sch
IP1
HENLEY AV
KEATS CR
3
BLAKE RD
COLERIDGE RD
MOORE RD
MACAULAY RD
BURKE CL
PALMCROFT RD
PEARCROFT RD
BROWNING RD
KIPLING RD
ARNOLD CL
19
BUNYAN CL
CONGREVE ROAD
FIRCROFT RD
ALDERCROFT RD
ALDERCROFT CL
BURNS RD
GARRICK WAY
BURKE RD
Castle Hill Recreation Gd
LARCHCROFT RD
STRATFORD ROAD
47
CONGREVE RD
BIRCHCROFT RD
LARCHCROFT CL
ancras tholic n Sch
CEDARCROFT RD
PRESTON DR
FIRCROFT ROAD
CHARLTON AV
WILLOWCROFT RD
ROSECROFT RD
CHESTERFIELD DR
TRANMERE GR
PINECROFT RD
HAZELCROFT RD
CLIVE AV
IPSWICH
2
LARCHCROFT RD
ELMCROFT RD
Dale Hall Prim Sch
HIGHFIELD RD
BEECHCROFT RD
JUNE AV
HENLEY ROAD
THE GROVE; HENLEY RD
ASHCROFT ROAD
VERE GDNS
CHELSEA CL
EVERTON CR
PO
Grove Farm
QUEENSDALE CL
KNIGHTSDALE RD
WHARFEDALE RD
DALE HALL LANE
BARONSDALE CL
KAREN CL
GH
RD
STER RD
NORWICH RD
DALES ROAD
QUEENSDALE RD
1
ONEHOUSE LA
VALLEY CL
KELVIN RD
CHELTENHAM AV
1 PRINCEDALE CL
2 WESTHOLME RD
SILVERDALE CL
DEBEN RD
CROMER RD
PARK VW RD
COTSWOLD AV
VALLEY ROAD
A1214
WOODSTONE AV
DALES VW RD
PINE AV
46
A1156
PINE VW RD
LWR DALES VW RD
CROMER RD
THOMPSON RD
BROOKFIELD RD
KENSINGTON ROAD
WESTHOLME ROAD
DALE HALL LANE
ELSMERE RD
15
A
SHERRINGTON ROAD
Liby
28
B
16
C
Water Tower
SPRINGFIELD LA
Broom Hill Swimming Pool
CONSTITUTION HILL
GREENWAYS CL
ST EDMUND'S PL
PARK
KITCHENER RD
Springfield Jun Sch
BROOM HILL RD
HENLEY ROAD
PO
PO
Springfield
TWOOD AVENUE
GRAHAM AV

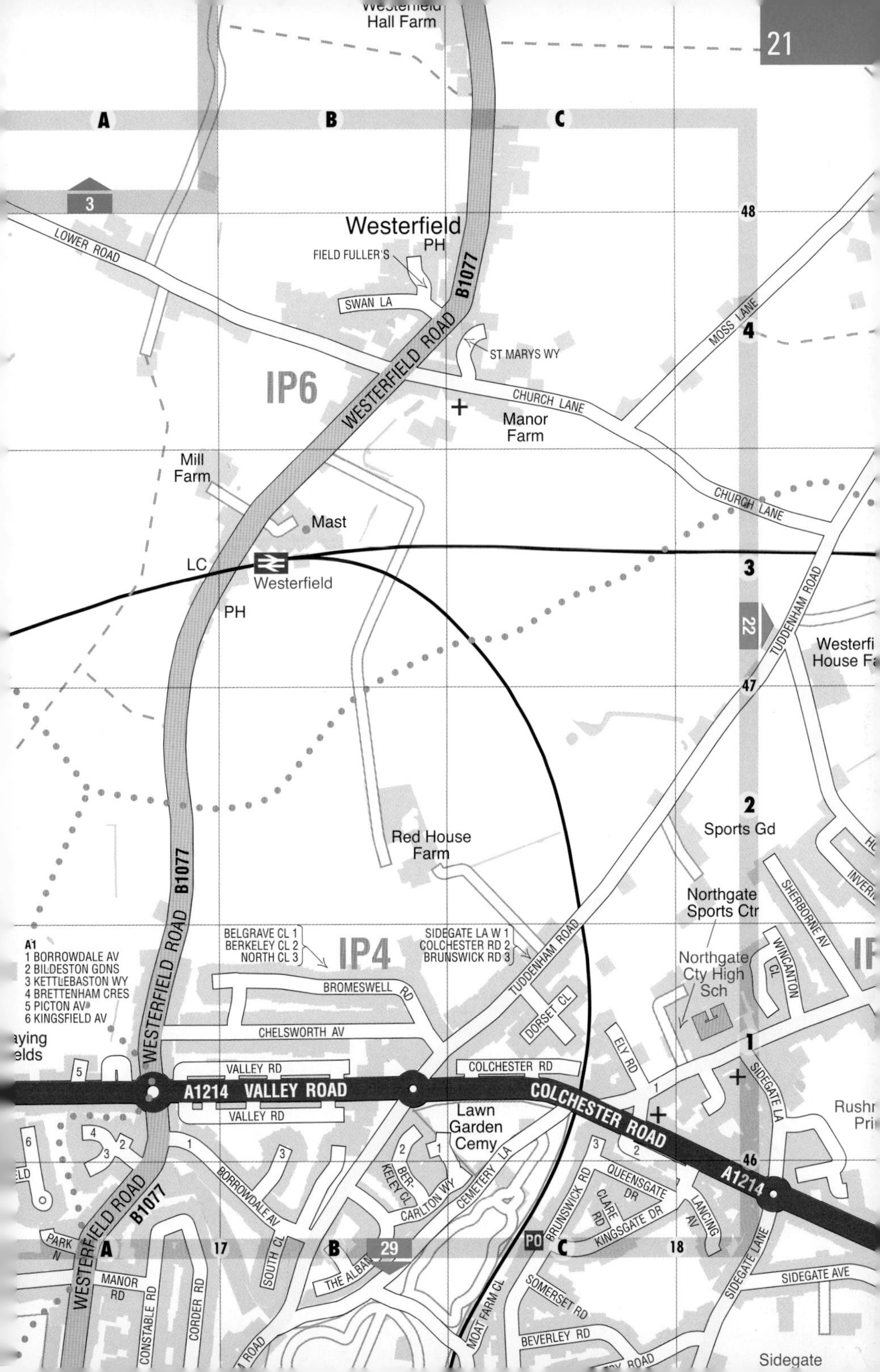
Westerfield Hall Farm
A
B
C
3
48
Westerfield
PH
FIELD FULLER'S
SWAN LA
B1077
LOWER ROAD
WESTERFIELD ROAD
ST MARYS WY
MOSS LANE
4
IP6
CHURCH LANE
Manor Farm
Mill Farm
Mast
CHURCH LANE
LC
Westerfield
PH
3
22
TUDDENHAM ROAD
Westerfield House Fa
47
2
Sports Gd
Red House Farm
Northgate Sports Ctr
SHERBORNE AV
A1
1 BORROWDALE AV
2 BILDESTON GDNS
3 KETTLEBASTON WY
4 BRETTENHAM CRES
5 PICTON AV
6 KINGSFIELD AV
BELGRAVE CL 1
BERKELEY CL 2
NORTH CL 3
IP4
SIDEGATE LA W 1
COLCHESTER RD 2
BRUNSWICK RD 3
TUDDENHAM ROAD
Northgate Cty High Sch
WINCANTON CL
BROMESWELL RD
DORSET CL
CHELSWORTH AV
ELY RD
1
VALLEY RD
COLCHESTER RD
A1214 VALLEY ROAD
COLCHESTER ROAD
SIDEGATE LA
Rushm Pri
VALLEY RD
Lawn Garden Cemy
BER-KELEY CL
CARLTON WY
CEMETERY LA
BORROWDALE AV
SOUTH CL
BRUNSWICK RD
QUEENSGATE DR
CLARE RD
KINGSGATE DR
LANCING AV
46
A1214
PARK N
A
17
B
29
PO
C
18
SIDEGATE LANE
SIDEGATE AVE
MANOR RD
CONSTABLE RD
CORDER RD
THE ALBAN
MOAT FARM CL
SOMERSET RD
BEVERLEY RD
Sidegate

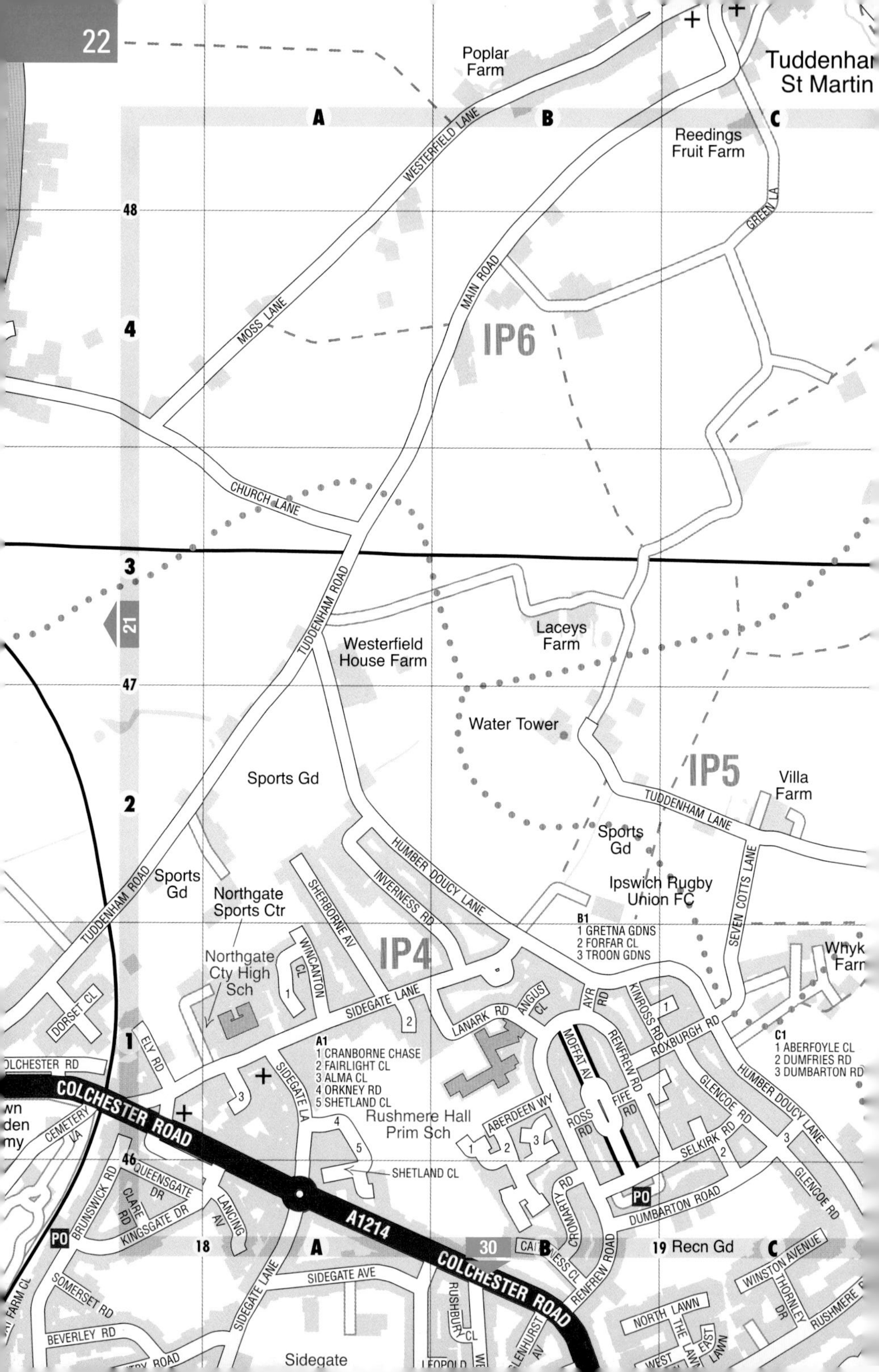
22
Poplar Farm
Tuddenham St Martin
Reedings Fruit Farm
A
B
C
WESTERFIELD LANE
GREEN LA
48
MAIN ROAD
MOSS LANE
4
IP6
CHURCH LANE
3
21
TUDDENHAM ROAD
Westerfield House Farm
Laceys Farm
47
Water Tower
Sports Gd
2
IP5
Villa Farm
TUDDENHAM LANE
Sports Gd
Sports Gd
Northgate Sports Ctr
HUMBER DOUCY LANE
INVERNESS RD
SHERBORNE AV
Ipswich Rugby Union FC
SEVEN COTTS LANE
B1
1 GRETNA GDNS
2 FORFAR CL
3 TROON GDNS
Northgate Cty High Sch
WINCANTON CL
IP4
Whyk Farm
TUDDENHAM ROAD
DORSET CL
SIDEGATE LANE
LANARK RD
ANGUS CL
AYR RD
KINROSS RD
ROXBURGH RD
1
ELY RD
A1
1 CRANBORNE CHASE
2 FAIRLIGHT CL
3 ALMA CL
4 ORKNEY RD
5 SHETLAND CL
MOFFAT AV
RENFREW RD
C1
1 ABERFOYLE CL
2 DUMFRIES RD
3 DUMBARTON RD
COLCHESTER RD
COLCHESTER ROAD
SIDEGATE LA
Rushmere Hall Prim Sch
ABERDEEN WY
ROSS RD
FIFE RD
GLENCOE RD
HUMBER DOUCY LANE
CEMETERY LA
SELKIRK RD
46
BRUNSWICK RD
QUEENSGATE DR
CLARE RD
SHETLAND CL
LANCING AV
CROMARTY RD
PO
DUMBARTON ROAD
GLENCOE RD
KINGSGATE DR
A1214
PO
18
A
30
CAITHNESS CL
19 Recn Gd
C
WINSTON AVENUE
SOMERSET RD
SIDEGATE AVE
RENFREW ROAD
THORNLEY DR
SIDEGATE LANE
RUSHBURY CL
COLCHESTER ROAD
NORTH LAWN
RUSHMERE
BEVERLEY RD
GLENHURST AV
THE LAWN
EAST LAWN
WEST
Sidegate
LEOPOLD

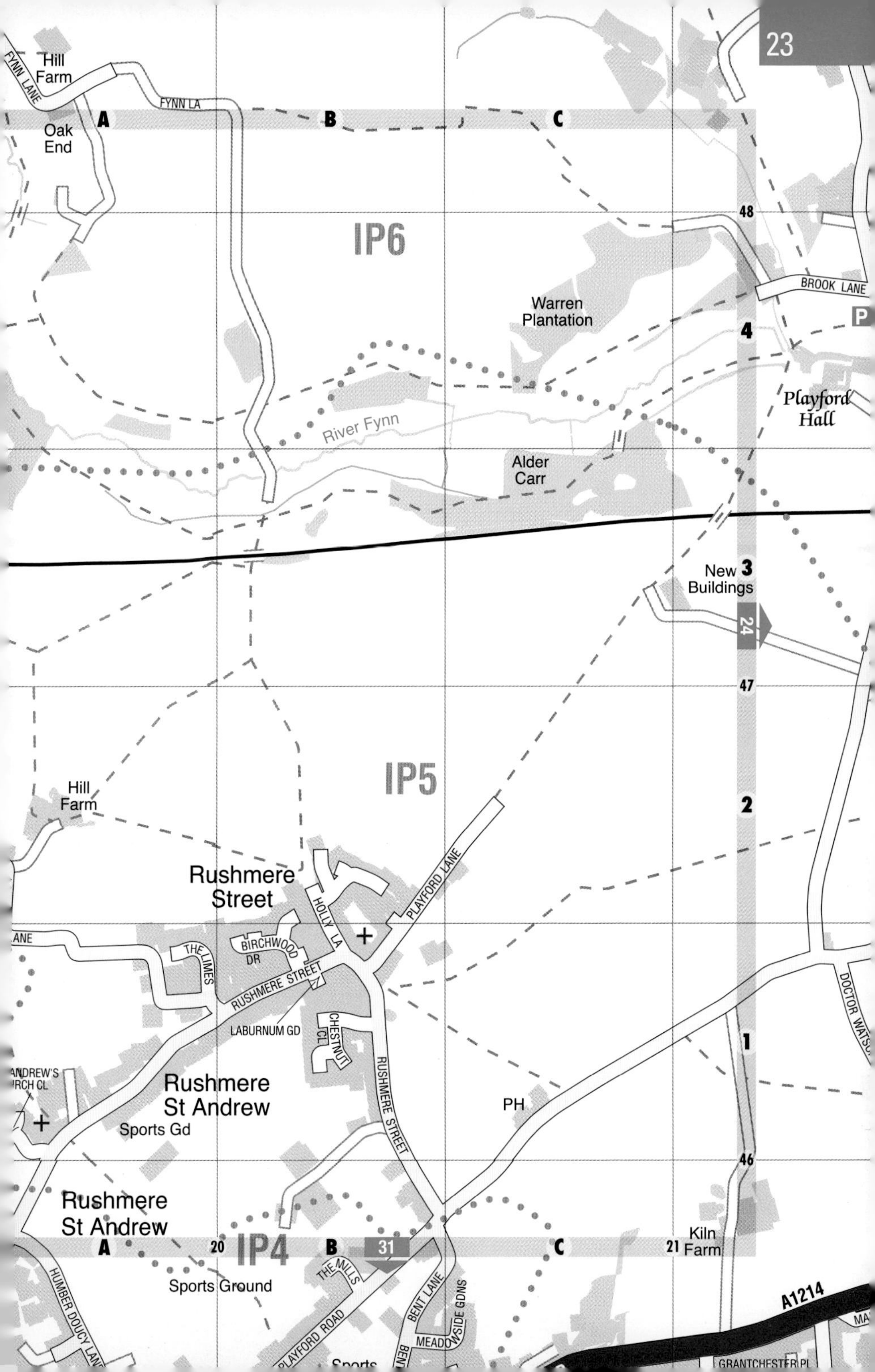
Hill Farm
FYNN LANE
FYNN LA
Oak End
A
B
C
IP6
48
BROOK LANE
P
Warren Plantation
4
Playford Hall
River Fynn
Alder Carr
New Buildings
3
24
47
IP5
Hill Farm
2
Rushmere Street
HOLLY LA
PLAYFORD LANE
LANE
THE LIMES
BIRCHWOOD DR
RUSHMERE STREET
LABURNUM GD
CHESTNUT CL
DOCTOR WATSO
1
ANDREW'S RCH CL
Rushmere St Andrew
Sports Gd
PH
46
Rushmere St Andrew
A
20
IP4
B
31
C
21
Kiln Farm
THE MILLS
Sports Ground
HUMBER DOUCY LANE
PLAYFORD ROAD
BENT LANE
MEADOWSIDE GDNS
A1214
GRANTCHESTER PL

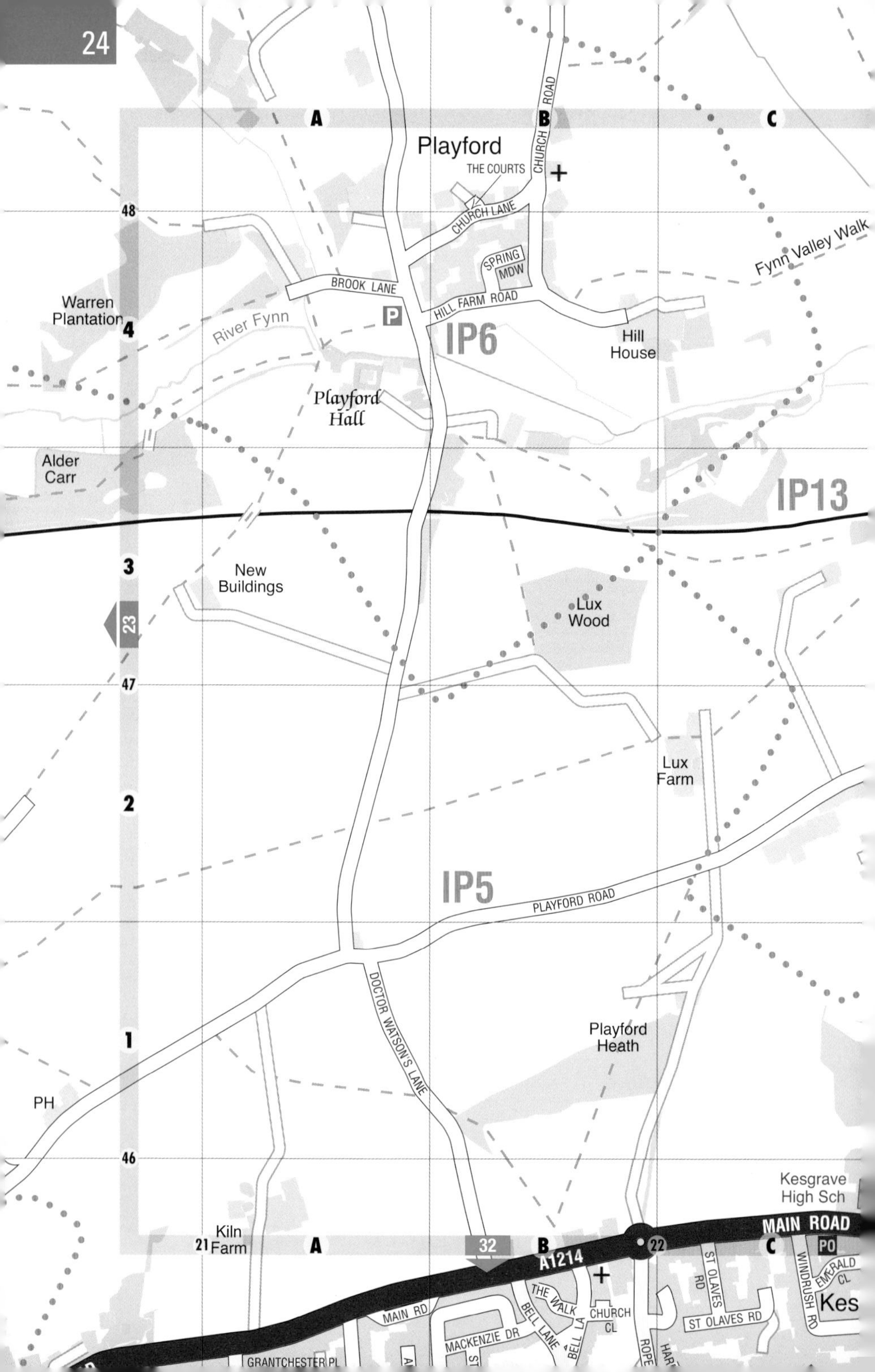
A
B
C
Playford
THE COURTS
CHURCH ROAD
CHURCH LANE
SPRING MDW
BROOK LANE
HILL FARM ROAD
Fynn Valley Walk
Warren Plantation
River Fynn
P
IP6
Hill House
Playford Hall
Alder Carr
IP13
New Buildings
Lux Wood
23
48
4
3
47
2
1
46
Lux Farm
IP5
PLAYFORD ROAD
DOCTOR WATSON'S LANE
Playford Heath
PH
Kiln Farm
21
32
A1214
22
MAIN ROAD
Kesgrave High Sch
PO
THE WALK
BELL LANE
BELL LA
CHURCH CL
ST OLAVES RD
ST OLAVES RD
WINDRUSH RD
EMERALD CL
Kes
MAIN RD
MACKENZIE DR
GRANTCHESTER PL
ROPE

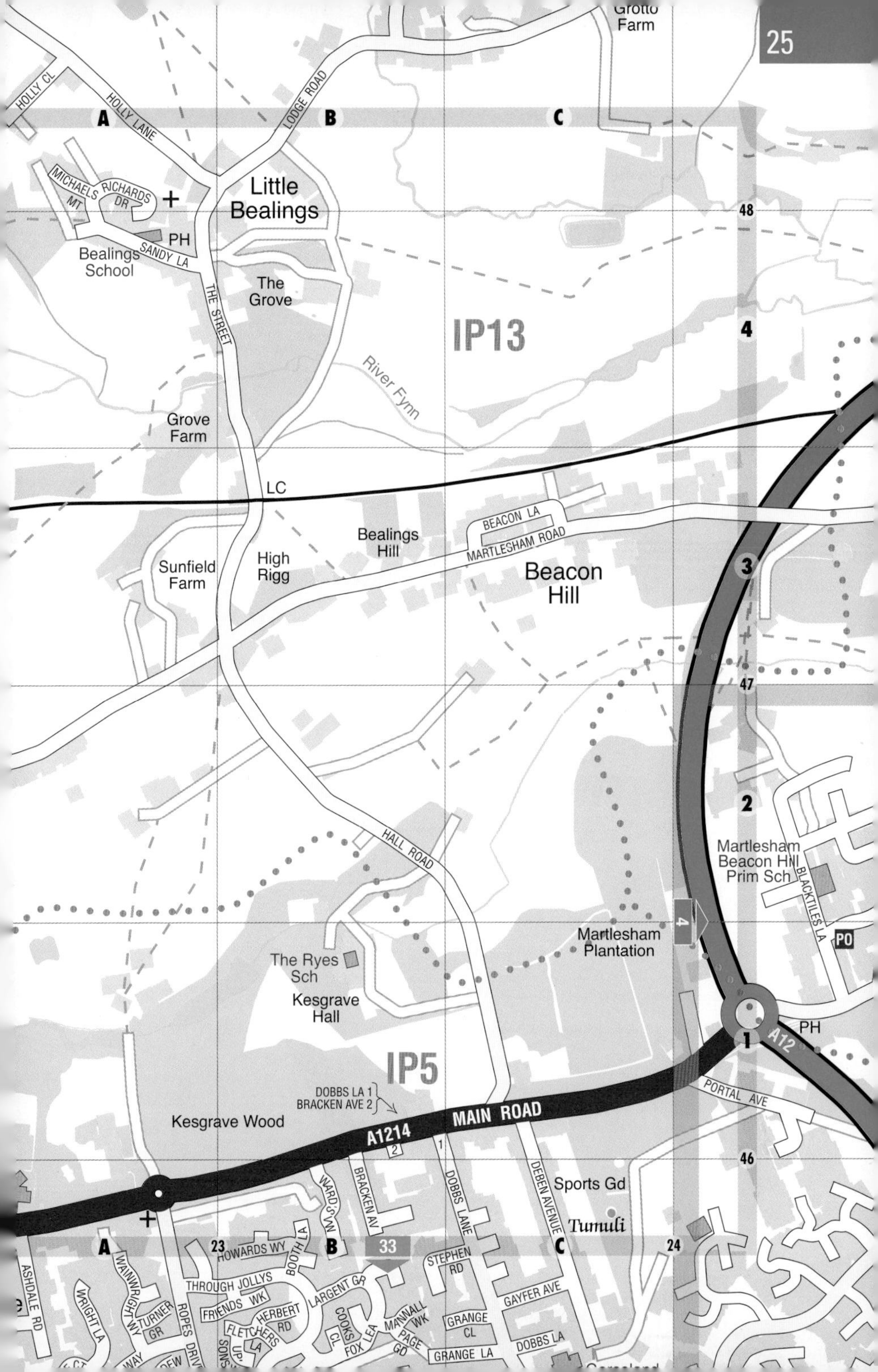

Grotto
Farm

HOLLY CL.

HOLLY LANE

LODGE ROAD

A **B** **C**

48

MICHAELS MT
RICHARDS DR
+
Little
Bealings

PH
SANDY LA

Bealings
School

THE STREET

The
Grove

IP13

4

River Fynn

Grove
Farm

LC

Sunfield
Farm

High
Rigg

Bealings
Hill

BEACON LA
MARTLESHAM ROAD

Beacon
Hill

3

47

2

Martlesham
Beacon Hill
Prim Sch

BLACKTILES LA

PO

HALL ROAD

The Ryes
Sch

Kesgrave
Hall

Martlesham
Plantation

4

IP5

1

A12

PH

DOBBS LA 1
BRACKEN AVE 2

Kesgrave Wood

A1214

2

MAIN ROAD

1

PORTAL AVE

DEBEN AVENUE

Sports Gd

46

+

A

23

HOWARDS WY

BOOTH LA

B

33

WARDS WY

BRACKEN AV

DOBBS LANE

Tumuli

C

24

WAINWRIGHT WY

WRIGHT LA

TURNER GR

THROUGH JOLLYS

FRIENDS WK

ROPES DRIVE

HERBERT RD

FLETCHERS

LARGENT GR

COOKS LEA

FOX LEA

UP SONES

STEPHEN RD

MINMALL WK

PAGE RD

GRANGE CL

GRANGE LA

DOBBS LA

GAYFER AVE

ASHDALE RD

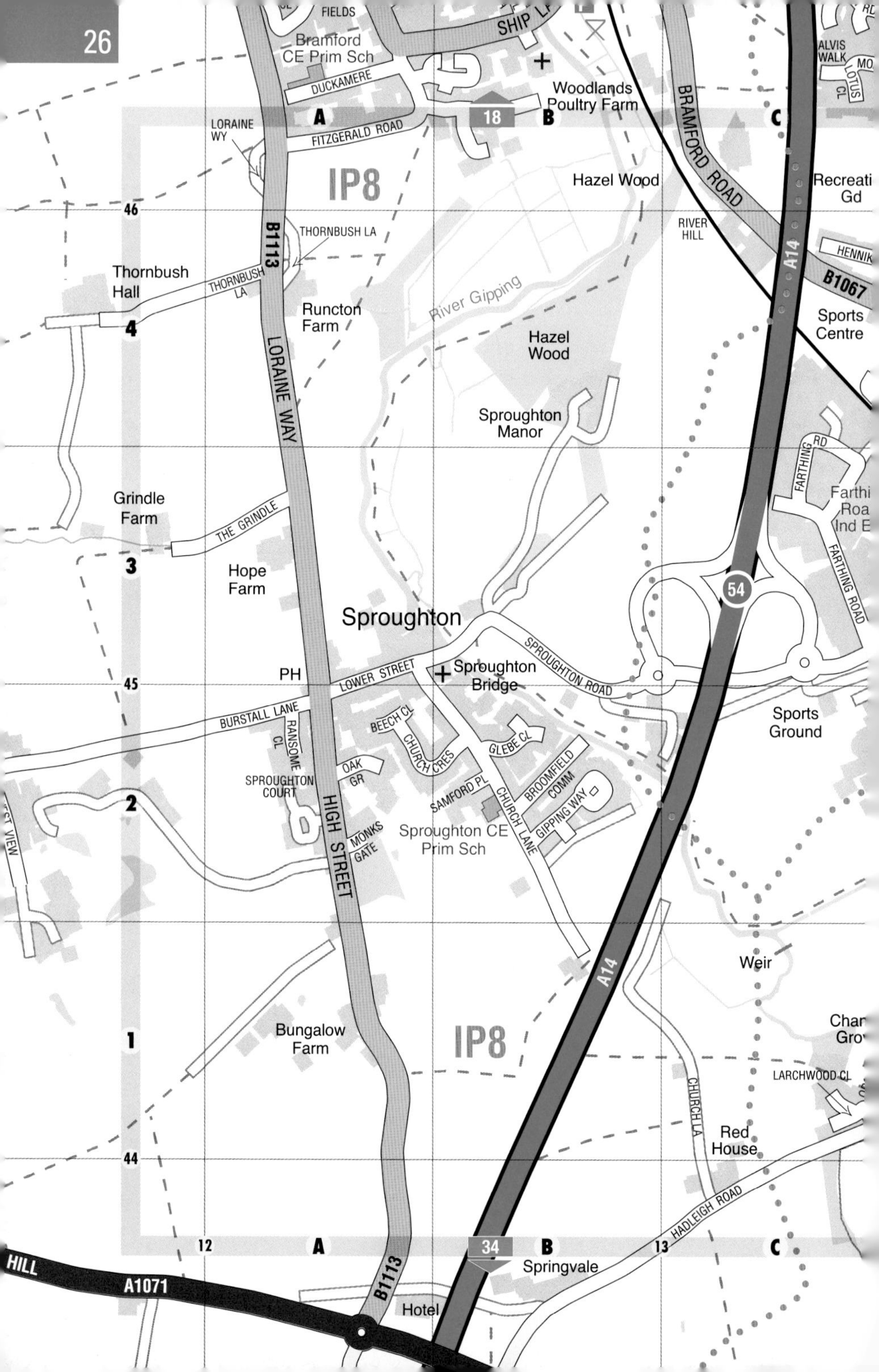
FIELDS
SHIP LA
Bramford CE Prim Sch
DUCKAMERE
Woodlands Poultry Farm
ALVIS WALK
LOTUS CL
A
18
B
C
LORAINE WY
FITZGERALD ROAD
BRAMFORD ROAD
IP8
Hazel Wood
Recreation Gd
46
B1113
THORNBUSH LA
RIVER HILL
A14
HENNIKER
B1067
Thornbush Hall
THORNBUSH LA
River Gipping
Runcton Farm
Sports Centre
4
Hazel Wood
LORAINE WAY
Sproughton Manor
FARTHING RD
Farthing Road Ind Est
Grindle Farm
THE GRINDLE
FARTHING ROAD
3
Hope Farm
54
Sproughton
SPROUGHTON ROAD
Sproughton Bridge
PH
LOWER STREET
45
BURSTALL LANE
RANSOME CL
BEECH CL
CHURCH CRES
GLEBE CL
Sports Ground
OAK GR
BROOMFIELD COMM
SPROUGHTON COURT
SAMFORD PL
GIPPING WAY
2
HIGH STREET
MONKS GATE
CHURCH LANE
Sproughton CE Prim Sch
A14
Weir
1
Bungalow Farm
IP8
LARCHWOOD CL
CHURCH LA
Red House
44
HADLEIGH ROAD
12
A
34
B
13
C
HILL
A1071
B1113
Springvale
Hotel

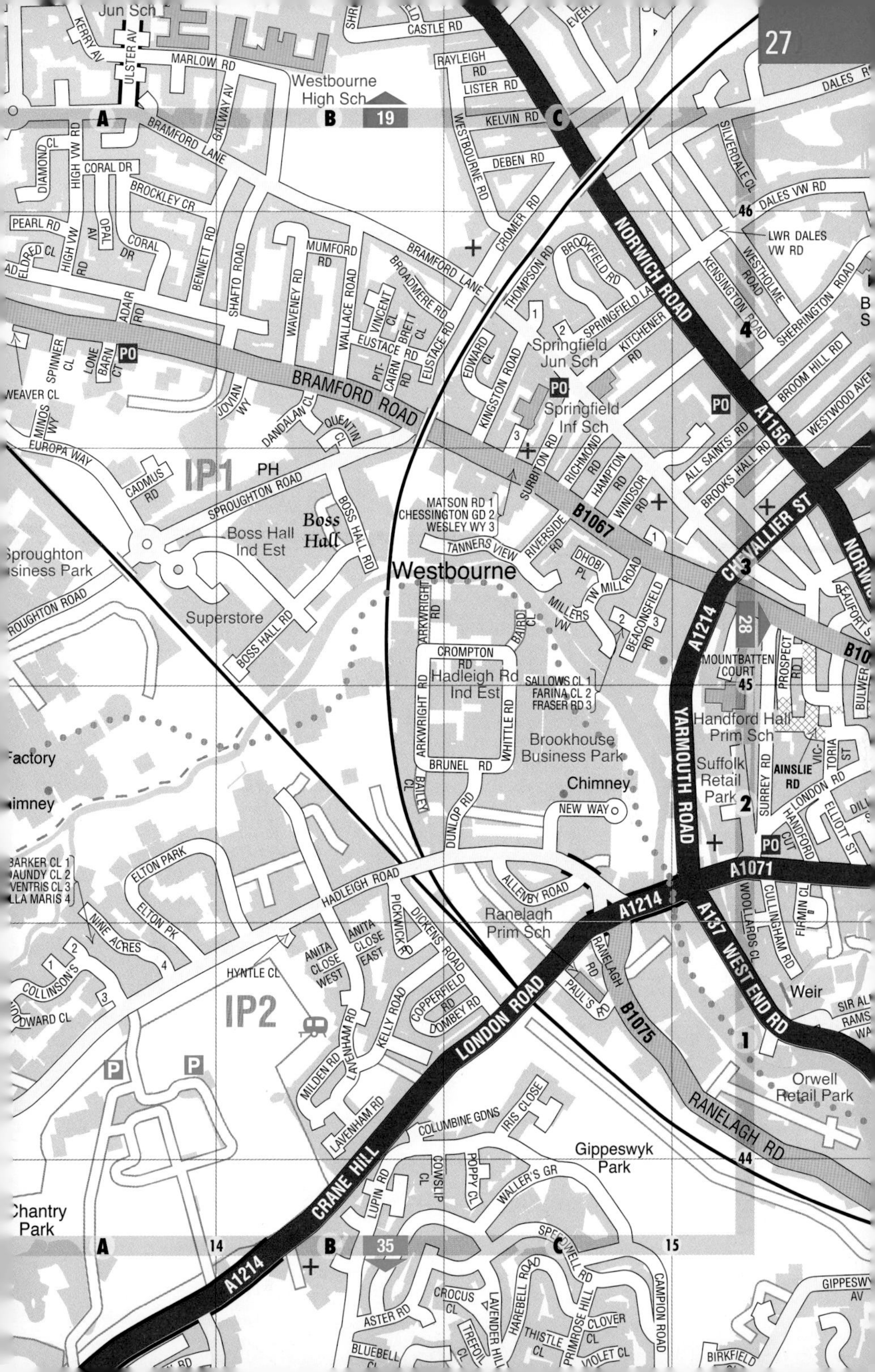
Jun Sch
KERRY AV
ULSTER AV
MARLOW RD
CASTLE RD
RAYLEIGH RD
LISTER RD
DALES RD
Westbourne High Sch
A
B
19
KELVIN RD
C
BRAMFORD LANE
GALWAY AV
DIAMOND CL
HIGH VW RD
CORAL DR
BROCKLEY CR
WESTBOURNE RD
DEBEN RD
SILVERDALE CL
DALES VW RD
46
LWR DALES VW RD
PEARL RD
OPAL AV
CORAL DR
BENNETT RD
SHAFTO ROAD
MUMFORD RD
BRAMFORD LANE
CROMER RD
NORWICH ROAD
ELDRED CL
HIGH VW RD
ADAIR RD
WAVENEY RD
WALLACE ROAD
BROADMERE RD
VINCENT CL
BRETT CL
EUSTACE RD
PIT-CAIRN RD
EUSTACE RD
THOMPSON RD
BROOKFIELD RD
SPRINGFIELD LA
KITCHENER RD
KENSINGTON ROAD
WESTHOLME ROAD
SHERRINGTON ROAD
4
SPINNER CL
LONE BARN CT
PO
WEAVER CL
BRAMFORD ROAD
EDWARD CL
KINGSTON ROAD
Springfield Jun Sch
PO
Springfield Inf Sch
BROOM HILL RD
WESTWOOD AVE
PO
A1156
MINOS WY
JOVIAN WY
DANDALAN CL
QUENTIN CL
EUROPA WAY
CADMUS RD
IP1
PH
SPROUGHTON ROAD
BOSS HALL RD
Boss Hall
Boss Hall Ind Est
SURBITON RD
RICHMOND RD
HAMPTON RD
WINDSOR RD
ALL SAINTS' RD
BROOKS HALL RD
MATSON RD 1
CHESSINGTON GD 2
WESLEY WY 3
B1067
TANNERS VIEW
RIVERSIDE RD
DHOBI PL
TW MILL ROAD
CHEVALLIER ST
NORWICH
3
Sproughton Business Park
SPROUGHTON ROAD
Westbourne
ARKWRIGHT RD
MILLERS VW
BEACONSFIELD RD
BEAUFORT ST
Superstore
BOSS HALL RD
BAIRD CL
CROMPTON RD
A1214
28
B10
Hadleigh Rd Ind Est
SALLOWS CL 1
FARINA CL 2
FRASER RD 3
MOUNTBATTEN COURT
PROSPECT RD
BULWER
45
ARKWRIGHT RD
WHITTLE RD
Brookhouse Business Park
YARMOUTH ROAD
Handford Hall Prim Sch
Factory
BRUNEL RD
BAILEY CL
Chimney
Suffolk Retail Park
SURREY RD
AINSLIE RD
VICTORIA ST
Chimney
DUNLOP RD
NEW WAY
LONDON RD
HANDFORD CUT
ELLIOTT ST
2
BARKER CL 1
DAUNDY CL 2
VENTRIS CL 3
ELTON PARK
HADLEIGH ROAD
ALLENBY ROAD
PO
A1071
ELTON PK
NINE ACRES
4
PICKWICK RD
DICKENS ROAD
ANITA CLOSE EAST
ANITA CLOSE WEST
Ranelagh Prim Sch
A1214
A137
WEST END RD
WOOLLARDS CL
CULLINGHAM RD
FIRMIN CL
HYNTLE CL
RANELAGH RD
PAUL'S RD
1
2
3
COLLINSON'S
EDWARD CL
IP2
KELLY ROAD
COPPERFIELD RD
DOMBEY RD
LONDON ROAD
B1075
Weir
SIR AL
RAMS
WA
1
LAVENHAM RD
MILDEN RD
P
P
Orwell Retail Park
COLUMBINE GDNS
IRIS CLOSE
RANELAGH RD
LAVENHAM RD
Gippeswyk Park
44
CRANE HILL
LUPIN RD
COWSLIP CL
POPPY CL
WALLER'S GR
Chantry Park
A
14
B
35
C
15
SPEEDWELL RD
A1214
HAREBELL ROAD
CAMPION ROAD
GIPPESWYK AV
CROCUS CL
LAVENDER HILL
ASTER RD
TREFOIL
PRIMROSE HILL
CLOVER CL
THISTLE CL
VIOLET CL
BLUEBELL
BIRKFIELD

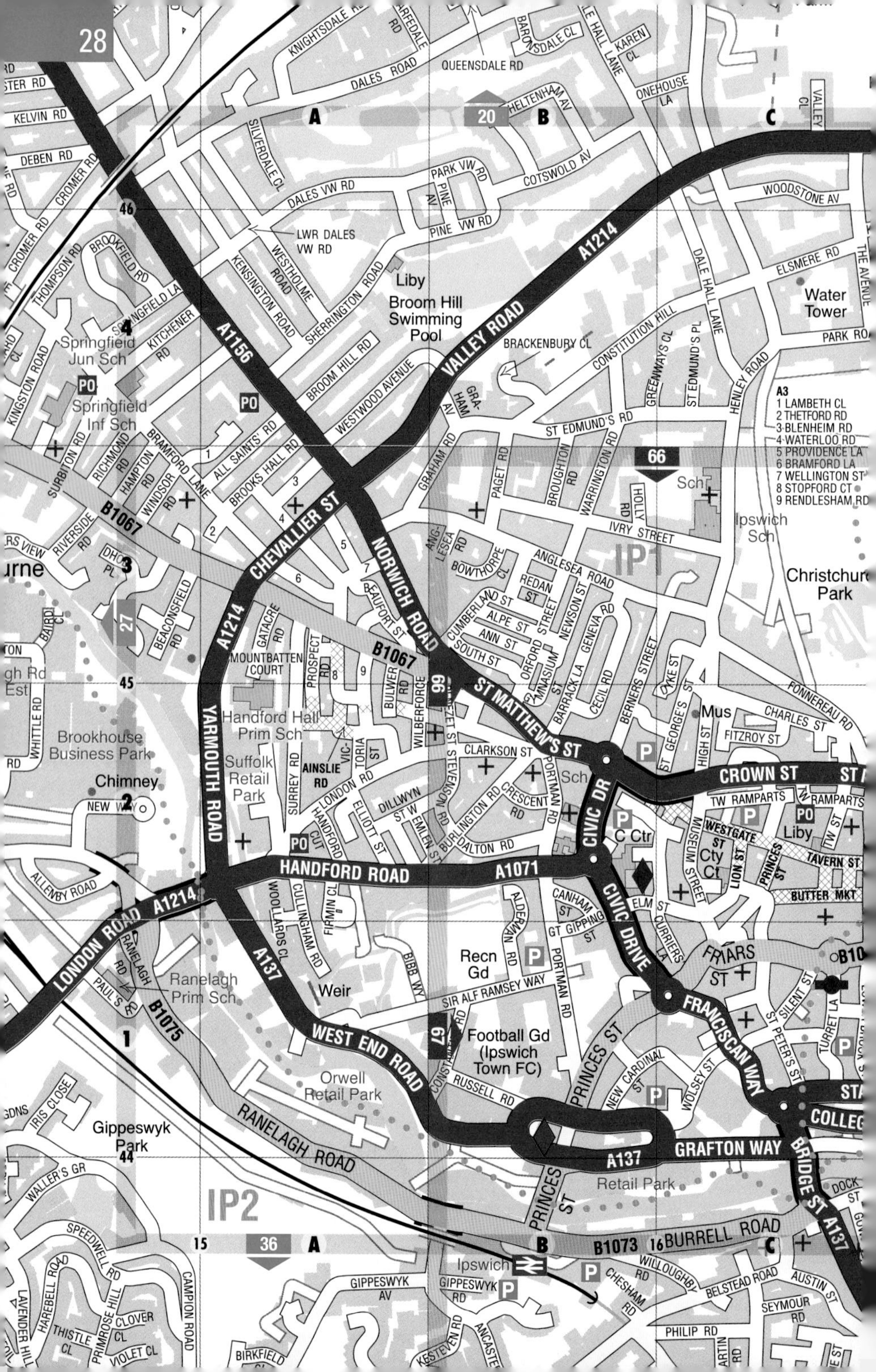
KNIGHTSDALE RD
QUEENSDALE RD
BARONSDALE CL
DALE HALL LANE
KAREN CL
DALES ROAD
ONEHOUSE LA
VALLEY CL
KELVIN RD
A
20
CHELTENHAM AV
B
C
DEBEN RD
CROMER RD
SILVERDALE CL
PARK VW RD
PINE AV
COTSWOLD AV
DALES VW RD
PINE VW RD
WOODSTONE AV
46
LWR DALES VW RD
A1214
THOMPSON RD
BROOKFIELD RD
KENSINGTON ROAD
WESTHOLME ROAD
SHERRINGTON ROAD
Liby
Broom Hill Swimming Pool
DALE HALL LANE
ELSMERE RD
THE AVENUE
Water Tower
SPRINGFIELD LA
4
KITCHENER RD
A1156
VALLEY ROAD
BRACKENBURY CL
CONSTITUTION HILL
GREENWAYS CL
ST EDMUND'S PL
PARK RD
Springfield Jun Sch
KINGSTON ROAD
BROOM HILL RD
HENLEY ROAD
PO
Springfield Inf Sch
WESTWOOD AVENUE
GRAHAM AV
A3
1 LAMBETH CL
2 THETFORD RD
3 BLENHEIM RD
4 WATERLOO RD
5 PROVIDENCE LA
6 BRAMFORD LA
7 WELLINGTON ST
8 STOPFORD CT
9 RENDLESHAM RD
ALL SAINTS' RD
ST EDMUND'S RD
SURBITON RD
RICHMOND RD
HAMPTON RD
BRAMFORD LANE
BROOKS HALL RD
GRAHAM RD
PAGET RD
BROUGHTON RD
WARRINGTON RD
66
Sch
WINDSOR RD
CHEVALLIER ST
HOLLY RD
Ipswich Sch
B1067
RIVERSIDE RD
IVRY STREET
RIVERS VIEW
DHOBI PL
3
NORWICH ROAD
ANGLESEA RD
BOWTHORPE CL
ANGLESEA ROAD
IP1
Christchurch Park
BAIRD CL
27
BEACONSFIELD RD
GATACRE RD
BEAUFORT ST
REDAN ST
NEWSON ST
CUMBERLAND ST
ALPE ST
ANN ST
SOUTH ST
ORFORD STREET
GENEVA RD
A1214
MOUNTBATTEN COURT
PROSPECT RD
B1067
BERNERS STREET
DYKE ST
45
BULWER RD
WILBERFORCE
99
GYMNASIUM ST
BARRACK LA
CECIL RD
FONNEREAU RD
WHITTLE RD
Brookhouse Business Park
YARMOUTH ROAD
Handford Hall Prim Sch
ST MATTHEW'S ST
ST GEORGE'S ST
Mus
CHARLES ST
FITZROY ST
HIGH ST
Suffolk Retail Park
SURREY RD
AINSLIE RD
VICTORIA ST
CLARKSON ST
STEVENSON RD
PORTMAN RD
Sch
CROWN ST
Chimney
LONDON RD
2
NEW WAY
DILLWYN ST W
BURLINGTON RD
CRESCENT RD
CIVIC DR
TW RAMPARTS
HANDFORD CUT
ELLIOTT ST
EMLEN ST
C Ctr
WESTGATE ST
MUSEUM STREET
PO
Liby
TW ST
PO
DALTON RD
Cty Ct
LION ST
PRINCES ST
TAVERN ST
HANDFORD ROAD
A1071
BUTTER MKT
ALLENBY ROAD
A1214
WOOLLARDS CL
CULLINGHAM RD
FIRMIN CL
ALDERMAN RD
CANHAM ST
ELM ST
LONDON ROAD
RANELAGH RD
GT GIPPING ST
CIVIC DRIVE
CURRIERS LA
FRIARS ST
A137
BIBB WAY
Recn Gd
PORTMAN RD
SIR ALF RAMSEY WAY
Ranelagh Prim Sch
PAUL'S RD
Weir
FRANCISCAN WAY
SILENT ST
TURRET LA
B1075
1
67
Football Gd (Ipswich Town FC)
PRINCES ST
NEW CARDINAL ST
ST PETER'S ST
WEST END ROAD
CONSTANTINE RD
WOLSEY ST
IRIS CLOSE
Orwell Retail Park
RUSSELL RD
COLLEGE
Gipeswyk Park
RANELAGH ROAD
A137
GRAFTON WAY
44
WALLER'S GR
BRIDGE ST
Retail Park
DOCK ST
IP2
PRINCES ST
SPEEDWELL RD
15
36
A
B
B1073
16
BURRELL ROAD
C
A137
Ipswich
WILLOUGHBY RD
CHESHAM RD
BELSTEAD ROAD
AUSTIN ST
GIPPESWYK AV
GIPPESWYK RD
HAREBELL ROAD
PRIMROSE HILL
CLOVER CL
SEYMOUR RD
THISTLE CL
VIOLET CL
CAMPION ROAD
LAVENDER HILL
BIRKFIELD
KESTEVEN RD
ANCASTER
PHILIP RD

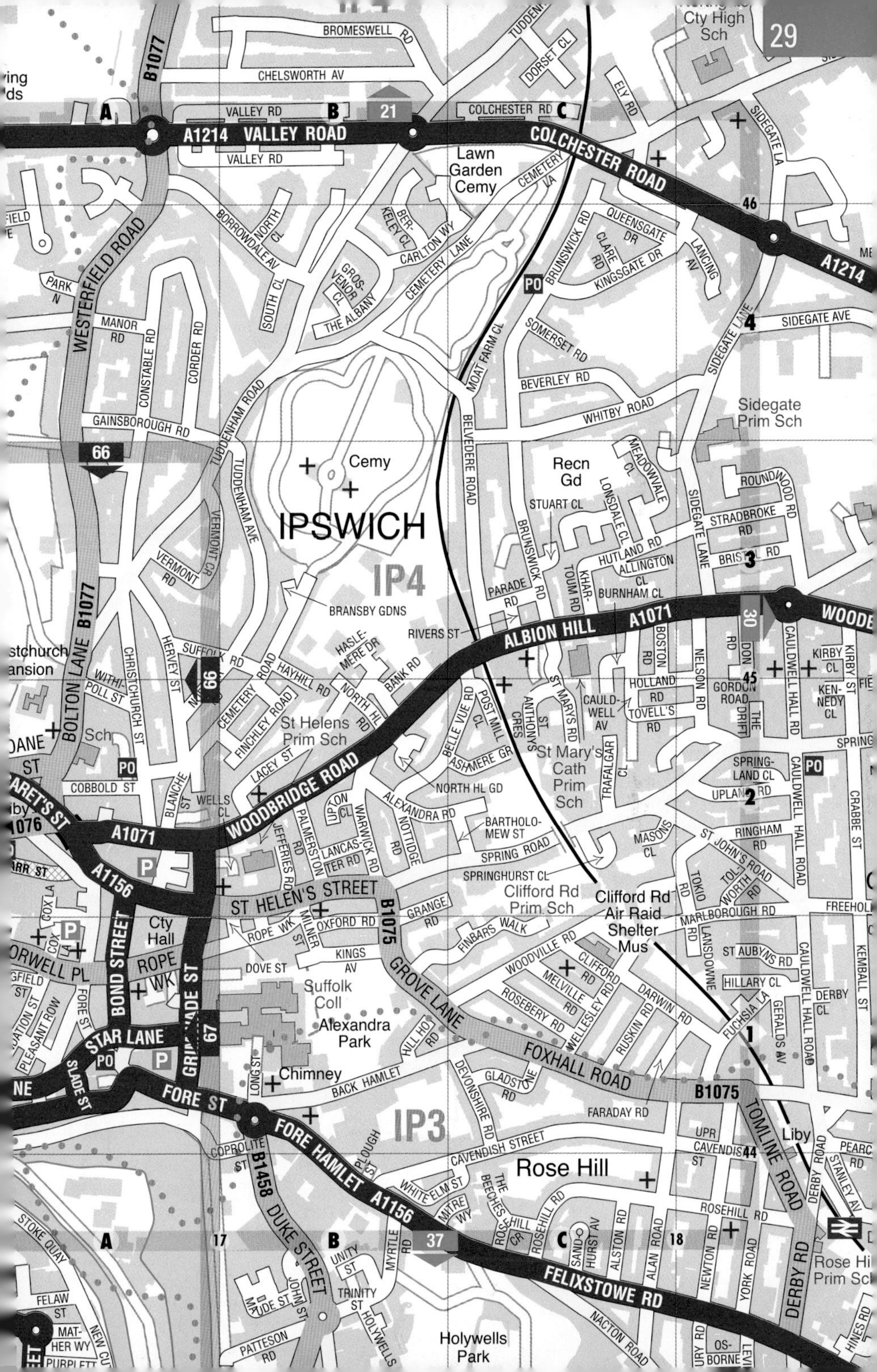

IPSWICH
IP4
IP3
A1214 VALLEY ROAD
VALLEY RD
COLCHESTER ROAD
COLCHESTER RD
A1214
BROMESWELL RD
CHELSWORTH AV
DORSET CL
ELY RD
SIDEGATE LA
City High Sch
B1077
WESTERFIELD ROAD
BORROWDALE AV
NORTH CL
SOUTH CL
BERKELEY CL
CARLTON WY
GROSVENOR CL
THE ALBANY
CEMETERY LANE
CEMETERY LA
Lawn Garden Cemy
BRUNSWICK RD
QUEENSGATE DR
CLARE RD
KINGSGATE DR
LANCING AV
SIDEGATE LANE
SIDEGATE AVE
MANOR RD
CONSTABLE RD
CORDER RD
GAINSBOROUGH RD
TUDDENHAM ROAD
TUDDENHAM AVE
MOAT FARM CL
SOMERSET RD
BEVERLEY RD
WHITBY ROAD
Sidegate Prim Sch
Cemy
BELVEDERE ROAD
Recn Gd
MEADOWVALE CL
LONSDALE CL
STUART CL
ROUNDWOOD RD
STRADBROKE RD
BRISTOL RD
HUTLAND RD
ALLINGTON CL
BURNHAM CL
KHARTOUM RD
PARADE RD
VERMONT CR
VERMONT RD
BRANSBY GDNS
RIVERS ST
ALBION HILL
A1071
WOODBRIDGE ROAD
BOLTON LANE B1077
CHRISTCHURCH ST
HERVEY ST
SUFFOLK RD
CEMETERY ROAD
HAYHILL RD
HASLEMERE DR
BANK RD
NORTH HL
NORTH HL RD
FINCHLEY ROAD
St Helens Prim Sch
BELLE VUE RD
POST MILL CL
ASHMERE GR
ST ANTHONY'S CRES
ST MARY'S RD
CAULDWELL AV
HOLLAND RD
TOVELL'S RD
BOSTON RD
NELSON RD
GORDON ROAD
THE DRIFT
CAULDWELL HALL RD
KIRBY CL
KIRBY ST
KENNEDY CL
WITHIPOLL ST
Sch
COBBOLD ST
LACEY ST
WELLS CL
BLANCHE ST
St Mary's Cath Prim Sch
TRAFALGAR CL
SPRINGLAND CL
UPLAND RD
CRABBE ST
ALEXANDRA RD
NOTTIDGE RD
UPTON CL
WARWICK RD
PALMERSTON RD
JEFFERIES RD
LANCASTER RD
BARTHOLOMEW ST
SPRING ROAD
MASONS CL
RINGHAM RD
ST JOHN'S ROAD
TOLWORTH RD
TOKIO RD
SPRINGHURST CL
Clifford Rd Prim Sch
Clifford Rd Air Raid Shelter Mus
MARLBOROUGH RD
FREEHOLD
A1156
BOND STREET
City Hall
ST HELEN'S STREET
B1075
ROPE WK
MILNER ST
OXFORD RD
GRANGE RD
FINBARS WALK
WOODVILLE RD
CLIFFORD RD
MELVILLE RD
ROSEBERY RD
WELLESLEY RD
DARWIN RD
RUSKIN RD
LANSDOWNE RD
ST AUBYNS RD
HILLARY CL
DERBY CL
GERALDS AV
FUCHSIA LA
KEMBALL ST
DOVE ST
KINGS AV
GROVE LANE
ORWELL PL
Suffolk Coll
Alexandra Park
HILL HO RD
FOXHALL ROAD
GRIMWADE ST
COX LA
STAR LANE
SLADE ST
FORE ST
PLEASANT ROW
Chimney
BACK HAMLET
DEVONSHIRE RD
GLADSTONE RD
FARADAY RD
B1075
TOMLINE ROAD
Liby
FORE HAMLET A1156
COPROLITE ST
B1458 DUKE STREET
PLOUGH ST
CAVENDISH STREET
UPR CAVENDISH ST
Rose Hill
WHITE ELM ST
MYTRE WY
THE BEECHES
ROSEHILL CR
ROSEHILL RD
SANDHURST AV
ALSTON RD
ALAN ROAD
NEWTON RD
YORK ROAD
DERBY RD
DERBY ROAD
STANLEY AV
STOKE QUAY
UNITY ST
MYRTLE RD
TRINITY ST
MAUDE ST
JOHN ST
HOLYWELLS
FELIXSTOWE RD
Holywells Park
NACTON ROAD
PATTESON RD
FELAW ST
MATHER WY
OSBORNE
HINES RD

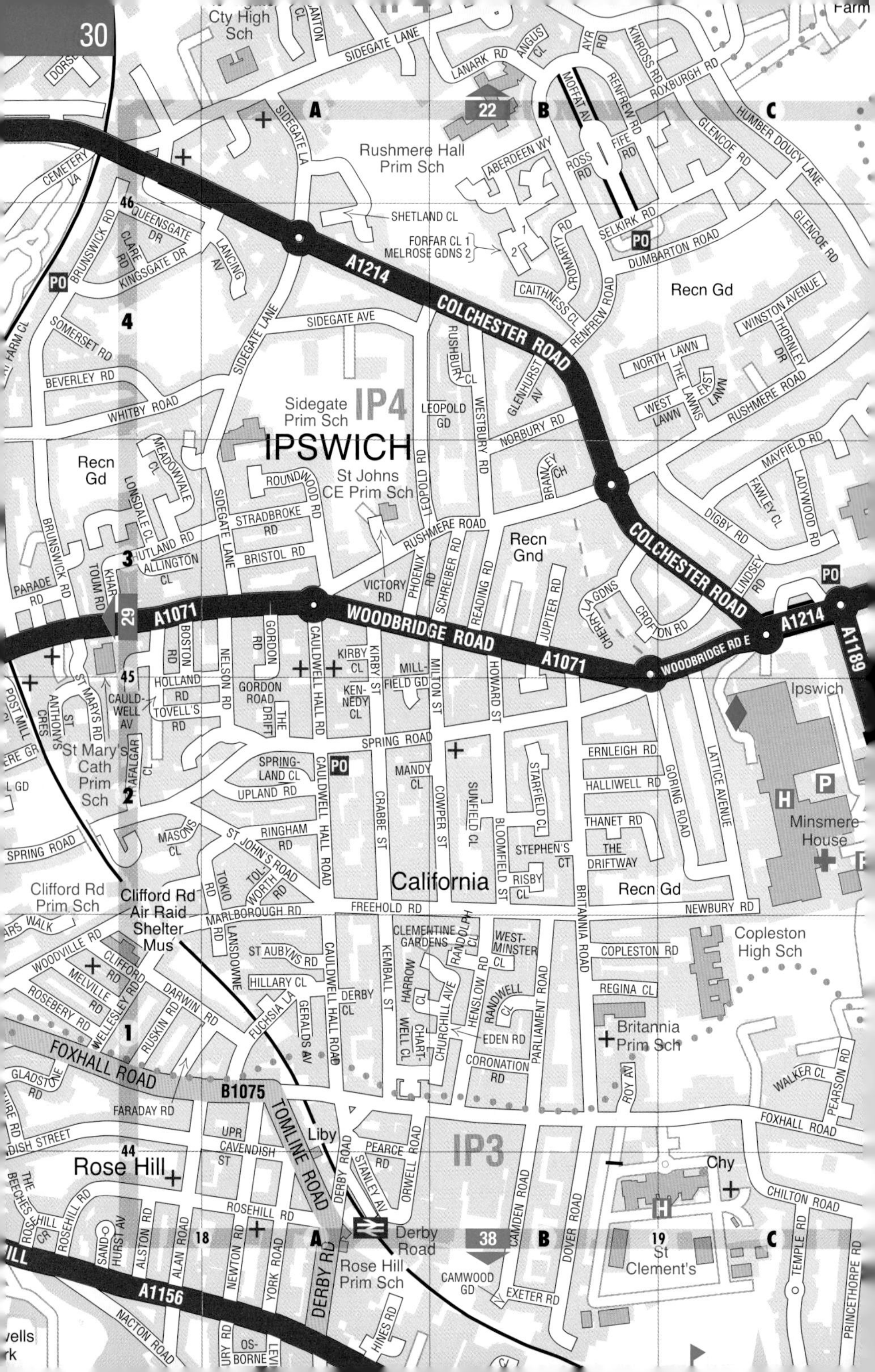
Cty High Sch
SIDEGATE LANE
LANARK RD
ANGUS CL
AYR RD
KINROSS RD
ROXBURGH RD
MOFFAT AV
RENFREW RD
HUMBER DOUCY LANE
A
22
B
C
GLENCOE RD
ABERDEEN WY
FIFE RD
ROSS RD
Rushmere Hall Prim Sch
CEMETERY LA
SIDEGATE LA
SHETLAND CL
FORFAR CL 1
MELROSE GDNS 2
SELKIRK RD
PO
DUMBARTON ROAD
46
BRUNSWICK RD
QUEENSGATE DR
CLARE RD
KINGSGATE DR
LANCING AV
A1214
CRONMARTY RD
CAITHNESS CL
RENFREW ROAD
Recn Gd
WINSTON AVENUE
THORNLEY DR
COLCHESTER ROAD
4
SOMERSET RD
SIDEGATE AVE
SIDEGATE LANE
RUSHBURY CL
GLENHURST AV
NORTH LAWN
THE AWNS
EAST LAWN
WEST LAWN
RUSHMERE ROAD
BEVERLEY RD
WHITBY ROAD
Sidegate Prim Sch
IP4
LEOPOLD GD
WESTBURY RD
NORBURY RD
IPSWICH
MAYFIELD RD
Recn Gd
MEADOWVALE CL
LONSDALE CL
ROUNDWOOD RD
St Johns CE Prim Sch
LEOPOLD RD
BRAMLEY CH
FAWLEY CL
LADYWOOD RD
DIGBY RD
BRUNSWICK RD
STRADBROKE RD
SIDEGATE LANE
RUSHMERE ROAD
Recn Gnd
RUTLAND RD
3
ALLINGTON CL
BRISTOL RD
PHOENIX RD
SCHREIBER RD
READING RD
JUPITER RD
LINDSEY RD
PO
PARADE RD
KHARTOUM RD
VICTORY RD
CHERRY LA GDNS
CROFTON RD
29
A1071
WOODBRIDGE ROAD
A1214
A1189
BOSTON RD
GORDON RD
CAULDWELL HALL RD
KIRBY CL
KIRBY ST
MILLFIELD GD
MILTON ST
HOWARD ST
A1071
WOODBRIDGE RD E
45
HOLLAND RD
NELSON RD
GORDON ROAD
KENNEDY CL
Ipswich
POST MILL CRES
ST ANTHONYS
ST MARYS RD
CAULDWELL AV
TOVELL'S RD
THE DRIFT
SPRING ROAD
ERNLEIGH RD
St Mary's Cath Prim Sch
TRAFALGAR CL
SPRINGLAND CL
PO
MANDY CL
STARFIELD CL
HALLIWELL RD
LATTICE AVENUE
GORING ROAD
2
UPLAND RD
CAULDWELL HALL ROAD
CRABBE ST
COWPER ST
SUNFIELD CL
THANET RD
H
P
Minsmere House
SPRING ROAD
MASONS CL
ST JOHN'S ROAD
RINGHAM RD
BLOOMFIELD ST
STEPHEN'S CT
THE DRIFTWAY
TOKIO RD
TOLWORTH RD
California
RISBY CL
BRITANNIA ROAD
Recn Gd
Clifford Rd Prim Sch
Clifford Rd Air Raid Shelter Mus
MARLBOROUGH RD
FREEHOLD RD
NEWBURY RD
WOODVILLE RD
CLIFFORD RD
LANSDOWNE RD
CLEMENTINE GARDENS
RANDOLPH CL
WESTMINSTER CL
Copleston High Sch
ST AUBYNS RD
KEMBALL ST
COPLESTON RD
MELVILLE RD
HILLARY CL
HARROW CL
HENSLOW RD
PARLIAMENT ROAD
ROSEBERY RD
DARWIN RD
WELLESLEY RD
RUSKIN RD
GERALDS AV
DERBY CL
CHURCHILL AVE
RANDWELL CL
REGINA CL
Britannia Prim Sch
1
FUCHSIA LA
WELL CL
CHARTWELL CL
EDEN RD
FOXHALL ROAD
CORONATION RD
ROY AV
WALKER CL
PEARSON RD
GLADSTONE RD
B1075
TOMLINE ROAD
FARADAY RD
FOXHALL ROAD
Liby
DISH STREET
UPR CAVENDISH ST
44
DERBY ROAD
PEARCE RD
ORWELL ROAD
IP3
Rose Hill
STANLEY AV
CAMDEN ROAD
DOVER ROAD
Chy
CHILTON ROAD
THE BEECHES
ROSEHILL CR
ROSEHILL RD
SANDHURST AV
ALSTON RD
ALAN RD
18
ROSEHILL RD
A
Derby Road
38
B
19
St Clement's
C
TEMPLE RD
PRINCETHORPE RD
NEWTON RD
YORK ROAD
DERBY RD
Rose Hill Prim Sch
CAMWOOD GD
EXETER RD
A1156
NACTON ROAD
HINES RD
OSBORNE

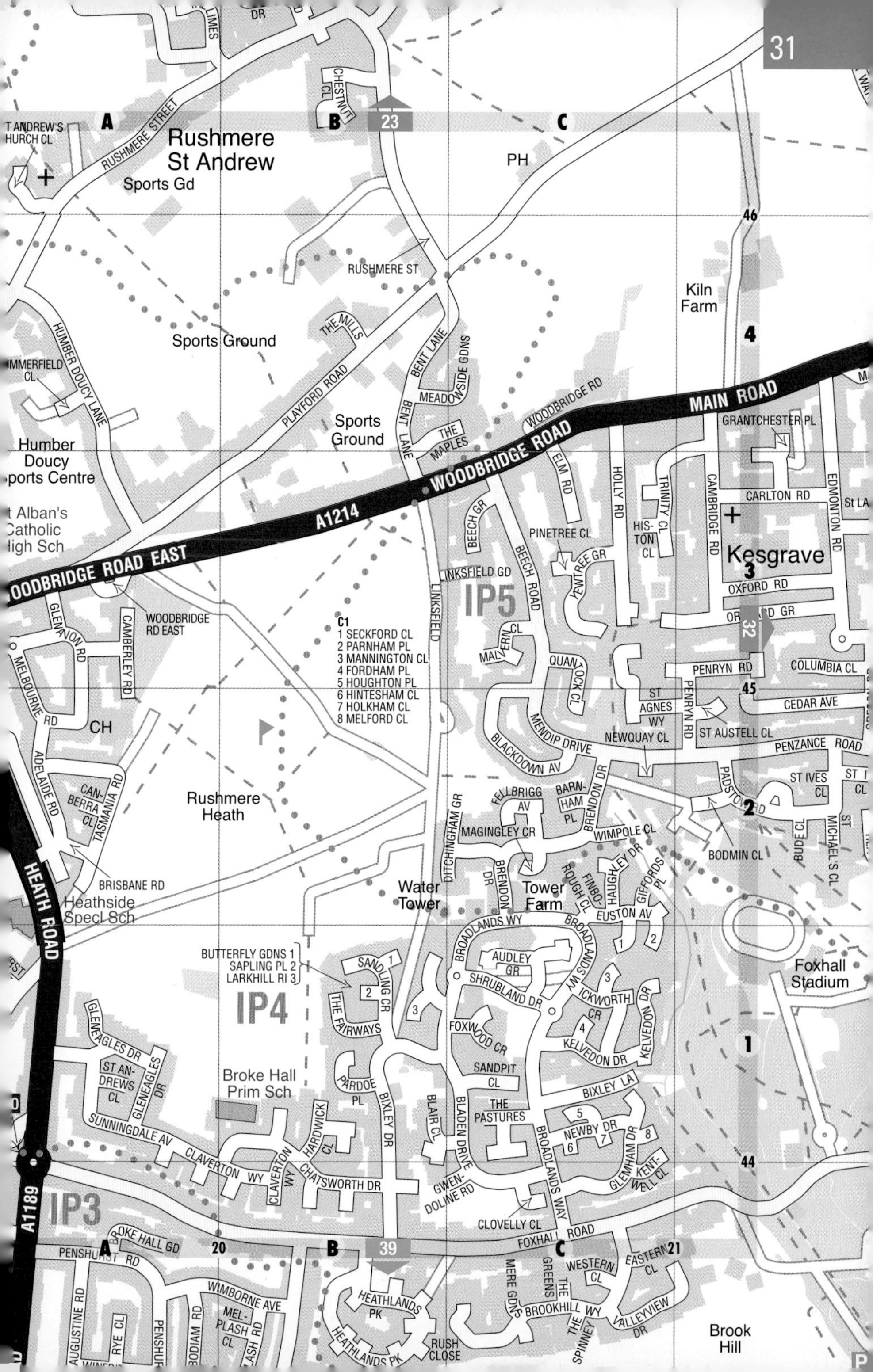
Rushmere St Andrew
Sports Gd
RUSHMERE STREET
CHESTNUT CL
23
PH
46
RUSHMERE ST
Sports Ground
THE MILLS
PLAYFORD ROAD
BENT LANE
MEADOWSIDE GDNS
Sports Ground
THE MAPLES
Kiln Farm
HUMBER DOUCY LANE
Humber Doucy Sports Centre
WOODBRIDGE ROAD
WOODBRIDGE RD
MAIN ROAD
A1214
WOODBRIDGE ROAD EAST
ELM RD
HOLLY RD
TRINITY CL
HIS-TON CL
CAMBRIDGE RD
GRANTCHESTER PL
CARLTON RD
EDMONTON RD
Kesgrave
OXFORD RD
32
BEECH GR
PINETREE CL
YEWTREE GR
LINKSFIELD GD
LINKSFIELD
IP5
BEECH ROAD
WOODBRIDGE RD EAST
CAMBERLEY RD
GLENAVON RD
MELBOURNE RD
C1
1 SECKFORD CL
2 PARNHAM PL
3 MANNINGTON CL
4 FORDHAM PL
5 HOUGHTON PL
6 HINTESHAM CL
7 HOLKHAM CL
8 MELFORD CL
MALVERN CL
QUANTOCK CL
ST AGNES WY
PENRYN RD
COLUMBIA CL
45
CEDAR AVE
ST AUSTELL CL
NEWQUAY CL
MENDIP DRIVE
BLACKDOWN AV
PENZANCE ROAD
ST IVES CL
CH
ADELAIDE RD
CANBERRA CL
TASMANIA RD
Rushmere Heath
FELBRIGG AV
BARNHAM PL
BRENDON DR
PADSTOW RD
DITCHINGHAM GR
MAGINGLEY CR
WIMPOLE CL
BODMIN CL
BUDE CL
ST MICHAEL'S CL
HEATH ROAD
BRISBANE RD
Heathside Specl Sch
Water Tower
Tower Farm
FINBOROUGH CL
HAUGHLEY DR
GIFFORDS PL
EUSTON AV
BROADLANDS WY
Foxhall Stadium
BUTTERFLY GDNS 1
SAPLING PL 2
LARKHILL RI 3
SANDLING CR
AUDLEY GR
SHRUBLAND DR
ICKWORTH CR
KELVEDON DR
IP4
THE FAIRWAYS
FOXWOOD CR
GLENEAGLES DR
ST ANDREWS CL
Broke Hall Prim Sch
PARDOE PL
BIXLEY DR
SANDPIT CL
BIXLEY LA
THE PASTURES
BLAIR CL
BLADEN DRIVE
NEWBY DR
GLEMHAM DR
FENTWELL CL
44
SUNNINGDALE AV
CLAVERTON WY
HARDWICK CL
CHATSWORTH DR
GWENDOLINE RD
BROADLANDS WAY
A1189
IP3
CLOVELLY CL
BROKE HALL GD
20
FOXHALL ROAD
39
21
PENSHURST RD
WIMBORNE AVE
HEATHLANDS PK
MERE GDNS
THE GREENS
WESTERN CL
EASTERN CL
BROOKHILL WY
VALLEYVIEW DR
THE SPINNEY
AUGUSTINE RD
RYE CL
BODIAM RD
MELPLASH CL
ASH RD
RUSH CLOSE
Brook Hill
A B C
1 2 3 4

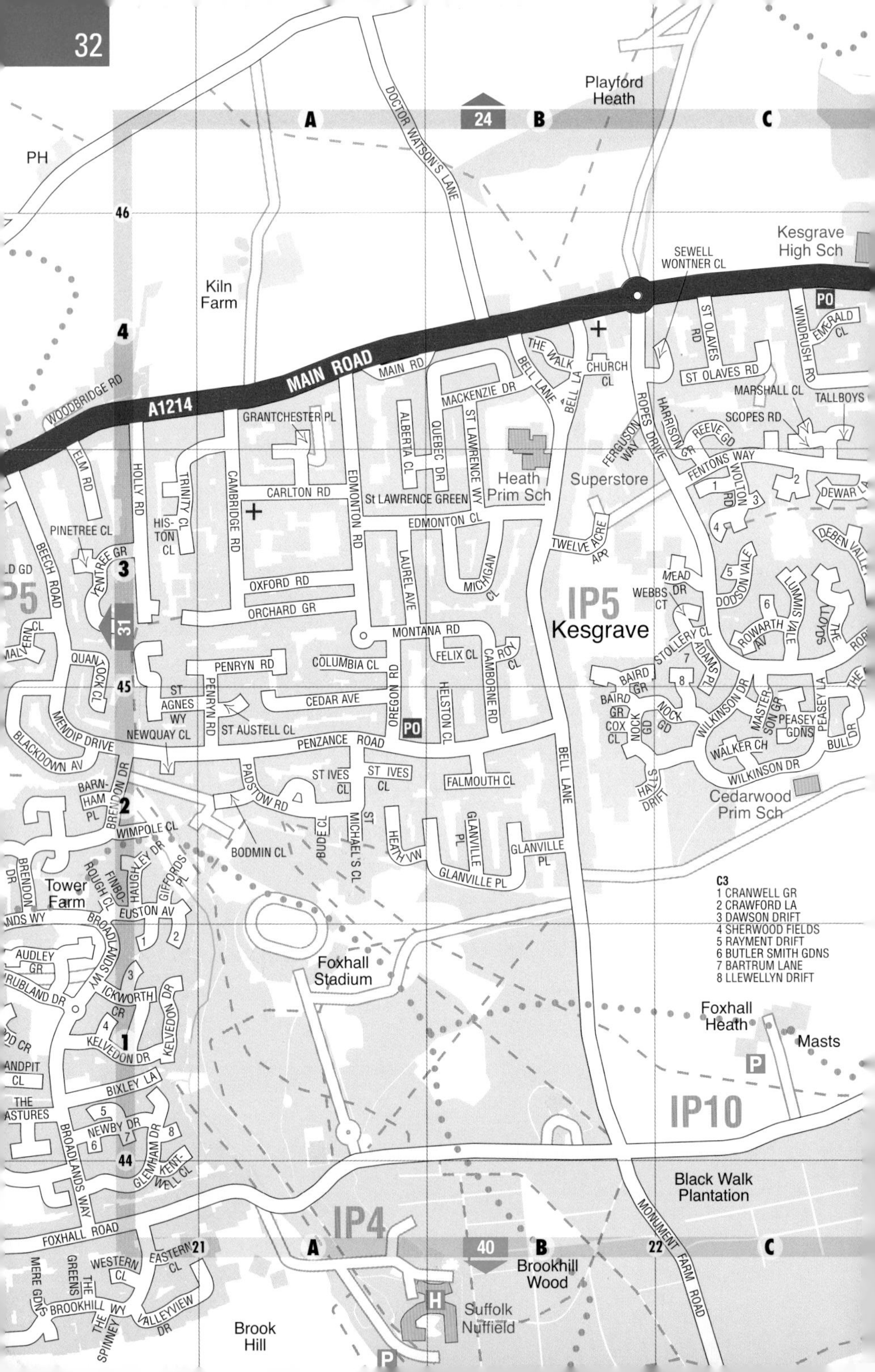
Playford Heath
A
24
B
C
PH
DOCTOR WATSON'S LANE
46
Kesgrave High Sch
SEWELL WONTNER CL
Kiln Farm
PO
4
MAIN ROAD
A1214
WOODBRIDGE RD
MAIN RD
THE WALK
BELL LANE
BELL LA
CHURCH CL
ST OLAVES RD
WINDRUSH RD
EMERALD CL
ST OLAVES RD
MARSHALL CL
TALLBOYS
MACKENZIE DR
GRANTCHESTER PL
ALBERTA CL
QUEBEC DR
ST LAWRENCE WAY
FERGUSON WAY
ROPES DRIVE
HARRISON GR
REEVE GD
SCOPES RD
FENTONS WAY
ELM RD
HOLLY RD
TRINITY CL
CAMBRIDGE RD
EDMONTON RD
Heath Prim Sch
Superstore
WOLTON RD
DEWAR LA
CARLTON RD
St LAWRENCE GREEN
HIS-TON CL
EDMONTON CL
TWELVE ACRE APR
PINETREE CL
PINETREE GR
LAUREL AVE
MICHIGAN CL
MEAD DR
DEBEN VALLEY
BEECH ROAD
3
OXFORD RD
WEBBS CT
DODSON VALE
LUMMIS VALE
ORCHARD GR
IP5
Kesgrave
ROWARTH AV
THE LLOYDS
31
MONTANA RD
STOLLERY CL
ADAMS PL
MALVERN CL
QUANTOCK CL
PENRYN RD
COLUMBIA CL
FELIX CL
ROY CL
CAMBORNE RD
BAIRD GR
45
CEDAR AVE
HELSTON CL
OREGON RD
ST AGNES WY
PENRYN RD
ST AUSTELL CL
NOCK GD
WILKINSON DR
MASTERSON GR
PEASEY GDNS
PEASEY LA
MENDIP DRIVE
NEWQUAY CL
PENZANCE ROAD
PO
COX CL
NOCK GD
BULL DR
BLACKDOWN AV
BELL LANE
WALKER CH
WILKINSON DR
BARNHAM PL
BRENDON DR
ST IVES CL
ST IVES CL
FALMOUTH CL
HALLS DRIFT
2
PADSTOW RD
Cedarwood Prim Sch
WIMPOLE CL
BUDE CL
ST MICHAEL'S CL
HEATH VW
GLANVILLE PL
GLANVILLE PL
BRENDON DR
HAUGHLEY DR
BODMIN CL
GIFFORDS PL
GLANVILLE PL
Tower Farm
FINBOROUGH CL
C3
1 CRANWELL GR
2 CRAWFORD LA
3 DAWSON DRIFT
4 SHERWOOD FIELDS
5 RAYMENT DRIFT
6 BUTLER SMITH GDNS
7 BARTRUM LANE
8 LLEWELLYN DRIFT
LANDS WY
BROADLANDS WY
EUSTON AV
AUDLEY GR
Foxhall Stadium
RUBLAND DR
ICKWORTH CR
Foxhall Heath
KELVEDON DR
Masts
KELVEDON DR
1
SANDPIT CL
BIXLEY LA
P
THE PASTURES
IP10
NEWBY DR
GLEMHAM DR
BROADLANDS WAY
44
KENTWELL CL
Black Walk Plantation
FOXHALL ROAD
IP4
MONUMENT FARM ROAD
21
A
40
B
22
C
WESTERN CL
EASTERN CL
Brookhill Wood
MERE GDNS
THE GREENS
BROOKHILL WY
VALLEYVIEW DR
THE SPINNEY
H
Suffolk Nuffield
Brook Hill
P

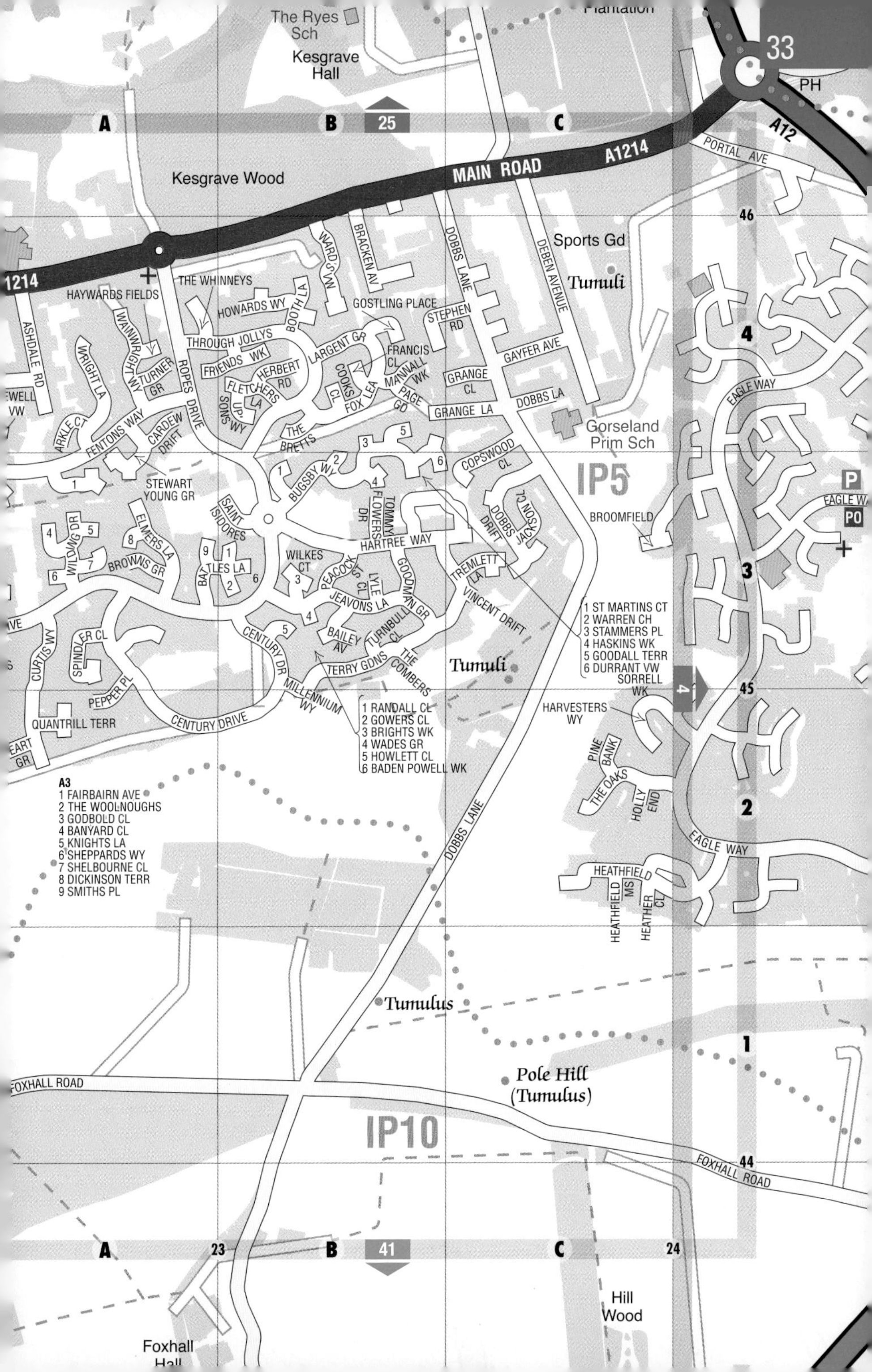

The Ryes Sch
Kesgrave Hall
Plantation
PH
A12
A B C
25
MAIN ROAD
A1214
Kesgrave Wood
PORTAL AVE
46
Sports Gd
Tumuli
DEBEN AVENUE
DOBBS LANE
BRACKEN AV
WARD'S VW
BOOTH LA
THE WHINNEYS
HAYWARDS FIELDS
HOWARDS WY
GOSTLING PLACE
STEPHEN RD
ASHDALE RD
WRIGHT LA
WAINWRIGHT WY
TURNER GR
ROPES DRIVE
THROUGH JOLLYS
FRIENDS WK
HERBERT RD
LARGENT GR
FRANCIS CL
COOKS CL
FOX LA
MANNALL WK
GRANGE CL
GAYFER AVE
FLETCHERS LA
UP' SONS WY
PAGE GD
GRANGE LA
DOBBS LA
EAGLE WAY
Gorseland Prim Sch
IP5
ARKLE CT
FENTONS WAY
CARDEW DRIFT
THE BRETTS
STEWART YOUNG GR
BUGSBY WY
COPSWOOD CL
TOMMY FLOWERS DR
SAINT ISIDORES
DOBBS DRIFT
JACKSON CL
BROOMFIELD
EAGLE WAY
P
PO
WILDING DR
ELMERS LA
BROWNS GR
BATTLES LA
WILKES CT
HARTREE WAY
PEACOCK ST
LYLE CL
GOODMAN GR
TREMLETT LA
JEAVONS LA
VINCENT DRIFT
1 ST MARTINS CT
2 WARREN CH
3 STAMMERS PL
4 HASKINS WK
5 GOODALL TERR
6 DURRANT VW
CURTIS WY
SPINDLER CL
CENTURY DR
BAILEY AV
TURNBULL CL
THE COMBERS
TERRY GDNS
Tumuli
SORRELL WK
45
4
PEPPER PL
MILLENNIUM WY
CENTURY DRIVE
HARVESTERS WY
QUANTRILL TERR
1 RANDALL CL
2 GOWERS CL
3 BRIGHTS WK
4 WADES GR
5 HOWLETT CL
6 BADEN POWELL WK
PINE BANK
THE OAKS
HOLLY END
A3
1 FAIRBAIRN AVE
2 THE WOOLNOUGHS
3 GODBOLD CL
4 BANYARD CL
5 KNIGHTS LA
6 SHEPPARDS WY
7 SHELBOURNE CL
8 DICKINSON TERR
9 SMITHS PL
DOBBS LANE
EAGLE WAY
HEATHFIELD
HEATHFIELD MS
HEATHER CL
Tumulus
1
FOXHALL ROAD
Pole Hill (Tumulus)
IP10
44
FOXHALL ROAD
A 23 B 41 C 24
Hill Wood
Foxhall Hall

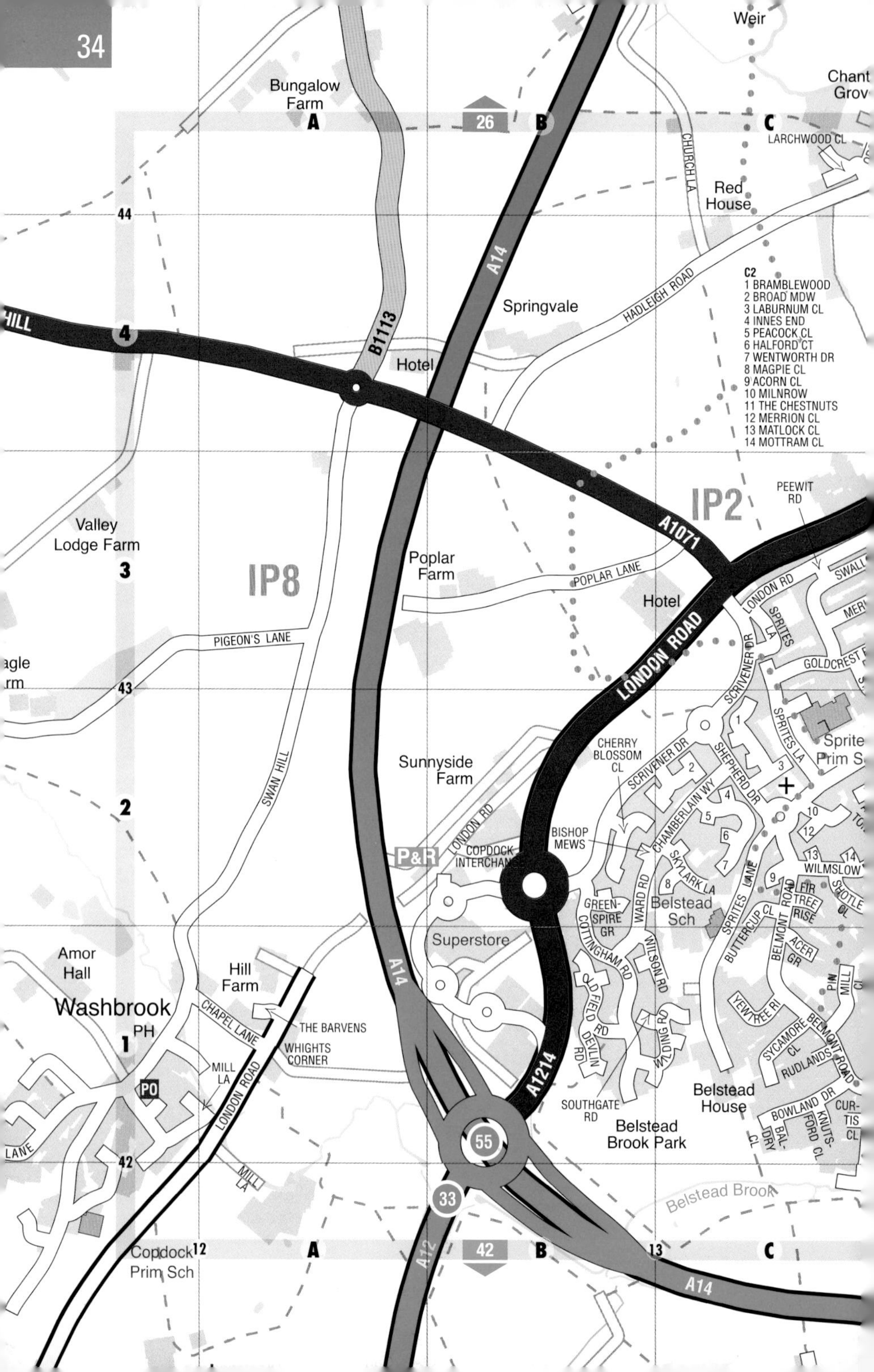
Weir
Bungalow Farm
Chant Grov
A
26
B
C
LARCHWOOD CL
CHURCH LA
Red House
44
A14
HADLEIGH ROAD
C2
1 BRAMBLEWOOD
2 BROAD MDW
3 LABURNUM CL
4 INNES END
5 PEACOCK CL
6 HALFORD CT
7 WENTWORTH DR
8 MAGPIE CL
9 ACORN CL
10 MILNROW
11 THE CHESTNUTS
12 MERRION CL
13 MATLOCK CL
14 MOTTRAM CL
Springvale
HILL
4
B1113
Hotel
IP2
PEEWIT RD
A1071
Valley Lodge Farm
3
IP8
Poplar Farm
POPLAR LANE
Hotel
LONDON RD
SPRITES LA
LONDON ROAD
PIGEON'S LANE
GOLDCREST
43
SCRIVENER DR
SPRITES LA
Sprite Prim S
CHERRY BLOSSOM CL
SHEPHERD DR
Sunnyside Farm
SWAN HILL
2
CHAMBERLAIN WY
BISHOP MEWS
LONDON RD
P&R
COPDOCK INTERCHANGE
SKYLARK LA
WILMSLOW
SPRITES LANE
FIR TREE RISE
GREEN-SPIRE GR
WARD RD
Belstead Sch
BUTTERCUP CL
BELMONT ROAD
ACER GR
Superstore
COTTINGHAM RD
WILSON RD
Amor Hall
A14
Hill Farm
OLD FIELD RD
PIN MILL CL
YEWTREE RI
Washbrook
CHAPEL LANE
THE BARVENS
WILDING RD
SYCAMORE CL
BELMONT ROAD
PH
1
WHIGHTS CORNER
DEVLIN RD
MILL LA
RUDLANDS
A1214
PO
LONDON ROAD
SOUTHGATE RD
Belstead House
BOWLAND DR
KNUTS-FORD CL
CURTIS CL
BALDRY CL
Belstead Brook Park
LANE
42
55
MILL LA
33
Belstead Brook
Copdock Prim Sch
12
A
A12
42
B
13
C
A14

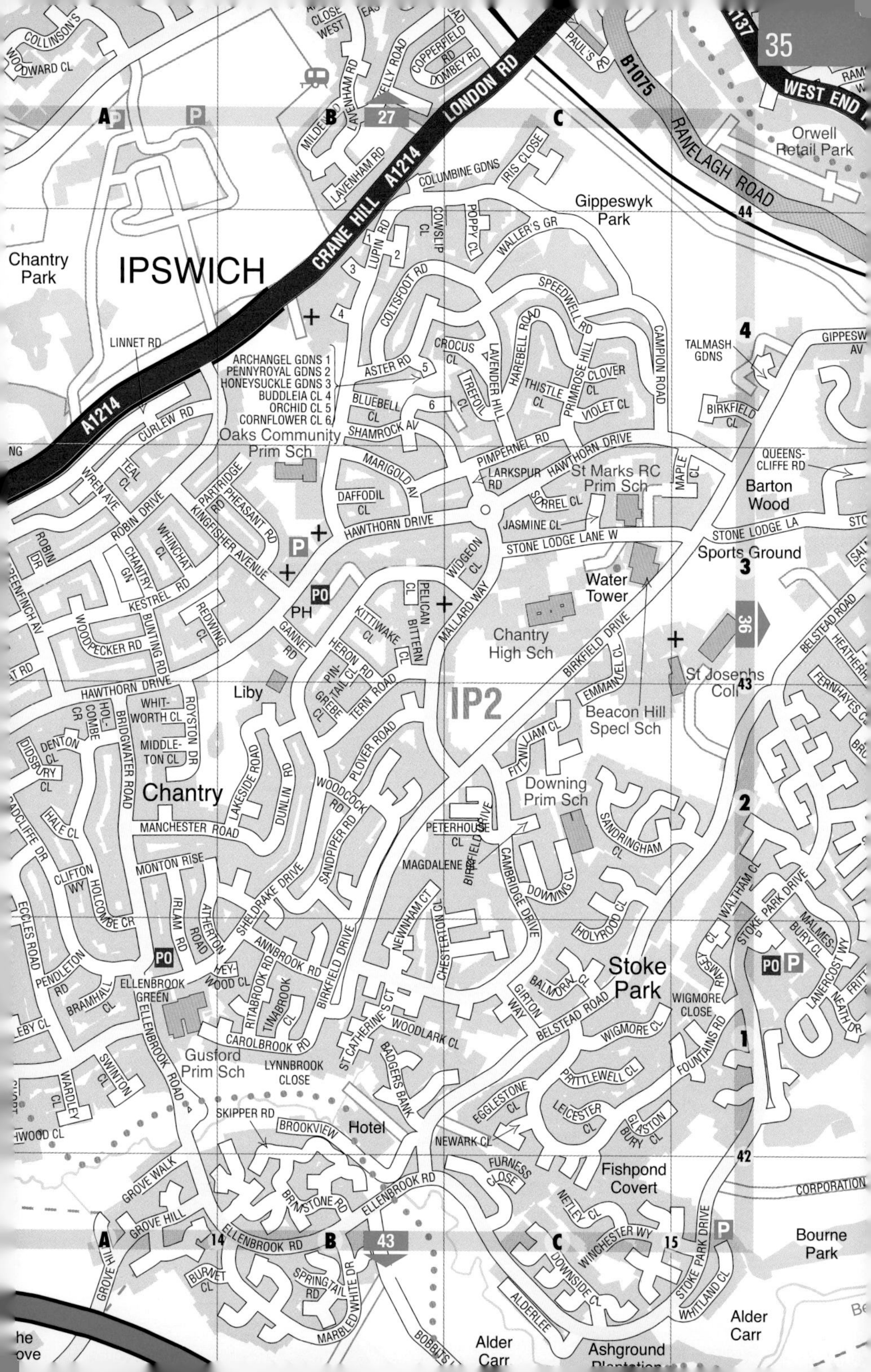

35
IPSWICH
Chantry Park
Chantry
IP2
A1214
CRANE HILL A1214
LONDON RD
B1075
RANELAGH ROAD
WEST END
Orwell Retail Park
Gippeswyk Park
27
36
43
44
42
14
15
A
B
C
1
2
3
4
COLLINSON'S
WOODWARD CL
CLOSE WEST
MILDEN RD
LAVENHAM RD
KELLY ROAD
COPPERFIELD RD
DOMBEY RD
PAUL'S RD
IRIS CLOSE
COLUMBINE GDNS
COWSLIP CL
POPPY CL
LUPIN RD
WALLER'S GR
COLTSFOOT RD
SPEEDWELL RD
CAMPION ROAD
CROCUS CL
LAVENDER HILL
HAREBELL ROAD
PRIMROSE HILL
THISTLE CL
CLOVER CL
VIOLET CL
TREFOIL CL
ASTER RD
BLUEBELL CL
SHAMROCK AV
MARIGOLD AV
DAFFODIL CL
PIMPERNEL RD
LARKSPUR RD
HAWTHORN DRIVE
SORREL CL
JASMINE CL
MAPLE CL
STONE LODGE LANE W
STONE LODGE LA
ARCHANGEL GDNS 1
PENNYROYAL GDNS 2
HONEYSUCKLE GDNS 3
BUDDLEIA CL 4
ORCHID CL 5
CORNFLOWER CL 6
LINNET RD
CURLEW RD
Oaks Community Prim Sch
St Marks RC Prim Sch
TALMASH GDNS
GIPPESWYK AV
BIRKFIELD CL
QUEENSCLIFFE RD
Barton Wood
Sports Ground
WREN AVE
TEAL CL
PARTRIDGE RD
PHEASANT RD
KINGFISHER AVENUE
ROBIN DRIVE
ROBIN DR
WHINCHAT CL
CHANTRY GN
KESTREL RD
REDWING CL
GREENFINCH AV
WOODPECKER RD
BUNTING RD
GANNET RD
PO
PH
KITTIWAKE CL
PELICAN CL
BITTERN CL
MALLARD WAY
WIDGEON CL
HERON RD
PINTAIL CL
GREBE CL
TERN ROAD
Water Tower
Chantry High Sch
BIRKFIELD DRIVE
EMMANUEL CL
St Josephs Coll
BELSTEAD ROAD
HEATHERHAYES
FERNHAYES CL
Beacon Hill Specl Sch
HAWTHORN DRIVE
Liby
WHITWORTH CL
ROYSTON DR
MIDDLETON CL
HOLCOMBE CR
BRIDGWATER ROAD
DENTON CL
DIDSBURY CL
LAKESIDE ROAD
DUNLIN RD
PLOVER ROAD
WOODCOCK RD
SANDPIPER RD
FITZWILLIAM CL
Downing Prim Sch
SANDRINGHAM CL
PETERHOUSE CL
MAGDALENE CL
BIRKFIELD DRIVE
CAMBRIDGE DRIVE
DOWNING CL
HOLYROOD CL
WALTHAM CL
STOKE PARK DRIVE
MALMESBURY CL
LANERCOST WY
NEATH DR
MANCHESTER ROAD
HALE CL
RADCLIFFE DR
CLIFTON WY
MONTON RISE
IRLAM RD
ATHERTON ROAD
SHELDRAKE DRIVE
ANNBROOK RD
NEWNHAM CT
CHESTERTON CL
ECCLES ROAD
PENDLETON RD
BRAMHALL CL
ELLENBROOK GREEN
ELLENBROOK ROAD
HEYWOOD CL
RITABROOK RD
TINABROOK CL
BIRKFIELD DRIVE
ST CATHERINE'S CT
WOODLARK CL
BADGERS BANK
GIRTON WAY
BALMORAL CL
Stoke Park
RAMSEY CL
WIGMORE CLOSE
WIGMORE CL
FOUNTAINS RD
PRITTLEWELL CL
CAROLBROOK RD
Gusford Prim Sch
LYNNBROOK CLOSE
SWINTON CL
WARDLEY CL
SKIPPER RD
BROOKVIEW
Hotel
EGGLESTONE CL
LEICESTER CL
GLASTONBURY CL
NEWARK CL
FURNESS CLOSE
Fishpond Covert
CORPORATION
GROVE WALK
GROVE HILL
BRIMSTONE RD
ELLENBROOK RD
NETLEY CL
WINCHESTER WY
STOKE PARK DRIVE
Bourne Park
BURNET CL
SPRINGTAIL RD
MARBLED WHITE DR
DOWNSIDE CL
WHITLAND CL
ALDERLEE
BOBBITS
Alder Carr
Ashground Plantation

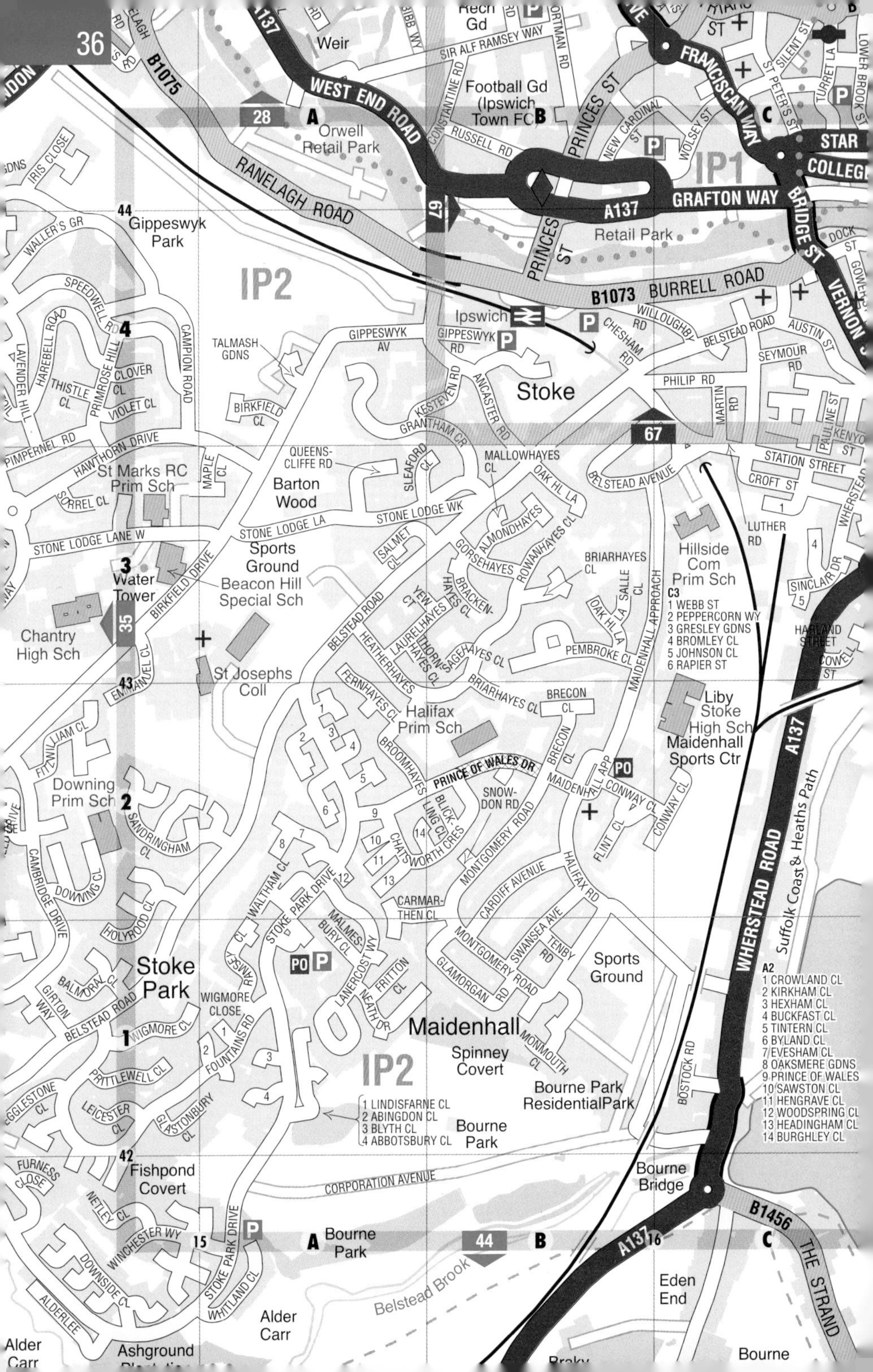
WEST END ROAD
Orwell Retail Park
Football Gd (Ipswich Town FC)
RANELAGH ROAD
Gippeswyk Park
IP2
IP1
GRAFTON WAY
BRIDGE ST
BURRELL ROAD
B1073
A137
B1075
Ipswich
Stoke
Barton Wood
Sports Ground
Beacon Hill Special Sch
St Marks RC Prim Sch
Water Tower
Chantry High Sch
St Josephs Coll
Halifax Prim Sch
Hillside Com Prim Sch
Maidenhall Sports Ctr
Downing Prim Sch
Stoke Park
Maidenhall
Spinney Covert
Bourne Park Residential Park
Bourne Park
Fishpond Covert
Bourne Bridge
Eden End
Alder Carr
Belstead Brook
WHERSTEAD ROAD
THE STRAND
B1456
CORPORATION AVENUE
BELSTEAD ROAD
STONE LODGE LANE W
BIRKFIELD DRIVE
MAIDENHALL APPROACH
MONTGOMERY ROAD
STOKE PARK DRIVE
Suffolk Coast & Heaths Path
C3
1 WEBB ST
2 PEPPERCORN WY
3 GRESLEY GDNS
4 BROMLEY CL
5 JOHNSON CL
6 RAPIER ST
A2
1 CROWLAND CL
2 KIRKHAM CL
3 HEXHAM CL
4 BUCKFAST CL
5 TINTERN CL
6 BYLAND CL
7 EVESHAM CL
8 OAKSMERE GDNS
9 PRINCE OF WALES
10 SAWSTON CL
11 HENGRAVE CL
12 WOODSPRING CL
13 HEADINGHAM CL
14 BURGHLEY CL
1 LINDISFARNE CL
2 ABINGDON CL
3 BLYTH CL
4 ABBOTSBURY CL

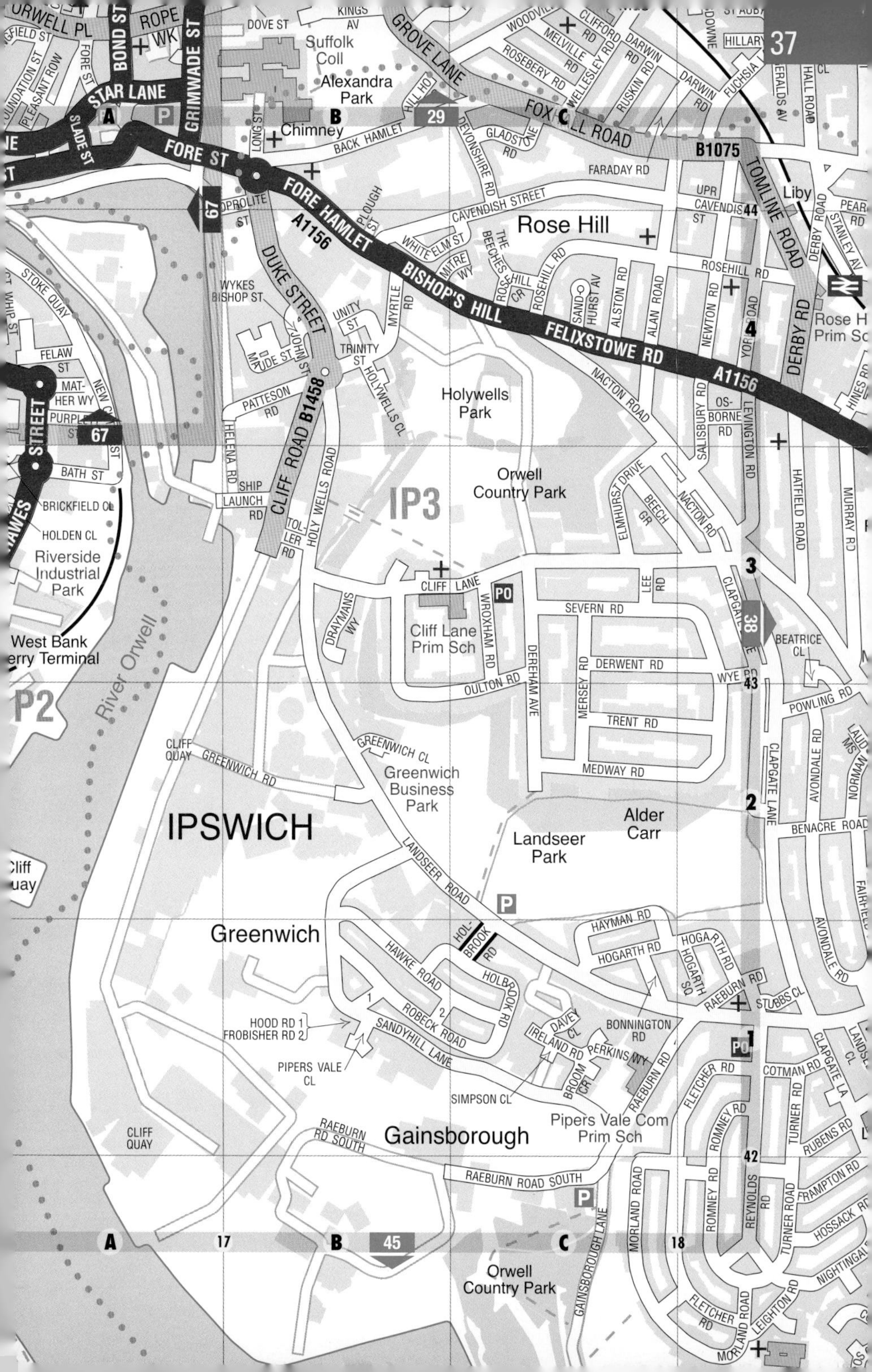

ORWELL PL
ROPE WK
BOND ST
GRIMWADE ST
DOVE ST
KINGS AV
Suffolk Coll
Alexandra Park
GROVE LANE
WOODVILLE
CLIFFORD RD
MELVILLE RD
DARWIN RD
ROSEBERY RD
WELLESLEY RD
RUSKIN RD
DARWIN RD
FUCHSIA
HILLARY
HALL RD
FORE ST
STAR LANE
PLEASANT ROW
SLADE ST
FOUNDATION ST
Chimney
LONG ST
HILL HO
BACK HAMLET
29
DEVONSHIRE RD
GLADSTONE RD
FOXHALL ROAD
B1075
FARADAY RD
TOMLINE ROAD
Liby
DERBY ROAD
STANLEY AV
67
COPROLITE ST
FORE HAMLET
A1156
PLOUGH ST
CAVENDISH STREET
UPR CAVENDISH ST
44
Rose Hill
WHITE ELM ST
MITRE WY
THE BEECHES
ROSEHILL RD
ROSEHILL CR
SANDHURST AV
ALSTON RD
ALAN ROAD
NEWTON RD
YORK ROAD
ROSEHILL RD
BISHOP'S HILL
FELIXSTOWE RD
DERBY RD
Rose Hill Prim Sch
STOKE QUAY
WHIP ST
WYKES BISHOP ST
DUKE STREET
UNITY ST
TRINITY ST
MYRTLE RD
JOHN ST
MAUDE ST
HOLYWELLS CL
FELAW ST
MATHER WY
NEW CUT
PURPLE ST
STREET
PATTESON RD
B1458
Holywells Park
NACTON ROAD
SALISBURY RD
OSBORNE RD
LEVINGTON RD
A1156
HINES RD
BATH ST
HELENA RD
CLIFF ROAD
HOLY WELLS ROAD
Orwell Country Park
HATFIELD ROAD
MURRAY RD
BRICKFIELD CL
HOLDEN CL
SHIP LAUNCH RD
IP3
ELMHURST DRIVE
BEECH GR
NACTON RD
Riverside Industrial Park
TOLLER RD
3
CLIFF LANE
PO
LEE RD
CLAPGATE
38
SEVERN RD
West Bank Ferry Terminal
DRAYMANS WY
Cliff Lane Prim Sch
WROXHAM RD
DEREHAM AVE
MERSEY RD
DERWENT RD
BEATRICE CL
WYE RD
43
OULTON RD
TRENT RD
POWLING RD
River Orwell
IP2
CLIFF QUAY
GREENWICH RD
GREENWICH CL
Greenwich Business Park
MEDWAY RD
CLAPGATE LANE
AVONDALE RD
NORMAN
2
BENACRE ROAD
IPSWICH
Alder Carr
Landseer Park
LANDSEER ROAD
P
Greenwich
HOLBROOK RD
HAYMAN RD
HOGARTH RD
HOGARTH SQ
HAWKE ROAD
AVONDALE RD
RAEBURN RD
STUBBS CL
HOOD RD 1
FROBISHER RD 2
ROBECK ROAD
SANDYHILL LANE
DAVEY CL
IRELAND RD
BONNINGTON RD
PERKINS WY
1
PO
PIPERS VALE CL
SIMPSON CL
BROOM CR
RAEBURN RD
FLETCHER RD
COTMAN RD
CLAPGATE LA
ROMNEY RD
TURNER RD
RUBENS RD
CLIFF QUAY
RAEBURN RD SOUTH
Gainsborough
Pipers Vale Com Prim Sch
42
RAEBURN ROAD SOUTH
MORLAND ROAD
ROMNEY RD
REYNOLDS RD
TURNER ROAD
FRAMPTON RD
HOSSACK RD
A
17
B
45
C
18
GAINSBOROUGH LANE
Orwell Country Park
FLETCHER RD
MORLAND ROAD
LEIGHTON RD
NIGHTINGALE

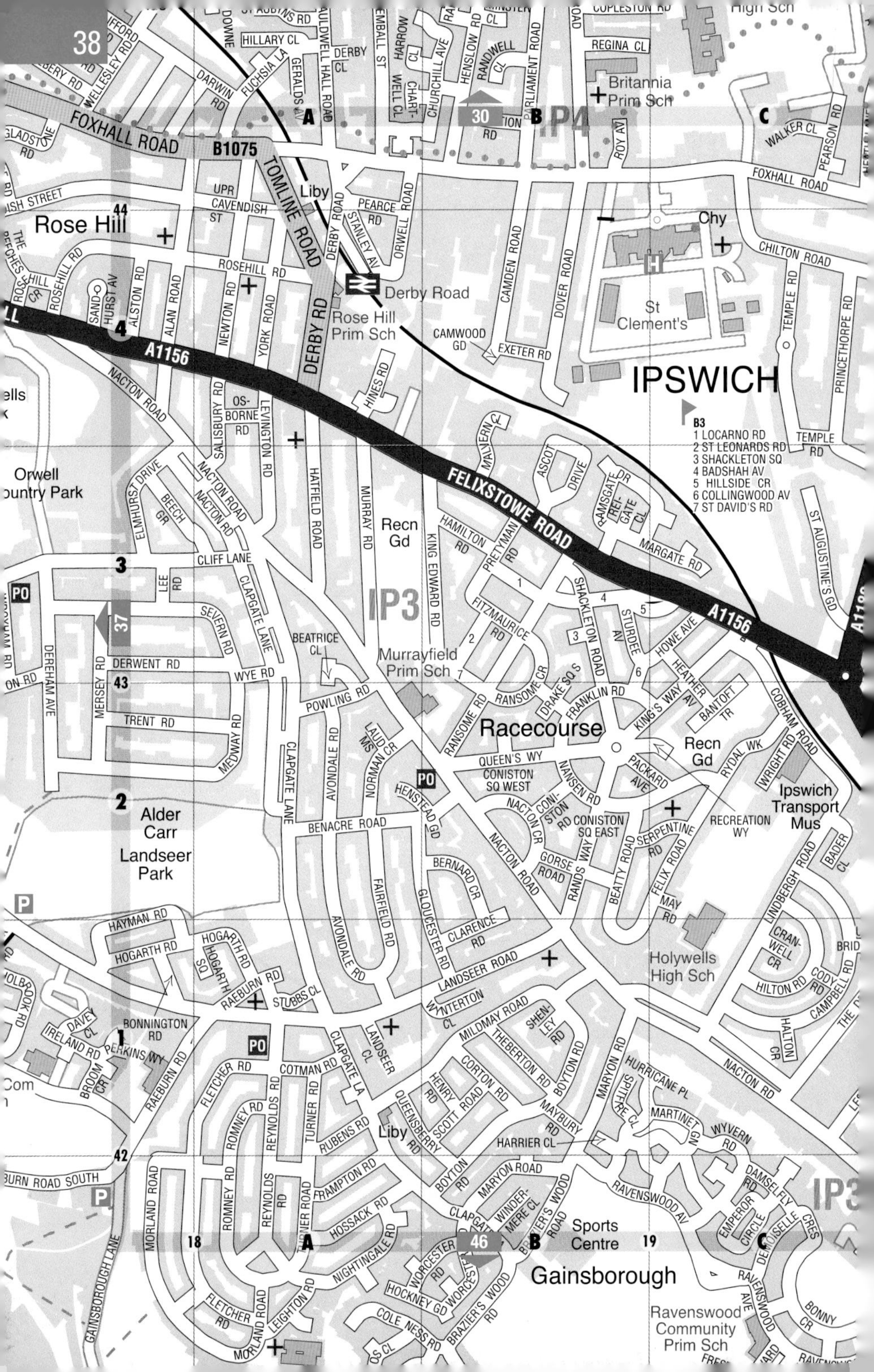
38
IPSWICH
Rose Hill
Racecourse
Gainsborough
Alder Carr
Landseer Park
Orwell Country Park
St Clement's
Britannia Prim Sch
Rose Hill Prim Sch
Murrayfield Prim Sch
Holywells High Sch
Ravenswood Community Prim Sch
Ipswich Transport Mus
Sports Centre
Derby Road
Liby
Chy
Recn Gd
PO
IP4
IP3
A1156
B1075
FOXHALL ROAD
FELIXSTOWE ROAD
TOMLINE ROAD
DERBY RD
NACTON ROAD
CLAPGATE LANE
LANDSEER ROAD
BENACRE ROAD
MARYON ROAD
RAVENSWOOD AV
COBHAM ROAD
GAINSBOROUGH LANE
B3
1 LOCARNO RD
2 ST LEONARDS RD
3 SHACKLETON SQ
4 BADSHAH AV
5 HILLSIDE CR
6 COLLINGWOOD AV
7 ST DAVID'S RD
30
37
46
A
B
C
18
19
42
43
44
1
2
3
4

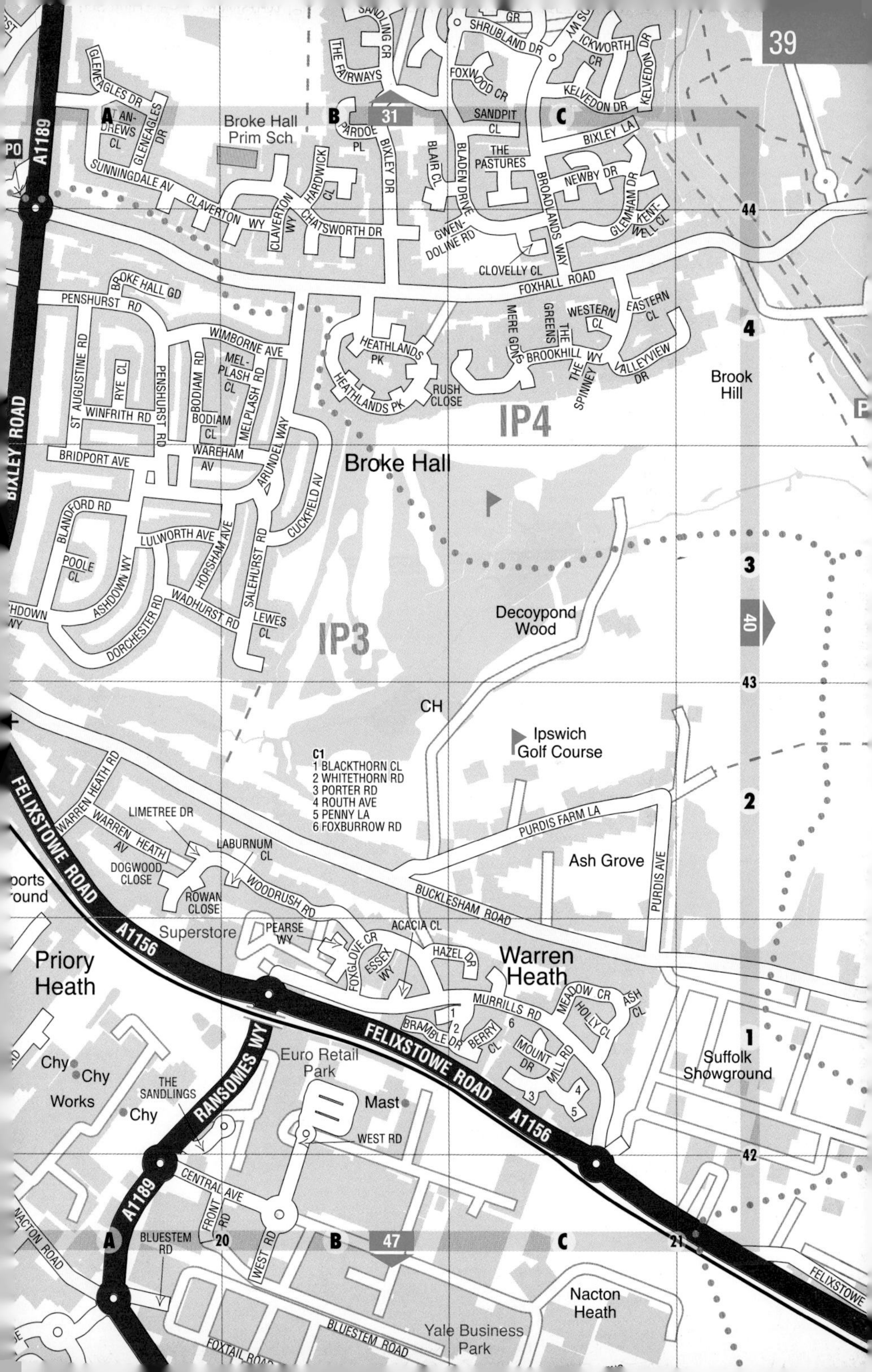

GLENEAGLES DR
ST ANDREWS CL
GLENEAGLES DR
Broke Hall Prim Sch
SUNNINGDALE AV
CLAVERTON WY
CLAVERTON WY
HARDWICK CL
CHATSWORTH DR
PARDOE PL
BIXLEY DR
31
SANDLING CR
THE FAIRWAYS
SHRUBLAND DR
ICKWORTH CR
KELVEDON DR
FOXWOOD CR
SANDPIT CL
BLAIR CL
BLADEN DRIVE
THE PASTURES
BIXLEY LA
NEWBY DR
BROADLANDS WAY
GLEMHAM DR
TENTWELL CL
GWENDOLINE RD
CLOVELLY CL
FOXHALL ROAD
A1189
BIXLEY ROAD
BROKE HALL GD
PENSHURST RD
WIMBORNE AVE
MELPLASH CL
MELPLASH RD
BODIAM RD
ST AUGUSTINE RD
RYE CL
PENSHURST RD
WINFRITH RD
BODIAM CL
WAREHAM AV
ARUNDEL WAY
BRIDPORT AVE
CUCKFIELD AV
HEATHLANDS PK
HEATHLANDS PK
RUSH CLOSE
MERE GDNS
THE GREENS
WESTERN CL
EASTERN CL
BROOKHILL WY
THE SPINNEY
VALLEYVIEW DR
IP4
Brook Hill
Broke Hall
BLANDFORD RD
POOLE CL
ASHDOWN WY
LULWORTH AVE
HORSHAM AVE
SALEHURST RD
DORCHESTER RD
WADHURST RD
LEWES CL
IP3
Decoypond Wood
CH
Ipswich Golf Course
40
C1
1 BLACKTHORN CL
2 WHITETHORN RD
3 PORTER RD
4 ROUTH AVE
5 PENNY LA
6 FOXBURROW RD
FELIXSTOWE ROAD
WARREN HEATH RD
WARREN HEATH AV
LIMETREE DR
LABURNUM CL
DOGWOOD CLOSE
ROWAN CLOSE
WOODRUSH RD
PURDIS FARM LA
Ash Grove
PURDIS AVE
BUCKLESHAM ROAD
A1156
Superstore
PEARSE WY
FOXGLOVE CR
ESSEX WY
ACACIA CL
HAZEL DR
Warren Heath
Priory Heath
MURRILLS RD
MEADOW CR
HOLLY CL
ASH CL
BRAMBLE DR
BERRY CL
MOUNT DR
MILL RD
FELIXSTOWE ROAD
A1156
Suffolk Showground
Euro Retail Park
Mast
RANSOMES WY
THE SANDLINGS
Chy
Chy
Works
Chy
WEST RD
A1189
CENTRAL AVE
FRONT RD
BLUESTEM RD
WEST RD
NACTON ROAD
47
Nacton Heath
Yale Business Park
BLUESTEM ROAD
FOXTAIL ROAD
FELIXSTOWE

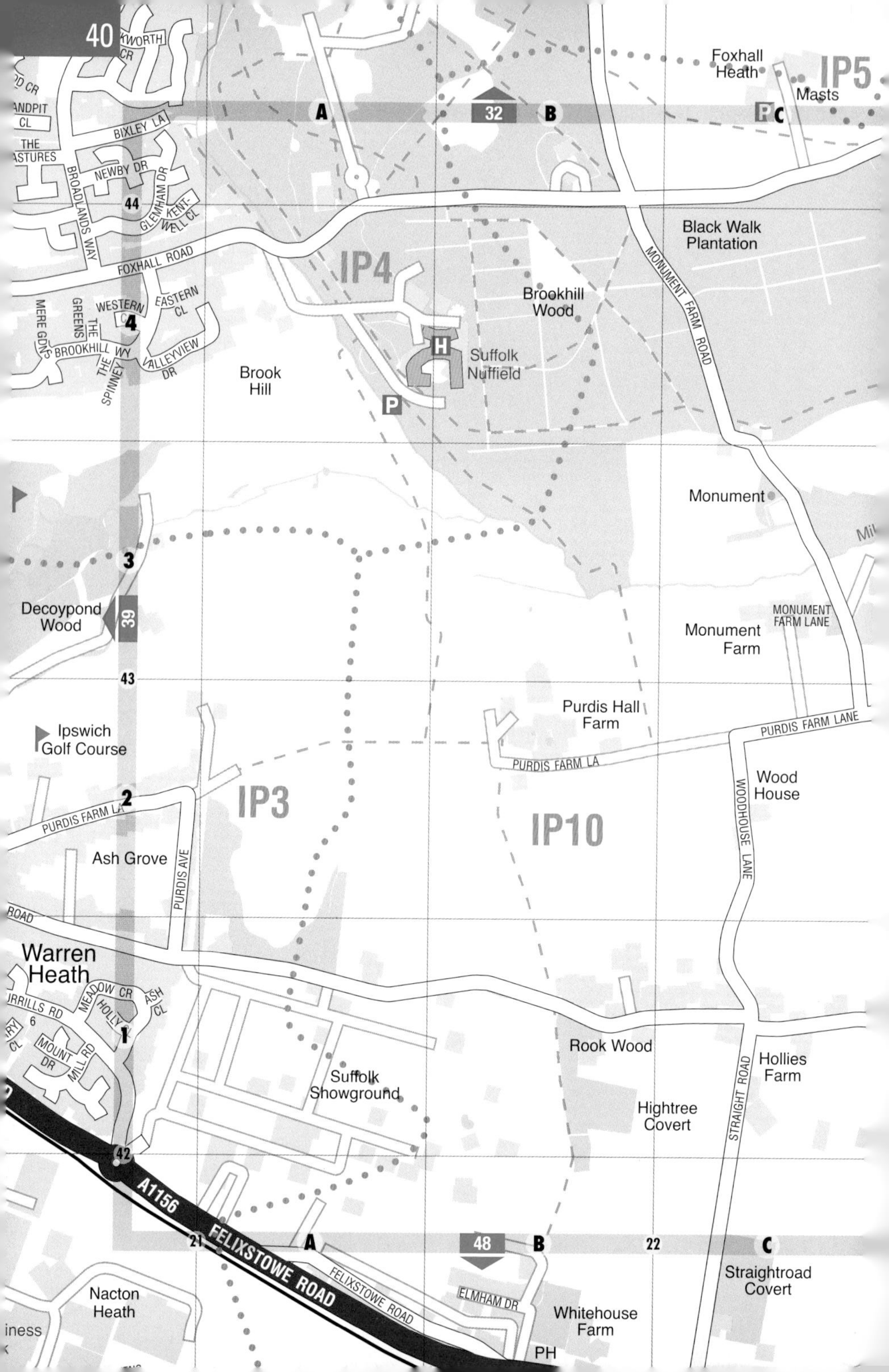

IP5

Foxhall
Heath

Masts

A

32

B

P **C**

Black Walk
Plantation

MONUMENT FARM ROAD

IP4

Brookhill
Wood

H

Suffolk
Nuffield

Brook
Hill

P

Monument

Mil

3

Monument
Farm

MONUMENT
FARM LANE

Decoypond
Wood

39

43

Purdis Hall
Farm

PURDIS FARM LANE

▶ Ipswich
Golf Course

PURDIS FARM LA

Wood
House

WOODHOUSE LANE

2

PURDIS FARM LA

IP3

IP10

Ash Grove

PURDIS AVE

ROAD

Warren
Heath

MEADOW CR

HOLLY

ASH CL

RRILLS RD

6

MOUNT DR

MILL RD

1

Rook Wood

Hollies
Farm

Suffolk
Showground

Hightree
Covert

STRAIGHT ROAD

42

A1156

FELIXSTOWE ROAD

Nacton
Heath

A

FELIXSTOWE ROAD

48

B

22

C

ELMHAM DR

Straightroad
Covert

Whitehouse
Farm

PH

iness

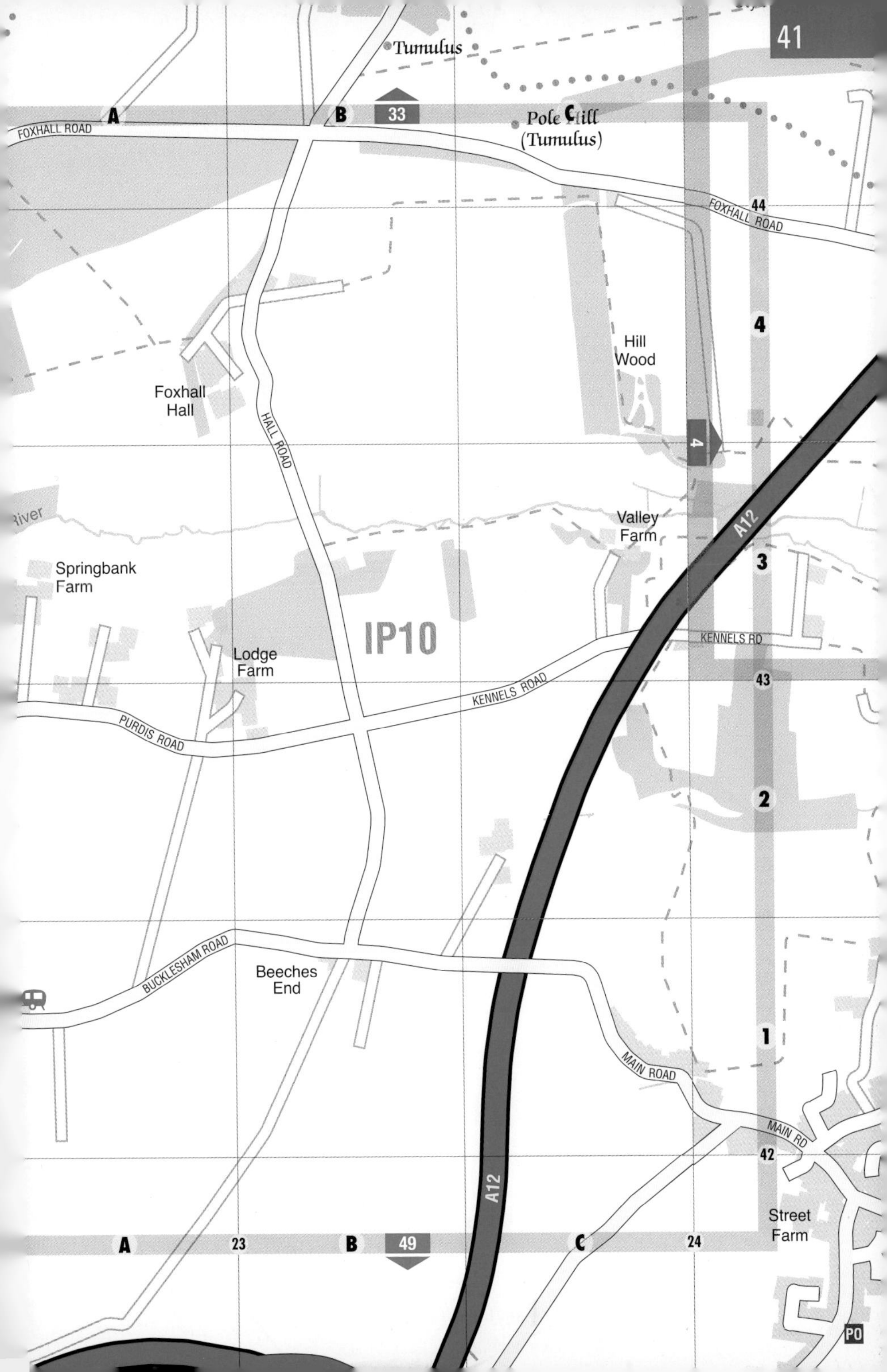
Tumulus
Pole Hill
(Tumulus)
33
FOXHALL ROAD
FOXHALL ROAD
Hill
Wood
Foxhall
Hall
HALL ROAD
River
Valley
Farm
Springbank
Farm
IP10
Lodge
Farm
KENNELS RD
KENNELS ROAD
PURDIS ROAD
A12
BUCKLESHAM ROAD
Beeches
End
MAIN ROAD
MAIN RD
Street
Farm
49
PO
A
B
C
23
24
44
43
42
1
2
3
4

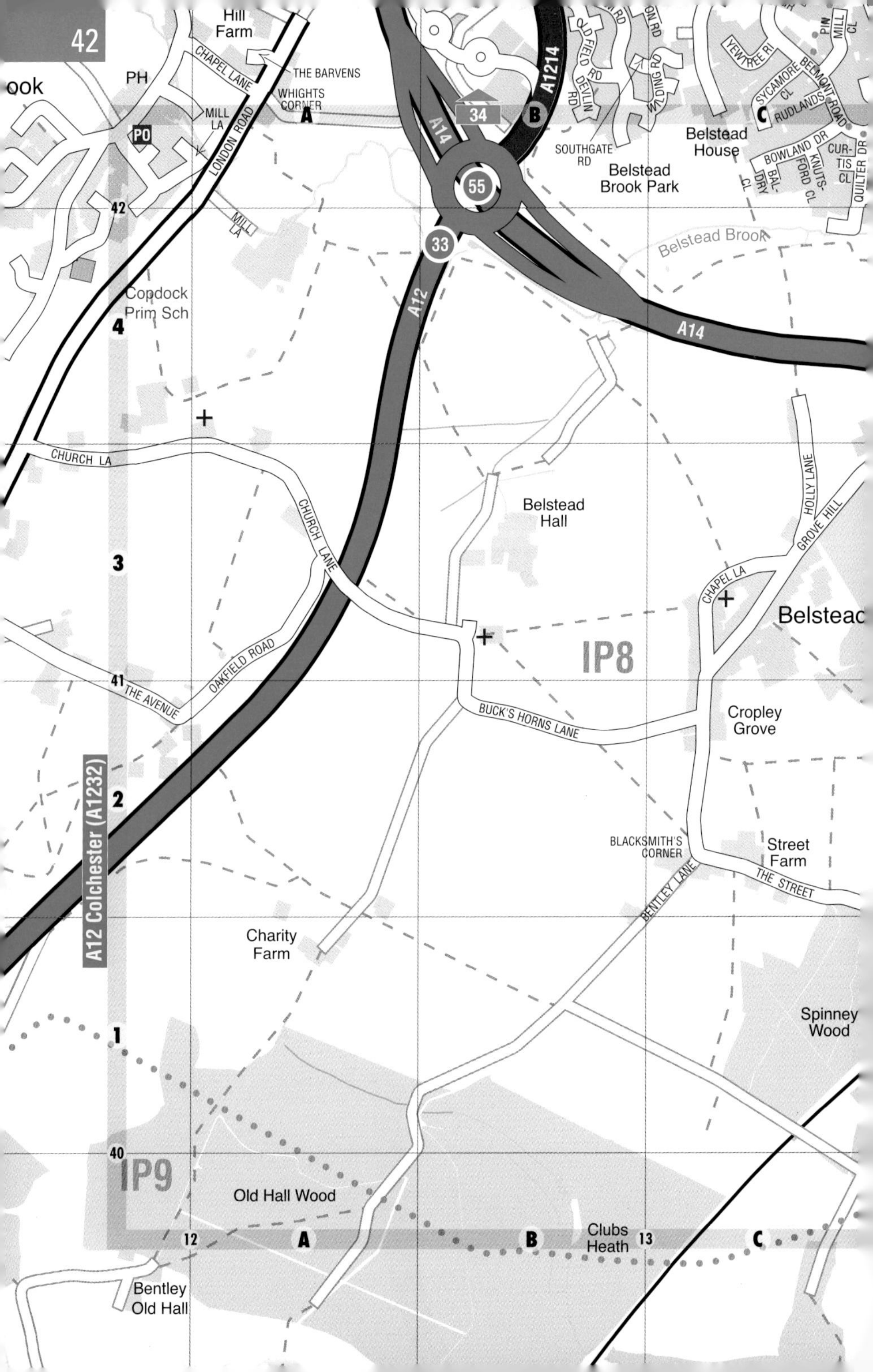
Hill Farm
PH
CHAPEL LANE
THE BARVENS
WHIGHTS CORNER
MILL LA
PO
LONDON ROAD
A
34
B
C
A14
A1214
55
33
A12
OLD FIELD RD
DEVLIN RD
WILDING RD
SOUTHGATE RD
Belstead Brook Park
Belstead House
YEWTREE RI
SYCAMORE CL
BELMONT ROAD
RUDLANDS
PIN MILL CL
BOWLAND DR
BALDRY CL
KNUTSFORD CL
CURTIS CL
QUILTER DR
Belstead Brook
Copdock Prim Sch
CHURCH LA
CHURCH LANE
OAKFIELD ROAD
THE AVENUE
Belstead Hall
HOLLY LANE
GROVE HILL
CHAPEL LA
Belstead
IP8
BUCK'S HORNS LANE
Cropley Grove
BLACKSMITH'S CORNER
Street Farm
THE STREET
BENTLEY LANE
Charity Farm
Spinney Wood
A12 Colchester (A1232)
IP9
Old Hall Wood
Clubs Heath
Bentley Old Hall
42
4
3
41
2
1
40
12
13

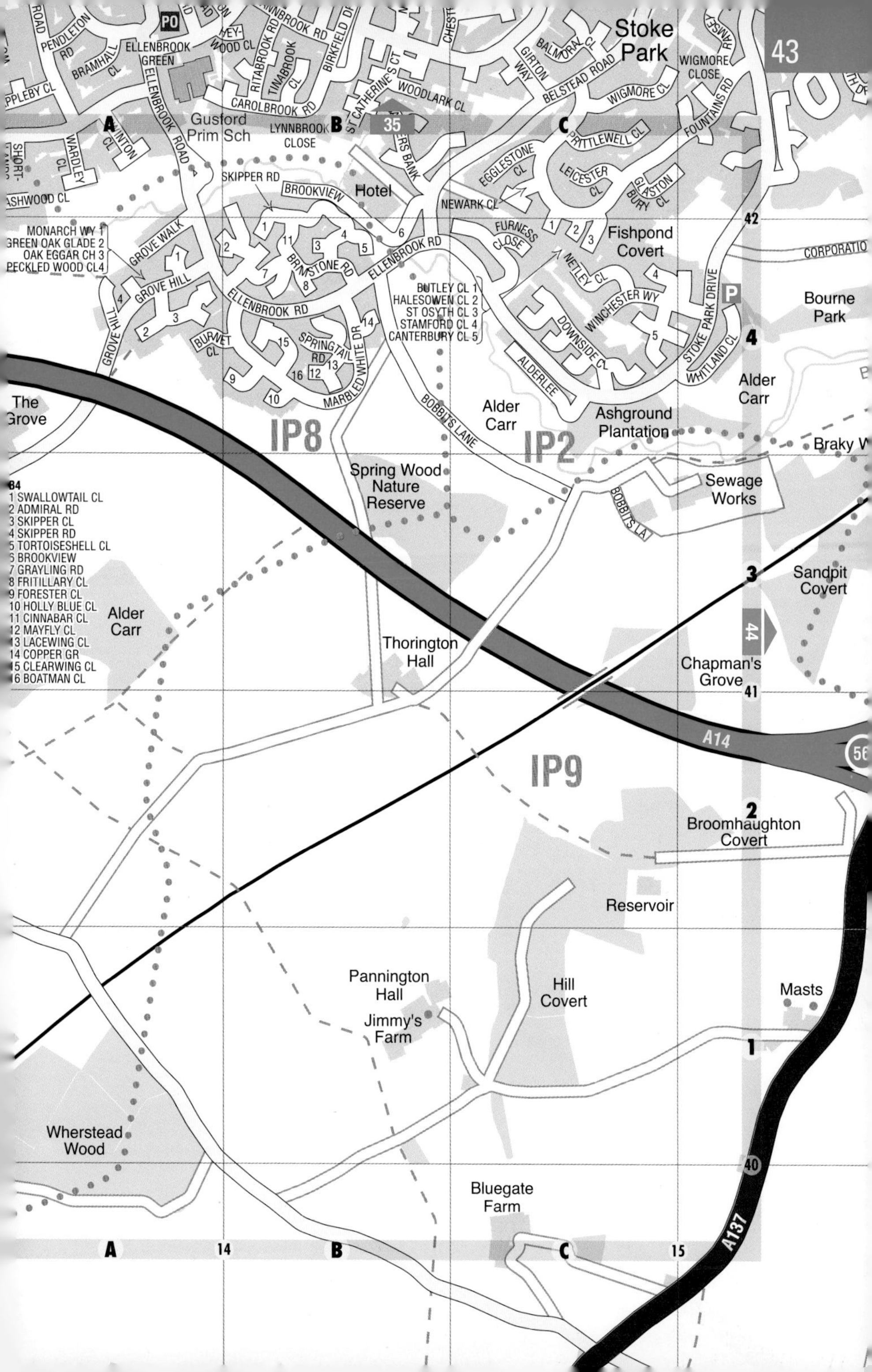
Stoke Park
Gusford Prim Sch
Hotel
Fishpond Covert
Bourne Park
Alder Carr
The Grove
IP8
IP2
Ashground Plantation
Spring Wood Nature Reserve
Sewage Works
Sandpit Covert
Thorington Hall
Chapman's Grove
A14
IP9
Broomhaughton Covert
Reservoir
Pannington Hall
Jimmy's Farm
Hill Covert
Masts
Wherstead Wood
Bluegate Farm
A137
MONARCH WY 1
GREEN OAK GLADE 2
OAK EGGAR CH 3
PECKLED WOOD CL 4
BUTLEY CL 1
HALESOWEN CL 2
ST OSYTH CL 3
STAMFORD CL 4
CANTERBURY CL 5
B4
1 SWALLOWTAIL CL
2 ADMIRAL RD
3 SKIPPER CL
4 SKIPPER RD
5 TORTOISESHELL CL
6 BROOKVIEW
7 GRAYLING RD
8 FRITILLARY CL
9 FORESTER CL
10 HOLLY BLUE CL
11 CINNABAR CL
12 MAYFLY CL
13 LACEWING CL
14 COPPER GR
15 CLEARWING CL
16 BOATMAN CL
ELLENBROOK RD
BOBBITS LANE
STOKE PARK DRIVE
CORPORATIO
Braky W
35
44
56
A
B
C
14
15
40
41
42

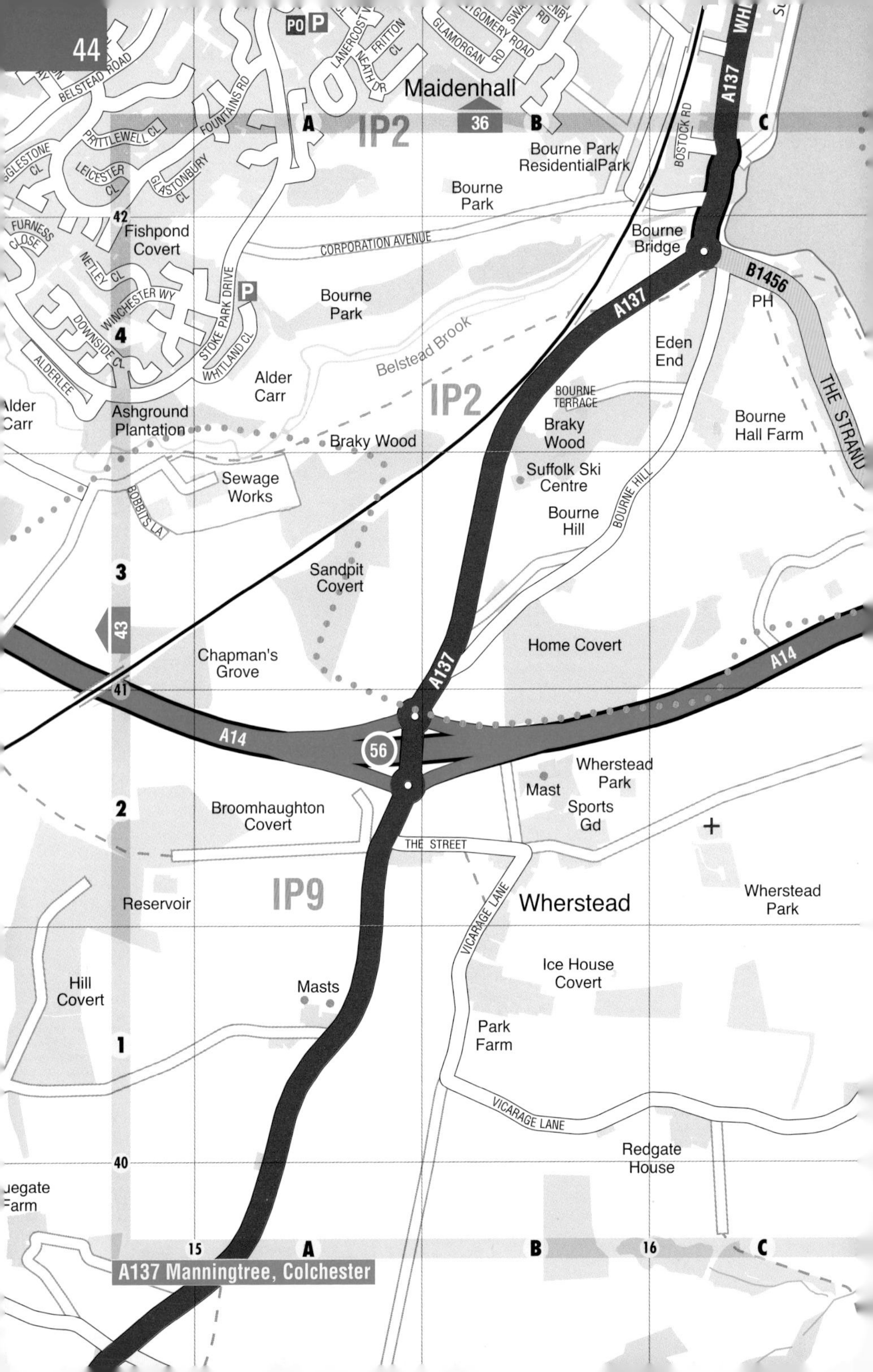

Maidenhall
36
IP2
A
B
C
BELSTEAD ROAD
FOUNTAINS RD
LANERCOST
NEATH DR
FRITTON CL
GLAMORGAN RD
MONTGOMERY ROAD
PRITTLEWELL CL
LEICESTER CL
GLASTONBURY CL
BOSTOCK RD
A137
Bourne Park ResidentialPark
Bourne Park
FURNESS CLOSE
Fishpond Covert
CORPORATION AVENUE
Bourne Bridge
NETLEY CL
WINCHESTER WY
STOKE PARK DRIVE
Bourne Park
B1456
PH
DOWNSIDE CL
WHITLAND CL
Belstead Brook
Eden End
ALDERLEE
Alder Carr
IP2
BOURNE TERRACE
THE STRAND
Bourne Hall Farm
Ashground Plantation
Braky Wood
Braky Wood
Sewage Works
Suffolk Ski Centre
BOBBITS LA
BOURNE HILL
Bourne Hill
Sandpit Covert
43
Home Covert
Chapman's Grove
A14
41
A14
56
Whersted Park
Mast
Sports Gd
Broomhaughton Covert
THE STREET
IP9
Reservoir
VICARAGE LANE
Wherstead
Wherstead Park
Ice House Covert
Hill Covert
Masts
Park Farm
VICARAGE LANE
Redgate House
40
15
16
A137 Manningtree, Colchester

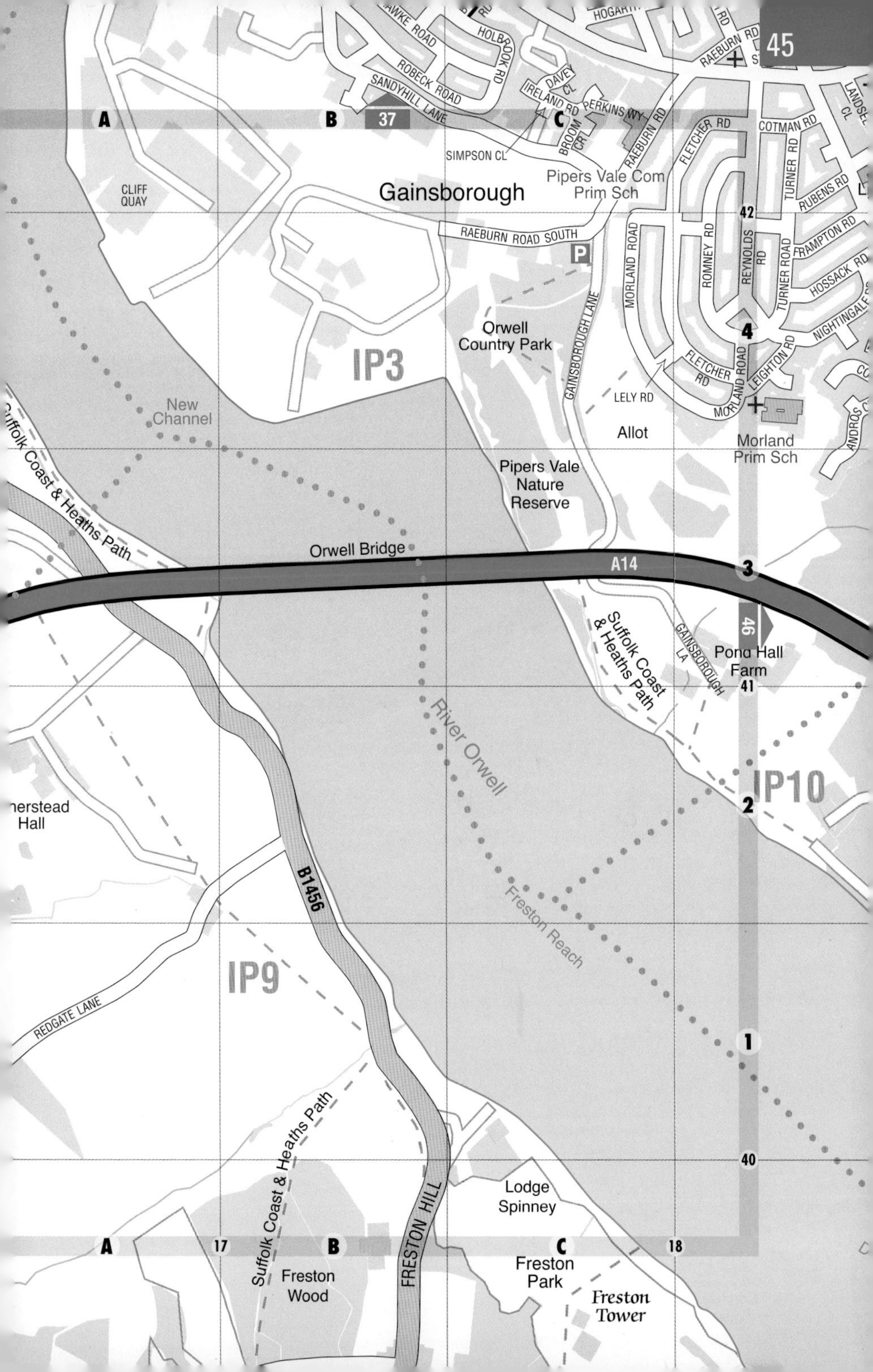
Gainsborough
CLIFF QUAY
SANDYHILL LANE
ROBECK ROAD
HOLBROOK RD
DAVEY CL
IRELAND RD
PERKINS WY
BROOM CR
SIMPSON CL
RAEBURN RD
FLETCHER RD
COTMAN RD
TURNER RD
RUBENS RD
Pipers Vale Com Prim Sch
RAEBURN ROAD SOUTH
MORLAND ROAD
ROMNEY RD
REYNOLDS RD
TURNER ROAD
FRAMPTON RD
HOSSACK RD
NIGHTINGALE RD
Orwell Country Park
GAINSBOROUGH LANE
LEIGHTON RD
LELY RD
Allot
Morland Prim Sch
IP3
New Channel
Suffolk Coast & Heaths Path
Pipers Vale Nature Reserve
Orwell Bridge
A14
GAINSBOROUGH LA
Pond Hall Farm
River Orwell
IP10
Freston Reach
B1456
IP9
REDGATE LANE
Lodge Spinney
FRESTON HILL
Freston Wood
Freston Park
Freston Tower

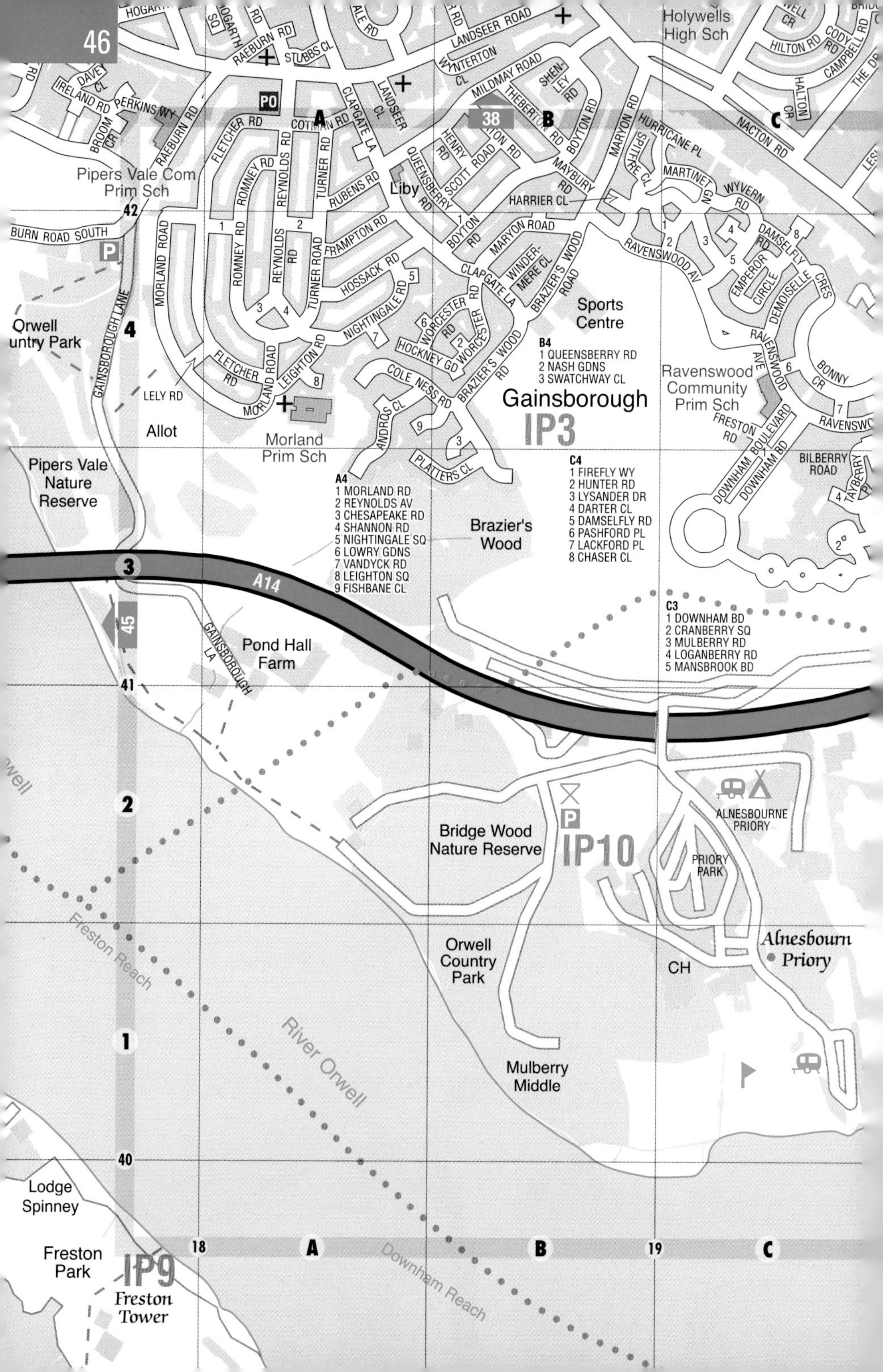
Holywells High Sch
Pipers Vale Com Prim Sch
Liby
Sports Centre
Ravenswood Community Prim Sch
Gainsborough
IP3
Orwell Country Park
Allot
Morland Prim Sch
Pipers Vale Nature Reserve
Brazier's Wood
Pond Hall Farm
Bridge Wood Nature Reserve
IP10
ALNESBOURNE PRIORY
PRIORY PARK
Alnesbourn Priory
CH
Orwell Country Park
Mulberry Middle
River Orwell
Freston Reach
Downham Reach
Lodge Spinney
Freston Park
IP9
Freston Tower
A14
38
45
B4
1 QUEENSBERRY RD
2 NASH GDNS
3 SWATCHWAY CL
A4
1 MORLAND RD
2 REYNOLDS AV
3 CHESAPEAKE RD
4 SHANNON RD
5 NIGHTINGALE SQ
6 LOWRY GDNS
7 VANDYCK RD
8 LEIGHTON SQ
9 FISHBANE CL
C4
1 FIREFLY WY
2 HUNTER RD
3 LYSANDER DR
4 DARTER CL
5 DAMSELFLY RD
6 PASHFORD PL
7 LACKFORD PL
8 CHASER CL
C3
1 DOWNHAM BD
2 CRANBERRY SQ
3 MULBERRY RD
4 LOGANBERRY RD
5 MANSBROOK BD
RAEBURN RD
STUBBS CL
LANDSEER ROAD
WYNTERTON CL
MILDMAY ROAD
SHENLEY RD
THEBERTON RD
BOYTON RD
MARYON RD
HURRICANE PL
NACTON RD
HILTON RD
CODY RD
CAMPBELL RD
HALTON CR
IRELAND RD
DAVEY CL
PERKINS WY
BROOM CR
FLETCHER RD
COTMAN RD
CLAPGATE LA
LANDSEER CL
ROMNEY RD
REYNOLDS RD
TURNER RD
RUBENS RD
QUEENSBERRY RD
HENRY RD
SCOTT ROAD
MAYBURY RD
SPITFIRE CL
MARTINET GN
WYVERN RD
HARRIER CL
BURN ROAD SOUTH
MORLAND ROAD
ROMNEY RD
REYNOLDS RD
TURNER ROAD
FRAMPTON RD
BOYTON RD
MARYON ROAD
RAVENSWOOD AV
DAMSELFLY RD
EMPEROR CIRCLE
DEMOISELLE CRES
HOSSACK RD
NIGHTINGALE RD
CLAPGATE LA
WINDERMERE CL
BRAZIER'S WOOD ROAD
WORCESTER RD
HOCKNEY GD
GAINSBOROUGH LANE
FLETCHER RD
LEIGHTON RD
MORLAND ROAD
LELY RD
COLE NESS RD
BRAZIER'S WOOD RD
RAVENSWOOD AVE
BONNY CR
RAVENSWOOD
FRESTON RD
DOWNHAM BOULEVARD
DOWNHAM BD
BILBERRY ROAD
TAYBERRY PL
ANDROS CL
PLATTERS CL
GAINSBOROUGH LA
A
B
C
18
19
40
41
42

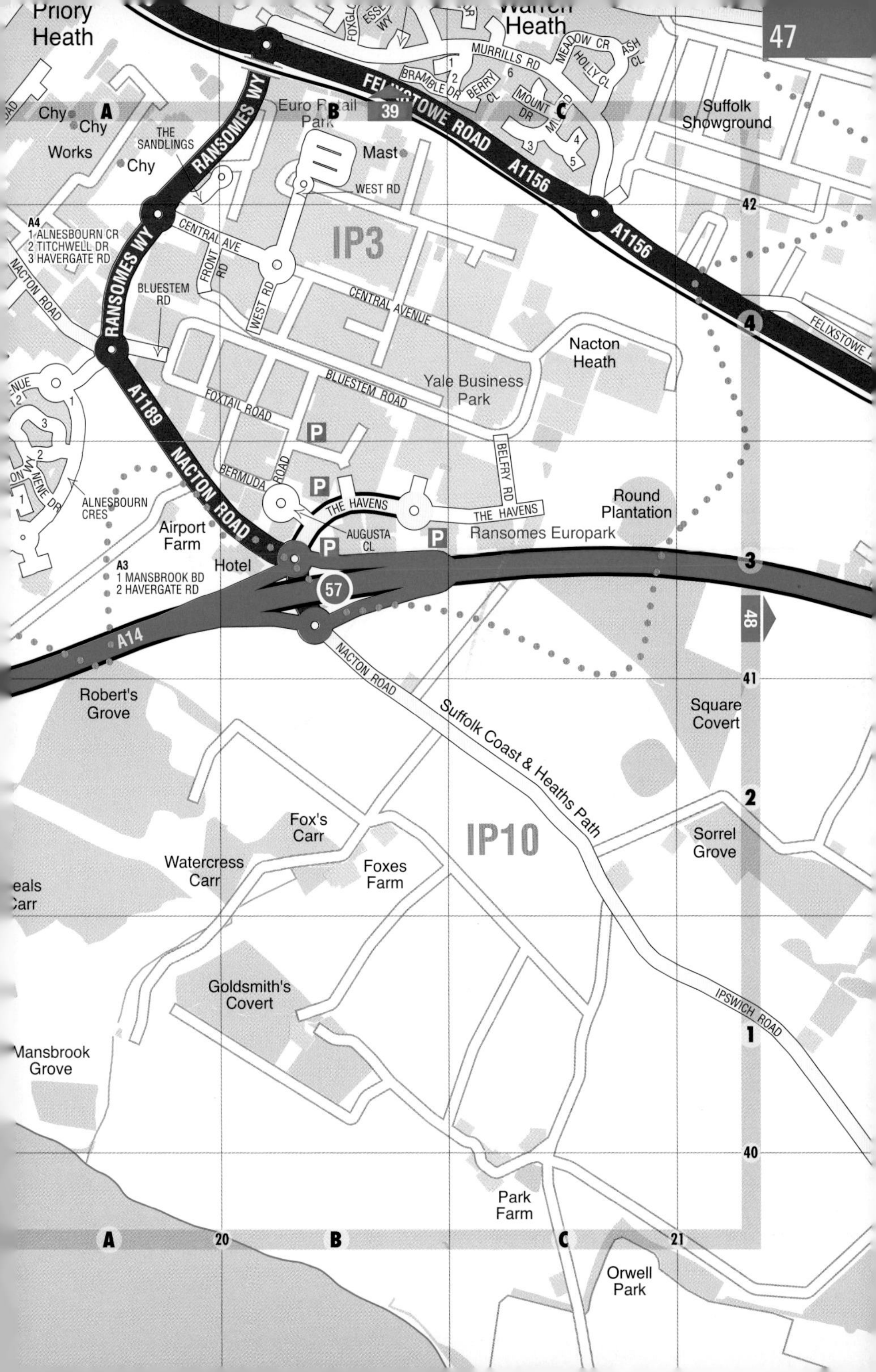

Priory Heath
Warren Heath
Chy
Chy
Works
Chy
A
B
C
39
Euro Retail Park
Mast
Suffolk Showground
THE SANDLINGS
RANSOMES WY
FELIXSTOWE ROAD
A1156
MURRILLS RD
MEADOW CR
HOLLY CL
ASH CL
BRAMBLE DR
BERRY CL
MOUNT DR
MILL RD
WEST RD
42
A4
1 ALNESBOURN CR
2 TITCHWELL DR
3 HAVERGATE RD
NACTON ROAD
CENTRAL AVE
FRONT RD
IP3
CENTRAL AVENUE
BLUESTEM RD
4
Nacton Heath
Yale Business Park
BLUESTEM ROAD
FOXTAIL ROAD
A1189
NACTON ROAD
BERMUDA ROAD
BELFRY RD
THE HAVENS
THE HAVENS
AUGUSTA CL
Round Plantation
Ransomes Europark
ALNESBOURN CRES
Airport Farm
Hotel
A3
1 MANSBROOK BD
2 HAVERGATE RD
57
3
A14
48
NACTON ROAD
41
Robert's Grove
Suffolk Coast & Heaths Path
Square Covert
2
IP10
Fox's Carr
Watercress Carr
Foxes Farm
Sorrel Grove
Goldsmith's Covert
IPSWICH ROAD
1
Mansbrook Grove
40
Park Farm
A
20
B
C
21
Orwell Park

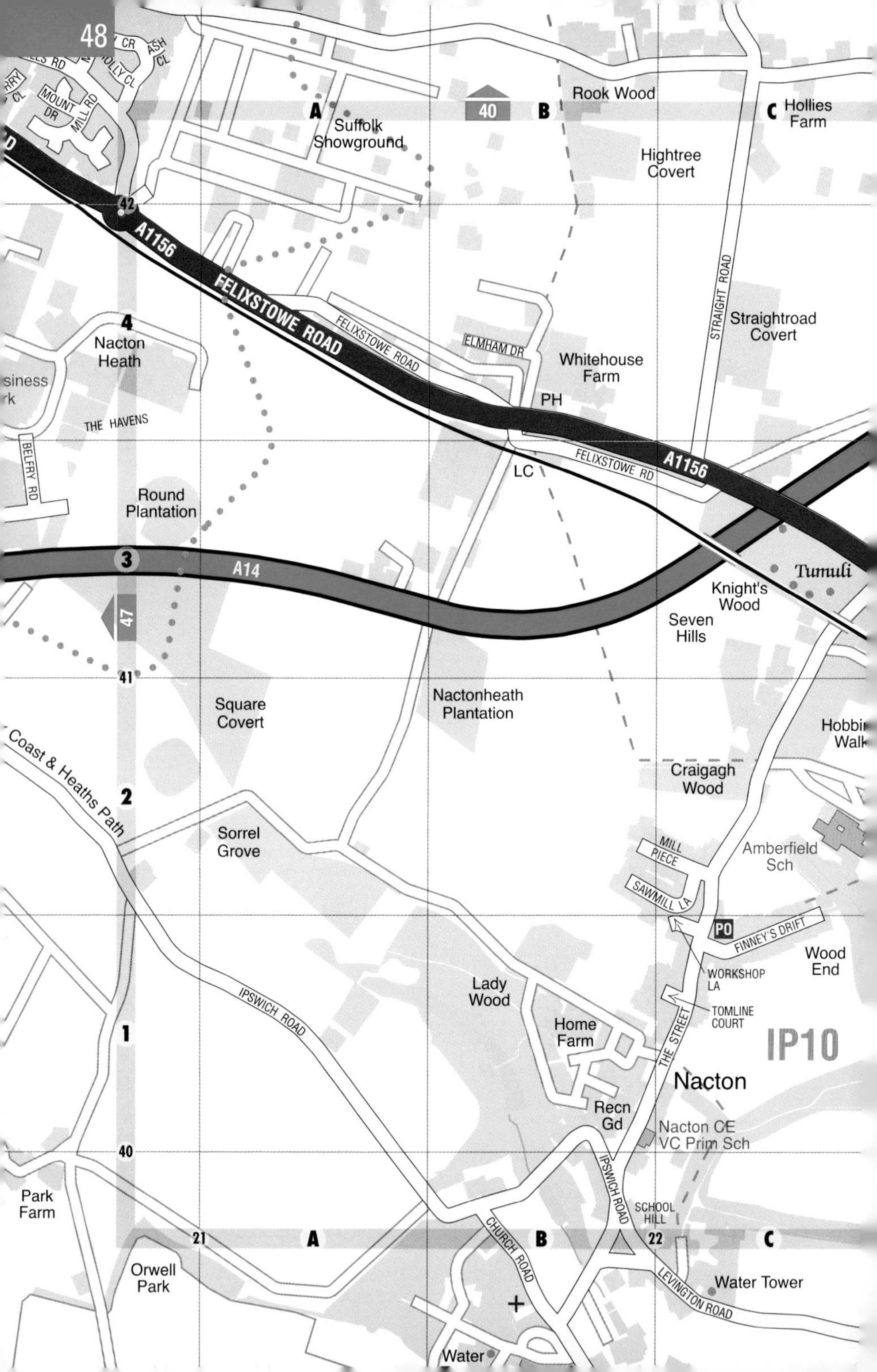

40
A
B
C
Rook Wood
Hollies Farm
Suffolk Showground
Hightree Covert
42
A1156
FELIXSTOWE ROAD
FELIXSTOWE ROAD
ELMHAM DR
Whitehouse Farm
PH
STRAIGHT ROAD
Straightroad Covert
4
Nacton Heath
THE HAVENS
BELFRY RD
FELIXSTOWE RD
A1156
LC
Round Plantation
3
A14
Tumuli
Knight's Wood
Seven Hills
47
41
Square Covert
Nactonheath Plantation
Coast & Heaths Path
2
Craigagh Wood
Sorrel Grove
MILL PIECE
Amberfield Sch
SAWMILL LA
PO
FINNEY'S DRIFT
WORKSHOP LA
Wood End
Lady Wood
TOMLINE COURT
IPSWICH ROAD
1
Home Farm
THE STREET
IP10
Nacton
Recn Gd
Nacton CE VC Prim Sch
40
IPSWICH ROAD
Park Farm
CHURCH ROAD
SCHOOL HILL
21
A
B
22
C
Orwell Park
LEVINGTON ROAD
Water Tower
Water

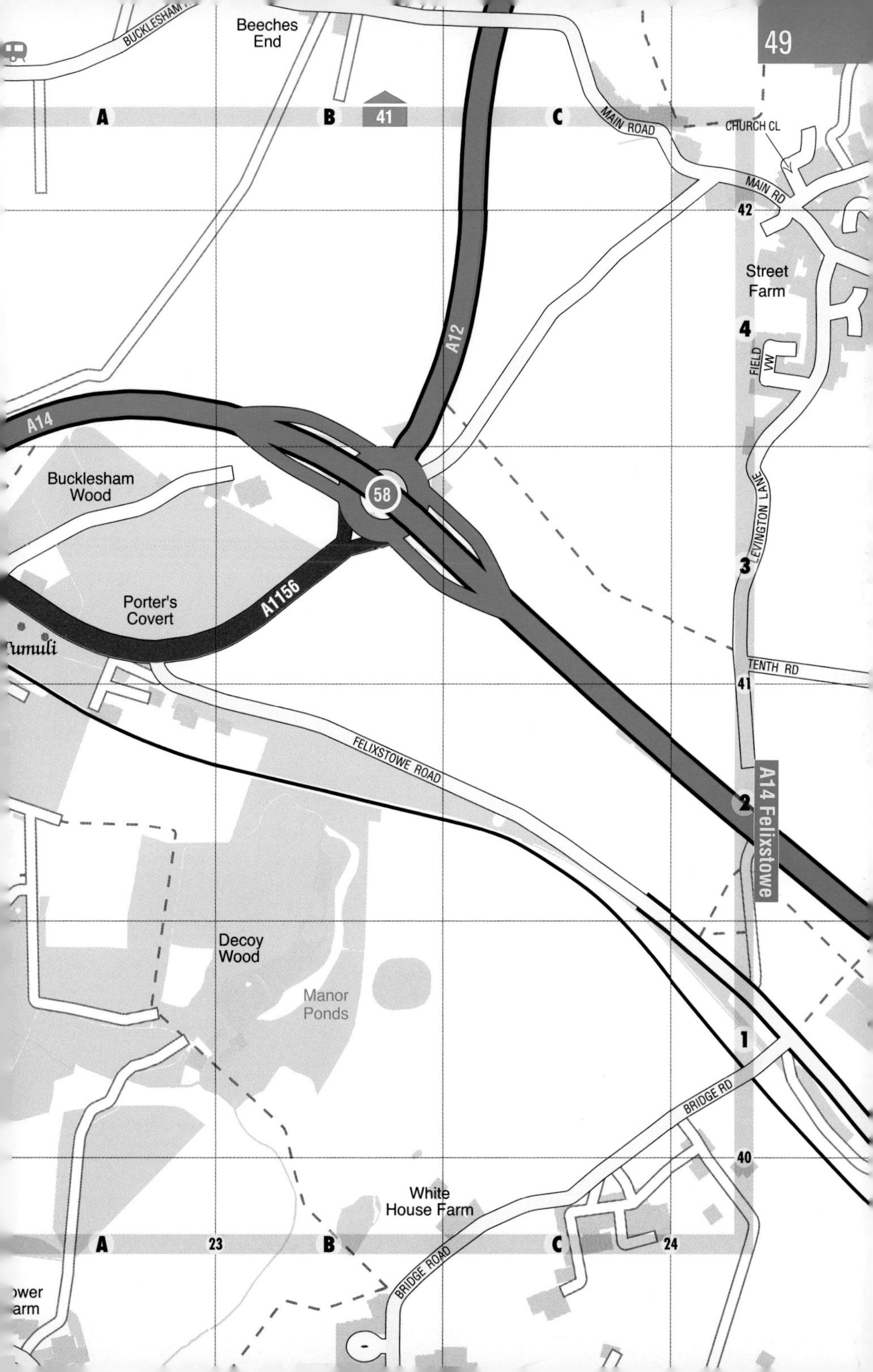
BUCKLESHAM
Beeches End
A
B
41
C
MAIN ROAD
CHURCH CL
MAIN RD
42
Street Farm
4
FIELD VW
A12
A14
Bucklesham Wood
58
LEVINGTON LANE
3
Porter's Covert
A1156
Tumuli
TENTH RD
41
FELIXSTOWE ROAD
A14 Felixstowe
2
Decoy Wood
Manor Ponds
1
BRIDGE RD
40
White House Farm
A
23
B
C
24
BRIDGE ROAD

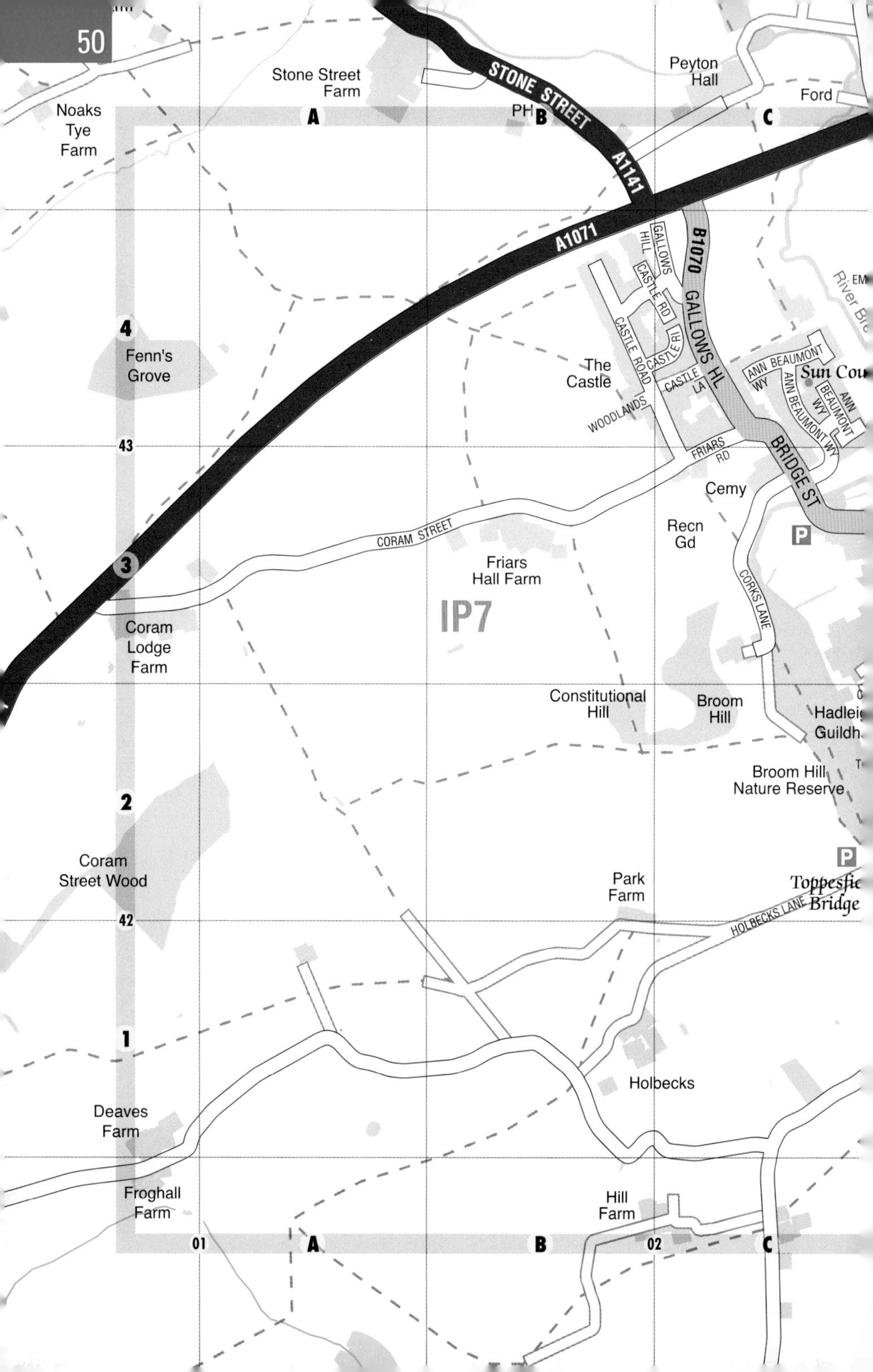

Stone Street Farm
STONE STREET
A1141
PH
Peyton Hall
Ford
Noaks Tye Farm
A
B
C
A1071
B1070
GALLOWS HILL
GALLOWS HL
CASTLE RD
CASTLE RI
CASTLE ROAD
CASTLE LA
WOODLANDS
The Castle
ANN BEAUMONT WY
Sun Cou
River Br
4
Fenn's Grove
43
FRIARS RD
BRIDGE ST
Cemy
Recn Gd
CORAM STREET
3
Friars Hall Farm
IP7
CORKS LANE
Coram Lodge Farm
Constitutional Hill
Broom Hill
Hadlei
Guildh
Broom Hill Nature Reserve
2
Coram Street Wood
Park Farm
Toppesfie Bridge
HOLBECKS LANE
42
1
Holbecks
Deaves Farm
Froghall Farm
Hill Farm
01
02

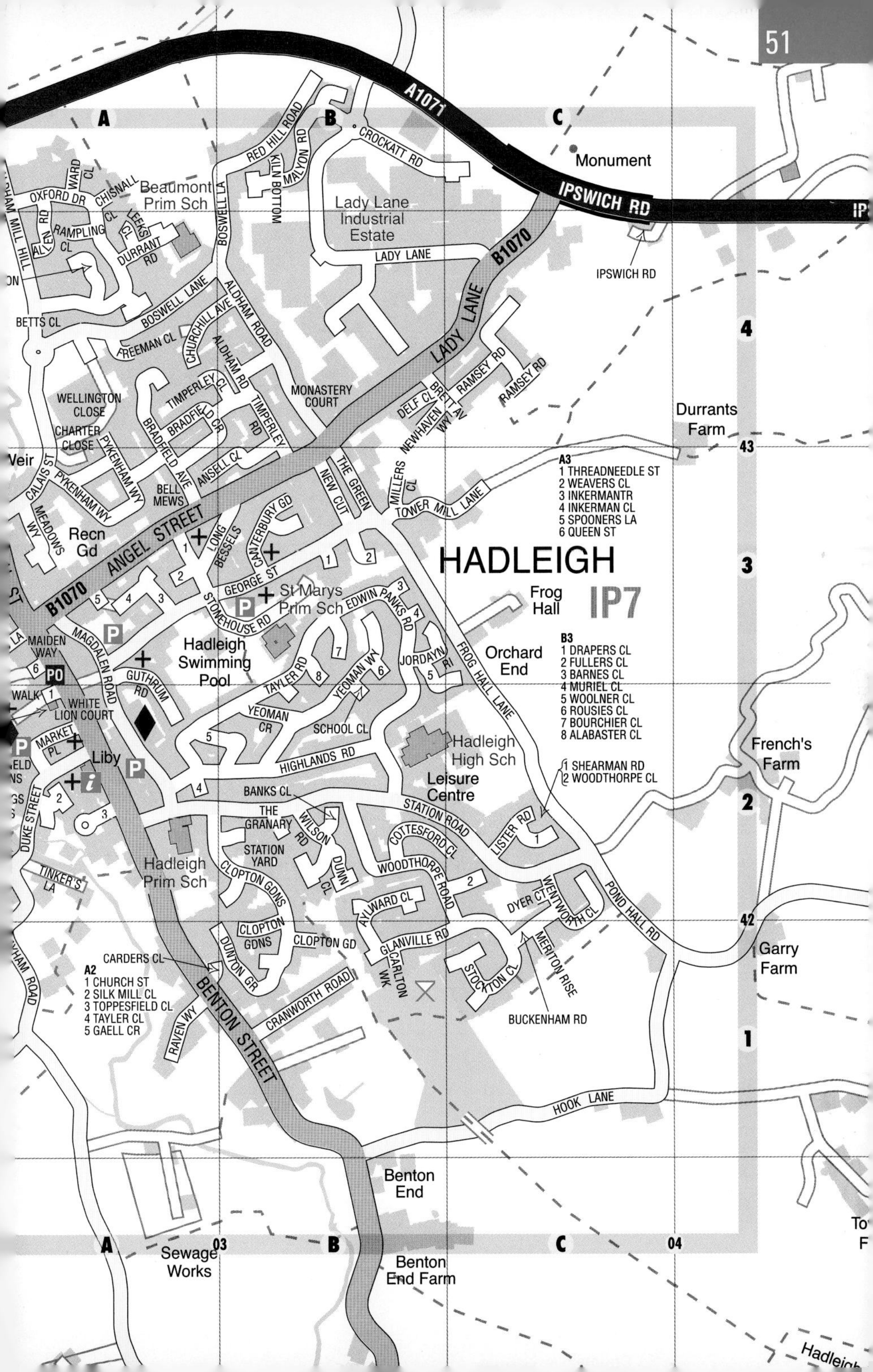
HADLEIGH
IP7
A1071
IPSWICH RD
B1070
Monument
Lady Lane Industrial Estate
LADY LANE
CROCKATT RD
RED HILL ROAD
MALYON RD
KILN BOTTOM
Beaumont Prim Sch
OXFORD DR
WARD CL
CHISNALL CL
RAMPLING CL
LEEKS CL
ALLEN RD
DURRANT RD
BOSWELL LA
BOSWELL LANE
BETTS CL
FREEMAN CL
CHURCHILL AVE
ALDHAM ROAD
ALDHAM RD
TIMPERLEY CL
TIMPERLEY RD
BRADFIELD CR
BRADFIELD AVE
WELLINGTON CLOSE
CHARTER CLOSE
PYKENHAM WY
CALAIS ST
MEADOWS WY
MONASTERY COURT
ANSELL CL
BELL MEWS
Recn Gd
ANGEL STREET
LONG BESSELS
CANTERBURY GD
GEORGE ST
NEW CUT
THE GREEN
MILLERS CL
TOWER MILL LANE
DELF CL
BRETT AV
NEWHAVEN WY
RAMSEY RD
Durrants Farm
A3
1 THREADNEEDLE ST
2 WEAVERS CL
3 INKERMANTR
4 INKERMAN CL
5 SPOONERS LA
6 QUEEN ST
St Marys Prim Sch
STONEHOUSE RD
EDWIN PANKS RD
MAGDALEN ROAD
MAIDEN WAY
Hadleigh Swimming Pool
GUTHRUM RD
TAYLER RD
YEOMAN WY
YEOMAN CR
SCHOOL CL
JORDAYN RI
Frog Hall
Orchard End
FROG HALL LANE
B3
1 DRAPERS CL
2 FULLERS CL
3 BARNES CL
4 MURIEL CL
5 WOOLNER CL
6 ROUSIES CL
7 BOURCHIER CL
8 ALABASTER CL
PO
WALK
WHITE LION COURT
MARKET PL
Liby
HIGHLANDS RD
Hadleigh High Sch
Leisure Centre
1 SHEARMAN RD
2 WOODTHORPE CL
French's Farm
DUKE STREET
BANKS CL
THE GRANARY
WILSON RD
STATION YARD
STATION ROAD
COTTESFORD CL
LISTER RD
Hadleigh Prim Sch
TINKER'S LA
CLOPTON GDNS
DUNN CL
WOODTHORPE ROAD
DYER CT
WENTWORTH CL
POND HALL RD
AYLWARD CL
GLANVILLE RD
CLOPTON GD
CARLTON WK
STOCKTON CL
MERITON RISE
Garry Farm
CARDERS CL
DUNTON GR
A2
1 CHURCH ST
2 SILK MILL CL
3 TOPPESFIELD CL
4 TAYLER CL
5 GAELL CR
BENTON STREET
CRANWORTH ROAD
RAVEN WY
BUCKENHAM RD
HOOK LANE
Benton End
Sewage Works
Benton End Farm
A
B
C
03
04
43
42
4
3
2
1
Weir
Hadleigh

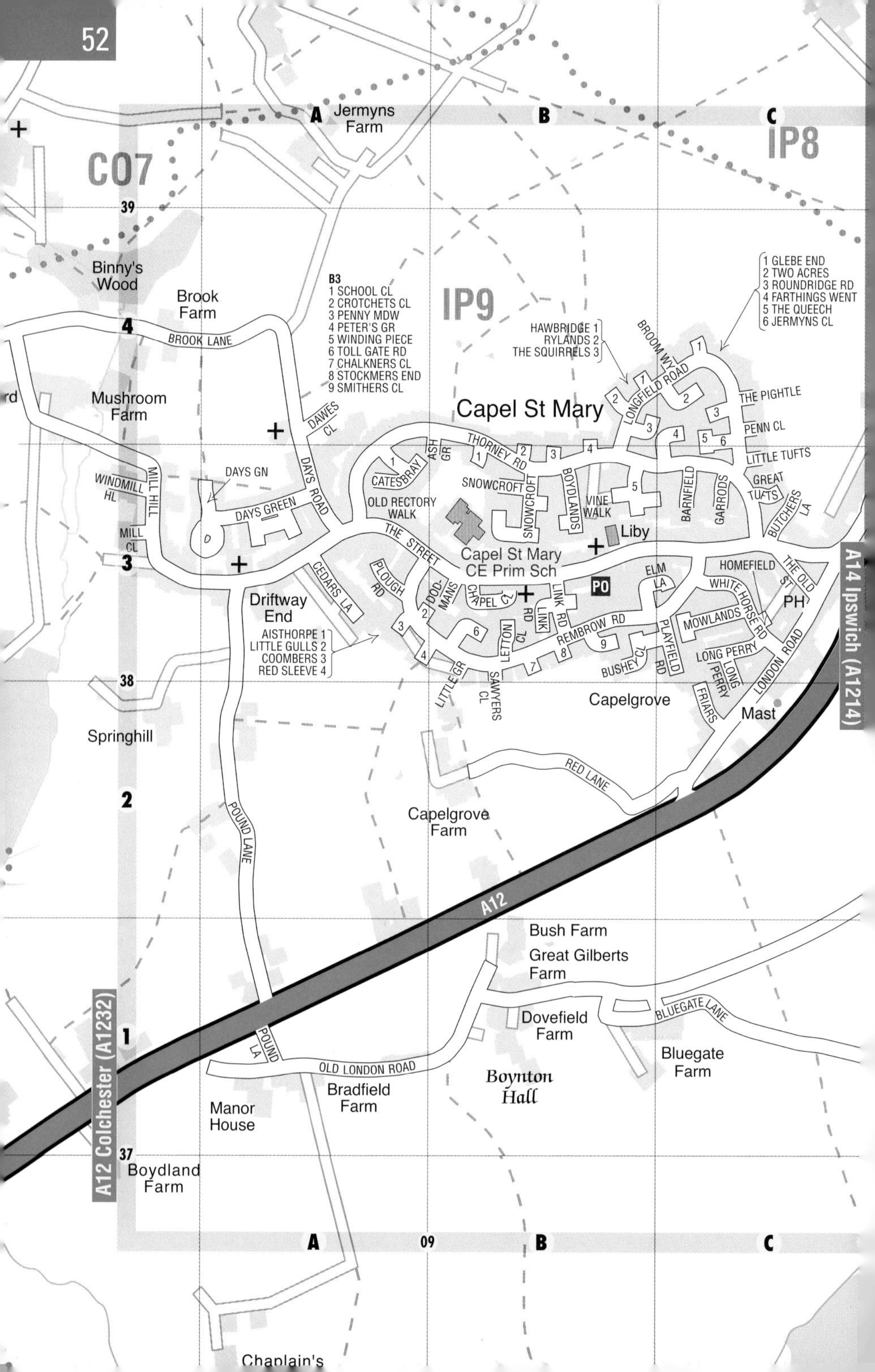

Jermyns Farm
A
B
C
IP8
CO7
39
Binny's Wood
Brook Farm
4
BROOK LANE
B3
1 SCHOOL CL
2 CROTCHETS CL
3 PENNY MDW
4 PETER'S GR
5 WINDING PIECE
6 TOLL GATE RD
7 CHALKNERS CL
8 STOCKMERS END
9 SMITHERS CL
IP9
HAWBRIDGE 1
RYLANDS 2
THE SQUIRRELS 3
1 GLEBE END
2 TWO ACRES
3 ROUNDRIDGE RD
4 FARTHINGS WENT
5 THE QUEECH
6 JERMYNS CL
BROOM WY
LONGFIELD ROAD
THE PIGHTLE
PENN CL
LITTLE TUFTS
GREAT TUFTS
BUTCHERS LA
Mushroom Farm
DAWES CL
Capel St Mary
THORNEY RD
ASH GR
CATESBRAY
SNOWCROFT
BOYDLANDS
VINE WALK
BARNFIELD
GARRODS
WINDMILL HL
MILL HILL
DAYS GN
DAYS ROAD
DAYS GREEN
OLD RECTORY WALK
MILL CL
3
THE STREET
Liby
Capel St Mary CE Prim Sch
HOMEFIELD
THE OLD ST
CEDARS LA
PLOUGH RD
DODMANS
CHAPEL CL
LINK RD
PO
ELM LA
WHITE HORSE RD
PH
Driftway End
AISTHORPE 1
LITTLE GULLS 2
COOMBERS 3
RED SLEEVE 4
LETTON CL
REMBROW RD
PLAYFIELD RD
MOWLANDS
LONG PERRY
LONDON ROAD
BUSHEY CL
LITTLE GR
SAWYERS CL
FRIARS
38
Capelgrove
Mast
Springhill
A14 Ipswich (A1214)
RED LANE
2
POUND LANE
Capelgrove Farm
A12
Bush Farm
Great Gilberts Farm
Dovefield Farm
BLUEGATE LANE
1
POUND LA
OLD LONDON ROAD
Bluegate Farm
Boynton Hall
Bradfield Farm
Manor House
A12 Colchester (A1232)
37
Boydland Farm
09
Chaplain's

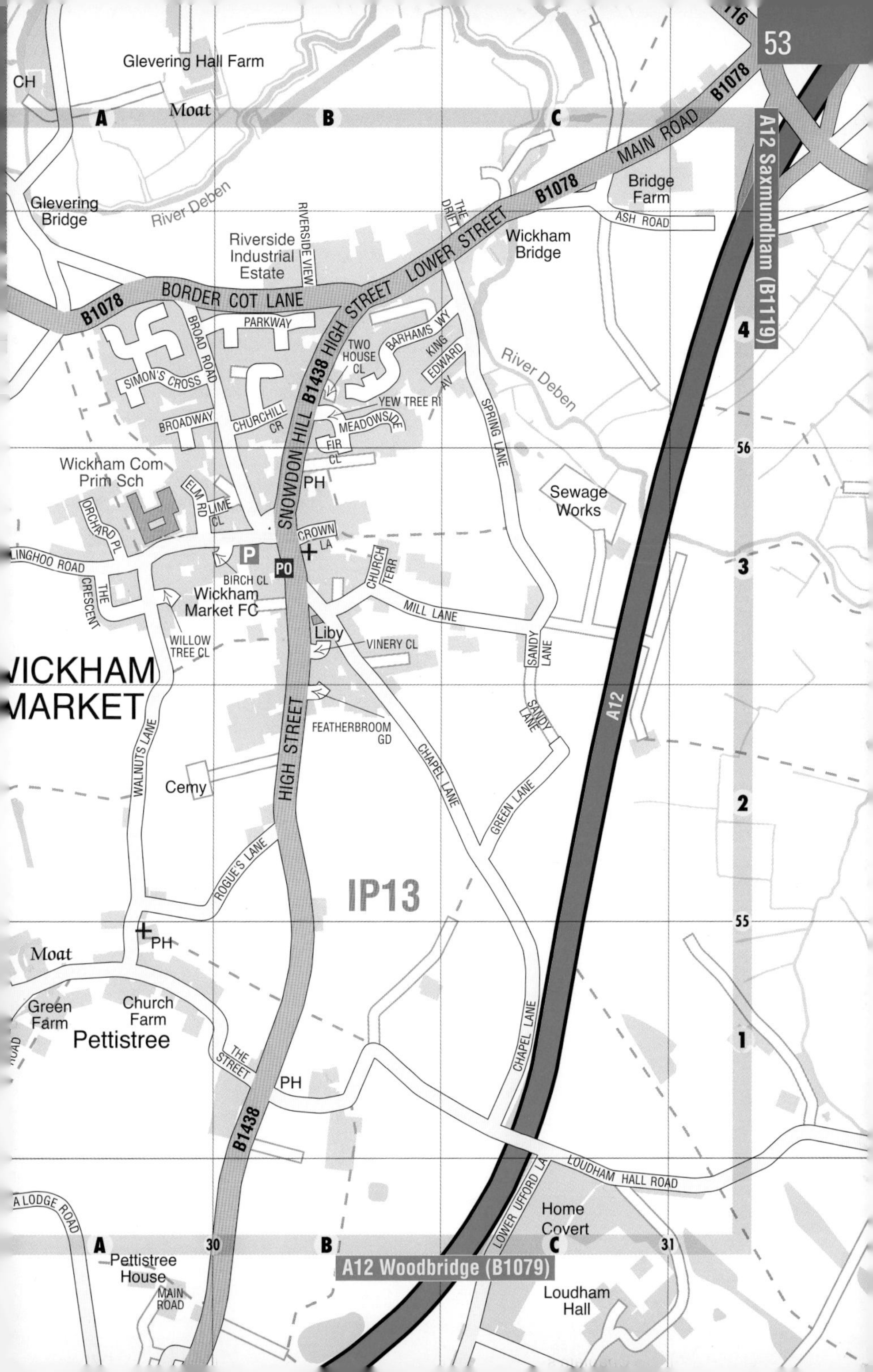

Glevering Hall Farm
CH
Moat
A
B
C
B1078
MAIN ROAD
A12 Saxmundham (B1119)
Bridge Farm
ASH ROAD
Glevering Bridge
River Deben
RIVERSIDE VIEW
Riverside Industrial Estate
THE DRIFT
LOWER STREET
Wickham Bridge
BORDER COT LANE
HIGH STREET
PARKWAY
BROAD ROAD
TWO HOUSE CL
BARHAMS WY
KING EDWARD AV
SIMON'S CROSS
SNOWDON HILL
B1438
YEW TREE RI
SPRING LANE
BROADWAY
CHURCHILL CR
MEADOWSIDE
FIR CL
Wickham Com Prim Sch
PH
Sewage Works
ELM RD
LIME CL
ORCHARD PL
CROWN LA
CHURCH TERR
LINGHOO ROAD
P
PO
BIRCH CL
THE CRESCENT
Wickham Market FC
MILL LANE
Liby
VINERY CL
SANDY LANE
WILLOW TREE CL
WICKHAM MARKET
FEATHERBROOM GD
CHAPEL LANE
A12
WALNUTS LANE
Cemy
GREEN LANE
ROGUE'S LANE
IP13
Moat
Green Farm
Church Farm
Pettistree
THE STREET
LOUDHAM HALL ROAD
LOWER UFFORD LA
Home Covert
LODGE ROAD
Pettistree House
MAIN ROAD
A12 Woodbridge (B1079)
Loudham Hall
1
2
3
4
55
56
30
31

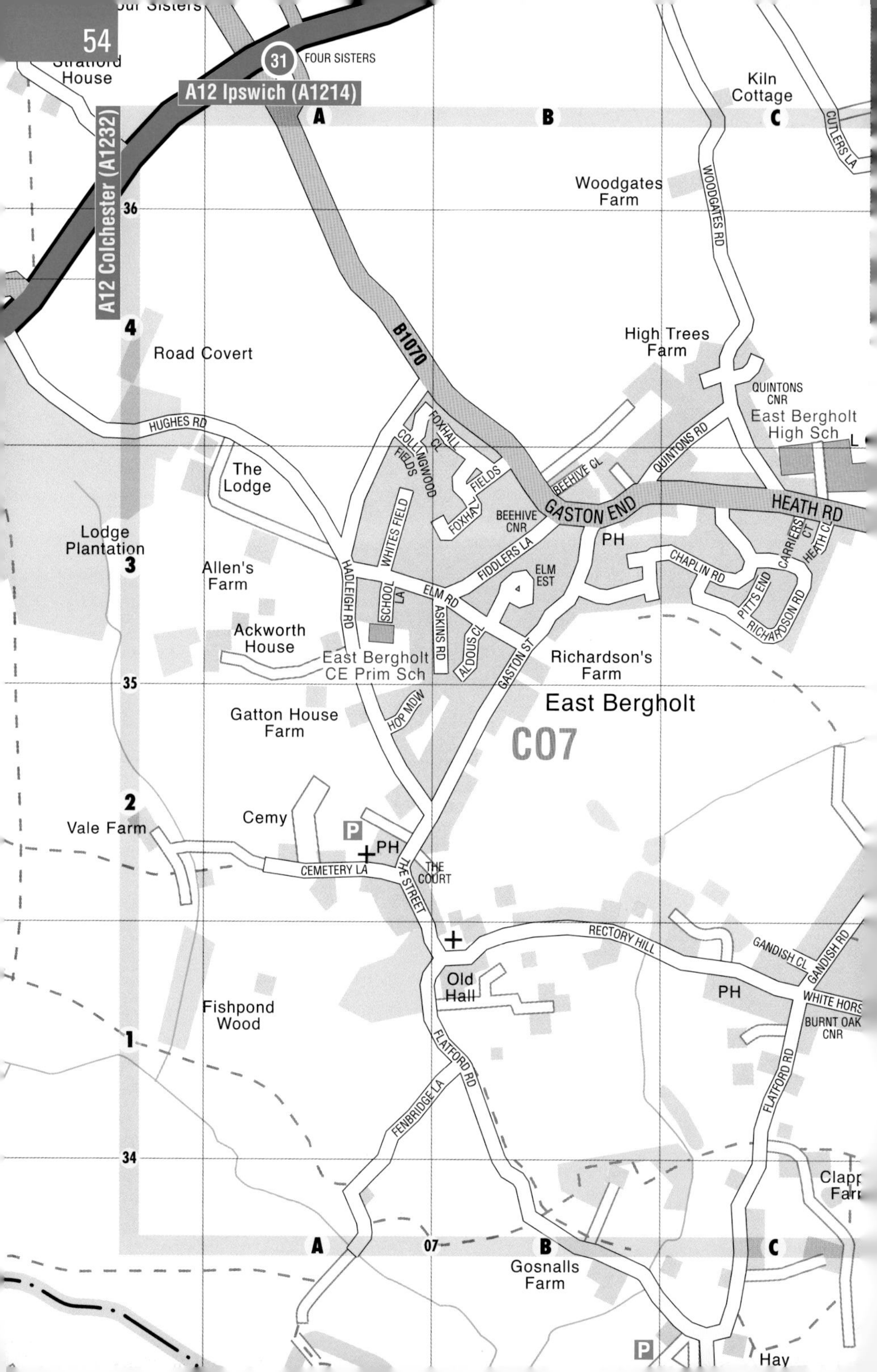
Four Sisters
Stratford House
31
FOUR SISTERS
A12 Ipswich (A1214)
A12 Colchester (A1232)
A
B
C
Kiln Cottage
CUTLERS LA
Woodgates Farm
WOODGATES RD
36
4
B1070
Road Covert
High Trees Farm
QUINTONS CNR
East Bergholt High Sch
HUGHES RD
FOXHALL CL
COLLINGWOOD FIELDS
FOXHALL FIELDS
BEEHIVE CL
QUINTONS RD
The Lodge
WHITES FIELD
BEEHIVE CNR
GASTON END
HEATH RD
Lodge Plantation
PH
CARRIERS CT
HEATH CL
3
Allen's Farm
HADLEIGH RD
FIDDLERS LA
ELM EST
CHAPLIN RD
SCHOOL LA
ELM RD
PITTS END
RICHARDSON RD
ASKINS RD
Ackworth House
ALDOUS CL
GASTON ST
RICHARDSON RD
East Bergholt CE Prim Sch
Richardson's Farm
35
East Bergholt
Gatton House Farm
HOP MDW
CO7
2
Cemy
Vale Farm
P
PH
CEMETERY LA
THE STREET
THE COURT
RECTORY HILL
GANDISH CL
GANDISH RD
Old Hall
PH
WHITE HORS
BURNT OAK CNR
Fishpond Wood
1
FLATFORD RD
FENBRIDGE LA
FLATFORD RD
34
Clapp Farm
A
07
B
C
Gosnalls Farm
P
Hay

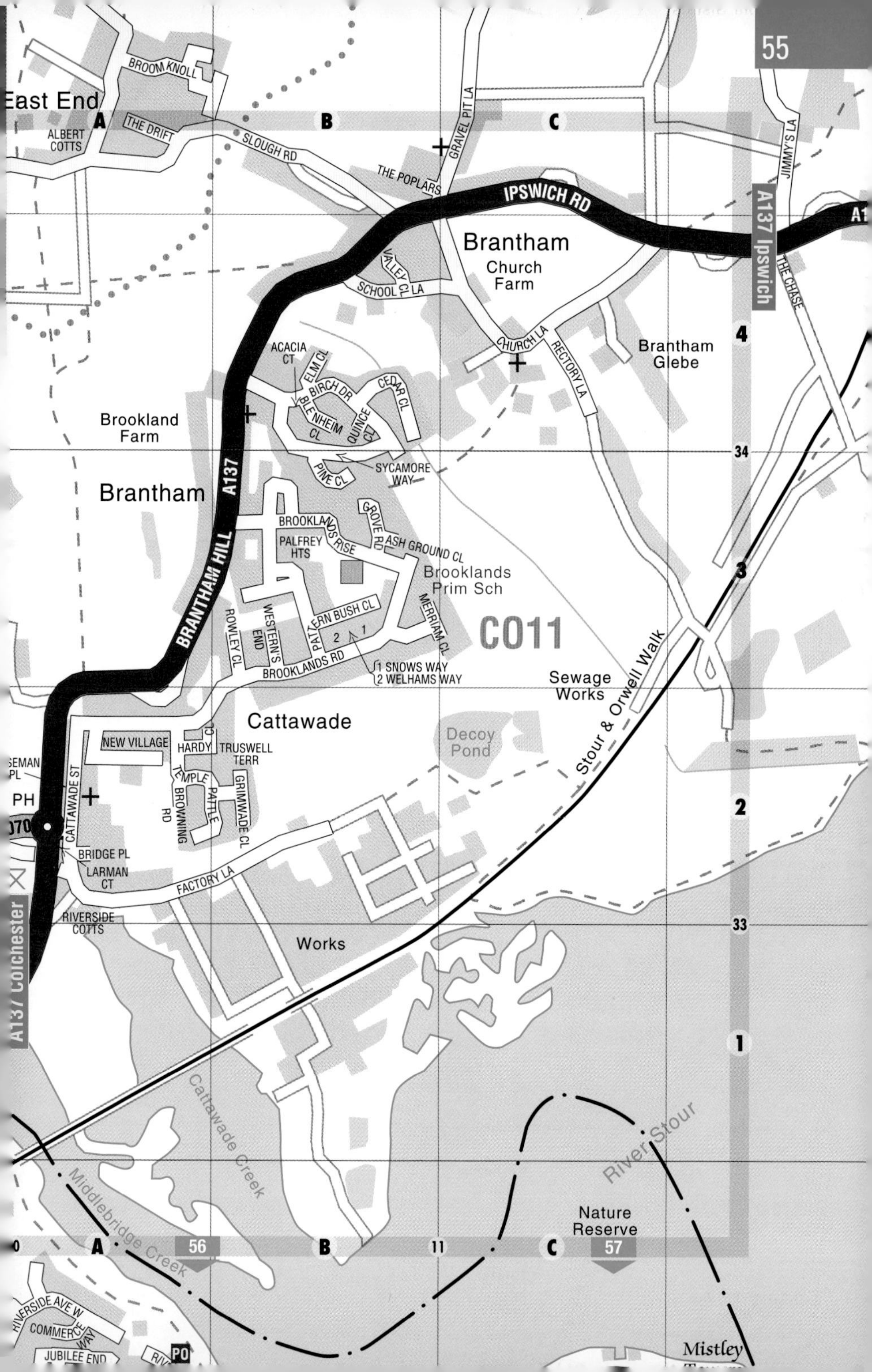
East End
BROOM KNOLL
ALBERT COTTS
THE DRIFT
SLOUGH RD
GRAVEL PIT LA
THE POPLARS
IPSWICH RD
JIMMY'S LA
A137 Ipswich
Brantham
Church Farm
VALLEY CL
SCHOOL LA
THE CHASE
CHURCH LA
RECTORY LA
Brantham Glebe
ACACIA CT
ELM CL
BIRCH DR
CEDAR CL
BLENHEIM CL
QUINCE CL
Brookland Farm
SYCAMORE WAY
PINE CL
Brantham
A137
BRANTHAM HILL
BROOKLANDS RISE
GROVE RD
ASH GROUND CL
PALFREY HTS
Brooklands Prim Sch
PATTERN BUSH CL
MERRIAM CL
ROWLEY CL
WESTERN'S END
CO11
BROOKLANDS RD
1 SNOWS WAY
2 WELHAMS WAY
Sewage Works
Stour & Orwell Walk
Cattawade
NEW VILLAGE
HARDY CL
TRUSWELL TERR
Decoy Pond
TEMPLE
PATTLE
GRIMWADE CL
BROWNING RD
CATTAWADE ST
PH
BRIDGE PL
LARMAN CT
FACTORY LA
RIVERSIDE COTTS
Works
A137 Colchester
Cattawade Creek
River Stour
Middlebridge Creek
Nature Reserve
56
57
RIVERSIDE AVE W
COMMERCE WAY
JUBILEE END
PO
Mistley
A
B
C
4
34
3
2
33
1
11

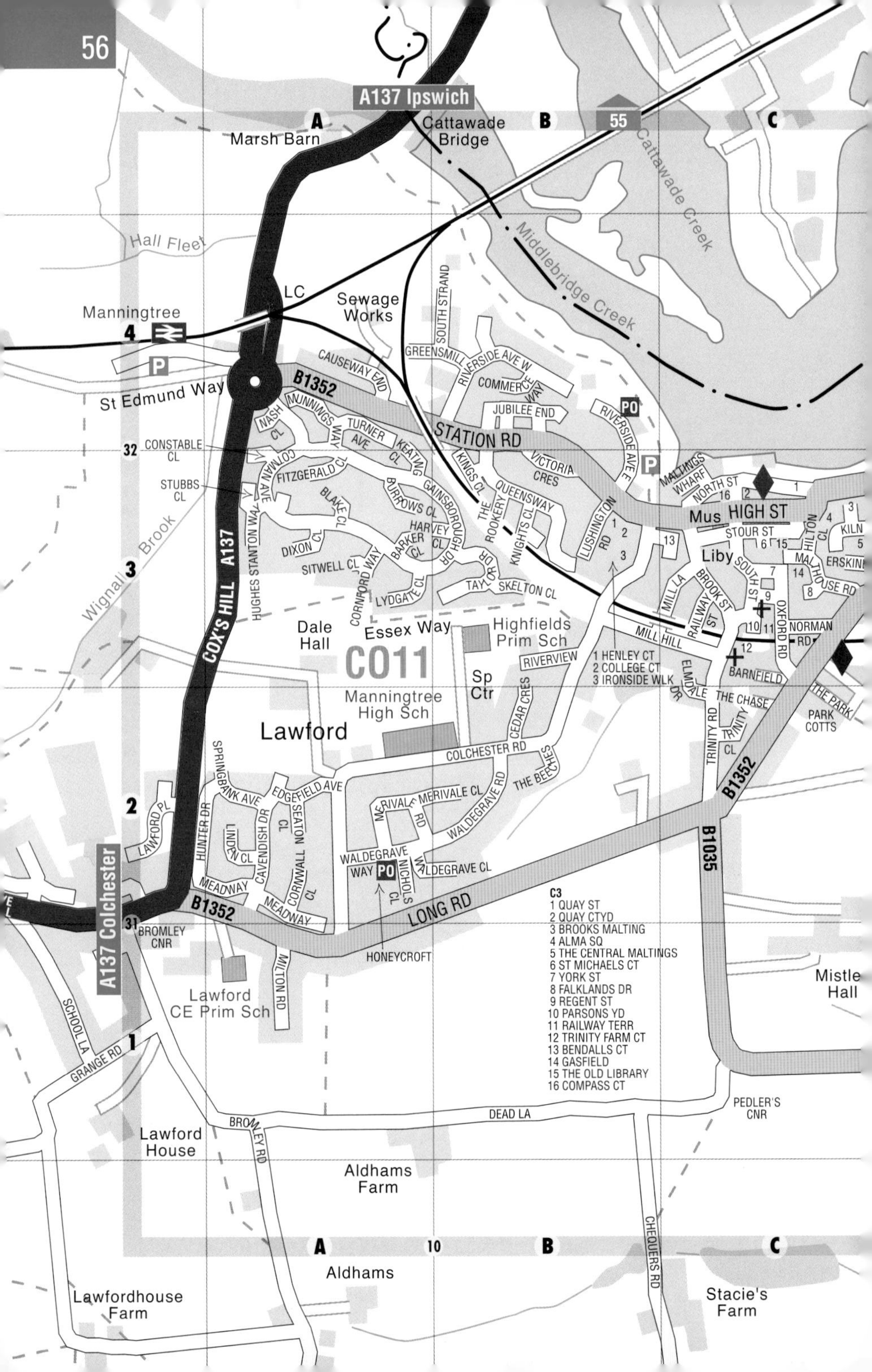

A137 Ipswich

A   B   55   C

Marsh Barn

Cattawade Bridge

Cattawade Creek

Hall Fleet

Middlebridge Creek

Manningtree

LC

Sewage Works

4

P

St Edmund Way

B1352

32 CONSTABLE CL

STUBBS CL

SOUTH STRAND

GREENSMILL
RIVERSIDE AVE W
COMMERCE WAY
JUBILEE END
STATION RD
RIVERSIDE AVE
PO
MALTINGS WHARF
NORTH ST
Mus HIGH ST
Liby

CAUSEWAY END
KINGS CL
VICTORIA CRES
QUEENSWAY
LLUSHINGTON RD
STOUR ST
HILTON
KILN
ERSKINE

NASH CL
MUNNINGS WAY
TURNER AVE
KEATING CL
GAINSBOROUGH DR
THE ROOKERY
KNIGHTS CL
MILL LA
BROOK ST
SOUTH ST
MALTHOUSE RD

3

Wignall Brook

COX'S HILL A137

HUGHES STANTON WAY

FITZGERALD CL
BLAKE CL
BURROWS CL
HARVEY CL
BARKER CL
LYDGATE CL
TAY
SKELTON CL

DIXON
SITWELL CL
CORNFORD WAY

Dale Hall

Essex Way

CO11

Highfields Prim Sch

RIVERVIEW

1 HENLEY CT
2 COLLEGE CT
3 IRONSIDE WLK

RAILWAY ST
MILL HILL
NORMAN RD
BARNFIELD

Manningtree High Sch

Sp Ctr

CEDAR CRES

ELMDALE

THE CHASE
TRINITY CL
PARK COTTS
THE PARK

Lawford

COLCHESTER RD

THE BEECHES

TRINITY RD

B1352

2

LAWFORD PL
SPRINGBANK AVE
HUNTER DR
EDGEFIELD AVE
SEATON RD
MERIVALE RD
MERIVALE CL
WALDEGRAVE RD

B1035

Mistle Hall

LINDEN CL
CAVENDISH DR
CORNWALL CL
WALDEGRAVE WAY
PO
NICHOLS CL
WALDEGRAVE CL

MEADWAY

B1352

31 BROMLEY CNR

MILTON RD

HONEYCROFT

LONG RD

C3
1 QUAY ST
2 QUAY CTYD
3 BROOKS MALTING
4 ALMA SQ
5 THE CENTRAL MALTINGS
6 ST MICHAELS CT
7 YORK ST
8 FALKLANDS DR
9 REGENT ST
10 PARSONS YD
11 RAILWAY TERR
12 TRINITY FARM CT
13 BENDALLS CT
14 GASFIELD
15 THE OLD LIBRARY
16 COMPASS CT

Lawford CE Prim Sch

1

SCHOOL LA
GRANGE RD

BROMLEY RD

DEAD LA

PEDLER'S CNR

Lawford House

Aldhams Farm

A   10   B   C

Aldhams

CHEQUERS RD

Stacie's Farm

Lawfordhouse Farm

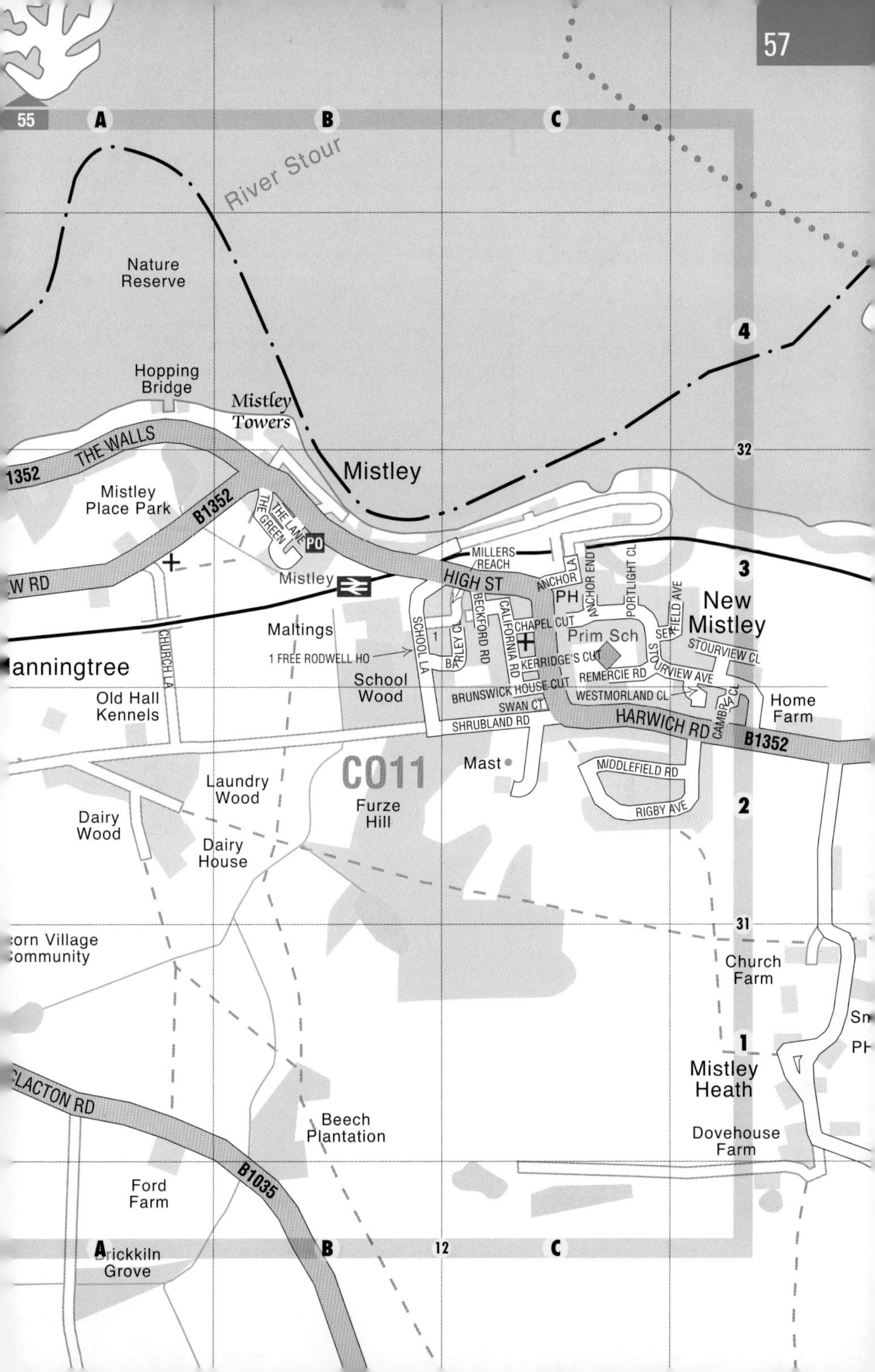

55
A
B
C
River Stour
Nature Reserve
Hopping Bridge
Mistley Towers
Mistley
THE WALLS
1352
Mistley Place Park
B1352
THE LANE
THE GREEN
PO
W RD
Mistley
MILLERS REACH
HIGH ST
ANCHOR LA
ANCHOR END
PORTLIGHT CL
FIELD AVE
New Mistley
PH
Maltings
SCHOOL LA
BECKFORD RD
CALIFORNIA RD
CHAPEL CUT
Prim Sch
SEA
STOURVIEW CL
STOURVIEW AVE
1 FREE RODWELL HO
KERRIDGE'S CUT
REMERCIE RD
anningtree
CHURCH LA
School Wood
BRUNSWICK HOUSE CUT
WESTMORLAND CL
Old Hall Kennels
SWAN CT
SHRUBLAND RD
HARWICH RD
CAMBRIA CL
B1352
Home Farm
CO11
Mast
MIDDLEFIELD RD
Laundry Wood
Furze Hill
RIGBY AVE
Dairy Wood
Dairy House
4
32
3
2
31
1
orn Village
ommunity
Church Farm
Mistley Heath
Dovehouse Farm
CLACTON RD
Beech Plantation
B1035
Ford Farm
Brickkiln Grove
12

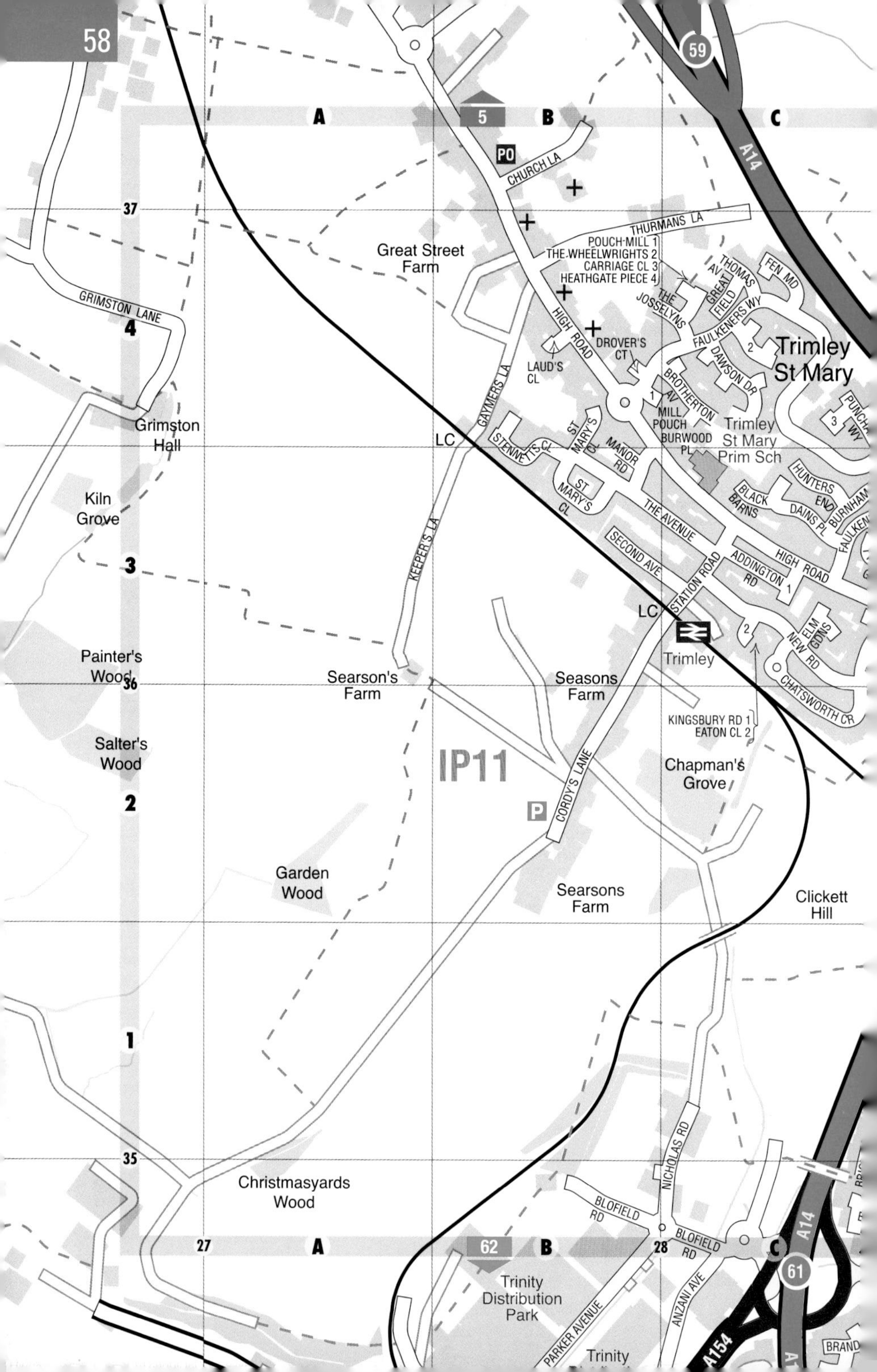
59
A
5
B
C
PO
CHURCH LA
A14
37
THURMANS LA
POUCH MILL 1
THE WHEELWRIGHTS 2
CARRIAGE CL 3
HEATHGATE PIECE 4
Great Street
Farm
THOMAS AV
FEN MD
GRIMSTON LANE
THE JOSSELYNS
GREAT FIELD
FAULKENERS WY
4
HIGH ROAD
DROVER'S CT
Trimley
St Mary
DAWSON DR
LAUD'S CL
BROTHERTON AV
GAYMERS LA
MILL
POUCH
BURWOOD PL
Trimley
St Mary
Prim Sch
PUNCHARD WY
Grimston
Hall
LC
STENNETTS CL
ST MARY'S CL
MANOR RD
Kiln
Grove
ST MARY'S CL
HUNTERS END
BLACK BARNS
DAINS PL
BURNHAM
THE AVENUE
KEEPER'S LA
SECOND AVE
HIGH ROAD
3
ADDINGTON RD
STATION ROAD
LC
ELM GDNS
NEW RD
Painter's
Wood
36
Searson's
Farm
Trimley
Seasons
Farm
CHATSWORTH CR
KINGSBURY RD 1
EATON CL 2
Salter's
Wood
IP11
Chapman's
Grove
2
CORDY'S LANE
P
Garden
Wood
Searsons
Farm
Clickett
Hill
1
NICHOLAS RD
35
Christmasyards
Wood
BLOFIELD RD
BLOFIELD RD
27
A
62
B
28
C
A14
61
ANZANI AVE
Trinity
Distribution
Park
PARKER AVENUE
Trinity
A154
BRAND

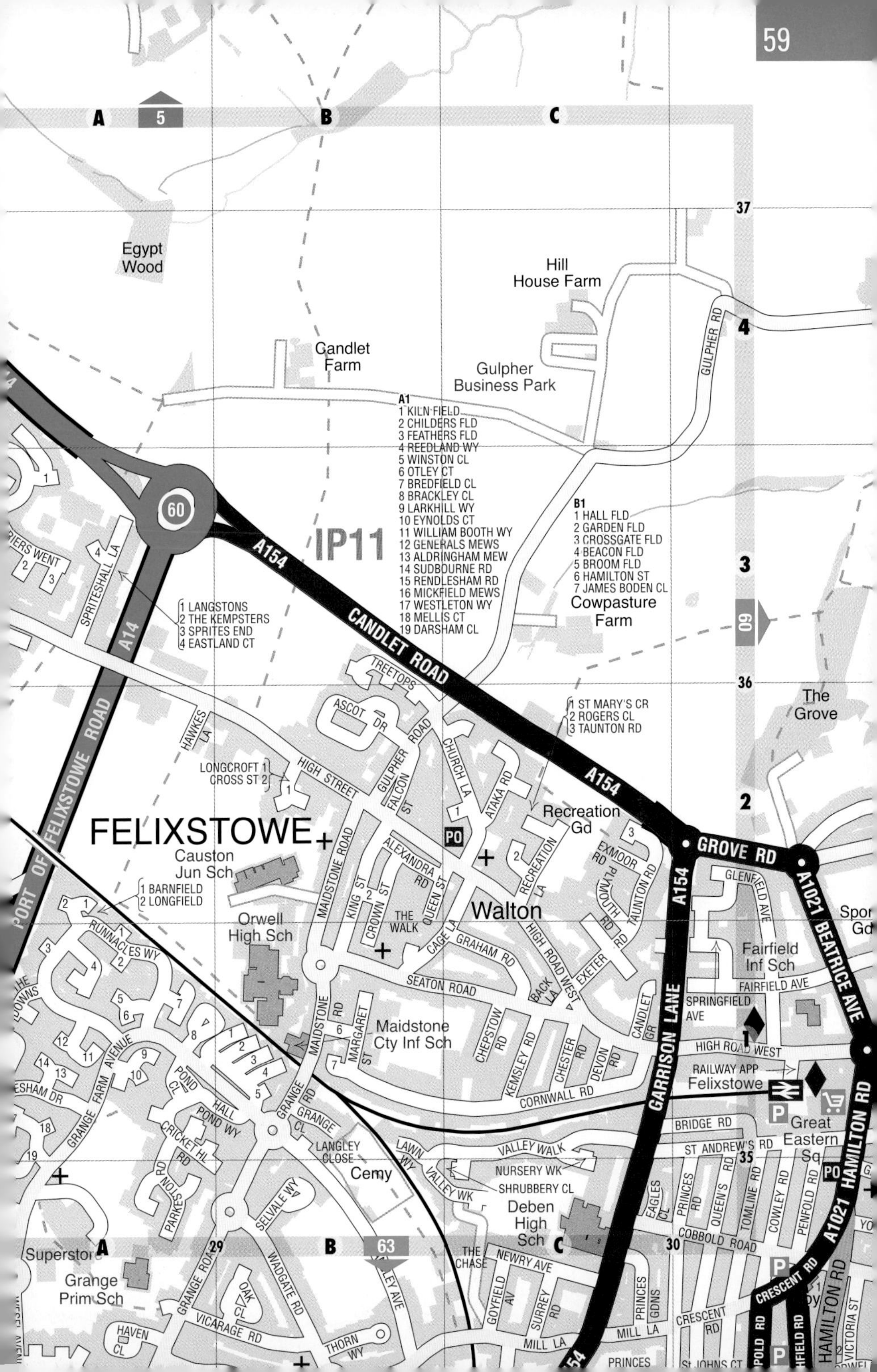
A
B
C
5
37
36
35
4
3
2
1
29
30
60
63
Egypt Wood
Hill House Farm
Candlet Farm
Gulpher Business Park
IP11
A1
1 KILN FIELD
2 CHILDERS FLD
3 FEATHERS FLD
4 REEDLAND WY
5 WINSTON CL
6 OTLEY CT
7 BREDFIELD CL
8 BRACKLEY CL
9 LARKHILL WY
10 EYNOLDS CT
11 WILLIAM BOOTH WY
12 GENERALS MEWS
13 ALDRINGHAM MEW
14 SUDBOURNE RD
15 RENDLESHAM RD
16 MICKFIELD MEWS
17 WESTLETON WY
18 MELLIS CT
19 DARSHAM CL
B1
1 HALL FLD
2 GARDEN FLD
3 CROSSGATE FLD
4 BEACON FLD
5 BROOM FLD
6 HAMILTON ST
7 JAMES BODEN CL
Cowpasture Farm
1 LANGSTONS
2 THE KEMPSTERS
3 SPRITES END
4 EASTLAND CT
A154
CANDLET ROAD
A14
FELIXSTOWE ROAD
PORT OF FELIXSTOWE
SPRITESHALL LA
GULPHER RD
TREETOPS
ASCOT DR
HAWKES LA
HIGH STREET
GULPHER ROAD
FALCON ST
CHURCH LA
ATAKA RD
1 ST MARY'S CR
2 ROGERS CL
3 TAUNTON RD
The Grove
LONGCROFT 1
CROSS ST 2
FELIXSTOWE
Causton Jun Sch
1 BARNFIELD
2 LONGFIELD
Orwell High Sch
MAIDSTONE ROAD
ALEXANDRA RD
KING ST
CROWN ST
THE WALK
QUEEN ST
PO
Recreation Gd
RECREATION LA
EXMOOR RD
PLYMOUTH RD
TAUNTON RD
Walton
GROVE RD
A1021 BEATRICE AVE
GLENFIELD AVE
Fairfield Inf Sch
Sports Gd
CAGE LA
GRAHAM RD
HIGH ROAD WEST
EXETER RD
BACK LA
SEATON ROAD
RUNNACLES WY
THE DOWNS
GRANGE FARM AVENUE
MAIDSTONE RD
MARGARET ST
Maidstone Cty Inf Sch
CHEPSTOW RD
KEMSLEY RD
CHESTER RD
DEVON RD
CANDLET GR
GARRISON LANE
FAIRFIELD AVE
SPRINGFIELD AVE
HIGH ROAD WEST
RAILWAY APP
Felixstowe
CORNWALL RD
POND CL
HALL POND WY
CRICKET HL RD
GRANGE RD
GRANGE CL
LANGLEY CLOSE
Cemy
LAWN WY
VALLEY WALK
NURSERY WK
SHRUBBERY CL
VALLEY WK
BRIDGE RD
ST ANDREW'S RD
Great Eastern Sq
PO
A1021 HAMILTON RD
Deben High Sch
EAGLES CL
PRINCES RD
QUEEN'S RD
TOMLINE RD
COWLEY RD
PENFOLD RD
COBBOLD ROAD
CRESCENT RD
PARKESTON RD
SELVALE WY
Superstore
Grange Prim Sch
GRANGE ROAD
WADGATE RD
OAK CL
THE CHASE
NEWRY AVE
GOYFIELD AV
SURREY RD
PRINCES GDNS
CRESCENT RD
HAVEN CL
VICARAGE RD
THORN WY
MILL LA
PRINCES
ST JOHNS CT
HAMILTON RD
VICTORIA ST

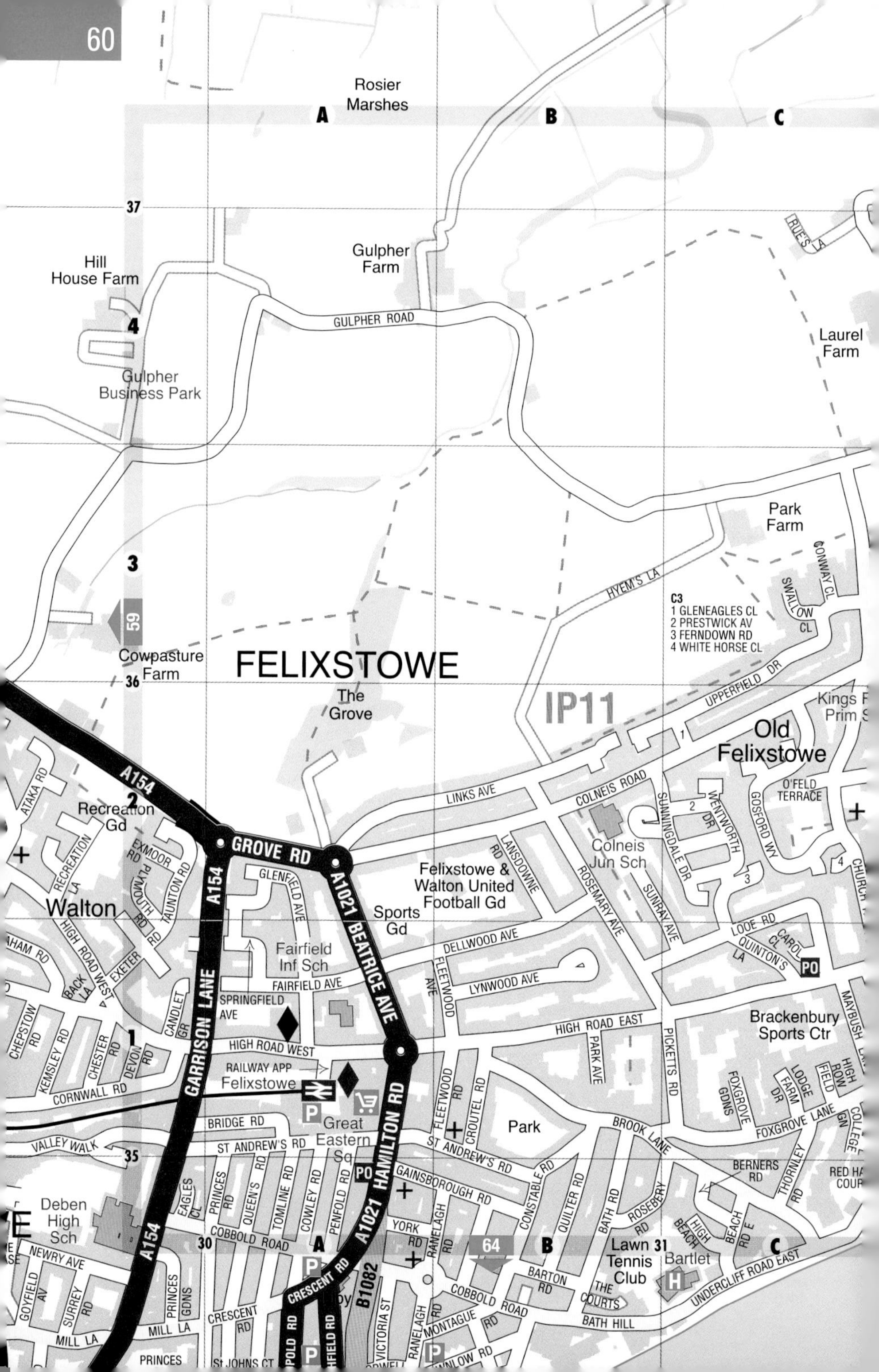

A   B   C

Rosier
Marshes

37

Gulpher
Farm

Hill
House Farm

4

GULPHER ROAD

Laurel
Farm

Gulpher
Business Park

FRIES LA

Park
Farm

3

CONWAY CL

SWALLOW CL

59

HYEM'S LA

C3
1 GLENEAGLES CL
2 PRESTWICK AV
3 FERNDOWN RD
4 WHITE HORSE CL

Cowpasture
Farm

36

FELIXSTOWE

UPPERFIELD DR

IP11

Kings F
Prim S

The
Grove

Old
Felixstowe

O'FELD
TERRACE

LINKS AVE

COLNEIS ROAD

WENTWORTH DR

GOSFORD WY

SUNNINGDALE DR

ATAXA RD

A154

Recreation
Gd

2

GROVE RD

A154

A1021 BEATRICE AVE

GLENFIELD AVE

LANSDOWNE RD

Colneis
Jun Sch

SURRAY AVE

CHURCH

EXMOOR RD

PLYMOUTH RD

TAUNTON RD

Felixstowe &
Walton United
Football Gd

ROSEMARY AVE

LOOE RD

CARD

QUINTON'S LA

PO

Walton

HIGH ROAD WEST

EXETER RD

Sports
Gd

DELLWOOD AVE

MAYBUSH

HIGH ROW

Fairfield
Inf Sch

FAIRFIELD AVE

FLEETWOOD AVE

LYNWOOD AVE

Brackenbury
Sports Ctr

LODGE
FARM

COLLEGE
GN

CHEPSTOW RD

KEMSLEY RD

CHESTER RD

DEVON RD

CANDLET RD

SPRINGFIELD
AVE

HIGH ROAD WEST

HIGH ROAD EAST

PARK AVE

PICKETTS RD

FOXGROVE GDNS

HORNLEY RD

HIGH FIELD

RED HA
COURT

1

BACK LA

HIGH ROAD WEST

RAILWAY APP
Felixstowe

FLEETWOOD RD

CROUTEL RD

FOXGROVE LANE

CORNWALL RD

BRIDGE RD

ST ANDREW'S RD

Great
Eastern
Sq

ST ANDREW'S RD

Park

BROOK LANE

BERNERS RD

ROSEBRY RD

VALLEY WALK

35

PO

GAINSBOROUGH RD

QUILTER RD

BATH RD

BEACH RD E

AHAM RD

GRAHAM RD

EAGLES CL

PRINCES RD

QUEEN'S RD

TOMLINE RD

COWLEY RD

PENFOLD RD

HAMILTON RD

YORK RD

RAMELAGH RD

CONSTABLE RD

BARTON RD

Lawn 31
Tennis
Club

HIGH BEACH

UNDERCLIFF ROAD EAST

Bartlet

H

Deben
High
Sch

E

NEWRY AVE

GOYFIELD AV

SURREY RD

A154

COBBOLD ROAD

CRESCENT RD

30

CRESCENT RD

POLD RD

FIELD RD

HFIELD RD

B1082

VICTORIA ST

64

COBBOLD ROAD

MONTAGUE RD

RANELAGH RD

BARTON RD

BATH HILL

THE
COURTS

A   B   C

PRINCES

MILL LA

MILL LA

PRINCES GDNS

ST JOHN'S CT

PDWELL

NLOW RD

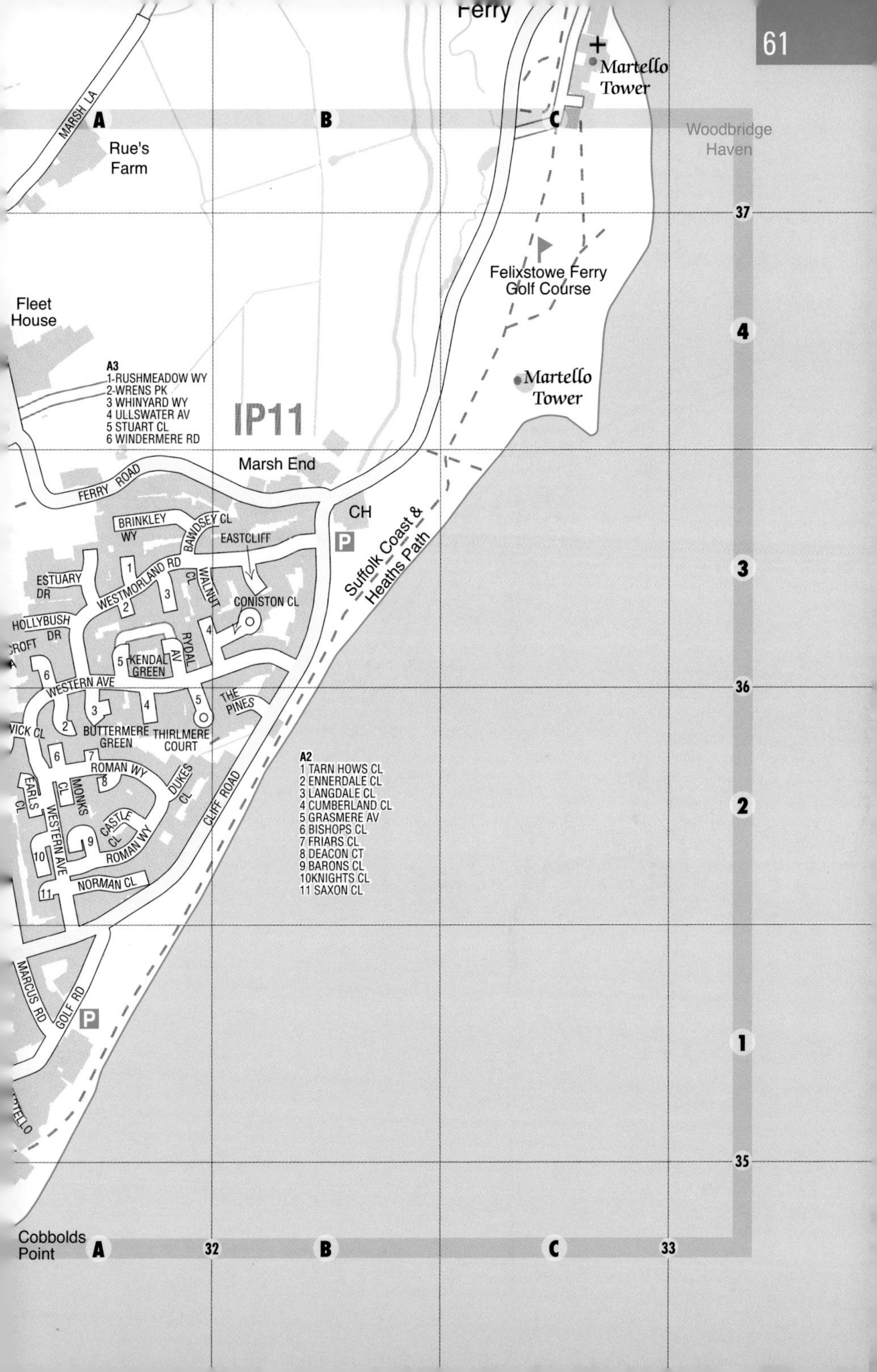

Ferry

+ Martello
Tower

A   B   C   Woodbridge
Haven

Rue's
Farm

37

Felixstowe Ferry
Golf Course

4

Fleet
House

A3
1-RUSHMEADOW WY
2-WRENS PK
3 WHINYARD WY
4 ULLSWATER AV
5 STUART CL
6 WINDERMERE RD

Martello
Tower

IP11

Marsh End

FERRY ROAD

CH

Suffolk Coast &
Heaths Path

BRINKLEY
WY

BAWDSEY CL

EASTCLIFF

P

ESTUARY
DR

WESTMORLAND RD

WALNUT CL

CONISTON CL

3

HOLLYBUSH
DR

CROFT

RYDAL AV

KENDAL
GREEN

WESTERN AVE

THE
PINES

36

VICK CL

BUTTERMERE
GREEN

THIRLMERE
COURT

A2
1 TARN HOWS CL
2 ENNERDALE CL
3 LANGDALE CL
4 CUMBERLAND CL
5 GRASMERE AV
6 BISHOPS CL
7 FRIARS CL
8 DEACON CT
9 BARONS CL
10 KNIGHTS CL
11 SAXON CL

ROMAN WY

DUKES CL

EARLS CL

WESTERN AVE

MONKS

CASTLE
CL

ROMAN WY

CLIFF ROAD

2

NORMAN CL

MARCUS RD

GOLF RD

P

1

MTELLO

35

Cobbolds
Point

A   32   B   C   33

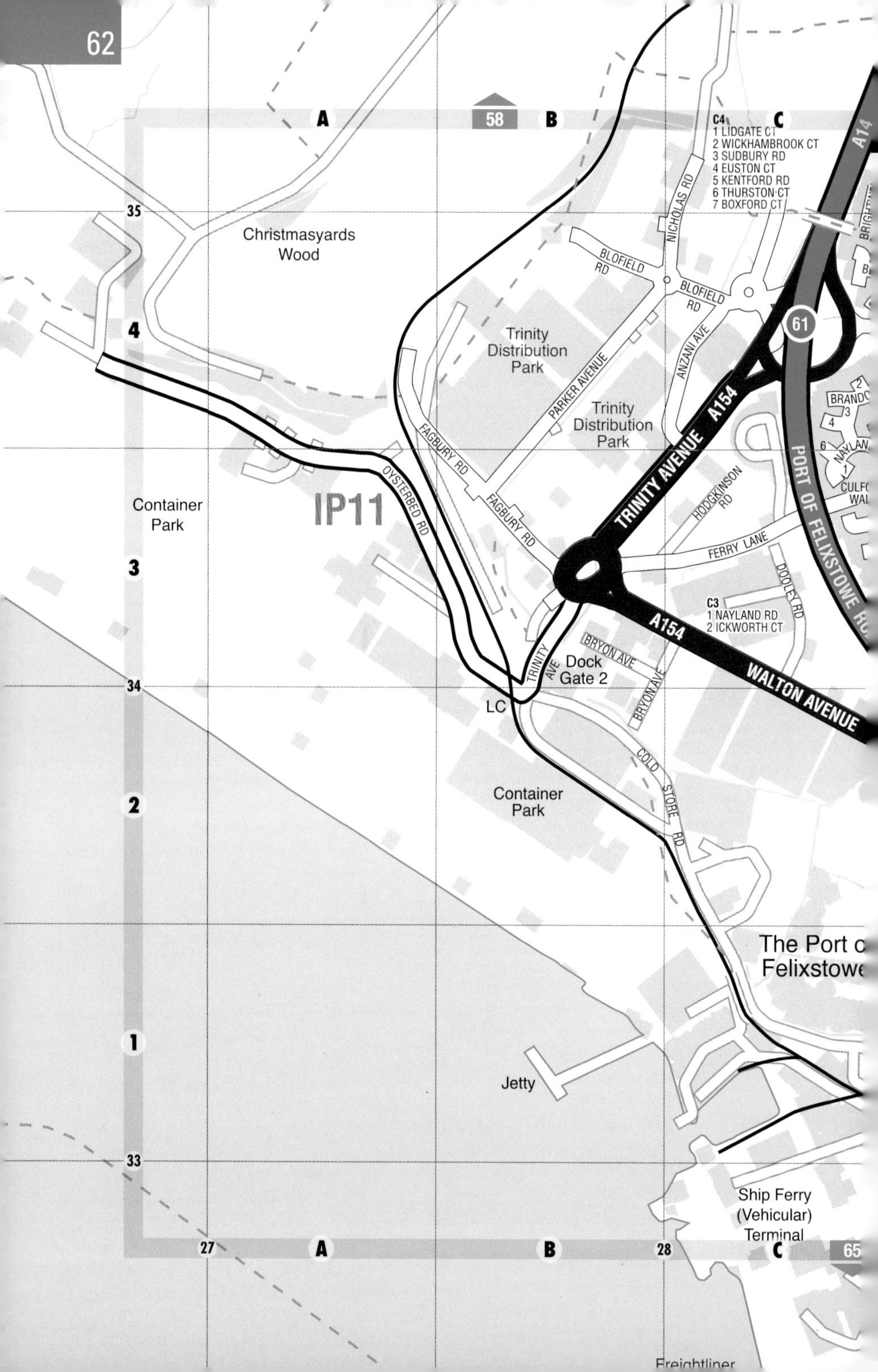

A
58
B
C4
1 LIDGATE CT
2 WICKHAMBROOK CT
3 SUDBURY RD
4 EUSTON CT
5 KENTFORD RD
6 THURSTON CT
7 BOXFORD CT
C

A14

35

Christmasyards
Wood

BLOFIELD
RD

BLOFIELD
RD

NICHOLAS RD

61

4

Trinity
Distribution
Park

PARKER AVENUE

ANZANI AVE

BRAND

B

NAYLA

6

CULF
WAI

Trinity
Distribution
Park

FAGBURY RD

OYSTERBED RD

Container
Park

IP11

3

FAGBURY RD

HODGKINSON
RD

TRINITY AVENUE A154

PORT OF FELIXSTOWE R

FERRY LANE

DOOLEY RD

A154

C3
1 NAYLAND RD
2 ICKWORTH CT

34

TRINITY AVE

BRYON AVE

Dock
Gate 2

BRYON AVE

WALTON AVENUE

LC

2

Container
Park

COLD STORE RD

The Port o
Felixstowe

1

Jetty

33

Ship Ferry
(Vehicular)
Terminal

27

A

B

28

C

65

Freightliner

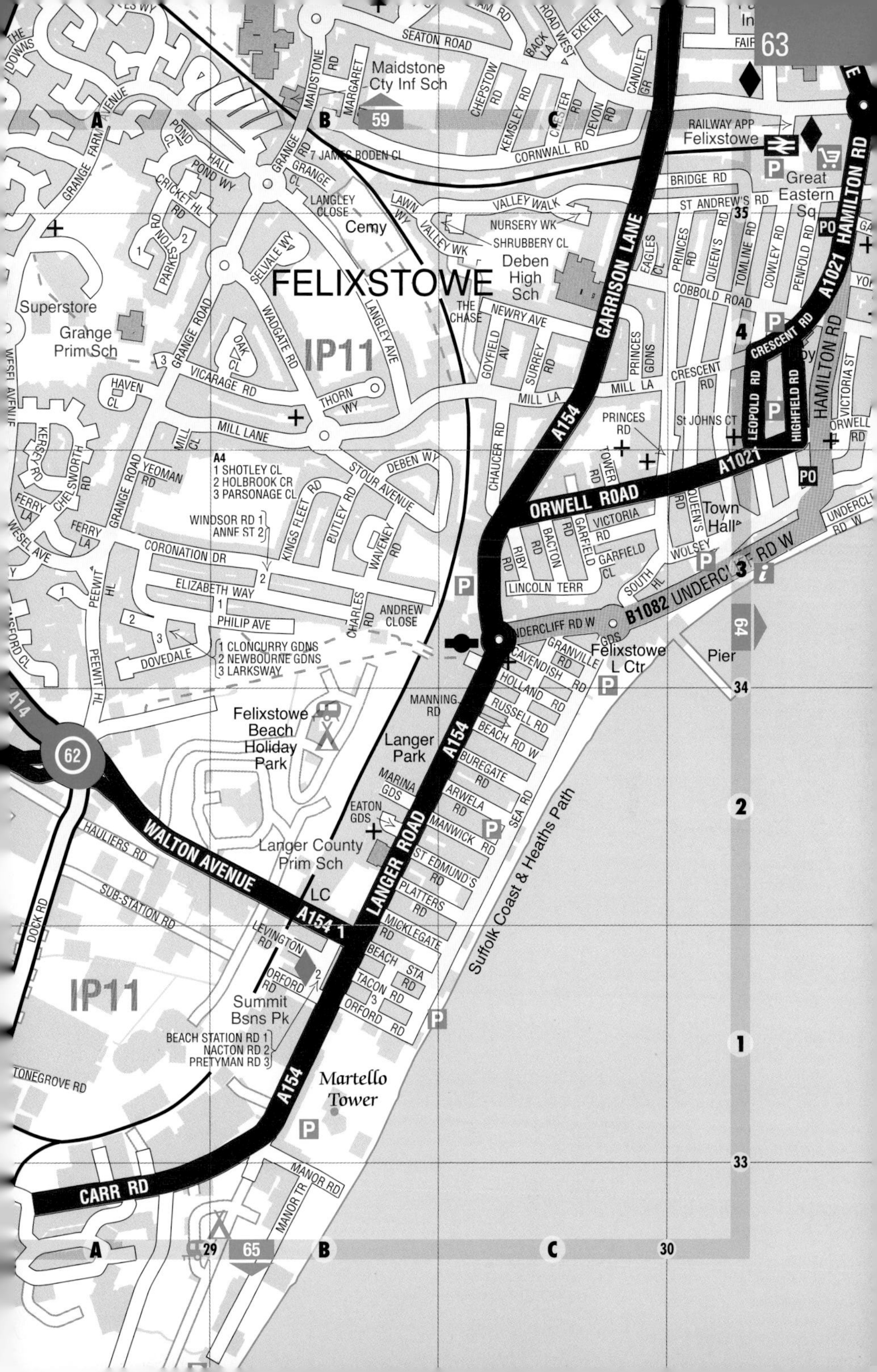
FELIXSTOWE
IP11
Maidstone Cty Inf Sch
SEATON ROAD
MAIDSTONE RD
MARGARET RD
CHEPSTOW RD
KEMSLEY RD
CHESTER RD
DEVON RD
CANDLET GR
BACK LA
EXETER RD
CORNWALL RD
RAILWAY APP
Felixstowe
Great Eastern Sq
BRIDGE RD
ST ANDREW'S RD
HAMILTON RD
A1021
7 JAMES BODEN CL
GRANGE RD
GRANGE CL
LANGLEY CLOSE
Cemy
LAWN WY
VALLEY WALK
VALLEY WK
NURSERY WK
SHRUBBERY CL
Deben High Sch
GARRISON LANE
EAGLES CL
PRINCES RD
QUEEN'S RD
TOMLINE RD
COWLEY RD
PENFOLD RD
PO
COBBOLD ROAD
CRESCENT RD
LEOPOLD RD
HIGHFIELD RD
VICTORIA ST
ORWELL RD
THE DOWNS
GRANGE FARM AVENUE
POND CL
POND HALL
POND WY
CRICKET HL RD
PARKES RD
TON RD
Superstore
Grange Prim Sch
SELVALE WY
WADGATE RD
LANGLEY AVE
THE CHASE
NEWRY AVE
GOYFIELD AV
SURREY RD
PRINCES GDNS
CRESCENT RD
GRANGE ROAD
OAK CL
VICARAGE RD
THORN WY
MILL LA
HAVEN CL
MILL LANE
MILL CL
A154
PRINCES RD
St JOHNS CT
TOWER RD
CHAUCER RD
KERSEY RD
CHELSWORTH RD
YEOMAN RD
A4
1 SHOTLEY CL
2 HOLBROOK CR
3 PARSONAGE CL
STOUR AVENUE
DEBEN WY
KINGS FLEET RD
BUTLEY RD
WAVENEY RD
ORWELL ROAD
FERRY LA
WESEL AVE
WINDSOR RD 1
ANNE ST 2
CORONATION DR
ELIZABETH WAY
PHILIP AVE
CHARLES RD
ANDREW CLOSE
VICTORIA RD
GARFIELD RD
GARFIELD CL
BACTON RD
RIBY RD
LINCOLN TERR
SOUTH HL
WOLSEY
Town Hall
QUEEN'S RD
B1082 UNDERCLIFF RD W
UNDERCLIFF RD W
PEEWIT HL
DOVEDALE
1 CLONCURRY GDNS
2 NEWBOURNE GDNS
3 LARKSWAY
GRANVILLE RD
CAVENDISH RD
HOLLAND RD
Felixstowe L Ctr
Pier
64
34
A14
62
Felixstowe Beach Holiday Park
MANNING RD
RUSSELL RD
BEACH RD W
Langer Park
BUREGATE RD
MARINA GDS
ARWELA RD
SEA RD
EATON GDS
MANWICK RD
HAULIERS RD
WALTON AVENUE
Langer County Prim Sch
LANGER ROAD
ST EDMUND'S RD
PLATTERS RD
Suffolk Coast & Heaths Path
2
LC
SUB-STATION RD
DOCK RD
A154
MICKLEGATE RD
LEVINGTON RD
BEACH STA RD
ORFORD RD
TACON RD
ORFORD RD
IP11
Summit Bsns Pk
BEACH STATION RD 1
NACTON RD 2
PRETYMAN RD 3
1
TONEGROVE RD
Martello Tower
33
CARR RD
MANOR RD
MANOR TR
A
B
C
29
65
30
59

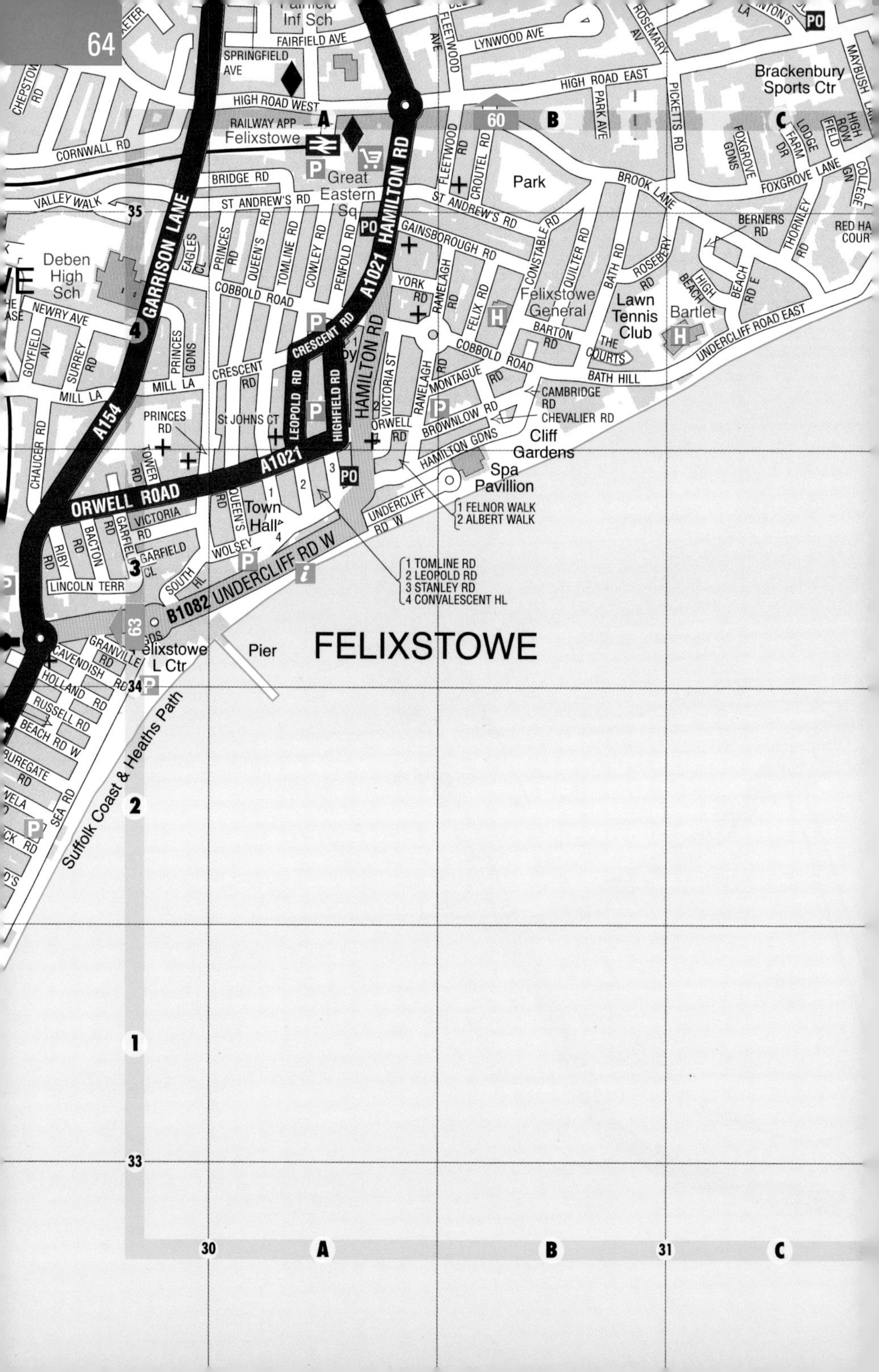

FELIXSTOWE

Pier

Town Hall

Spa Pavillion

Cliff Gardens

Felixstowe General

Lawn Tennis Club

Bartlet

Park

Brackenbury Sports Ctr

Deben High Sch

Great Eastern Sq

Felixstowe

RAILWAY APP

1 FELNOR WALK
2 ALBERT WALK

1 TOMLINE RD
2 LEOPOLD RD
3 STANLEY RD
4 CONVALESCENT HL

1 TOMLINE RD
2 LEOPOLD RD
3 STANLEY RD
4 CONVALESCENT HL

THE COURTS

CAMBRIDGE RD
CHEVALIER RD

Suffolk Coast & Heaths Path

Felixstowe L Ctr

GARRISON LANE
ORWELL ROAD
HIGH ROAD WEST
HIGH ROAD EAST
CRESCENT RD
HAMILTON RD
HIGHFIELD RD
LEOPOLD RD
UNDERCLIFF RD W
UNDERCLIFF ROAD EAST
BATH HILL

A154
A1021
B1082

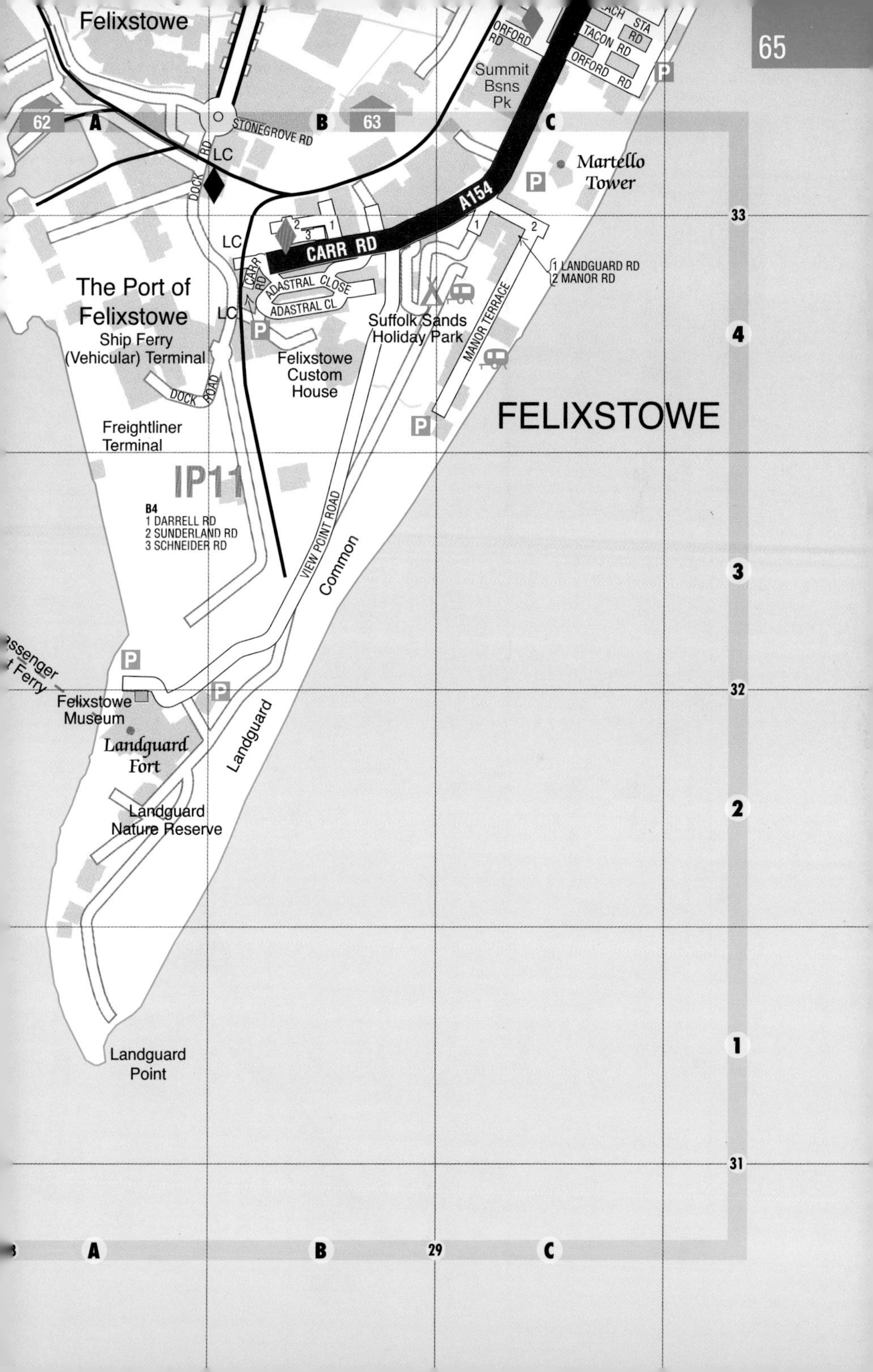

Felixstowe

STONEGROVE RD

62 A

B

63

C

Summit
Bsns
Pk

ORFORD
RD

TACON
RD

ACH
STA

ORFORD RD

P

LC

A154

P

Martello
Tower

33

LC

CARR RD

1

2

1 LANDGUARD RD
2 MANOR RD

ADASTRAL CLOSE

ADASTRAL CL

LC

P

The Port of
Felixstowe

Ship Ferry
(Vehicular) Terminal

Felixstowe
Custom
House

Suffolk Sands
Holiday Park

MANOR TERRACE

4

Freightliner
Terminal

IP11

P

FELIXSTOWE

B4
1 DARRELL RD
2 SUNDERLAND RD
3 SCHNEIDER RD

VIEW POINT ROAD

Common

DOCK ROAD

3

ssenger
Ferry

P

P

32

Felixstowe
Museum

Landguard
Fort

Landguard

Landguard
Nature Reserve

2

Landguard
Point

1

31

A

B

29

C

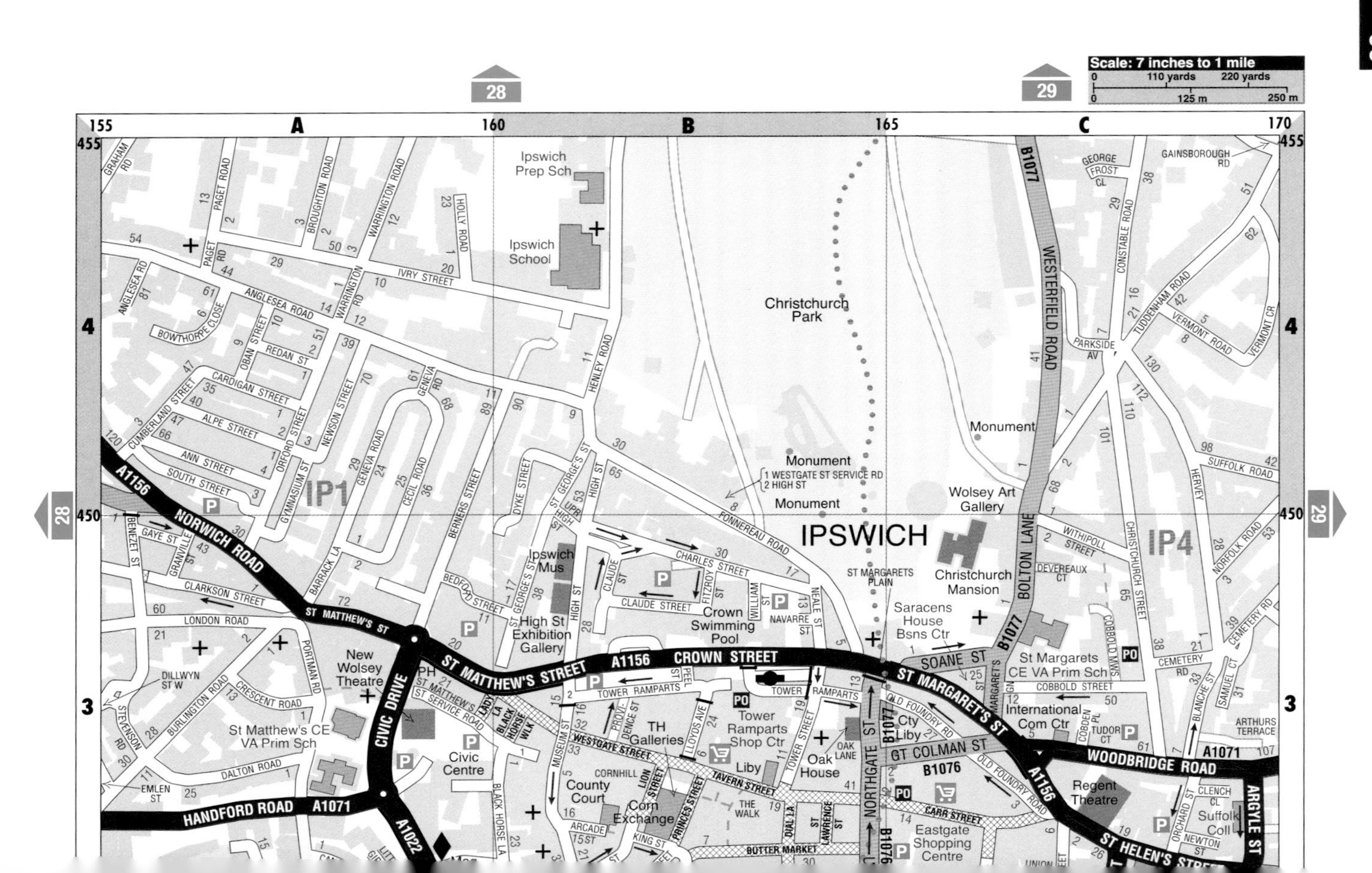
Scale: 7 inches to 1 mile
0 110 yards 220 yards
0 125 m 250 m
28
29
155 A 160 B 165 C 170
455
450
4
3
IPSWICH
IP1
IP4
Christchurch Park
Monument
1 WESTGATE ST SERVICE RD
2 HIGH ST
Wolsey Art Gallery
Christchurch Mansion
Saracens House Bsns Ctr
St Margarets CE VA Prim Sch
International Com Ctr
Ipswich Prep Sch
Ipswich School
Ipswich Mus
High St Exhibition Gallery
Crown Swimming Pool
Tower Ramparts Shop Ctr
TH Galleries
Liby
Cty Liby
Oak House
County Court
Corn Exchange
Civic Centre
New Wolsey Theatre
St Matthew's CE VA Prim Sch
Eastgate Shopping Centre
Regent Theatre
Suffolk Coll
WESTERFIELD ROAD
BOLTON LANE
B1077
CROWN STREET
A1156
ST MATTHEW'S STREET
ST MARGARET'S ST
NORWICH ROAD
CIVIC DRIVE
HANDFORD ROAD
A1071
A1022
WOODBRIDGE ROAD
ARGYLE ST
ST HELEN'S STREET
NORTHGATE ST
GT COLMAN ST
B1076
FONNEREAU ROAD
HENLEY ROAD
BERNERS STREET
CHRISTCHURCH STREET
TUDDENHAM ROAD
VERMONT ROAD
CONSTABLE ROAD
SUFFOLK ROAD
NORFOLK ROAD
CEMETERY RD
TOWER RAMPARTS
TAVERN STREET
PRINCES STREET
WESTGATE STREET
BUTTER MARKET
CARR STREET
OLD FOUNDRY RD
ANGLESEA ROAD
IVRY STREET
GENEVA ROAD
CECIL ROAD
LONDON ROAD
BURLINGTON ROAD
CLARKSON STREET
PORTMAN RD
DALTON ROAD
CHARLES STREET
CLAUDE STREET
SOANE ST
COBBOLD STREET

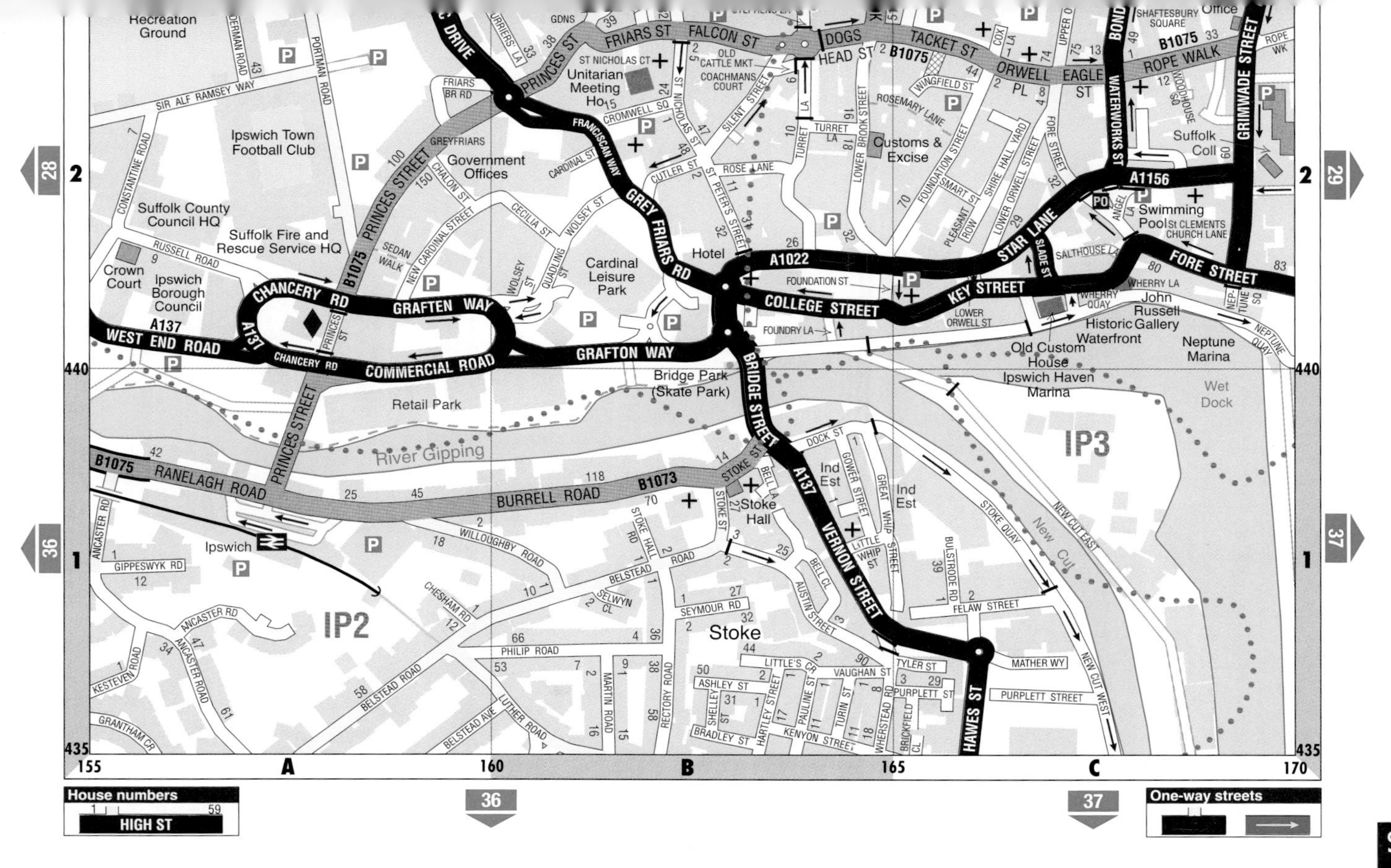
Recreation Ground
PORTMAN ROAD
SIR ALF RAMSEY WAY
CONSTANTINE ROAD
Ipswich Town Football Club
Suffolk County Council HQ
Suffolk Fire and Rescue Service HQ
RUSSELL ROAD
Crown Court
Ipswich Borough Council
A137
WEST END ROAD
CHANCERY RD
PRINCES ST
GRAFTEN WAY
COMMERCIAL ROAD
GRAFTON WAY
B1075
PRINCES STREET
GREYFRIARS
Government Offices
CHALON ST
SEDAN WALK
NEW CARDINAL STREET
CECILIA ST
WOLSEY ST
QUADLING ST
CARDINAL ST
FRIARS BR RD
FRANCISCAN WAY
GREY FRIARS RD
Cardinal Leisure Park
Hotel
DRIVE
PRINCES ST
FRIARS ST
FALCON ST
ST NICHOLAS CT
Unitarian Meeting Ho
CROMWELL SQ
ST NICHOLAS ST
OLD CATTLE MKT
COACHMANS COURT
SILENT STREET
CUTLER ST
ST PETER'S STREET
ROSE LANE
TURRET LA
LOWER BROOK STREET
Customs & Excise
ROSEMARY LANE
WINGFIELD ST
DOGS HEAD ST
B1075
TACKET ST
ORWELL PL
EAGLE ST
FOUNDATION STREET
SMART ST
PLEASANT ROW
SHIRE HALL YARD
LOWER ORWELL STREET
FORE STREET
UPPER O
COX LA
BOND
WATERWORKS ST
SHAFTESBURY SQUARE
ROPE WALK
ROPE WK
WOODHOUSE SQ
Suffolk Coll
GRIMWADE STREET
A1156
ANGEL LA
Swimming Pool
ST CLEMENTS CHURCH LANE
STAR LANE
SLADE ST
SALTHOUSE LA
FORE STREET
WHERRY LA
WHERRY QUAY
NEP-TUNE SQ
A1022
FOUNDATION ST
COLLEGE STREET
KEY STREET
LOWER ORWELL ST
FOUNDRY LA
John Russell Historic Gallery
Waterfront
Old Custom House
Neptune Marina
NEPTUNE QUAY
Ipswich Haven Marina
Wet Dock
Bridge Park (Skate Park)
BRIDGE STREET
Retail Park
River Gipping
PRINCES STREET
B1075
RANELAGH ROAD
BURRELL ROAD
B1073
STOKE ST
Ind Est
DOCK ST
GOWER STREET
GREAT WHIP STREET
LITTLE WHIP ST
A137
VERNON STREET
BELL LA
Stoke Hall
STOKE HALL RD
BELSTEAD ROAD
IP3
STOKE QUAY
New Cut
NEW CUT EAST
NEW CUT WEST
BULSTRODE RD
FELAW STREET
MATHER WY
PURPLETT STREET
HAWES ST
ANCASTER RD
GIPPESWYK RD
Ipswich
IP2
WILLOUGHBY ROAD
CHESHAM RD
SELWYN CL
SEYMOUR RD
Stoke
PHILIP ROAD
MARTIN ROAD
RECTORY ROAD
KESTEVEN ROAD
ANCASTER ROAD
GRANTHAM CR
BELSTEAD ROAD
BELSTEAD AVE
LUTHER ROAD
BELL CL
AUSTIN STREET
LITTLE'S CR
VAUGHAN ST
TYLER ST
PURPLETT ST
ASHLEY ST
SHELLEY ST
BRADLEY ST
HARTLEY STREET
PAULINE ST
TURIN ST
KENYON STREET
WHERSTEAD RD
BRICKFIELD CL
28
29
36
37
2
1
440
435
155
A
160
B
165
C
170
House numbers
HIGH ST
One-way streets

Index

Street names are listed alphabetically and show the locality, the Postcode district, the page number and a reference to the square in which the name falls on the map page

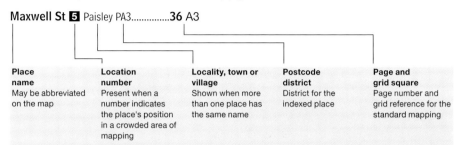

Maxwell St **5** Paisley PA3..............36 A3

Place name	Location number	Locality, town or village	Postcode district	Page and grid square
May be abbreviated on the map	Present when a number indicates the place's position in a crowded area of mapping	Shown when more than one place has the same name	District for the indexed place	Page number and grid reference for the standard mapping

Towns and villages are listed in CAPITAL LETTERS
Public and commercial buildings are highlighted in **magenta**. **Places of interest** are highlighted in blue with a star *

Abbreviations used in the index

Acad	**Academy**	Ct	**Court**	Hts	**Heights**	Pl	**Place**
App	**Approach**	Ctr	**Centre**	Ind	**Industrial**	Prec	**Precinct**
Arc	**Arcade**	Ctry	**Country**	Inst	**Institute**	Prom	**Promenade**
Ave	**Avenue**	Cty	**County**	Int	**International**	Rd	**Road**
Bglw	**Bungalow**	Dr	**Drive**	Intc	**Interchange**	Recn	**Recreation**
Bldg	**Building**	Dro	**Drove**	Junc	**Junction**	Ret	**Retail**
Bsns, Bus	**Business**	Ed	**Education**	L	**Leisure**	Sh	**Shopping**
Bvd	**Boulevard**	Emb	**Embankment**	La	**Lane**	Sq	**Square**
Cath	**Cathedral**	Est	**Estate**	Liby	**Library**	St	**Street**
Cir	**Circus**	Ex	**Exhibition**	Mdw	**Meadow**	Sta	**Station**
Cl	**Close**	Gd	**Ground**	Meml	**Memorial**	Terr	**Terrace**
Cnr	**Corner**	Gdn	**Garden**	Mkt	**Market**	TH	**Town Hall**
Coll	**College**	Gn	**Green**	Mus	**Museum**	Univ	**University**
Com	**Community**	Gr	**Grove**	Orch	**Orchard**	Wk, Wlk	**Walk**
Comm	**Common**	H	**Hall**	Pal	**Palace**	Wr	**Water**
Cott	**Cottage**	Ho	**House**	Par	**Parade**	Yd	**Yard**
Cres	**Crescent**	Hospl	**Hospital**	Pas	**Passage**		
Cswy	**Causeway**	HQ	**Headquarters**	Pk	**Park**		

Index of towns, villages, streets, hospitals, industrial estates, railway stations, schools, shopping centres, universities and places of interest

68 Abb–Arw

A

Abbey Sch The IP12 . . 15 B4
Abbotsbury Cl IP2 . . . . 36 A1
Abbots Hall* IP14 . . . . . 7 A1
Abbots Hall Prim Sch
IP14 . . . . 6 C1
Abbot's Hall Rd IP14 . . . 7 A1
Aberdeen Way IP4 . . . . 22 B1
Aberfoyle Cl **1** IP4 . . 22 C1
Abingdon Cl IP2 . . . . . . 36 A1
Acacia Cl IP3 . . . . 39 B1
Acacia Ct CO11 . . . . . . 55 B4
Acer Gr IP8 . . . . 34 C1
Acorn Cl **9** IP8 . . . . . . 34 C2
Acorn Way IP5 . . . . 4 B3
Acton Cl IP8 . . . . 18 A2
Acton Gdns **1** IP8 . . . 18 A2
Acton Rd IP8 . . . . 18 A2
Adair Rd IP1 . . . . 27 A4

Adams Pl IP5 . . . . 32 C3
Adastral Cl IP11 . . . . . 65 B4
Addington Rd IP11 . . . 58 C3
Adelaide Rd IP4 . . . . . . 31 A2
Admiral Rd **2** IP8 . . . . 43 B4
Admirals Wlk IP12 . . . . 12 B3
Agate Cl **2** IP1 . . . . . . 19 A1
Ainslie Rd IP1 . . . . 28 A2
Aisthorpe IP9 . . . . 52 A3
AKENHAM IP1 . . . . 17 B2
Alabaster Cl **8** IP7 . . 51 B3
Alan Rd IP3 . . . . 37 C4
Alasdair Pl **9** IP6 . . . . 16 B4
Alban Sq **2** IP12 . . . . . 4 A4
Albany The IP4 . . . . 29 B4
Alberta Cl IP5 . . . . 32 A4
Albert Wlk IP11 . . . . . . 64 B3
Albion Hill IP4 . . . . 29 C3
Alder Carr Farm & Ctyd
Craft Ctr* IP6 . . . . . 11 B3
Aldercroft Cl IP1 . . . . . 20 B3
Aldercroft Rd IP1 . . . . 20 B3
Alderlee IP2 . . . . 43 C4
Alderman Rd IP1 . . . . . 67 A2

Aldham Gdns IP14 . . . . . 9 B4
Aldham Rd IP7 . . . . 51 B4
Aldis Ave IP14 . . . . 9 A4
Aldous Cl CO7 . . . . 54 B3
Aldringham Mews **13**
IP11 . . . . 59 A1
Alexander Dr IP6 . . . . . 10 C3
Alexandra Rd
Felixstowe IP11 . . . . . 59 B2
Ipswich IP4 . . . . 29 B2
Allenby Rd IP2 . . . . 27 C2
Allen Rd IP7 . . . . 51 A4
Alley Rd IP10 . . . . 5 B3
Allington Cl IP4 . . . . . . 29 C3
All Saints' Rd IP1 . . . . . 28 A3
Alma Cl **3** IP4 . . . . . . 22 A1
Alma Sq **4** CO11 . . . . 56 C3
Almondhayes IP2 . . . . 36 B3
Alnesbourn Cres
1 Gainsborough
IP2 . . . . 47 A4
Ipswich IP3 . . . . 47 A3
Alnesbourne Priory
IP10 . . . . 46 C2

Alpe St IP1 . . . . 66 A4
Alpha Bsns Pk IP1 . . . . 19 A3
Alston Rd IP3 . . . . 37 C4
Alvis Wlk IP1 . . . . 18 C1
Amberfield Sch
IP10 . . . . 48 C2
Ancaster Rd IP2 . . . . . . 67 A1
Anchor End CO11 . . . . . 57 C3
Anchor La CO11 . . . . . . 57 C3
Anderson Cl IP6 . . . . . . 10 C3
Anderson's Way **8**
IP12 . . . . 14 C4
Andrew Cl IP11 . . . . . . 63 B3
Andros Cl IP3 . . . . 46 A3
Angela Cl IP12 . . . . 4 A4
Angel La
Ipswich IP4 . . . . 67 C2
2 Woodbridge IP12 . . 12 C1
Angel Rd IP8 . . . . 18 A2
Angel St IP7 . . . . 51 A3
Anglesea Rd IP1 . . . . . . 66 A4
Anglia Parkway N
IP1 . . . . 19 A4

Anglia Parkway S
IP1 . . . . 19 A3
Angus Cl IP4 . . . . 22 B1
Anita Cl E IP2 . . . . 27 B1
Anita Cl W IP2 . . . . 27 B1
Ann Beaumont Way
IP7 . . . . 50 C4
Annbrook Rd IP2 . . . . . 35 B1
Anne St IP11 . . . . 63 B3
Ann St IP1 . . . . 66 A4
Ansell Cl IP7 . . . . 51 A3
Anson Rd **7** IP5 . . . . . . 4 A3
Antrim Rd IP1 . . . . 19 A1
Anzani Ave IP11 . . . . . . 62 C4
Appleby Cl IP8 . . . . 34 C1
Arcade St IP1 . . . . 66 B3
Archangel Gdns IP2 . . 35 B4
Argyle St IP4 . . . . 66 C3
Arkle Ct IP5 . . . . 33 A3
Arkwright Rd IP2 . . . . . 27 B2
Arnold Cl IP1 . . . . 19 C3
Arthurs Terr IP4 . . . . . . 66 C3
Arundel Way IP3 . . . . . 39 B3
Arwela Rd IP11 . . . . 63 C2

Ascot Dr
Felixstowe IP11 . . . . 59 B2
Ipswich IP3 . . . . 38 B3
Ashbocking Rd IP6 . . . . 3 C4
Ashburnham Rd IP6 . . 10 C2
Ash Cl
Warren Heath IP3 . . . . . 39 C1
Woodbridge IP12 . . . . . . 15 A4
Ashcroft Rd IP1 . . . . . . 20 A1
Ashdale Rd IP5 . . . . 33 A4
Ashdown Way IP3 . . . . 39 A3
Ash Gd Cl 10 IP11 . . . . . . 5 B1
Ash Gr IP9 . . . . 52 B3
Ash Ground Cl CO11 . . 55 B3
Ashley St IP2 . . . . 67 B1
Ashmere Gr IP4 . . . . . . 29 C2
Ashton Cl IP2 . . . . 34 C2
Askins Rd CO7 . . . . 54 B3
Aspen Cl
Claydon IP6 . . . . 16 C4
3 Woodbridge IP12 . . . 13 A2
Aster Rd IP2 . . . . 35 B4
Aston Cl IP1 . . . . 18 C1
Ataka Rd IP11 . . . . 59 C2
Atherton Rd IP2 . . . . . . 35 A2
Audley Gr IP4 . . . . 31 C1
Augusta Cl IP10 . . . . . . 47 B3
Austin St IP2 . . . . 67 B1
Avenue The
Felixstowe IP11 . . . . 58 B3
Ipswich IP1 . . . . 20 C1
Woodbridge IP12 . . . . . . 15 B4
Avocet La 23 IP5 . . . . 4 A3
Avondale Rd IP3 . . . . . . 38 A2
Aylward Cl IP7 . . . . 51 B1
Ayr Rd IP4 . . . . 22 B1

B

Back Hamlet IP3 . . . . . 29 B1
Back La
Claydon IP6 . . . . 16 B4
Felixstowe IP11 . . . . 59 C1
Back Rd IP10 . . . . 5 B3
Bacon Rd 7 IP6 . . . . 2 C3
Bacton Rd IP11 . . . . 63 C3
Baden Powell Wlk
IP5 . . . . 33 B3
Bader Cl IP3 . . . . 38 C2
Bader Ct 25 IP5 . . . . 4 A3
Badgers Bank IP2 . . . . . 35 B1
Badshah Ave 4 IP3 . . . 38 B3
Bailey Ave IP5 . . . . 33 B3
Bailey Cl IP2 . . . . 27 B2
Baird Cl IP2 . . . . 27 C3
Baird Gr IP5 . . . . 32 B2
Bakers La 1 IP12 . . . . . 15 B4
Baldry Cl IP8 . . . . 34 C1
Baldwin Rd IP14 . . . . 8 C4
Ballater Cl IP1 . . . . 19 B4
Balliol Cl IP12 . . . . 14 B3
Balmoral Cl IP2 . . . . . . 35 C1
Bank Rd IP4 . . . . 29 B2
Banks Cl IP7 . . . . 51 B2
Bantoft Terr IP3 . . . . . . 38 C2
Banyard Cl 4 IP5 . . . . 33 A3
BARHAM IP6 . . . . 3 A4
Barham Picnic Site Visitor Ctr★ IP6 . . . . . . 2 B4
Barhams Way IP13 . . . 53 B4
Barker Cl
Ipswich IP2 . . . . 27 A1
Lawford CO11 . . . . 56 A3
Barley Cl CO11 . . . . 57 C3
Barnes Cl 3 IP7 . . . . . . 51 B3
Barnfield
Capel St Mary IP9 . . . . . 52 C3
Felixstowe IP11 . . . . 59 A2
Manningtree CO11 . . . . . 56 C3
Barnham Pl IP5 . . . . . . 31 C2
Barons Cl 9 IP11 . . . . . 61 A2
Baronsdale Cl IP1 . . . . 20 B1
Barrack La IP1 . . . . 66 A3
Barrack Sq IP5 . . . . 4 A3
Barrett's La IP6 . . . . . . 10 C2
Bartholomew St IP4 . . 29 C2
Bartlet Hospl IP11 . . . . 64 C4
Barton Rd
Felixstowe IP11 . . . . 64 B4
Woodbridge IP12 . . . . . . 12 B3
Bartrum La 7 IP5 . . . . 32 C3
Barvens The IP8 . . . . . . 34 A1
Bath Hill IP11 . . . . 64 B4
Bath Rd IP11 . . . . 64 B4
Bath St IP2 . . . . 37 A3
Battles La IP5 . . . . 33 A3
Bawdsey Cl IP11 . . . . . . 61 A3
Beach Rd E IP11 . . . . . . 64 C4
Beach Rd W IP11 . . . . . 63 C2
Beach Sta Rd IP11 . . . . 63 B1
Beacon Field 4
IP11 . . . . 59 B1
BEACON HILL IP13 . . . 25 C3
Beacon Hill Specl Sch IP2 . . . . 35 C2
Beacon La IP13 . . . . 25 C3
Beaconsfield Rd
Ipswich IP1 . . . . 27 C3
3 Woodbridge IP12 . . . 12 C1
Bealings Sch IP13 . . . . 25 A4
Beardmore Pk 10 IP5 . . 4 A3
Beatrice Ave IP11 . . . . 60 A1
Beatrice Cl IP3 . . . . 38 A3
Beatty Rd IP3 . . . . 38 B2
Beaufort St IP1 . . . . 28 A3
Beaumont Way IP14 . . . 6 B1
Becketts The IP14 . . . . . 6 B4
Beckford Rd CO11 . . . . 57 C3
Bedford St IP1 . . . . 66 A3
Beech Cl IP8 . . . . 26 A2
Beechcroft Rd IP1 . . . . 19 C2
Beeches The
Claydon IP6 . . . . 16 B4
Ipswich IP3 . . . . 37 C4
Lawford CO11 . . . . 56 B2
Beech Gr IP3 . . . . 37 C3
Beech Rd IP5 . . . . 31 C3
Beech Terr IP14 . . . . 7 A3
Beech Way IP12 . . . . . . 15 A3
Beehive Cl CO7 . . . . 54 B3
Beehive Cnr CO7 . . . . . 54 B3
Belfry Rd IP3 . . . . 47 C3
Belgrave Cl IP4 . . . . 21 B1
Bell Cl IP2 . . . . 67 B1
Belle Vue Rd IP4 . . . . . . 29 C2
Bell La IP2 . . . . 67 B1
Bell Mews IP7 . . . . 51 A3
Belmont Rd IP8 . . . . . . 34 C1
BELSTEAD IP8 . . . . 42 C3
Belstead Ave IP2 . . . . . 67 A1
Belstead Rd IP2 . . . . . . 67 A1
Belstead Sch IP8 . . . . . 34 C2
Belvedere Rd IP4 . . . . . 29 C4
Benacre Rd IP3 . . . . 38 A2
Bendalls Ct 13 CO11 . . 56 C3
Benezet St IP1 . . . . 66 A3
Bennett Rd IP1 . . . . 19 B1
Bent La IP4 . . . . 31 B4
Bentley La IP8 . . . . 42 C1
Bentley Rd IP1 . . . . 18 C2
Benton St IP7 . . . . 51 A1
Beresford Dr IP12 . . . . 12 B3
Berkeley Cl IP4 . . . . 21 B1
Bermuda Rd IP10 . . . . . 47 A3
Bernard Cres IP3 . . . . . 38 B2
Berners Rd IP11 . . . . . . 64 C4
Berners St IP1 . . . . 66 A3
Berry Cl IP3 . . . . 39 C1
Betts Ave IP5 . . . . 4 A3
Betts Cl IP7 . . . . 51 A4
Beverley Rd IP4 . . . . . . 29 C4
Bibb Way IP1 . . . . 28 A1
Bilberry Rd IP3 . . . . 46 C3
Bildeston Gdns 2
IP1 . . . . 21 A1
Bildeston Rd IP14 . . . . . 8 A1
Bilney Rd IP12 . . . . 12 A1
Birch Cl
Wickham Market IP13 . . . . 53 B3
Woodbridge IP12 . . . . . . 15 A3
Birchcroft Rd IP1 . . . . . 20 B2
Birch Dr CO11 . . . . 55 B4
Birch Gr IP5 . . . . 4 A2
Birchwood Cty Prim Sch IP5 . . . . 4 A3
Birchwood Dr IP5 . . . . 23 B1
Birkfield Cl IP2 . . . . 36 A4
Birkfield Dr IP2 . . . . . . 35 B1
Bishop Mews IP8 . . . . . 34 B2
Bishops Cl 6 IP11 . . . . 61 A2
Bishop's Hill IP3 . . . . . 37 B4
Bittern Cl IP2 . . . . 35 B3
Bixley Dr IP4 . . . . 31 B1
Bixley La IP4 . . . . 31 C1
Bixley Rd IP3 . . . . 39 A3
Black Barns IP11 . . . . . 58 C3
Blackdown Ave IP5 . . . 31 C2
Black Horse La IP1 . . . 66 A3
Black Horse Wlk
IP1 . . . . 66 B3
Blacksmith's Cnr
IP8 . . . . 42 C2
Blackthorn Cl 1
IP3 . . . . 39 C1
Blacktiles La IP12 . . . . . 4 A4
Bladen Dr IP4 . . . . 31 C1
Blair Cl IP4 . . . . 31 B1
Blake Cl CO11 . . . . 56 A3
Blakenham Woodland Gdn★ IP6 . . . . 2 A2
Blake Rd
Ipswich IP1 . . . . 19 C3
Stowmarket IP14 . . . . 6 B3
Blakes Cl IP12 . . . . 13 B3
Blanche St IP4 . . . . 66 C3
Blandford Rd IP3 . . . . . 39 A3
Blenheim Cl CO11 . . . . 55 B4
Blenheim Rd 3 IP1 . . 28 A3
Blickling Cl IP2 . . . . 36 B2
Blofield Rd IP11 . . . . . . 62 B4
Bloomfield St IP4 . . . . 30 B2
Blue Barn Cl 13 IP11 . . . 5 B1
Bluebell Cl IP2 . . . . 35 B4
Bluebell Gr IP6 . . . . 11 A1
Bluegate La IP9 . . . . . . 52 C1
Bluestem Rd IP3 . . . . . 47 A4
Blyford Way IP11 . . . . . 62 C4
Blyth Cl IP2 . . . . 36 A1
Boatman Cl 16 IP8 . . . . 43 B4
Bobbits La
Pinewood IP9 . . . . 43 B4
Wherstead IP9 . . . . 44 A3
Bodiam Cl IP3 . . . . 39 A4
Bodiam Rd IP3 . . . . 39 A4
Bodmin Cl IP5 . . . . 32 A2
Bolton La IP1 . . . . 66 C3
Bond St
Ipswich IP4 . . . . 67 C2
Stowmarket IP14 . . . . 7 A3
Bonnington Rd IP3 . . . 37 C1
Bonny Cres IP3 . . . . 46 C4
Booth La IP5 . . . . 33 B4
Border Cot La IP13 . . . 53 A4
Borrett Pl IP12 . . . . 14 B3
Borrowdale Ave 1
IP4 . . . . 21 A1
Bosmere Prim Sch IP6 . . . . 11 A2
Boss Hall Ind Est IP1 . . . . 27 B3
Boss Hall Rd IP1 . . . . . . 27 B3
Bostock Rd IP2 . . . . 36 C1
Boston Rd IP4 . . . . 29 C3
Boswell La IP7 . . . . 51 A4
Boulters Cl IP14 . . . . 6 B2
Boulters Way IP14 . . . . . 6 B2
Bourchier Cl 7 IP7 . . . 51 B3
Bourne Hill IP2 . . . . 44 B3
Bourne Pk Residential Park IP2 . . . . 36 B1
Bourne Terr IP2 . . . . . . 44 B4
Bowland Dr IP8 . . . . . . 34 C1
Bowthorpe Cl IP1 . . . . 66 A4
Boxford Cl 2 IP14 . . . . . 9 B3
Boxford Ct 7 IP11 . . . . 62 C4
Boydlands IP9 . . . . 52 B3
Boyton Rd IP3 . . . . 38 B1
Bracken Ave IP5 . . . . . . 25 B1
Brackenbury Cl IP1 . . . 28 B4
Brackenbury Sports Ctr IP11 . . . . 60 C1
Brackenhayes Cl
IP2 . . . . 36 B3
Brackley Cl 8 IP11 . . . 59 A1
Bradfield Ave IP7 . . . . . 51 A4
Bradfield Cres IP7 . . . . 51 A4
Bradley St IP2 . . . . 67 B1
Bramble Dr IP3 . . . . 39 B1
Bramblewood 1
IP8 . . . . 34 C2
BRAMFORD IP8 . . . . . . 18 A2
Bramford CE Prim Sch IP8 . . . . 18 A1
Bramford Ct IP14 . . . . . . 9 B4
Bramford La
Ipswich IP1 . . . . 19 A1
6 Ipswich IP1 . . . . 28 A3
Bramford Meadows Nature Reserve★ IP1 . . . . 18 B3
Bramford Rd
Bramford IP8 . . . . 18 B1
Ipswich IP1 . . . . 27 B4
Bramhall Cl IP2 . . . . . . 35 A1
Bramley Chase IP4 . . . 30 B3
Brandon Rd IP11 . . . . . 62 C4
Bransby Gdns IP4 . . . . 29 B3
BRANTHAM 55 C4
Brantham Hill CO11 . . . 55 A3
Brazier's Wood Rd
IP3 . . . . 46 B4
Brecon Cl IP2 . . . . 36 B2
Bredfield Cl 7 IP11 . . 59 A1
Bredfield Rd IP12 . . . . . 12 C3
Bredfield St IP12 . . . . . 12 B1
Brendon Dr IP5 . . . . . . 31 C2
Brett Ave IP7 . . . . 51 B4
Brett Cl IP1 . . . . 27 B4
Brettenham Cres 4
IP1 . . . . 21 A1
Betts The IP5 . . . . 33 B4
Breydon Way IP3 . . . . . 46 C3
Briarhayes Cl IP2 . . . . . 36 B3
Briarwood Rd IP12 . . . 14 C3
Brickfield Cl IP2 . . . . . . 67 C1
Brickfields The IP14 . . . 6 C2
Brick Kiln Cl 15 IP11 . . . 5 B1
Bridge Pk (Skate Park)★ IP1 . . . . 67 B1
Bridge Pl CO11 . . . . 55 A2
Bridge Rd IP11 . . . . 60 A1
Bridge St
Hadleigh IP7 . . . . 50 C4
Ipswich IP1 . . . . 67 B2
Needham Market IP6 . . . 11 A3
Stowmarket IP14 . . . . 7 C1
Bridge Wood Nature Reserve★ IP3 . . . . 46 B2
Bridgewood Rd
IP12 . . . . 12 A1
Bridgwater Rd IP2 . . . . 35 A2
Bridport Ave IP3 . . . . . 39 A3
Brights Wlk IP5 . . . . . . 33 B3
BRIGHTWELL IP10 . . . . . 4 A1
Brightwell Cl IP11 . . . . 62 C4
Brimstone Rd IP8 . . . . 43 B4
Brinkley Way IP11 . . . . 61 A3
Brisbane Rd IP4 . . . . . . 31 A2
Bristol Rd IP4 . . . . 30 A3
Britannia Prim Sch IP4 . . . . 30 B1
Britannia Rd IP4 . . . . . . 30 B2
Britten Ave IP14 . . . . 6 C3
Broadlands Way IP4 . . 31 C1
Broad Meadow 2
IP8 . . . . 34 C2
Broadmere Rd IP1 . . . . 27 B4
Broad Rd IP13 . . . . 53 A4
Broadway IP13 . . . . 53 A4
Brock La IP13 . . . . 14 A2
Brockley Cres IP1 . . . . 19 A1
Broke Ave IP8 . . . . 18 B2
BROKE HALL IP4 . . . . . 39 B3
Broke Hall Gdns IP3 . . 39 A4
Broke Hall Prim Sch IP4 . . . . 31 B1
Bromeswell Rd IP4 . . . 21 B1
Bromley Cl 4 IP2 . . . . 36 C3
Bromley Rd CO11 . . . . . 56 A1
Brook Cl IP14 . . . . 6 B3
Brookfield Rd IP1 . . . . 27 C4
Brookhill Way IP4 . . . . 39 C4
Brookhouse Bsns Pk IP2 . . . . 27 C2
Brook La
Felixstowe IP11 . . . . 60 B1
Playford IP6 . . . . 24 A4
Trimley St Martin IP10 . . . 5 C2
Brooklands Prim Sch CO11 . . . . 55 B3
Brooklands Rd CO11 . . 55 B3
Brooklands Rise
CO11 . . . . 55 B3
Brooks Hall Rd IP1 . . . 28 A3
Brooks Malting 3
CO11 . . . . 56 C3
Brook St
Manningtree CO11 . . . . . 56 C3
Woodbridge IP12 . . . . . . 12 C1
Brookview
6 Ipswich IP2 . . . . 43 B4
Pinewood IP2 . . . . 35 B1
Broom Cres IP3 . . . . . . 37 C1
Broomfield
17 Martlesham Heath IP5 . . . . 4 A3
Martlesham IP5 . . . . 33 C3
Broom Field 5 IP11 . . 59 B1
Broomfield Comm
IP8 . . . . 26 B2
Broomfield Mews 18
IP5 . . . . 4 A3
Broomhayes IP2 . . . . . . 36 A2
Broomheath IP12 . . . . . 15 A2
BROOM HILL IP12 . . . . 14 C2
Broom Hill Nature Reserve★ IP7 . . . . 50 C2
Broom Hill Rd IP1 . . . . 28 A4
Broom Hill Swimming Pool IP1 . . . . 28 A4
Broom Way IP9 . . . . 52 B4
Brotherton Ave IP11 . . 58 B4
Broughton Rd IP1 . . . . 66 A4
Browning Rd
Brantham CO11 . . . . 55 A2
Ipswich IP1 . . . . 19 C3
Brownlow Rd IP11 . . . . 64 A4
Browns Gr IP5 . . . . 33 A3
Brunel Rd IP2 . . . . 27 B2
Brunswick House Cut
CO11 . . . . 57 C2
Brunswick Rd IP4 . . . . 21 C1
Bryon Ave IP11 . . . . 62 B2
Buckenham Rd IP7 . . . 51 C1
Buckfast Cl 4 IP2 . . . 36 A2
Buckingham Cl 4
IP12 . . . . 4 A4
Bucklesham Rd
Ipswich IP3 . . . . 39 B2
Kirton IP10 . . . . 5 B4
Buck's Horns La IP8 . . 42 B2
Buddleia Cl IP2 . . . . . . 35 B4
Bude Cl IP5 . . . . 32 A2
Bugsby Way IP5 . . . . . . 33 B3
Bullard's La IP12 . . . . . 12 A1
Bull Dr IP5 . . . . 32 C2
Bullen Cl IP8 . . . . 18 A2
Bullen La 5 IP8 . . . . . . 18 A2
Bulstrode Rd IP2 . . . . . 67 C1
Bulwer Rd IP1 . . . . 28 A2
Bunting Rd IP2 . . . . 35 A3
Bunyan Cl IP1 . . . . 20 A3
Buregate Rd IP11 . . . . . 63 C2
Bures Cl IP14 . . . . 9 B4
Burgess Pl 22 IP5 . . . . . . 4 A3
Burghley Cl 14 IP2 . . . . 36 A2
Burke Cl IP1 . . . . 20 A3
Burke Rd 7 IP1 . . . . . . 20 A3
Burkitt Rd IP12 . . . . 12 A1
Burlington Rd IP1 . . . . 66 A3

Burnet Cl IP8. . . . . .43 A4
Burnham Cl
  Felixstowe IP11 . . . . . . .58 C3
  Ipswich IP4 . . . . .29 C3
Burns Rd IP1 . . . . .19 B3
Burnt House La IP10 . . . 5 B3
Burnt Oak Cnr CO7 . . .54 C1
Burrell Rd IP2 . . . . .67 B1
Burrows Cl CO11 . . . . . .56 A3
Burton Dr IP6 . . . . .10 C3
Burwood Pl IP1 . . . . . . .58 C4
Bury Hill IP12 . . . . .12 C3
Bury Hill IP12 . . . . .12 C3
Bury Rd
  Ipswich IP1 . . . . .19 A4
  Stowmarket IP14 . . . . . . 6 C4
Bury St **3** IP14 . . . . 7 A2
Bushey Cl IP9 . . . . .52 B3
Bushman Gdns **3**
  IP8 . . . . .18 A2
Butchers La IP9 . . . . . .52 C3
Butler Smith Gdns **6**
  IP5 . . . . .32 C3
Butley Cl IP2 . . . . .43 C4
Butley Rd IP11 . . . . . . .63 B3
Buttercup Cl IP8 . . . . . .34 C1
Butterfly Gdns IP4 . . . .31 B1
Buttermarket Sh Ctr
  IP1 . . . . .66 B3
Buttermere Gn IP11 . .61 A2
Butter Mkt IP1 . . . . . . .66 B3
Buttrum's Mill★
  IP12 . . . . .12 A1
Byland Cl **6** IP2 . . . . . .36 A2
Byron Rd IP1 . . . . .19 B4

C

Cadmus Rd IP1 . . . . . . .27 A3
Cage La IP11 . . . . .59 B1
Caithness Cl IP4 . . . . . .30 B4
Calais St IP7 . . . . .51 A3
CALIFORNIA IP4 . . . . . .30 B2
California IP12 . . . . . . .14 B3
California Rd CO11 . . . .57 C3
Camberley Rd IP4 . . . . .31 A3
Camborne Rd IP5 . . . . .32 B3
Cambridge Dr IP2 . . . .35 C2
Cambridge Rd
  Felixstowe IP11 . . . . . .64 B4
  Ipswich IP5 . . . . .32 A3
Camden Rd IP3 . . . . . . .38 B4
Campbell Rd IP3 . . . . . .38 C1
Campion Cres IP14 . . . . 8 C4
Campion Rd IP2 . . . . . .35 C4
Camwood Gdns IP3 . . .38 B4
Canberra Cl IP4 . . . . . .31 A2
Candlet Gr IP11 . . . . . .59 C1
Candlet Rd IP11 . . . . . .59 B3
Canham St IP1 . . . . . . .66 A3
Canterbury Cl IP2 . . . .43 C4
Canterbury Gdns
  IP7 . . . . .51 B3
Capel Cl **4** IP1 . . . . 5 B1
Capel Dr IP11 . . . . .62 C4
Capel Hall La IP11 . . . . . 5 C1
CAPEL ST MARY IP9 . .52 B3
Capel St Mary CE Prim
  Sch IP9 . . . . .52 B3
Carders Cl IP7 . . . . .51 A1
Cardew Drift IP5 . . . . . .33 A4
Cardiff Ave IP2 . . . . . . .36 B1
Cardigan St IP1 . . . . . .66 A4
Cardinalls Rd IP14 . . . . 7 A3
Cardinal Pk IP1 . . . . . . .67 B2
Cardinal St IP1 . . . . . . .67 B2
Carlford Cl **14** IP5 . . . . 4 A3
Carlow Mews **13**
  IP12 . . . . .12 C1
Carlton Rd IP5 . . . . . . .32 A3
Carlton Way IP4 . . . . . .29 B4
Carlton Wlk IP7 . . . . . .51 B1
Carlyle Cl IP1 . . . . .19 C4
Carmarthen Cl IP2 . . .36 A2

Carmelite Pl **14**
  IP12 . . . . .12 C1
Carol Ave **9** IP12 . . . . . 4 A4
Carolbrook Rd IP2 . . . .35 B1
Carol Cl IP11 . . . . .60 C1
Carriage Cl IP11 . . . . . .58 C4
Carriers Ct CO7 . . . . . . .54 C3
Carr Rd IP11 . . . . .65 B4
Carr St IP4 . . . . .66 C3
Castle Cl IP11 . . . . .61 A2
CASTLE HILL IP1 . . . . .20 A3
Castle Hill Inf Sch
  IP1 . . . . .20 A3
Castle Hill Jun Sch
  IP1 . . . . .20 A3
Castle La IP7 . . . . .50 C4
Castle Rd
  Hadleigh IP7 . . . . .50 B4
  Ipswich IP1 . . . . .19 B1
Castle Rise IP7 . . . . . . .50 B4
Castle St IP12 . . . . .12 C1
Catesbray IP9 . . . . .52 A3
Catherine Rd IP12 . . . .12 A2
CATTAWADE 55 B2
Cattawade St CO11 . . .55 A2
Cauldwell Ave IP4 . . . .29 C2
Cauldwell Hall Rd
  IP4 . . . . .30 A1
Causeway End CO11 . .56 A4
Causeway The IP6 . . . .11 A2
Causton Jun Sch
  IP14 . . . . .59 B2
Cavan Rd IP1 . . . . .19 A2
Cavendish Dr CO11 . . .56 A2
Cavendish Rd
  Felixstowe IP11 . . . . . .63 C3
  Stowmarket IP14 . . . . . 7 C4
Cavendish St IP3 . . . . . .37 C4
Cecilia St IP1 . . . . .67 B2
Cecil Rd IP1 . . . . .66 A4
Cedar Ave IP5 . . . . .32 A2
Cedar Cl CO11 . . . . .55 B4
Cedar Cres CO11 . . . . . .56 B2
Cedarcroft Rd IP1 . . . .19 C2
Cedars La IP9 . . . . .52 A3
Cedarwood Prim Sch
  IP5 . . . . .32 C2
Cemetery La
  East Bergholt CO7 . . . .54 A2
  Ipswich IP4 . . . . .21 C1
  Woodbridge IP12 . . . . .14 C4
Cemetery Rd IP4 . . . . .66 C3
Central Ave IP3 . . . . . . .47 A4
Central Maltings The **5**
  CO11 . . . . .56 B3
Century Dr IP5 . . . . . . .33 B3
Chaffinch Way IP14 . . . 7 C3
Chainhouse Rd IP6 . . . .11 A1
Chalkeith Rd IP6 . . . . . .11 B1
Chalk Hill La IP6 . . . . . . 2 A3
Chalkners Cl **7** IP9 . . .52 B3
Chalon St IP1 . . . . .67 A2
Chamberlain Way
  IP8 . . . . .34 C2
Chancery Rd IP1 . . . . . .67 A2
Chandlers Wlk IP14 . . . 9 A4
Chandos Ct **8** IP12 . . . . 4 A4
Chandos Dr **5** IP12 . . . 4 A4
CHANTRY IP2 . . . . .35 A2
Chantry Gn IP2 . . . . . . .35 A3
Chantry High Sch
  IP2 . . . . .35 C3
Chapel Cl IP9 . . . . .52 B3
Chapel Cut CO11 . . . . . .57 C3
Chapel Field IP8 . . . . . .18 A2
Chapel La
  Belstead IP8 . . . . .42 C3
  Copdock & Washbrook
  IP8 . . . . .34 A1
  Wickham Market
  IP13 . . . . .53 B2
Chapel St IP12 . . . . .12 C1
Chaplin Rd CO7 . . . . . . .54 C3
Charles Ind Est IP14 . . . 7 B3
Charles Rd IP11 . . . . . . .63 B3
Charles St IP1 . . . . .66 B3
Charlton Ave IP1 . . . . . .19 C2

Charter Cl IP7 . . . . .51 A4
Chartwell Cl IP4 . . . . . .30 A1
Chaser Cl **8** IP3 . . . . . .46 C4
Chase The
  Felixstowe IP11 . . . . . .63 C4
  Manningtree CO11 . . . .56 C2
  20 Martlesham Heath
  IP5 . . . . 4 A3
Chatsworth Cres
  Felixstowe IP11 . . . . . .58 C3
  Ipswich IP2 . . . . .36 A2
Chatsworth Dr IP4 . . . .39 B4
Chattisham Cl IP10 . . . 9 B3
Chaucer Rd
  Felixstowe IP11 . . . . . .63 C3
  Ipswich IP1 . . . . .19 C3
Chelsea Cl IP1 . . . . .19 C1
Chelsworth Ave IP4 . . .21 B1
Chelsworth Rd IP11 . . .63 A3
Chelsworth Way IP1 . . . 9 B3
Cheltenham Ave IP1 . .20 B1
Chepstow Rd
  Felixstowe IP11 . . . . . .59 C1
  Ipswich IP1 . . . . .20 B4
Chequers Rise IP6 . . . . 2 A3
Cherry Blossom Cl
  IP8 . . . . .34 B2
Cherryfields IP8 . . . . . .18 A1
Cherry La Gdns IP4 . . .30 B3
Cherry Tree Rd
  Stowmarket IP14 . . . . . 6 C4
  Woodbridge IP12 . . . . .15 A4
Chesapeake Rd **3**
  IP3 . . . . .46 A4
Chesham Rd IP2 . . . . . .67 A1
Chessington Gdns
  IP1 . . . . .27 C4
Chesterfield Dr IP1 . . .19 C2
Chester Rd IP11 . . . . . . .59 C1
Chesterton Cl IP2 . . . . .35 C1
Chestnut Cl IP5 . . . . . . .23 B1
Chestnut Dr IP6 . . . . . .16 B4
Chestnut Gr **2** IP14 . . . 7 B1
Chestnuts The **11**
  IP2 . . . . .34 C2
Chevalier Rd IP11 . . . . .64 B4
Chevallier St IP1 . . . . . .28 A3
Childer Rd IP14 . . . . 7 A2
Childers Field **2**
  IP11 . . . . .59 A1
Chilton Ave IP14 . . . . . . 6 C2
Chilton Com Prim Sch
  IP14 . . . . 6 C3
Chilton Rd IP3 . . . . .38 C4
Chilton Way IP14 . . . . . 6 B3
Chilton Way Sports
  Club IP14 . . . . 6 A3
Christchurch Dr
  IP12 . . . . .14 B3
Christchurch Mansion★
  IP1 . . . . .67 A4
Christchurch St IP4 . . .66 C3
Church Cl IP5 . . . . .32 B4
Church Cres IP8 . . . . . . .26 A2
Church Gn IP8 . . . . .18 B1
Churchill Ave
  Hadleigh IP7 . . . . .51 A4
  Ipswich IP4 . . . . .30 B1
Churchill Cl **7** IP11 . . . .63 A3
Churchill Cres IP13 . . .53 B4
Church La
  Brantham CO11 . . . . . .55 C4
  Claydon IP6 . . . . .17 A4
  Copdock & Washbrook
  IP8 . . . . .42 A3
  Felixstowe IP11 . . . . . .59 B2
  Henley IP6 . . . . 3 C3
  Kirton IP10 . . . . 5 C3
  Martlesham CO11 . . . . .57 A3
  Mistley CO11 . . . . .57 A3
  Playford IP6 . . . . .24 B4
  Sproughton IP8 . . . . . .26 B2
  Westerfield IP6 . . . . . . .23 B2
Churchman Cl IP12 . . .13 A4
Church Meadows **1**
  IP6 . . . . 3 B4

Church Rd
  Combs IP14 . . . . 9 B2
  Felixstowe IP11 . . . . . .60 C2
  Stowmarket IP14 . . . . . 9 A3
Church St
  1 Hadleigh IP7 . . . . . .51 A2
  Woodbridge IP12 . . . . .12 C1
Church Terr IP13 . . . . . .53 B3
Church View Cl IP12 . .13 B3
Church Wlk
  Hadleigh IP7 . . . . .50 C2
  Stowmarket IP14 . . . . . 7 A2
Cinnabar Cl **11** IP8 . . . .43 B4
Civic Dr IP1 . . . . .67 A2
Clacton Rd CO11 . . . . . .57 A1
Clapgate La IP3 . . . . . . .38 A1
Clare Ave IP12 . . . . .14 C4
Clare Cl IP14 . . . . 9 B3
Clarence Rd IP3 . . . . . . .38 B1
Clare Rd IP4 . . . . .29 C4
Clarkson St IP1 . . . . . . .66 A3
Claude St IP1 . . . . .66 B3
Claverton Way IP4 . . . .31 A1
CLAYDON IP6 . . . . .16 B4
Claydon High Sch
  IP6 . . . . .16 B4
Claydon Prim Sch
  IP6 . . . . 2 C3
Clayton Ct IP12 . . . . . . .14 B3
Clearwing Cl **15** IP8 . .43 B4
Clementine Gdns
  IP4 . . . . .30 A1
Clench Cl IP4 . . . . .66 C3
Cliff La IP3 . . . . .37 B3
Cliff La Prim Sch
  IP3 . . . . .37 B3
Clifford Rd IP4 . . . . .29 C1
Clifford Rd Air Raid
  Shelter Mus★ IP4 . . . .29 C1
Clifford Rd Prim Sch
  IP4 . . . . .29 C2
Cliff Quay IP3 . . . . .37 A2
Cliff Rd
  Felixstowe IP11 . . . . . .61 A2
  Ipswich IP3 . . . . .37 B3
Clifton Way IP2 . . . . . . .35 A2
Clive Ave IP1 . . . . .20 B2
Cloncurry Gdns
  IP11 . . . . .63 A3
Clopton Gdns IP7 . . . . .51 B1
Clovelly Cl IP4 . . . . .39 C4
Clover Cl
  Ipswich IP2 . . . . .35 C4
  Needham Market IP6 . .11 A1
Clovers Cl IP14 . . . . 6 C2
Coachmans Ct IP1 . . . .67 B2
Cobbold Mews IP4 . . . .66 C3
Cobbold Rd
  Felixstowe IP11 . . . . . .64 A4
  Woodbridge IP12 . . . . .12 A3
Cobbold St IP4 . . . . .66 C3
Cobden Pl IP4 . . . . .66 C3
Cobham Rd IP3 . . . . . . .38 C2
Cody Rd IP3 . . . . .38 C1
Colchester Rd
  Ipswich IP4 . . . . .21 C1
  Lawford CO11 . . . . .56 B2
Cold Store Rd IP11 . . . .62 B2
Cole Ness Rd IP3 . . . . . .46 A4
Coleridge Rd IP1 . . . . . .19 C3
College Ct CO11 . . . . . . .56 B3
College Gn IP11 . . . . . . .60 C1
College St IP3 . . . . .67 B2
Collett's Wlk IP12 . . . .12 A1
Collingwood Ave **6**
  IP3 . . . . .38 B3
Collingwood Fields
  CO7 . . . . .54 A4
Collingwood Rd
  IP12 . . . . .12 B3
Collinson's IP2 . . . . . . .27 A1
Colneis Jun Sch
  IP11 . . . . .60 B2
Colneis Rd IP11 . . . . . . .60 B2
Coltsfoot Rd IP2 . . . . . .35 B4
Columbia Cl IP5 . . . . . .32 A3

Columbine Gdns
  IP2 . . . . .27 B1
Combers The IP5 . . . . .33 B3
COMBS IP14 . . . . 8 C1
COMBS FORD IP14 . . . 9 A4
Combs Ford Prim Sch
  IP14 . . . . 9 B2
Combs La IP14 . . . . 9 A4
Combs Mid Sch IP14 . . 9 C3
Combs Wood Dr IP14 . . 9 A3
Combs Wood Nature
  Reserve★ IP14 . . . . . . 9 B2
Commerce Way
  CO11 . . . . .56 B4
Commercial Rd IP1 . . .67 A1
Compass Ct **16** CO11 . .56 C3
Conach Rd IP2 . . . . .12 A1
Congreve Rd IP1 . . . . . .20 A3
Coniston Cl IP11 . . . . . .61 B3
Coniston Rd IP3 . . . . . . .38 B2
Coniston Sq E IP3 . . . . .38 B2
Coniston Sq W IP3 . . . .38 B2
Connaught Rd IP1 . . . .19 A2
Constable Cl CO11 . . . .56 A3
Constable Rd
  Felixstowe IP11 . . . . . .64 B4
  Ipswich IP4 . . . . .66 C4
Constable Way IP14 . . . 6 B2
Constantine Rd IP1 . . .67 A2
Constitution Hill
  Ipswich IP1 . . . . .28 B4
  2 Needham Market
  IP6 . . . . .11 A3
Convalescent Hill
  IP11 . . . . .64 A3
Conway Cl
  Felixstowe IP11 . . . . . .60 C3
  Ipswich IP2 . . . . .36 B2
Cooks Cl IP5 . . . . .33 B4
Coombers IP9 . . . . .52 A3
Coopers Rd **30** IP5 . . . . 4 A3
Cooper's Rd IP3 . . . . 3 A4
Coopers Way **4** IP6 . . . 2 B3
Copdock Intc IP8 . . . . .34 B2
Copleston High Sch
  IP4 . . . . .30 C1
Copleston Rd IP4 . . . . .30 B1
Copperfield Rd IP2 . . . .27 B1
Copper Gr **14** IP8 . . . . .43 B4
Coppice Cl IP12 . . . . . . .12 C2
Coprolite St IP3 . . . . . . .29 B1
Copswood Cl IP5 . . . . . .33 C3
Coral Dr IP1 . . . . .19 A1
Coram St IP7 . . . . .50 A3
Corder Rd IP4 . . . . .29 A4
Cordy's La IP11 . . . . . . .58 B2
Corks La IP7 . . . . .50 C3
Cormorant Dr IP14 . . . 7 C1
Cornflower Cl IP2 . . . . .35 B4
Cornford Way CO11 . . .56 A3
Cornhill IP1 . . . . .66 B3
Cornwall Cl IP11 . . . . . .56 A4
Cornwall Rd IP11 . . . . .59 C1
Coronation Dr IP11 . . .63 A3
Coronation Rd IP4 . . . .30 B1
Corporation Ave IP2 . .36 B1
Corton Rd IP3 . . . . .38 B1
Cotman Ave CO11 . . . . .56 A3
Cotman Rd IP3 . . . . .38 A1
Cotswold Ave IP1 . . . . .20 B1
Cottesford Cl IP7 . . . . . .51 B2
Cottingham Rd IP8 . . .34 B2
Courts The IP11 . . . . . . .64 B4
Court The CO7 . . . . .54 A2
Cowell St IP2 . . . . .36 C3
Cowley Rd IP11 . . . . . . .64 A4
Cowper St IP4 . . . . .30 B2
Cowslip Cl IP2 . . . . .35 B4
Cowslip Way IP6 . . . . . .11 A1
Cox Cl IP5 . . . . .32 B2
Cox La IP4 . . . . .67 C2
Cox's Hill CO11 . . . . . . .56 A3
Coytes Gdns IP1 . . . . . .67 B2
Crabbe St IP4 . . . . .30 A2
Craig Cl **7** IP11 . . . . 5 B1
Cranberry Sq **2** IP3 . .46 C3

Cranborne Chase 1
IP4 . . . . 22 A1
Crane Cl IP12 . . . . . . 14 B3
Crane Hill London Rd
IP2 . . . . 35 B4
Cranwell Cres IP3 . . 38 C1
Cranwell Gr 1 IP5 . . 32 C3
Cranworth Rd IP7 . . 51 B1
Crawford La 2 IP5 . . 32 C3
Creeting Hills IP6 . . . 11 C4
Creeting Rd IP14 . . . . 7 B2
Crescent Rd
Felixstowe IP11 . . . . . . 64 A4
Ipswich IP1 . . . . 66 A3
Crescent The
Stowmarket IP14 . . . . . . 9 A4
Wickham Market
IP13 . . . . 53 A3
Cricket Hill Rd IP11. . 59 A1
Crocus Cl IP2 . . . . 35 C4
Croft La IP10 . . . . 5 A3
Crofton Rd IP4 . . . . . . 30 B3
Croft St IP2 . . . . 36 C3
Cromarty Rd IP4 . . . . 30 B4
Cromer Rd IP1 . . . . . . 19 C1
Crompton Rd IP2. . . . 27 C3
Cromwell Sq IP1 . . . . 67 B2
Crossgate Field 3
IP11 . . . . 59 B1
Crossley Gdns IP1 . . 18 C2
Cross St IP11 . . . . 59 B2
Crotchets Cl 2 IP9 . . 52 B3
Croutel Rd IP11 . . . . . 60 B1
Crowe St IP14 . . . . 7 A2
Crow La IP14 . . . . 7 A1
Crowland Cl 1 IP2 . . 36 A2
Crowley Rd IP6 . . . . . 11 A2
Crown Cl 10 IP12 . . . . 4 A4
Crown La IP13 . . . . . . 53 B3
Crown Pl IP12 . . . . . . 15 B4
Crown St
Felixstowe IP11 . . . . . . 59 B1
Ipswich IP1 . . . . 66 B3
Needham Market IP6. . . 11 A3
Stowmarket IP14 . . . . . . 7 A3
Crown Swimming Pool
IP1 . . . . 66 B3
Crowswell Ct 6 IP11 . . 5 B1
Croxton IP10. . . . . 5 C3
Cuckfield Ave IP3 . . . 39 B3
Culford Wlk IP11 . . . . 62 C3
Cullingham Rd IP1 . . 28 A2
Cumberland Cl 4
IP11 . . . . 61 A2
Cumberland Mews
IP12 . . . . 15 B4
Cumberland St
Ipswich IP1 . . . . 66 A4
Woodbridge IP12 . . . . 15 B4
Curlew Rd IP2 . . . . . . 35 A4
Curriers' La IP1 . . . . . 67 A2
Curtis Cl IP8 . . . . 34 C1
Curtis Way IP5 . . . . . 33 A3
Curwen Rd IP14 . . . . . 6 C2
Cutler St IP1 . . . . 67 B2

D
Daffodil Cl IP2 . . . . . . 35 B3
Daimler Rd IP1. . . . . . 18 C2
Dains Pl IP11. . . . . 58 C3
Daires La IP12. . . . . . . 13 B3
Dale Hall La IP1 . . . . 20 B1
Dale Hall Prim Sch
IP1 . . . . 20 B2
Dales Rd IP1 . . . . 20 A1
Dales View Rd IP1 . . 20 A1
Dalton Rd IP11 . . . . . . 58 C3
Damselfly Rd 5 IP3 . . 46 C4
Dandalan Cl IP1 . . . . . 27 B4
Danes Cl IP14 . . . . 6 C1
Danescourt Ave IP14 . . 6 C1
Darrell Rd 1 IP1 . . . . 65 B4
Darsham Cl 19 IP11 . . 59 A1
Darter Cl 4 IP3 . . . . . 46 C4
Darwin Rd IP4. . . . . . . 29 C1
Dashwood Cl IP8. . . . 34 C1

Daundy Cl IP2 . . . . 27 A1
Davey Cl IP3 . . . . 37 C1
Dawes Cl IP9 . . . . 52 A4
Dawson Dr IP11 . . . . . 58 C4
Dawson Drift 3 IP5 . . 32 C3
Days Gn IP9 . . . . 52 A3
Days Rd IP9 . . . . 52 A3
Deacon Cl 8 IP11. . . . 61 A2
Dead La CO11 . . . . 56 B1
Deben Ave
Ipswich IP5 . . . . 33 C4
Martlesham IP5 . . . . . . 25 C1
Deben High Sch
IP11 . . . . 63 C4
Deben Mill Bsns Ctr
IP12 . . . . 13 A2
Deben Pool IP12 . . . . 15 B4
Deben Rd
Ipswich IP1 . . . . 19 C1
Woodbridge IP12 . . . . 13 A3
Debenside The IP12 . . 13 B3
Deben Valley Dr IP5 . . 32 C3
Deben Way IP11 . . . . 63 B3
Defoe Rd IP1 . . . . 20 A4
Delf Cl IP7 . . . . 51 B4
Delius Cl 1 IP14 . . . . . 6 C3
Dellwood Ave IP11 . . 60 B1
Demesne Gdns 6
IP5 . . . . 4 A3
Denton Cl IP2 . . . . . . 35 A2
Derby Cl IP4 . . . . 30 A1
Derby Rd IP3. . . . . . . 38 A4
Dereham Ave IP3. . . . 37 C3
Derwent Rd IP3 . . . . . 37 C3
Devereaux Ct IP4. . . . 66 C3
Devlin Rd IP8 . . . . . . 34 B1
Devon Rd IP11 . . . . . . 59 C1
Devonshire Rd IP3 . . 29 C1
Dewar La IP5. . . . . . . 32 C3
Dhobi Pl IP1 . . . . 27 C3
Dial La IP1 . . . . 66 B3
Diamond Cl IP1 . . . . . 19 A1
Dickens Rd IP2 . . . . . 27 B2
Dickinson Terr 8
IP5 . . . . 33 A3
Didsbury Cl IP2 . . . . . 35 A2
Digby Cl 5 IP5. . . . . . . 4 A2
Digby Rd IP4 . . . . 30 C3
Dillwyn St W IP1 . . . . 66 A3
Ditchingham Gr IP4 . . 31 C2
Dixon Cl CO11 . . . . . . 56 A3
Dobbs Drift IP5 . . . . . 33 C3
Dobbs La IP5. . . . . . . 25 B1
Dock La IP12. . . . . 13 B3
Dock Rd IP11. . . . . . . 62 C1
Dock St IP2 . . . . 67 B1
Doctor Watson's La
IP5 . . . . 24 A1
Dodmans IP9 . . . . 52 B3
Dodson Vale IP5. . . . . 32 C3
Dogs Head St IP4. . . . 67 B2
Dogwood Cl IP3 . . . . 39 A2
Dombey Rd IP2. . . . . . 27 B1
Donegal Rd IP1 . . . . . 19 A2
Dooley Rd IP11. . . . . . 62 C3
Dorchester Rd IP3. . . 39 A3
Doric Pl IP12 . . . . 15 B4
Dorset Cl IP4. . . . . . . 21 C1
Dovedale IP11. . . . . . . 63 A3
Dover Rd IP3. . . . . . . 38 B4
Dove St IP4 . . . . 29 B1
Downham Bvd IP3. . . 46 C3
Downing Cl
Ipswich IP2 . . . . 35 C2
2 Woodbridge IP12 . . 14 C4
Downing Prim Sch
IP2 . . . . 35 C2
Downside IP14 . . . . . . 6 B2
Downside Cl IP2. . . . . 43 C4
Downs The IP11 . . . . . 59 A1
Drake Cl IP14 . . . . 6 A2
Drake Sq S IP3 . . . . . 38 B2
Drapers Cl 1 IP7. . . . . 51 B3
Draymans Way IP3 . . 37 B3
Drift Cl IP6. . . . . 11 A2
Drift The
Ipswich IP3 . . . . 38 C1

Drift The *continued*
Ipswich IP4 . . . . 30 A2
24 Martlesham Heath
IP5 . . . . 4 A3
Driftway The IP4 . . . . 30 B2
Drive The IP5. . . . . 4 B3
Drover's Ct IP11. . . . . 58 B4
Drury Rd IP6 . . . . 16 B4
Drybridge Hill IP12 . . 14 C4
Dryden Rd IP1. . . . . . . 20 A3
Duckamere IP8 . . . . . 18 A1
Dukes Cl IP11 . . . . 61 A2
Duke's Meadow
IP12 . . . . 14 B3
Duke's Pk IP12 . . . . . 14 B2
Duke St
Hadleigh IP7. . . . . 51 A2
Ipswich IP3 . . . . 37 B4
Dumbarton Rd 3
IP4 . . . . 22 C1
Dumfries Rd 2 IP4. . . 22 C1
Dunlin Rd IP2 . . . . 35 B2
Dunlop Rd IP2 . . . . . . 27 C2
Dunn Cl IP7 . . . . 51 B2
Dunton Gr IP7 . . . . . . 51 B1
Durrant Rd IP7 . . . . . 51 A4
Durrant View IP5 . . . . 33 B3
Dyer Ct IP7. . . . . 51 C2
Dyke St IP1 . . . . 66 B3

E
Eagles Cl IP11. . . . . . . 63 C4
Eagle St IP4. . . . . 67 C2
Eagle Way IP5. . . . . . . 4 A3
Earls Cl IP11 . . . . 61 A2
EAST BERGHOLT. . . 54 B2
East Bergholt CE Prim
Sch CO7. . . . . 54 A3
East Bergholt High Sch
CO7. . . . . 54 C3
Eastcliff IP11. . . . . 61 B3
Eastern Cl IP14 . . . . . 39 C4
Eastgate Sh Ctr IP4 . . 66 C3
Eastland Ct IP11. . . . . 59 A3
East Lawn IP14 . . . . . 30 C4
Eastward Pl IP14 . . . . . 6 C3
Eaton Cl IP11. . . . . . . 58 C3
Eaton Gdns IP11. . . . . 63 B2
Eccles Rd IP2 . . . . . . 35 A2
Eddowes Rd 6 IP6 . . . 2 C3
Eden Rd IP4. . . . . 30 B1
Edgar Ave IP11 . . . . . . 9 A3
Edgecomb Rd IP14 . . . 9 A3
Edgefield Ave CO11. . . 56 A2
Edinburgh Cl IP11. . . . 7 B2
Edinburgh Gdns IP6 . . 2 C3
Edmonton Cl IP5 . . . . 32 A3
Edmonton Rd IP5. . . . 32 A3
Edward Cl IP11 . . . . . 27 C4
Edward Fitzgerald Ct
IP12 . . . . 12 A2
Edwin Ave IP12 . . . . . 12 B3
Edwin Panks Rd IP7 . . 51 B3
Edwin Terr IP12 . . . . . 12 B2
Egglestone Cl IP2 . . . 35 C1
Eldred Cl IP1 . . . . 27 A4
Eliot Way 4 IP14 . . . . . 6 B4
Elizabeth Way
Felixstowe IP11 . . . . . . 63 A3
Stowmarket IP14 . . . . . . 7 B2
Ellenbrook Gn IP2. . . 35 A1
Ellenbrook Rd
Ipswich IP2 . . . . 35 A1
Pinewood IP9 . . . . 43 B4
Elliott St IP1 . . . . 28 A2
Elm Cl CO11 . . . . 55 B4
Elmcroft La IP11 . . . . 60 C3
Elmcroft Rd IP1 . . . . . 20 A2
Elmdale Dr CO11 . . . . 56 C2
Elmers La IP5 . . . . . . 33 A3
Elm Est CO7 . . . . 54 B3
Elm Gdns IP1. . . . . . . 58 C3
Elmham Dr IP10 . . . . . 48 B4
Elmhurst Dr IP3 . . . . . 37 C3
Elm La IP9 . . . . 52 B3

Elm Rd
East Bergholt CO7 . . . . 54 B3
Ipswich IP5 . . . . 31 C3
Stowmarket IP14 . . . . . . 6 C2
Wickham Market
IP13 . . . . 53 A3
Elmsett Cl IP14 . . . . . . 9 C3
Elm St IP1 . . . . 66 B3
Elsmere Rd IP1. . . . . . 28 C4
Elton Pk IP2. . . . . 27 A2
Ely Rd
5 Claydon IP6. . . . . . . 2 C3
Ipswich IP4 . . . . 21 C1
Emerald Cl IP5 . . . . . . 32 C4
Emlen St IP1 . . . . 66 A3
Emmanuel Cl IP2. . . . 35 C2
Emmerson Way IP7. . 51 A4
Emperor Circ IP3. . . . 46 C4
Ennerdale Cl 2
IP11 . . . . 61 A2
Epsom Dr IP1 . . . . 20 A4
Ernleigh Rd IP4 . . . . . 30 B2
Erskine Rd CO11. . . . . 56 C3
Essex Way IP3. . . . . . 39 B1
Estuary Dr IP11. . . . . . 61 A3
Europa Way IP1 . . . . . 27 A4
Euro Ret Pk IP3 . . . . . 39 B1
Eustace Rd IP1. . . . . . 27 B4
Euston Ave IP4 . . . . . 31 C2
Euston Ct 4 IP11. . . . . 61 A3
Everton Cres IP1 . . . . 19 C1
Evesham Cl 7 IP2. . . . 36 A2
Exeter Rd
9 Claydon IP6. . . . . . . 2 C3
Felixstowe IP11 . . . . . . 59 C1
Ipswich IP3 . . . . 38 B4
Exmoor Rd IP11 . . . . . 59 C2

F
Factory La CO11 . . . . . 55 A2
Fagbury Rd IP11. . . . . 62 A4
Fairbairn Ave 1
IP5 . . . . 33 A3
Fairfax Gdns IP6 . . . . 11 B2
Fairfield Ave IP11 . . . . 60 C4
Fairfield Hill IP7 . . . . . 7 A2
Fairfield Inf Sch
IP11 . . . . 60 A1
Fairfield Rd IP3 . . . . . 38 A2
Fairlight Cl 2 IP4 . . . . 22 A1
Fairways The IP4 . . . . 31 B1
Falcon St
Felixstowe IP11 . . . . . . 59 B2
Ipswich IP1 . . . . 67 B2
FALKENHAM IP10 . . . . 5 C3
Falkenham Rd IP10. . . 5 C3
Falklands Dr 8
CO11. . . . . 56 C3
Falmouth Cl IP5 . . . . . 32 B2
Faraday Rd IP3. . . . . . 29 C1
Farina Cl IP7 . . . . 27 C3
Farlingaye High Sch
IP12 . . . . 12 A2
Farlingayes IP12 . . . . 12 B3
Farriers Cl 15 IP5. . . . . 4 A3
Farrier's Rd IP14 . . . . . 8 C3
Farriers Went IP11 . . . 59 A3
Farthing Rd IP1 . . . . . 26 C3
Farthing Rd Ind Est
IP1 . . . . 26 C3
Farthings Went IP9. . . 52 C4
Faulkeners Way
IP11 . . . . 58 C3
Fawley Cl IP4 . . . . 30 C3
Fayrefield Rd IP12. . . . 13 A3
Feathers Field 3
IP11 . . . . 59 A1
Felaw St IP2 . . . . 67 C1
Felix Cl IP5. . . . . 32 B3
Felix Rd
Felixstowe IP11 . . . . . . 64 B4
Ipswich IP3 . . . . 38 C2
FELIXSTOWE IP11. . . . 63 B4

Felixstowe General
Hospl IP11 . . . . 64 B4
Felixstowe Leisure Ctr
IP11 . . . . 63 C3
Felixstowe Mus ★
IP11 . . . . 65 A1
Felixstowe Rd
Ipswich IP3 . . . . 37 C4
8 Martlesham IP5 . . . . 4 A3
Felixstowe Sta IP11 . . 60 A1
Fellbrigg Ave IP5. . . . 31 C2
Felnor Wlk IP11. . . . . . 64 B3
Felsham Ct IP14 . . . . . 9 C3
Fenbridge La CO7 . . . . 54 A1
Fen Meadow IP11 . . . 58 C4
Fenn Cl IP14 . . . . 9 A3
Fentons Way IP5 . . . . 32 C3
Fen Wlk IP12. . . . . 15 A4
Ferguson Way IP5. . . . 32 B4
Ferndown Rd 3
IP11 . . . . 60 C2
Fernhayes Cl IP2 . . . . 36 A3
Fernhill Cl IP12. . . . . . 12 C3
Ferry La IP11 . . . . 62 C3
Ferry Quay IP12 . . . . . 15 B4
Ferry Rd IP11 . . . . 61 A3
Fiddlers Hill CO3 . . . . 65 A1
Fiddlers La CO7 . . . . . 54 B3
Field Fuller's IP6 . . . . 21 B4
Fife Rd IP4. . . . . 22 B1
Finbars Wlk IP4 . . . . . 29 C1
Finborough Cl IP4. . . . 31 C2
Finborough Rd IP14 . . . 6 B2
Finchley Rd IP4 . . . . . 29 B2
Finney's Drift IP10. . . 48 C1
Fir Cl IP13. . . . . 53 B3
Fircroft Rd IP1 . . . . . . 20 A2
Firecrest Dr 2 IP4. . . . 7 C3
Firefly Way 1 IP3 . . . . 46 C4
Firmin Cl IP1. . . . . 28 A2
Fir Tree Rise IP8 . . . . 34 C2
Fishbane Cl 9 IP3. . . . 46 A4
Fishers The IP5. . . . . . 25 C3
Fitzgerald Cl CO11. . . 56 A3
Fitzgerald Rd
Bramford IP8 . . . . 18 A1
Woodbridge IP12 . . . . 12 C2
Fitzmaurice Rd IP3. . . 38 B3
Fitzroy St IP1. . . . . . . 66 B3
Fitzwilliam Cl
Ipswich IP2 . . . . 35 C2
6 Woodbridge IP12 . . 14 C4
Flatford Cl IP11 . . . . . . 9 B3
Fleetwood Ave IP11 . . 60 B1
Fleetwood Rd IP11. . . 60 B1
Fletcher Cl 3 IP6 . . . . . 2 B3
Fletcher Rd IP3 . . . . . 38 A1
Fletchers La IP5. . . . . 33 B4
Flindell Dr IP8 . . . . . . 18 A2
Flint Cl IP2. . . . . 36 B2
Flordon Rd IP6. . . . . . 11 B3
Foden Ave IP1. . . . . . . 18 C2
Fonnereau Rd IP1 . . . 66 B3
Ford Cl IP14 . . . . 9 B4
Fordham Pl 4 IP4. . . . 31 C1
Ford View Rd IP14 . . . . 9 B4
Fore Hamlet IP3. . . . . 29 B1
Fore St IP14 . . . . 67 C2
Forester Cl 9 IP8 . . . . 43 B4
Foresters Wlk 6 IP6 . . 2 B2
Forest La 3 IP5 . . . . . . 4 A2
Forfar Cl
2 Ipswich IP4. . . . . . . 22 B1
Ipswich IP4 . . . . 30 B4
Foundation St IP4. . . . 67 B2
Foundry La IP11. . . . . . 67 B2
Fountains Rd IP2. . . . . 36 A3
Foxburrow Rd 6
IP3 . . . . 39 C1
Fox Cl IP11 . . . . 7 A2
Foxglove Ave IP6 . . . . 11 A4
Foxglove Cres IP3 . . . 39 B1
Foxgrove Gdns IP11 . . 60 C1
Foxgrove La IP11. . . . . 60 C1

Foxhall Cl CO7........ 54 B4
Foxhall Fields CO7.... 54 B3
Foxhall Rd
　Foxhall IP10 .... 4 A1
　Ipswich IP3 .... 29 C1
Foxhall Stadium IP4.. 32 A1
Fox Lea IP5 .... 33 B4
Foxtail Rd IP3 ...... 46 A4
Foxwood Cres IP4 ... 31 C1
Frampton Rd IP3 .... 46 A4
Franciscan Way IP1 .. 67 B2
Francis Cl IP5 .... 33 B4
Franklin Rd IP3 ..... 38 B2
Fraser Rd
　Bramford IP8 .... 18 B2
　Ipswich IP1 .... 27 C3
Freehold Rd
　Ipswich IP4 .... 30 A2
　Needham Market IP6.. 10 C4
Freeman Ave 4 IP6 ... 3 B4
Freeman Cl IP7....... 51 A4
Free Rodwell Ho
　CO11................ 57 B3
Friars IP9 .... 52 C2
Friars Bridge Rd
　IP1 .... 67 A2
Friars Cl 7 IP11...... 61 A2
Friars Ct IP12 ...... 13 B3
Friars Rd IP7 .... 50 C3
Friars St IP1 .... 67 B2
Friends Wlk IP3 ..... 46 A4
Fritillary Cl 8 IP8 ... 43 B4
Fritton Cl IP2....... 36 A1
Frobisher Rd IP3 .... 37 B1
Frog Hall La IP7 ..... 51 C3
Front Rd IP3 .... 47 A4
Fuchsia La IP4 ...... 30 A1
Fullers Cl 2 IP7...... 51 B3
Furness Cl IP2 ...... 43 C4
Fynn Rd IP12........ 14 B3

G

Gaell Cres 5 IP7..... 51 A2
GAINSBOROUGH
　Ipswich IP3 .... 37 C1
　Ipswich IP3 .... 46 B4
Gainsborough Ctr
　IP3 .... 46 B4
Gainsborough Dr
　CO11................ 56 B3
Gainsborough La
　IP3 .... 45 C4
Gainsborough Rd
　Felixstowe IP11 ..... 64 A4
　Ipswich IP4 .... 66 C4
　Stowmarket IP14 ..... 6 B2
Gallows Hill IP14 .... 50 B4
Galway Ave IP1 ...... 19 B1
Gandish Cl CO7....... 54 C1
Gannet Rd IP2....... 35 B3
Garden Field 2
　IP11 .... 59 B1
Garfield Cl IP11 ..... 63 C3
Garfield Rd IP11 .... 63 C3
Garrick Way IP11 .... 20 A3
Garrison La IP11 .... 63 C4
Garrods IP9......... 52 C3
Gascoigne Dr 3 IP6... 3 B4
Gasfield 14 CO11 ..... 56 C3
Gaston End CO7 ..... 54 B3
Gaston St CO7....... 54 B3
Gatacre Rd IP1 ..... 28 A3
Gaye St IP1 .... 66 A3
Gayfer Ave IP5 ..... 33 C4
Gaymers La IP11 .... 58 B4
　Gdn Room The *
　IP6 .... 11 A3
Generals Mews 12
　IP11 .... 59 A1
Geneva Rd IP1 ...... 66 A4
George Frost Cl IP4.. 66 C4
George St IP7 .... 51 B3
Geralds Ave IP4 ..... 30 A1

Giffords Pl IP4 ...... 31 C2
Gilbert Cl IP6 .... 10 C3
Gippeswyk Ave IP2 ... 36 A4
Gippeswyk Rd IP2 .... 67 A1
Gipping Pl IP14....... 7 A3
Gipping Rd IP6 ...... 2 B3
Gippingstone Rd
　IP8 .... 18 A1
Gipping Way
　Bramford IP8......... 18 B2
　Sproughton IP8 ...... 26 B2
　Stowmarket IP14 ..... 7 A3
Gipsy La IP6......... 10 C4
Girton Cl IP12 ...... 14 B4
Girton Way IP2...... 35 C1
Gladstone Rd
　Ipswich IP3 .... 29 C1
　6 Woodbridge IP12 .. 12 C1
Glamorgan Rd IP2.... 36 B1
Glanville Pl IP5...... 32 B2
Glanville Rd IP7 ..... 51 B1
Glastonbury Cl IP2 .. 35 C1
Glebe Cl IP8......... 26 B2
Glebe End IP9....... 52 C4
Glebe Way 1 IP6...... 2 C3
Glemham Dr IP4 ..... 39 C4
Glemsford Cl IP11 ... 63 A3
Glemsford Rd IP14 ... 9 B4
Glenavon Rd IP4 .... 31 A3
Glencoe Rd IP4...... 22 C1
Gleneagles Cl 1
　IP11 .... 60 C2
Gleneagles Dr IP4.... 31 A1
Glenfield Ave IP11 ... 60 A2
Glenhurst Ave IP4 ... 30 B4
Gloster Rd IP5 ...... 4 A3
Gloucester Rd IP3.... 38 A2
Gobbitts Yd IP12..... 15 B4
Godbold Cl 3 IP5..... 33 A3
Goddard Rd IP1 ..... 18 C3
Goddard Rd E IP1 ... 19 A3
Godfrey's Wood
　IP12 .... 12 C3
Goldcrest Rd IP2 .... 34 C3
Goldsmith Rd IP1..... 19 B3
Golf Rd IP11......... 61 A1
Gonville Cl 1 IP12 ... 14 C4
Goodall Terr IP15 .... 33 B4
Goodman Gr IP5 ..... 33 B3
Goodwood Cl IP1..... 20 B4
Gordon Rd
　California IP4 .... 30 A2
　Ipswich IP4 .... 30 A3
Goring Rd IP4 .... 30 C2
Gorsehayes IP2 ..... 36 B3
Gorseland Prim Sch
　IP5 .... 33 C4
Gorse Rd IP3 .... 38 B2
Gosford Way IP11 .... 60 C2
Gostling Pl IP5....... 33 B4
Gowers Cl IP5 ...... 33 B3
Gower St IP2 .... 67 B1
Gowle Rd IP14 ...... 6 C4
Goyfield Ave IP11 .... 63 C4
Graften Way IP11 .... 67 A2
Grafton Way IP1 ..... 67 B2
Graham Ave IP1 ..... 28 B4
Graham Rd
　Felixstowe IP11 ...... 59 C1
　Ipswich IP1 .... 66 A4
Granary The IP7 ..... 51 B2
Grange Cl
　Felixstowe IP11 ...... 59 B1
　Ipswich IP5 .... 33 C4
Grange Ct IP12...... 13 A2
Grange Farm Ave
　IP11 .... 59 A1
Grange La IP5....... 33 B4
Grange Prim Sch
　IP11 .... 63 A4
Grange Rd
　Felixstowe IP11 ...... 63 A3
　Ipswich IP4 .... 30 A3
Grantchester Pl IP5 .. 32 A4
Grantham Cres IP2 ... 67 A1
Granville Rd IP11 .... 63 C3
Granville St IP1 ..... 66 A3

Grasmere Ave 5
　IP11 .... 61 A2
Grayling Rd 7 IP8.... 43 B4
Gray's Orch IP10 .... 5 C3
GREAT BLAKENHAM
　IP6 .... 2 B3
Great Colman St
　IP4 .... 66 C3
Great Eastern Sq
　IP11 .... 60 A1
Great Field IP11 ..... 58 C4
Great Gipping St
　IP1 .... 67 A2
Great Tufts IP9 ..... 52 C3
Great Whip St IP2 ... 67 B1
Grebe Cl
　Ipswich IP2 .... 35 B2
　Stowmarket IP14 ..... 6 A2
Greenfinch Ave IP2... 35 A3
Green La
　3 Martlesham IP12 ... 4 A4
　Pettistree IP13....... 53 C2
　Tuddenham St Martin
　IP6 .... 22 C4
Green Man Way
　IP12 .... 13 A2
Green Oak Glade
　IP8 .... 43 A4
Greensmill CO11...... 56 B4
Greenspire Gr IP8 .... 34 B2
Greens The IP4....... 39 C4
Green The
　Hadleigh IP7......... 51 B3
　Mistley CO11 .... 57 B3
Greenways Cl IP1 .... 28 B4
GREENWICH IP3 ..... 37 B1
Greenwich Bsns Pk
　IP3 .... 37 B2
Greenwich Cl IP3 .... 37 B2
Greenwich Rd IP3.... 37 A2
Gresley Gdns 3 IP2 .. 36 C3
Gretna Gdns 1 IP4 ... 22 B1
Greyfriars
　Ipswich IP1 .... 67 A2
　Woodbridge IP12...... 14 B4
Grey Friars Rd IP1.... 67 B2
Grimston La IP11...... 5 A1
Grimwade Cl CO11.... 56 B3
Grimwade St IP4 ..... 67 C2
Grinstead Gdns IP6... 11 B1
GRINSTEAD HILL
　IP6 .... 11 B1
Grinstead Hill IP6 ... 11 B1
Grosvenor Cl IP4 .... 29 B4
Grove Gdns IP12..... 12 A2
Grove; Henley Rd The
　IP1 .... 20 C2
Grove Hill IP8 .... 42 C3
Grove La IP4 .... 29 B1
Grove Rd
　Brantham CO11........ 55 B3
　Felixstowe IP11 ...... 60 A2
　Woodbridge IP13...... 12 A2
Grove The
　12 Martlesham Heath
　IP5 .... 4 A3
　Stowmarket IP14 ..... 7 B1
　5 Woodbridge IP12 .. 13 A2
Grove Wlk IP8....... 43 A4
Gulpher Bsns Pk
　IP11 .... 59 C4
Gulpher Rd IP11...... 59 B2
Gusford Prim Sch
　IP2 .... 35 A1
Guston Gdns IP10 ... 5 C3
Guthrum Rd IP7...... 51 A4
Gwendoline Rd IP4... 39 B4
Gymnasium St IP1... 66 A3

H

Hackney Rd IP12..... 13 A2
Hackney's Cnr IP6.... 2 A3
Hackney Terr IP12 ... 13 A2
HADLEIGH IP7 .... 51 C2
　Hadleigh Guildhall *
　IP7 .... 51 A2

Hadleigh High Sch
　IP7 .... 51 C2
Hadleigh Prim Sch
　IP7 .... 51 A2
Hadleigh Rd
　East Bergholt CO7 .... 54 A3
　Ipswich IP2 .... 27 B2
Hadleigh Rd Ind Est
　IP2 .... 27 C2
Hadleigh Swimming
　Pool IP7 .... 51 A3
Hale Cl IP2.......... 35 A2
Halesowen Cl IP2 ... 43 C4
Halford Ct 6 IP8..... 34 C2
Halifax Prim Sch
　IP2 .... 36 A2
Halifax Rd IP2....... 36 B2
Hall Farm Cl IP12 ... 13 A4
Hall Farm Rd IP12 ... 13 A4
Hall Field 1 IP11..... 59 B1
Halliwell Rd IP4 ..... 30 B2
Hall La IP6 .... 17 A4
Hall Pond Way IP11.. 59 A1
Hall Rd
　Foxhall IP10 .... 41 B4
　Little Bealings IP5 .... 25 B2
　Stowmarket IP14 ..... 6 B4
Halls Drift IP5....... 32 B2
Halton Cres IP3 ..... 38 C1
Hamblin Rd IP12 .... 12 C1
Hamblin Wlk IP12 ... 12 C1
Hamilton Gdns IP11 .. 64 A3
Hamilton Rd
　Felixstowe IP11 ...... 64 A4
　Ipswich IP3 .... 38 B3
Hamilton St 6 IP11 .. 59 B1
Hamilton Way IP14 ... 7 A3
Hampton Rd IP11..... 27 C3
Handford Cut IP1..... 28 A2
Handford Hall Prim Sch
　IP1 .... 28 A2
Handford Rd IP1 ..... 66 A3
Hardwick Cl IP4...... 31 B1
Hardy Cl CO11....... 55 A2
Hardy Cres IP1 ...... 19 C4
Harebell Rd IP2...... 35 C4
Hargrave Ave IP6..... 11 A1
Harland St IP2 ...... 36 C3
Harrier Cl IP3 .... 38 B1
Harrison Gr IP5 ..... 32 C4
Harrow Cl IP4........ 30 A1
Hartest Way IP14 .... 9 C3
Hartley St IP2 ...... 67 B1
Hartree Way IP5 ..... 33 B3
Harvesters Way
　2 Martlesham Heath
　IP5 .... 4 A2
　Martlesham IP5 ...... 33 C2
Harvey Cl CO11...... 56 B3
Harvey's La IP6...... 3 A4
Hasketon Rd IP13 .... 12 A2
Haskins Wlk IP5 ..... 33 B3
Haslemere Dr IP4 ... 29 B3
Hatfield Rd IP3 ..... 38 A3
Haughgate Cl IP12 ... 12 B2
Haugh La IP12....... 12 B2
Haughley Dr IP4..... 31 C2
Hauliers Rd IP11 .... 63 A2
Haven Cl IP11....... 63 A4
Havens The IP10..... 47 B3
Havergate Rd 3
　IP3 .... 47 A4
Hawbridge IP9....... 52 B4
Hawes St IP2........ 67 C1
Hawke Rd IP3 .... 37 B1
Hawker Dr IP5 ...... 4 A3
Hawkes La IP11 ..... 59 A2
Hawks Mill St IP6 ... 11 A3
Hawthorn Dr IP2..... 35 A2
Hawthorn Pl IP12..... 12 A2
Hayhill Rd IP4....... 29 B3
Hayman Rd IP3....... 37 C1
Haywards Fields
　IP5 .... 33 A4
Hazelcroft Rd IP1 ... 20 B2
Hazel Dr IP3 .... 39 B1
Hazel Rise IP6....... 16 B4

Hazlitt Rd 6 IP1 ..... 20 A3
Headingham Cl 13
　IP2 .... 36 A2
Heath Cl CO7........ 54 C3
Heath Ct 12 IP11..... 5 B1
Heather Ave IP3 ..... 38 C2
Heather Cl IP5....... 33 C2
Heathercroft Rd IP1.. 20 A3
Heatherhayes IP2.... 36 A3
Heathfield IP5....... 33 C2
Heathfield Mews
　IP5 .... 33 C2
Heathfields IP11..... 5 B2
Heathgate Piece
　IP11 .... 58 C4
Heath La IP4........ 30 C1
Heathlands Pk IP4.... 39 B4
Heath Prim Sch IP5 .. 32 B2
Heath Rd
　East Bergholt CO7 .... 54 C3
　Ipswich IP4 .... 30 C1
Heathside Specl Sch
　IP4 .... 31 A2
Heath View IP5...... 32 A2
Helena Rd IP3....... 37 B4
Helston Cl IP5....... 32 B3
Henderson Cl IP8 .... 18 A1
Hengrave Cl 11 IP2 ... 36 A2
HENLEY IP6.......... 3 B4
Henley Ave IP1...... 20 B3
Henley Ct CO11...... 56 B3
Henley Prim Sch IP6 .. 3 C3
Henley Rd
　Henley IP1 .... 3 B3
　Ipswich IP1 .... 66 B4
Henniker Rd IP1..... 26 C4
Henry Rd IP3........ 38 B1
Henslow Rd IP4 ..... 30 B1
Henstead Gdns IP3 ... 38 A2
Herbert Rd IP5 ...... 33 B4
Hereford Dr 14 IP6 ... 2 C3
Heron Cl IP4......... 6 A2
Heron Rd IP2........ 35 B3
Hervey St IP4........ 66 C4
Hessett Cl IP14...... 9 C3
Hexham Cl 3 IP2 .... 36 A2
Heywood Cl IP2...... 35 A1
Hibbard Rd IP8...... 18 C2
High Beach IP11...... 64 C4
Highfield App 1
　IP1 .... 19 C1
Highfield Dr IP6...... 16 C4
Highfield Rd
　Felixstowe IP11 ...... 64 A4
　Ipswich IP1 .... 19 C2
Highfields Prim Sch
　CO11................ 56 B3
High Hall Cl 2 IP11 ... 5 B1
Highlands Cl IP6 .... 10 C3
Highlands Rd IP7..... 51 B2
High Rd
　Felixstowe IP11 ...... 58 B4
　Trimley St Martin IP11.. 5 A2
High Rd E IP11....... 60 B1
High Rd W IP11...... 59 C1
High Row Field IP11.. 60 C1
　High St Ex Gall *
　IP1 .... 66 B3
High St
　Felixstowe IP11 ...... 59 B2
　Hadleigh IP7......... 51 A3
　Ipswich IP1 .... 66 B3
　Manningtree CO11..... 56 C3
　Mistley CO11 .... 57 B2
　Needham Market IP6.. 11 A3
　Pettistree IP13....... 53 B2
　Sproughton IP8 ...... 26 A2
　Wickham Market
　IP13 .... 53 B4
High View Rd IP4 .... 19 A1
Hillary Cl IP4........ 30 A1
Hillcrest App IP8 .... 18 B2
Hill Farm Rd IP6..... 24 B4
Hill House La IP6 .... 10 C4
Hill House Rd IP4..... 29 B1
Hill Rise IP14........ 9 A3
Hillside IP14......... 9 A3

Hillside Com Prim Sch
IP2 . . . . .36 C3
Hillside Cres **5** IP3. . .38 B3
Hill View Bsns Pk
IP6 . . . . .16 C2
Hilly Fields IP12 . . . . . .14 C4
Hilton Cl CO11. . . . . . . .56 C3
Hilton Rd
Ipswich IP3 . . . . .38 C1
Martlesham Heath IP5. . . .4 A3
Hines Rd IP3 . . . . .38 A4
Hintesham Cl **6** IP4. .31 C1
Hintlesham Cl **8**
IP14 . . . . .9 B3
Hintlesham Dr IP11. . . .63 A4
Histon Cl IP5 . . . . .31 C3
Hockney Gdns IP3. . . .46 A4
Hodgkinson Rd IP11. . .62 C3
Hogarth Rd IP3. . . . . . .37 C1
Hogarth Sq IP3. . . . . . .38 A1
Holbecks La IP7. . . . . . .50 C1
Holbrook Cres IP11. . . .63 A4
Holbrook Rd IP3 . . . . . .37 C1
Holcombe Cres IP2. . . .35 A2
Holden Cl IP2 . . . . .37 A3
Holfen Cl IP12. . . . . .4 B4
Holkham Cl **7** IP4. . .31 C1
Holland Rd
Felixstowe IP11 . . . . . . .63 C3
Ipswich IP4 . . . . .29 C2
Hollingsworth Rd **3**
IP14 . . . . .7 B1
Holly Blue Cl **10** IP8. .43 B4
Hollybush Dr IP11 . . . .61 A3
Holly Cl IP3 . . . . .39 C1
Hollycroft Cl **5** IP1. . .20 A3
Holly End IP5 . . . . .33 C2
Holly La
Belstead IP8. . . . . .42 C3
Rushmere St Andrew
IP5 . . . . .23 B2
Holly Rd IP1. . . . . .66 A4
Holst Mead IP14. . . . . . .6 C4
Holt's La IP6 . . . . .11 C4
Holyrood Cl IP2 . . . . . .35 C1
Holywells Cl IP3. . . . . . .37 B4
Holywells High Sch
IP3 . . . . .38 C1
Holy Wells Rd IP3 . . . .37 B3
Homefield IP9. . . . . . . .52 C2
Homer Cl IP1. . . . . .19 C4
Honeycroft CO11. . . . . .56 A2
Honeysuckle Gdns
IP2 . . . . .35 B4
Hood Dr IP6. . . . . .2 A3
Hood Rd IP3 . . . . .37 B1
Hook La IP7. . . . . .51 C1
Hope Cres IP12. . . . . . .12 C2
Horsham Ave IP3. . . . . .39 A3
Hossack Rd IP3 . . . . . . .46 A4
Houghton Pl **5** IP4. .31 C1
Howard St IP14. . . . . . .30 B3
Howards Way IP5. . . . . .33 A4
Howe Ave IP3 . . . . .38 C3
Howlett Cl IP5. . . . . . . .33 B3
Hoxne Cl **5** IP14 . . . . .9 B3
Hugh Ager Cl **5** IP14. .9 A3
Hughes Stanton Way
CO11. . . . . .56 A3
Humber Doucy La
IP4 . . . . .22 A2
Humber Doucy Sports
Ctr IP4. . . . . .31 A3
Hunt Cl IP14 . . . . .9 A3
Hunter Rd **2** IP2. . . .46 C4
Hunters End IP11. . . . .58 C3
Hunters Ride **21** IP5 . .4 A3
Hurricane Pl IP13 . . . . .38 B1
Hurstlea Cl IP6. . . . . . .11 A3
Hurstlea Rd IP6 . . . . . .10 C3
Hutland Rd IP4. . . . . . .29 C3
Hyem's La IP11. . . . . . .60 B3
Hyntle Cl IP2. . . . . .27 B1

I

Ickworth Cres IP4 . . . .31 C1
Ickworth Ct **2** IP11. . .62 C3
Iliffe Way IP14. . . . . .7 A2
Inkerman Cl **4** IP7 . .51 A3
Inkerman Terr **3**
IP7 . . . . .51 A3
Innes End **4** IP8 . . . .34 C2
Inverness Rd IP4 . . . . . .22 A2
IPSWICH IP1 . . . . .66 B3
Ipswich Hospl IP4. . . . .30 C3
Ipswich Mus * IP1. . . .66 B3
Ipswich Prep Sch
IP1 . . . . .66 B4
Ipswich Rd
Claydon IP6. . . . . .16 B4
Hadleigh IP7. . . . . .51 C4
Nacton IP10. . . . . .48 A1
Needham Market IP6. . . .11 B2
Newbourne IP12 . . . . . . .4 C1
Stowmarket IP14. . . . . . . .9 B4
Woodbridge IP12. . . . . . .14 C3
Ipswich Sch IP1. . . . . . .66 B4
Ipswich St IP14. . . . . . . .7 A2
Ipswich Sta IP2 . . . . . . .67 A1
Ipswich Transport
Mus * IP3. . . . . .38 C2
Ireland Rd IP3. . . . . . . .37 C1
Iris Cl IP2. . . . . .27 C1
Irlam Rd IP2 . . . . .35 A2
Ironside Wlk CO11. . . . .56 B3
Ivry St IP1. . . . . .66 A4

J

Jack's Gn Rd IP6 . . . . . .11 B4
Jack's La IP14. . . . . .8 A2
Jackson Cl IP5 . . . . .33 C3
Jackson Way IP6 . . . . . .11 A2
Jacob Way **11** IP12 . . .12 C1
James Boden Cl **7**
IP11 . . . . .59 B1
Jasmine Cl
9 Felixstowe IP11 . . . . .5 B1
Ipswich IP2 . . . . .35 C3
Jeavons La IP5. . . . . . . .33 B3
Jefferies Rd IP1. . . . . . .29 B2
Jenners Cl **1** IP12. . .13 A2
Jermyns IP1. . . . . .52 C4
Jewell View IP5 . . . . . . .33 A4
Jimmy's Farm * IP9. .43 B1
John Russell Gall *
IP3 . . . . .67 C2
Johnson Cl **5** IP2. . .36 C3
John St IP3 . . . . .37 B4
John Swain Cl IP6. . . . .10 C3
Jordayn Rise IP7. . . . . .51 B3
Josselyns The IP11 . . . .58 B4
Jovian Way IP1. . . . . . . .27 B4
Jubilee Ave IP14 . . . . . .9 A4
Jubilee Cl
11 Claydon IP6. . . . . . . .2 C3
11 Felixstowe IP11 . . . . .5 B1
Jubilee End CO11. . . . . .56 B4
June Ave IP1. . . . . .20 B2
Jupiter Rd IP4. . . . . . . .30 B3

K

Karen Cl IP1 . . . . .20 B1
Keating Cl CO11. . . . . . .56 A3
Keats Cres IP1 . . . . .19 C3
Keeper's La IP11 . . . . . .58 A3
Kelly Rd IP2. . . . . .27 B1
Kelvedon Dr IP4. . . . . . .31 C1
Kelvin Rd IP4. . . . . .19 C1
Kemball St IP4 . . . . . . .30 A1
Kempsters The IP11 . . .59 A3
Kempton Cl **4** IP1. . .20 A3
Kempton Rd IP1. . . . . . .20 A3
Kemsley Rd IP11 . . . . . .59 C1
Kendal Gn IP11. . . . . . .61 A3
Kennedy Cl IP4. . . . . . . .30 A2
Kennels Rd
Brightwell IP10. . . . . . . .4 A1
Foxhall IP10 . . . . .41 C2

Kensington Rd
Ipswich IP1 . . . . .28 A4
Stowmarket IP14. . . . . . .7 A1
Kentford Rd **5** IP11 . .62 C4
Kent Rd IP14 . . . . .6 C3
Kentwell Cl IP4. . . . . . .39 C4
Kenyon St IP2. . . . . . . .67 B1
Kerridge's Cut CO11 . .57 C3
Kerry Ave IP1 . . . . .19 A1
Kersey Cl IP14. . . . . .9 B3
Kersey Rd IP11. . . . . . . .63 A4
KESGRAVE IP5 . . . . . . .32 C4
Kesgrave High Sch
IP5 . . . . .32 C4
Kesteven Rd IP2. . . . . . .67 A1
Kestrel Rd IP2. . . . . . . .35 A3
Keswick Cl IP11. . . . . . .60 C2
Kettlebaston Way **3**
IP1 . . . . .21 A1
Key St IP3. . . . . .67 C2
Khartoum Rd IP4. . . . . .29 C3
Kidz Kingdom * IP5. . .4 A3
Kildare Ave IP1. . . . . . .19 A2
Kiln Cotts IP14 . . . . .6 C1
Kiln Field **1** IP11. . . .59 A1
Kiln La CO11. . . . . .56 C3
King Edward Ave
IP13 . . . . .53 B4
King Edward Rd IP3 . .38 B3
Kingfisher Ave IP2. . . . .35 A3
Kingfisher Dr IP6. . . . . .2 A3
Kings Ave IP4 . . . . .29 B1
Kingsbury Rd IP11. . . . .58 C3
Kings Cl
Lawford CO11. . . . . .56 B3
Woodbridge IP12. . . . . .14 C4
Kingsfield Ave IP1. . . . .29 A4
Kings Fleet Prim Sch
IP11 . . . . .60 C2
Kings Fleet Rd IP11. . . .63 B3
Kingsgate Dr IP4 . . . . .29 C4
Kingsley Cl **8** IP1 . . .20 A3
Kingsmead Cl **3**
IP14 . . . . .6 C3
Kingsmead Rd IP14. . . .6 C3
King St
Felixstowe IP11 . . . . . . .59 B2
Ipswich IP1. . . . . .66 B3
KINGSTON IP12 . . . . . .15 A2
Kingston Farm Rd
IP12 . . . . .15 B4
Kingston Rd
Ipswich IP1 . . . . .27 C4
Woodbridge IP12. . . . . .15 B4
Kingsway IP12 . . . . .13 A1
King's Way IP3 . . . . . . .38 B2
King William St **3**
IP6 . . . . .11 A3
Kinross Rd IP4 . . . . . . .22 B1
Kipling Rd IP11. . . . . . .19 C3
Kipling Way IP14 . . . . . .6 B4
Kirby Cl IP4 . . . . .30 A3
Kirby St IP4 . . . . .30 A3
Kirkham Cl **2** IP2 . . .36 A2
KIRTON IP10 . . . . .5 C3
Kirton Rd IP11 . . . . .5 B1
Kitchener Rd IP1 . . . . . .27 C4
Kittiwake Cl IP2 . . . . . .35 B3
Knights Cl
10 Felixstowe IP11. . . . .61 C1
Lawford CO11. . . . . .56 B3
Knightsdale Rd IP1. . . .20 A1
Knights La **5** IP5. . . .33 A3
Knutsford Cl IP8. . . . . .34 C1
Kyson Hill * IP12. . . . .15 A2
Kyson Prim Sch
IP12 . . . . .14 B4

L

Laburnum Cl
Ipswich IP3 . . . . .39 A2
3 Ipswich IP8. . . . . .34 C2
Laburnum Gdns IP5 . .23 B1
Lacewing Cl **13** IP8 . .43 B4
Lacey St IP4 . . . . .29 B2
Lachlan Gn IP12. . . . . . .12 B3

Lackford Pl **7** IP3. . . .46 C4
Lacon Rd **2** IP8. . . . . .18 A2
Lady La
Hadleigh IP7. . . . . .51 B4
Ipswich IP1 . . . . .66 A3
Lady La Ind Est IP7. . . .51 B4
Lady Margaret Gdns
IP12 . . . . .14 B4
Ladywood Rd IP4. . . . . .30 C3
Lagonda Dr IP1 . . . . . . .18 C1
Lake Side IP14 . . . . .6 C2
Lakeside Rd IP2 . . . . . . .35 B2
Lamberts La IP5. . . . . . .23 A2
Lambeth Cl **1** IP1. . .28 A3
Lambourne Rd IP1 . . . .20 B4
Lanark Rd IP4 . . . . .22 B1
Lancaster Dr **8** IP5 . .4 A2
Lancaster Rd IP4 . . . . . .29 B2
Lancaster Way **10** IP6. .2 C4
Lancers The IP12 . . . . . .14 C3
Lancing Ave IP4 . . . . . .30 A4
Landguard Fort *
IP11 . . . . .65 A1
Landguard Nature
Reserve * IP11 . . . . . . .65 A1
Landguard Rd IP11 . . . .65 C4
Landseer Cl IP3 . . . . . . .38 A1
Landseer Rd IP3. . . . . . .37 B2
Lanercost Way IP2 . . . .36 A1
Lane The CO11. . . . . . . .57 B3
Langdale Cl **3** IP11 . .61 A2
Langer Prim Sch
IP11 . . . . .63 B2
Langer Rd IP11. . . . . . . .63 B2
Langford Cl IP14 . . . . . .6 B4
Langley Ave IP11 . . . . . .63 B4
Langley Cl IP11. . . . . . .59 B1
Langstons IP11. . . . . . . .59 A3
Lansdowne Rd
Felixstowe IP11 . . . . . . .60 B2
Ipswich IP4 . . . . .30 A1
Lapwing Rd IP2 . . . . . . .35 A3
Larchcroft Cl IP1. . . . . .20 A2
Larchcroft Rd IP1 . . . . .20 A2
Larchwood Cl IP8 . . . . .26 C1
Largent Gr IP5 . . . . .33 B4
Larkhill Rise IP4. . . . . . .31 B1
Larkhill Way **9** IP11. .59 A1
Lark Rise **23** IP5 . . . . .4 A3
Larkspur Rd IP2 . . . . . .35 C3
Larksway IP11. . . . . .63 A3
Larman Ct CO11. . . . . . .55 A2
La Salle Cl IP2. . . . . . . .36 B3
Lattice Ave IP4 . . . . . . .30 C2
Laud Mews IP3. . . . . . .38 A2
Laud's Cl IP11. . . . . . . .58 B4
Laurel Ave IP5. . . . . . . .32 A3
Laurel Dr **13** IP6. . . . . .2 B3
Laurelhayes IP2. . . . . . .36 A3
Laurel Way **6** IP6 . . .16 B4
Lavender Hill IP2. . . . . .35 C4
Lavenham Rd IP2. . . . . .27 B1
Lavenham Way **4**
IP14 . . . . .9 B3
LAWFORD 56 A2
Lawford CE Prim Sch
CO11. . . . . .56 A1
Lawns The IP4. . . . . . . .30 C4
Lawn Way IP11. . . . . . . .59 B1
Law's Drift IP10 . . . . . . .5 A3
Layham Gdns IP14. . . . .9 C3
Layham Rd IP7 . . . . .51 A1
Leeks Cl IP7. . . . . .51 A4
Leeks Hill IP12 . . . . . . .12 C3
Lee Rd IP3 . . . . .37 C3
Leggatt Dr IP8 . . . . . . .18 A2
Leicester Cl IP2 . . . . . . .35 C1
Leighton Rd IP3 . . . . . . .38 A4
Leighton Sq **8** IP3 . .46 A4
Lely Rd IP3. . . . . .45 C4
Leopold Gdns IP4 . . . . .30 B4
Leopold Rd
Felixstowe IP11 . . . . . . .64 A3
Ipswich IP4 . . . . .30 B3
Leslie Rd IP3. . . . . .38 C1
Letton Cl IP9 . . . . .52 B3

Levington Rd
Felixstowe IP11 . . . . . . .63 B1
Ipswich IP3 . . . . .38 A4
Lewes Cl IP3 . . . . .39 B3
Lidgate Ct **1** IP11 . . .62 C4
Lilac Wlk IP6 . . . . .11 A1
Lime Cl IP13 . . . . .53 A3
Limecroft Cl **1** IP1. . .20 A3
Limekiln Cl **7** IP6. . .16 B4
Lime Kiln Quay IP12 . .13 A1
Lime Kiln Quay Rd
IP12 . . . . .13 A1
Limerick Cl IP1. . . . . . . .19 B2
Limes Ave IP8 . . . . .18 C2
Limes The IP5 . . . . .23 A1
Limetree Cl IP6 . . . . . . .11 B2
Limetree Dr IP3 . . . . . . .39 A2
Lime Tree Pl IP14. . . . . .7 B1
Lincoln Cl IP1 . . . . .20 B3
Lincoln Gdns **8** IP6 . .2 C3
Lincoln Terr IP11 . . . . . .63 C3
Lindbergh Rd IP3. . . . . .38 C1
Linden Cl CO11. . . . . . . .56 A2
Lindisfarne Cl IP2 . . . . .36 A1
Lindsey Rd IP4 . . . . . . .30 C3
Lindsey Way IP11 . . . . . .9 B3
Lingfield Rd IP1 . . . . . . .20 B4
Lingside **1** IP5. . . . . . .4 A2
Link Rd IP9 . . . . .52 B3
Links Ave IP11. . . . . . . .60 B2
Linksfield IP5. . . . . .31 B3
Linksfield Gdns IP5. . . .31 B3
Linnet Rd IP2 . . . . .35 A4
Lion La IP6. . . . . .11 B1
Lion St IP1 . . . . .66 B3
Lister Rd
Hadleigh IP7. . . . . .51 C2
Ipswich IP1 . . . . .19 C1
LITTLE BLAKENHAM
IP8 . . . . .2 A1
Little Gipping St IP1. . .66 B3
Little Gr IP9 . . . . .52 B2
Little Gulls IP9 . . . . .52 A3
Little St John's St **8**
IP12 . . . . .12 C1
Little's Cres IP2 . . . . . . .67 B1
Little Tufts IP9. . . . . . . .52 C3
Little Whip St IP2. . . . . .67 B1
Llewellyn Drift **8**
IP5 . . . . .32 C3
Lloyds Ave IP1. . . . . . . .66 B3
Lloyds The IP5. . . . . . . .32 C3
Locarno Rd **1** IP3 . . .38 B3
Lockington Cl **4**
IP14 . . . . .7 B1
Lockington Cres IP14. . .7 A1
Lockington Rd IP14. . . .7 A1
Lockington Wlk IP14 . . .7 A1
Lockwood Cl **1**
IP12 . . . . .12 C1
Lodge Farm Dr IP11 . .60 C2
Loganberry Rd **4**
IP3 . . . . .46 C3
London Rd
Capel St Mary IP9 . . . . .52 C2
Copdock & Washbrook
IP8 . . . . .34 A1
Ipswich IP1 . . . . .66 A3
Pinewood IP8. . . . . .34 B2
Lone Barn Ct IP1 . . . . . .27 A4
Long Bessels IP7. . . . . . .51 A3
Longcroft IP11 . . . . .59 B2
Long Field IP11 . . . . . . .59 A2
Longfield Rd IP9 . . . . . .52 B4
Long Perry IP9 . . . . .52 C3
Long Rd CO11 . . . . .56 B2
Long St IP3 . . . . .29 B1
Lonsdale Cl IP4 . . . . . . .29 C3
Looe Rd IP11. . . . . .60 C1
Loraine Way IP8. . . . . . .18 A1
Lotus Cl IP1 . . . . .18 C1
Lovetofts Dr IP1. . . . . . .19 A1
Lower Brook St IP4. . . .67 B2
Lower Cres IP6. . . . . . . .2 B4

Lower Dales View Rd
IP1 . . . . 28 A4
Lower Orwell St IP4 . . 67 C2
Lower Rd IP6 . . . . 21 A4
Lower St
Sproughton IP8 . . . . . . 26 A2
Wickham Market
IP13 . . . . 53 B4
Lowry Gdns 6 IP3 . . 46 A4
Lowry Way IP14 . . . . . . 6 B3
Lucena Ct IP14 . . . . 6 C2
Ludbrook Cl IP1 . . . . . . 10 C3
Ludlow Cl IP1 . . . . 20 B4
Luff Meadow IP6 . . . . . 11 A3
Lugano Ave IP12 . . . . . . 4 B3
Lulworth Ave IP3 . . . . . 39 A3
Lummis Vale IP5 . . . . . . 32 C3
Lupin Rd IP2 . . . . 35 B4
Lupin Way IP6 . . . . 11 A1
Lushington Rd CO11 . . 56 B3
Luther Rd IP2 . . . . 67 B1
Lydgate Cl CO11 . . . . . 56 A3
Lydgate Rd IP14 . . . . . . 6 C3
Lyle Cl IP5 . . . . 31 B4
Lyndhurst Ave IP4 . . . . 30 C1
Lynnbrook Cl IP2 . . . . . 11 A1
Lynwood Ave IP11 . . . . 60 B1
Lysander Dr 3 IP3 . . 46 C4

M

MacAulay Rd IP1 . . . . . 19 C3
Mackenzie Dr IP5 . . . . 32 B4
Magdalen Dr IP12 . . . . 14 B3
Magdalene Cl IP2 . . . . 35 C2
Magdalen Rd IP7 . . . . 51 A3
Magingley Cres IP4 . . 31 C2
Magpie Cl 8 IP8 . . . . 34 C2
MAIDENHALL IP2 . . . . 36 B1
Maidenhall App IP2 . . 36 B2
Maidenhall Sports Ctr
IP2 . . . . 36 C2
MAIDENSGRAVE
IP12 . . . . 14 C3
Maiden Way IP7 . . . . . 51 A3
Maidstone Cty Inf Sch
IP11 . . . . 59 B1
Maidstone Rd IP11 . . . 59 B1
Main Rd
Bucklesham IP10 . . . . . 41 C1
Henley IP6 . . . . 3 B4
Ipswich IP5 . . . . 32 A4
Martlesham IP12 . . . . . 14 A1
Tuddenham St Martin
IP6 . . . . 22 B4
Maitland Rd IP6 . . . . . 11 B1
Mallard Way
Ipswich IP2 . . . . 35 C3
Stowmarket IP14 . . . . . 6 A2
Mallowhayes Cl IP2 . . 36 B4
Malmesbury Cl IP2 . . . 36 B4
Malthouse Rd CO11 . . 56 C3
Maltings Mews IP7 . . 51 A2
Maltings Wharf
CO11 . . . . 56 C3
Maltsters Wlk IP14 . . . 8 C3
Malvern Cl IP3 . . . . . . 38 B3
Manchester Rd IP2 . . 35 A4
Mandy Cl IP4 . . . . 30 A2
Mannall Wlk IP5 . . . . . 33 B4
Manning Rd IP11 . . . . 63 B2
Mannington Cl 3
IP4 . . . . 31 C1
MANNINGTREE 57 A3
Manningtree High Sch
CO11 . . . . 56 A2
Manningtree Mus★
CO11 . . . . 56 C3
Manor Rd
Felixstowe IP11 . . . . . . 58 B4
Ipswich IP4 . . . . 29 A4
11 Martlesham Heath
IP5 . . . . 4 A3

Manor Rd continued
Trimley St Martin
IP11 . . . . 65 C4
IP3 . . . . 46 C3
Mansfield Ave IP1 . . . 19 C2
Manthorp Cl IP12 . . . . 13 A4
Manwick Rd IP11 . . . . . 63 B2
Maple Cl IP2 . . . . 36 A3
Maple Gr IP6 . . . . 2 B4
Maples The IP5 . . . . . 31 B4
Marbled White Dr
IP9 . . . . 43 B4
Marcus Rd IP11 . . . . . 61 A1
Margaret Rd 2 IP14 . . 6 C3
Margaret St IP11 . . . . 59 B1
Margate Rd IP3 . . . . . . 38 B3
Marigold Ave IP2 . . . . 35 B3
Marina Gdns IP11 . . . . 63 B2
Market Pl
Hadleigh IP7 . . . . 51 A2
Stowmarket IP14 . . . . . 7 A2
Marlborough Rd
IP4 . . . . 30 A1
Marlow Rd IP1 . . . . . . 19 A1
Marriott's Wlk 5
IP14 . . . . 7 A2
Marshall Cl IP5 . . . . . 32 C4
Marsh La IP11 . . . . 60 C4
Martello La IP11 . . . . . 61 A1
Martinet Gn IP3 . . . . . 38 C1
Martin Rd IP2 . . . . 67 B1
Martinsyde 9 IP5 . . . . 4 A3
MARTLESHAM IP12 . . . 4 A4
Martlesham Beacon Hill
Prim Sch IP12 . . . . . . 4 A4
MARTLESHAM HEATH
IP5 . . . . 4 B2
Martlesham Heath
Control Twr Mus★ 31
IP5 . . . . 4 A3
Martlesham Rd IP13 . . 25 C3
Maryon Rd IP3 . . . . . . 38 B1
Masefield Rd IP14 . . . . 6 B4
Mason Ct 1 IP6 . . . . . 2 B3
Masons Cl IP4 . . . . . . 29 C2
Masterson Gr IP5 . . . . 32 C2
Mather Way IP1 . . . . . 67 C1
Matlock Cl 13 IP8 . . . . 34 C2
Matson Rd IP1 . . . . . . 27 C4
Maude St IP3 . . . . 37 B4
Maudslay Rd IP1 . . . . 18 C2
Maybury Rd IP3 . . . . . 38 B1
Maybush La IP11 . . . . 60 C1
Maycroft Cl 2 IP1 . . . . 20 A3
Mayfield La IP11 . . . . . 4 A2
Mayfield Rd IP4 . . . . . 30 C3
Mayfields 6 IP5 . . . . . 4 A2
Mayfly Cl 12 IP8 . . . . 43 B4
May Rd IP3 . . . . 38 C2
Mead Dr IP5 . . . . 32 C3
Meadow Cl 8 IP11 . . . 5 B1
Meadow Cres IP3 . . . . 39 C1
Meadowlands IP10 . . . 5 B3
Meadow Sh Ctr The
IP14 . . . . 7 A2
Meadowside IP13 . . . . 53 B4
Meadowside Gdns
IP4 . . . . 31 B4
Meadows Way IP7 . . . 51 A3
Meadowvale Cl IP4 . . 29 C4
Meadow View IP6 . . . . 10 C3
Meadway CO11 . . . . . . 56 A2
Medway Rd IP3 . . . . . 37 C2
Melbourne Rd IP4 . . . 31 A3
Melford Cl 8 IP4 . . . . 31 C1
Melford Rd IP14 . . . . . 9 C4
Melford Way IP11 . . . . 62 C3
Mellis Ct 18 IP11 . . . . 59 A1
Melplash Cl IP3 . . . . . 39 B4
Melplash Rd IP3 . . . . . 39 B4
Melrose Gdns IP4 . . . . 30 B4
MELTON IP12 . . . . 13 B4
Melton CP Sch IP12 . . 13 B3
Melton Grange Rd
IP12 . . . . 12 C2
Melton Hill IP12 . . . . . 13 A2

Melton Meadow Rd 4
IP12 . . . . 13 A2
Melton Rd IP12 . . . . . . 13 A2
Melton Sta IP12 . . . . . 13 C3
Melville Rd IP4 . . . . . . 29 C1
Mendip Dr IP5 . . . . . . 31 C2
Meredith Rd IP1 . . . . . 19 B2
Mere Gdns IP4 . . . . . . 39 C4
Meriton Rise IP7 . . . . . 51 C1
Merivale Cl CO11 . . . . 56 B2
Merivale Rd CO11 . . . . 56 A2
Merlin Rd IP2 . . . . 34 C3
Merriam Ct CO11 . . . . . 55 B3
Merrion Cl 12 IP8 . . . 34 C2
Mersey Rd IP3 . . . . . . 37 C2
Michigan Cl IP5 . . . . . 32 B3
Mickfield Mews 16
IP11 . . . . 59 A1
Micklegate Rd IP11 . . 63 B2
Middlefield Rd CO11 . . 57 C2
Middleton Cl IP2 . . . . 35 A2
Mid Suffolk Leisure Ctr
IP14 . . . . 6 B3
Milano Ave IP12 . . . . . 4 B3
Milden Cl 6 IP14 . . . . . 9 B3
Milden Rd IP2 . . . . 27 B1
Mildmay Rd IP3 . . . . . 38 B1
Mill Cl IP11 . . . . 63 A4
Millennium Way IP5 . . 33 B3
Millers Cl
Hadleigh IP7 . . . . 51 B3
Stowmarket IP14 . . . . . 8 C3
Millers Ct 5 IP6 . . . . . 2 B3
Millers Reach CO11 . . 57 C3
Millers View IP1 . . . . . 27 C3
Mill Field IP8 . . . . 18 B2
Millfield Ave IP14 . . . . 6 A4
Millfield Gdns IP4 . . . 30 A3
Mill Hill CO11 . . . . . . 56 B3
MILL HILLS IP12 . . . . 12 C2
Mill La
Bramford IP8 . . . . 18 B1
Combs IP14 . . . . 8 B1
Copdock & Washbrook
IP8 . . . . 34 A1
Felixstowe IP11 . . . . . . 63 C4
9 Great Blakenham
IP6 . . . . 2 B3
Henley IP6 . . . . 3 B4
Manningtree CO11 . . . . 56 C3
Wickham Market
IP13 . . . . 53 B3
Woodbridge IP12 . . . . 12 C1
Mill Piece IP10 . . . . . 48 C2
Mill Pouch IP11 . . . . . 58 C4
Mill Rd IP3 . . . . 39 C1
Mills The IP4 . . . . 31 B4
Mill View Cl IP12 . . . . 12 A1
Milner St IP4 . . . . 29 B2
Milnrow 10 IP8 . . . . . 34 C2
Milton Rd CO11 . . . . . 56 A1
Milton Rd E IP14 . . . . . 7 B2
Milton Rd N 4 IP14 . . . 7 B2
Milton Rd S IP14 . . . . . 7 B2
Milton St IP4 . . . . 30 B3
Minos Way IP1 . . . . . . 27 A4
Minsmere House Hospl
IP4 . . . . 30 C2
MISTLEY 57 B3
Mistley Norman CE
Prim Sch CO11 . . . . . 57 C3
Mistley Place Park★
CO11 . . . . 57 B3
Mistley Sta CO11 . . . . 57 B3
Mistley Towers★
CO11 . . . . 57 B4
Mistley Way IP12 . . . . 12 B2
Mitford Cl IP1 . . . . 20 A4
Mitre Way IP3 . . . . 37 B4
Moat Farm Cl IP4 . . . 29 C4
Mockbeggars Hall★
IP8 . . . . 16 B2
Moffat Ave IP2 . . . . . . 35 A4
Monarch Way IP8 . . . . 43 A4
Monastery Ct IP7 . . . . 51 A4
Monks Cl IP11 . . . . . . 61 A2
Monks Gate IP8 . . . . . 26 A2

Monmouth Cl IP2 . . . . 36 B1
Montague Rd IP11 . . . 64 A4
Montana Rd IP5 . . . . . 32 A3
Montgomery Rd IP2 . . 36 B1
Monton Rise IP2 . . . . 35 A2
Monument Farm La
IP10 . . . . 40 C3
Monument Farm Rd
IP10 . . . . 40 B4
Moore Rd IP1 . . . . 19 C3
Moorfield Rd IP12 . . . 12 A1
Moor's Way IP12 . . . . 12 A1
Morgan Ct 3 IP6 . . . . 16 B4
Morgan Dr IP1 . . . . . . 18 C1
Morgan Meadow
IP14 . . . . 8 C2
Morland Prim Sch
IP3 . . . . 46 A4
Morland Rd 1 IP3 . . . 46 A4
Morley Ave IP12 . . . . . 14 B4
Mornington Ave 2
IP1 . . . . 19 C1
Morris Way IP6 . . . . . 11 A2
Moss La IP6 . . . . 21 C4
Mottram Cl 14 IP8 . . . 34 C2
Mountbatten Ct IP1 . . 28 A3
Mount Dr IP3 . . . . 39 C1
Mowlands IP9 . . . . 52 C3
Mulberry Gdns 11 IP6 . 2 B3
Mulberry Rd 3 IP3 . . 46 C3
Mumford Rd IP1 . . . . . 27 B4
Munnings Way CO11 . . 56 A4
Muriel Cl 4 IP7 . . . . . 51 B3
Murrayfield Prim Sch
IP3 . . . . 38 A3
Murray Rd IP3 . . . . . . 38 A3
Murrills Rd IP3 . . . . . . 39 B1
Museum of E Anglian
Life★ IP14 . . . . 7 A1
Museum St IP1 . . . . . . 66 B3
Myrtle Rd IP3 . . . . 37 B4

N

NACTON IP10 . . . . . . 48 C1
Nacton CE VC Prim Sch
IP10 . . . . 48 C1
Nacton Cres IP3 . . . . 38 B2
Nacton Rd
Felixstowe IP11 . . . . . . 63 B1
Ipswich IP10 . . . . 47 A3
Nansen Rd IP3 . . . . . . 38 B2
Nash Cl CO11 . . . . 56 A4
Nash Gdns 2 IP3 . . . . 46 B4
Naughton Gdns 8
IP14 . . . . 9 B3
Naunton Rd IP12 . . . . 12 A1
Navarre St IP1 . . . . . . 66 B3
Naverne Meadow
IP12 . . . . 12 C1
Nayland Rd 1 IP11 . . 62 C3
Naylor Cl IP14 . . . . 6 B3
Neale St IP1 . . . . 66 B3
Neath Dr IP2 . . . . 36 A1
Needham Lake Nature
Reserve & Visitor
Ctr★ IP6 . . . . 11 B2
NEEDHAM MARKET
IP6 . . . . 11 B3
Needham Mkt Mid Sch
IP6 . . . . 11 A2
Needham Mkt Sta
IP6 . . . . 11 B2
Needham Rd IP14 . . . . 9 B4
Needham Rd W IP14 . . 9 C4
Nelson Rd IP4 . . . . 30 A3
Nelson Way IP12 . . . . 12 B3
Nene Dr IP3 . . . . 47 A3
Neptune Quay IP4 . . . 67 C2
Neptune Sq IP4 . . . . . 67 C2
Netley Cl IP2 . . . . 43 C4
Newark Cl IP2 . . . . . . 35 C1
Newbourne Gdns
IP11 . . . . 63 A3
Newbourne Rd
Brightwell IP10 . . . . . . 4 A1
Martlesham IP12 . . . . . 4 B4

Newbourne Rd continued
Waldringfield IP12 . . . . 4 C2
Newbury Rd IP4 . . . . . 30 C2
Newby Dr IP4 . . . . 31 C1
New Cardinal St IP1 . . 67 A2
New Cut IP7 . . . . 51 B3
New Cut E IP3 . . . . 67 C1
New Cut W IP7 . . . . . . 67 C1
Newell Rise IP6 . . . . . 16 B4
Newhaven Way IP7 . . . 51 B4
Newnham Ave IP12 . . . 14 B4
Newnham Ct IP2 . . . . . 35 B1
Newquay Cl IP5 . . . . . 31 C2
New Quay Ct IP12 . . . 13 A1
New Quay La IP12 . . . 13 A2
New Quay Terr IP12 . . 13 A2
New Rd
Felixstowe IP11 . . . . . . 58 C3
Mistley CO11 . . . . 57 A3
Newry Ave IP11 . . . . . . 63 C4
Newson St IP1 . . . . . . 66 A4
New St 9 IP12 . . . . . . 12 C1
Newton Rd
Ipswich IP3 . . . . 38 A4
Stowupland IP14 . . . . . 7 A4
Newton St IP4 . . . . 66 C3
New Village CO11 . . . . 55 A2
New Way IP2 . . . . 27 C2
New Wolsey Theatre★
IP1 . . . . 66 A3
Nicholas Rd IP11 . . . . 62 C4
Nichols Cl CO11 . . . . . 56 A2
Nightingale Rd IP3 . . . 46 A4
Nightingale Sq 5
IP3 . . . . 46 A4
Nine Acres IP2 . . . . . . 27 A2
Nock Gdns IP5 . . . . . . 32 C2
Norbury Rd IP4 . . . . . . 30 B3
Norfolk Rd IP4 . . . . . . 66 C3
Norman Cl
Felixstowe IP11 . . . . . . 61 A2
Woodbridge IP12 . . . . 12 C3
Norman Cres IP3 . . . . 38 A2
Normandy Cl IP14 . . . . 9 A3
Norman Rd CO11 . . . . 56 C3
North Cl IP4 . . . . 21 B1
Northgate Cty High Sch
IP4 . . . . 22 A1
Northgate Sports Ctr
IP4 . . . . 22 A2
Northgate St IP4 . . . . 66 B3
North Hill IP12 . . . . . . 12 B2
North Hill Gdns IP4 . . 29 B2
North Hill Rd IP4 . . . . 29 B2
North Lawn IP4 . . . . . . 30 B4
North St CO11 . . . . . . 56 C3
Norwich Rd
Barham IP6 . . . . 2 B4
Claydon IP6 . . . . 16 B4
Ipswich IP1 . . . . 66 A3
Nottidge Rd IP4 . . . . . 29 B2
Nunn Cl 1 IP12 . . . . . 4 A4
Nursery Wlk IP11 . . . . 63 C4

O

Oak Cl IP11 . . . . 63 B4
Oakdene IP10 . . . . 5 B3
Oak Eggar Chase
IP8 . . . . 43 A4
Oakfield Rd IP8 . . . . . 42 A2
Oak Gr IP8 . . . . 26 A2
Oak Hill La IP2 . . . . . . 36 B3
Oak La IP1 . . . . 66 B3
Oaks Com Prim Sch
Chantry IP2 . . . . 35 B4
Ipswich IP2 . . . . 35 B3
Oaksmere Gdns 8
IP2 . . . . 36 A2
Oaks The IP5 . . . . 33 C2
Oban St IP1 . . . . 66 A4
O'feld Terr IP11 . . . . . 60 C2
Old Barrack Rd IP12 . . 14 C4
Old Cattle Mkt IP1 . . . 67 B2
OLD FELIXSTOWE
IP11 . . . . 60 C2
Oldfield Rd IP8 . . . . . . 34 B1

Old Foundry Rd IP4.. 66 C3
Old Hall Cl **2** IP6..... 3 B4
Old Ipswich Rd IP6 .. 16 B3
Old Kirton Rd IP11.... 5 B1
Old Library The **15**
  CO11............... 56 C3
Old London Rd IP9 ... 52 A1
Old Maltings App
  IP12................ 13 A2
Old Maltings Ct
  IP12................ 13 A1
Old Norwich Rd IP1 .. 16 C1
Old Paper Mill La **8**
  IP6................ 16 B4
Old Rectory Cl **2** IP6 .. 2 C3
Old Rectory Wlk IP9 . 52 A3
Old St The IP9........ 52 C3
Olympus Cl IP1....... 18 C2
Onehouse La IP1...... 20 C1
Onehouse Rd IP14..... 6 B2
Opal Ave
  1 Ipswich IP1..... 19 A1
  Ipswich IP1......... 27 A4
Orchard Cl IP12...... 12 C3
Orchard Gate
  1 Needham Market
  IP6................ 11 A3
Orchard Gr
  Claydon IP6........ 16 B3
  Ipswich IP5......... 32 A3
Orchard Pl IP13....... 53 A3
Orchard Rd **6** IP8.... 18 A2
Orchard St IP4........ 66 C3
Orchid Cl IP2......... 35 B4
Orchid Way IP6....... 11 A1
Oregon Rd IP5....... 32 A2
Orford Rd IP11........ 63 B1
Orford St IP1......... 66 A4
Orkney Rd **4** IP4..... 22 A1
Orwell Ct IP12........ 14 C3
Orwell Ctry Pk* IP3.. 37 C3
Orwell High Sch
  IP11................ 59 B1
Orwell Pl IP4......... 67 C2
Orwell Rd
  Felixstowe IP11..... 63 C3
  Ipswich IP3......... 38 A4
  Stowmarket IP14..... 9 A4
Orwell Ret Pk IP2.... 28 A1
Osborne Rd IP3...... 38 A4
Osier Cl IP12......... 13 A2
Osiers The IP1........ 7 A3
Otley Cl **6** IP11...... 59 A1
Oulton Rd IP3........ 37 C2
Oxford Dr IP12....... 14 B3
Oxford Rd
  Ipswich IP4........ 29 B1
  Manningtree CO11... 56 C3

P

Packard Ave IP3...... 38 B2
Packard Pl IP8....... 18 B2
Paddocks The **3** IP5... 4 A3
Padstow Rd IP5...... 32 A2
Page Gdns IP5....... 33 B4
Page's Cl IP14........ 6 C2
Paget Cl IP6......... 10 C3
Paget Rd IP1......... 66 A4
Palfrey Hts CO11..... 55 B3
Palmcroft Cl **10** IP1.. 20 A3
Palmcroft Rd IP1..... 20 A3
Palmerston Rd IP4... 29 C3
Paper Mill La IP8..... 18 B4
Parade Rd IP4........ 29 C3
Pardoe Pl IP4........ 31 B1
Park Ave IP11........ 60 B1
Park Cl **5** IP5........ 4 A3
Parker Ave IP11...... 62 B4
Parkers Pl **1** IP5..... 4 A3
Parkeston Rd IP11.... 63 A4
Park La IP10......... 5 C4
Park N IP1........... 29 A4
Park Rd
  Combs IP14........ 8 B2

Park Rd continued
  Ipswich IP1......... 28 C4
  Needham Market IP6.. 11 A2
Parkside Ave IP4..... 66 C4
Park The CO11........ 56 C2
Park View Rd IP1..... 20 B1
Parkway IP13......... 53 B4
Parliament Rd IP4.... 30 B1
Parnell Cl IP1........ 19 C3
Parnell Rd IP1........ 19 C3
Parnham Pl **2** IP4... 31 C1
Parsonage Cl IP11.... 63 A4
Parsons Yd **10** CO11.. 56 C2
Partridge Rd IP2..... 35 A3
Pashford Pl **8** IP3.... 46 C4
Pastures The IP4...... 31 C1
Pattern Bush Cl
  CO11............... 55 B3
Patteson Rd IP3...... 37 B4
Pauline St IP2........ 67 B1
Paul's Rd IP2......... 27 C1
Peacock Cl **6** IP8.... 34 C2
Peacock St IP1....... 33 B3
Pearce Rd IP3........ 38 A4
Pearcroft Rd IP1...... 20 B3
Pearl Rd IP1......... 27 A4
Pearse Way IP3....... 39 B1
Pearson Rd IP4...... 30 C1
Peart Gr IP5......... 33 A2
Peasey Gdns IP5..... 32 C2
Peasey La IP5........ 32 C2
Pedler's Cnr CO11.... 56 C1
Peel St IP1.......... 66 B3
Peel Yd **2** IP5........ 4 A3
Peewit Hill IP11....... 63 A3
Peewit Rd IP2........ 34 C3
Pelican Cl IP2........ 35 B3
Pembroke Ave IP12.. 14 C4
Pembroke Cl IP2..... 36 B3
Pendleton Rd IP2.... 35 A1
Penfold Rd IP11...... 64 A4
Penn Cl IP9.......... 52 C4
Penny La **5** IP3...... 39 C1
Penny Meadow **3**
  IP9................ 52 B3
Pennyroyal Gdns
  IP2................ 35 B4
Penryn Rd IP5....... 32 A3
Penshurst Rd IP3.... 39 A4
Penzance Rd IP3..... 32 A2
Peppercorn Way **2**
  IP2................ 36 C3
Pepper Pl IP5........ 33 A2
Perkins Way IP3..... 37 C1
Pesthouse La IP6..... 2 B4
Peterhouse Cl IP2.... 35 C2
Peterhouse Cres
  IP12............... 14 B4
Peter's Gr **4** IP9..... 52 B3
PETTISTREE IP13..... 53 A1
Pheasant Rd IP2..... 35 B3
Philip Ave IP11....... 63 B3
Philip Rd IP2......... 67 B1
Phillipps Rd **3** IP6... 2 C3
Phillips Cres IP6..... 11 B2
Phoenix Rd IP4...... 30 A3
Phoenix Way IP14.... 7 C3
Picketts Rd IP11...... 60 C1
Pickwick Rd IP2...... 27 B2
Picton Ave **5** IP1.... 21 A1
Pigeon's La IP8....... 34 A3
Pightle The
  Capel St Mary IP9... 52 C4
  4 Needham Market
  IP6................ 11 A3
Pimpernel Rd IP2.... 35 C3
Pine Ave IP1......... 20 B1
Pine Bank IP5........ 33 C2
Pine Cl CO11......... 55 B3
Pinecroft Rd IP1...... 20 A2
Pinecroft Way IP6.... 11 B2
Pines The
  Claydon IP6........ 16 B4
  Felixstowe IP11..... 61 B2
Pinetree Cl IP15...... 31 C3
Pineview Cl IP14...... 7 A1
Pine View Rd IP1..... 28 B4

Pinewood IP12....... 14 C3
Pin Mill Cl IP8....... 34 C1
Pintail Cl IP2......... 35 B3
Pipers Vale Cl IP3.... 37 B1
Pipers Vale Com Prim
  Sch
  Gainsborough IP3... 37 C1
  Ipswich IP3......... 37 C1
Pipers Vale Nature
  Reserve* IP3........ 45 C3
Pitcairn Rd IP1....... 27 B4
Pitts End CO7........ 54 C3
Platten Cl IP6........ 10 C3
Platters Cl IP3....... 46 A3
Platters Rd IP11...... 63 B2
Playfield Rd IP9...... 52 C3
Playford La IP5....... 23 B2
Playford Rd
  Ipswich IP4......... 31 B4
  Playford IP5......... 2 B3
Pleasant Row IP4.... 67 C2
Plough Rd IP9........ 52 A3
Plough St IP3........ 37 B4
Plover Rd IP2........ 35 B2
Plummers Dell **11** IP6 . 2 B3
Plymouth Rd IP11.... 59 C2
Pole Hill (Tumulus)*
  IP10............... 33 C1
Polstead Cl IP14...... 9 C4
Pond Cl IP11......... 59 A1
Pond End IP6........ 3 C4
Pond Hall Rd IP7..... 51 C2
Poole St IP3......... 39 A3
Poplar Cl **4** IP6...... 16 B4
Poplar Hill IP4........ 9 B4
Poplar La IP8........ 34 B3
Poppy Cl IP2......... 27 C1
Portal Ave IP5....... 4 A4
Porter Rd **3** IP3...... 39 C1
Portland Cres **4**
  IP12............... 14 C4
Portlight Cl CO11..... 57 C3
Portman Rd IP1...... 67 A2
Portman's Wlk IP1... 28 A1
Port of Felixstowe Rd
  IP11............... 62 C3
Post Mill Cl IP4...... 29 C2
Post Office La IP12... 14 A1
Pouch Mill IP11...... 58 B4
Pound La
  Bramford IP8....... 2 A1
  Capel St Mary IP9.. 52 A1
  Hadleigh IP7........ 50 C3
  Stowmarket IP14.... 7 A3
Powling Rd IP3....... 38 A2
Prentice Rd IP14..... 7 B2
Preston Dr IP1....... 19 C2
Prestwick Ave **2**
  IP11............... 60 C2
Pretyman Rd
  Felixstowe IP11..... 63 B1
  Ipswich IP3......... 38 B3
Priestly Cl IP14...... 6 B4
Priestly Rd IP6....... 11 A2
Primrose Hill IP2..... 35 C4
Primrose Way IP6.... 11 A1
Princedale Cl IP1..... 20 A1
Prince of Wales Dr **9**
  IP2................ 36 A2
Princes Gdns IP11.... 63 C4
Princes Rd IP11...... 63 C4
Princes St IP2........ 67 A1
Princethorpe Rd
  IP3................ 38 C4
PRIORY HEATH IP3... 39 A1
Priory Pk IP10........ 46 C4
Priory Rd IP11........ 60 C1
Prittlewell Cl IP2..... 35 C1
Prospect Rd IP1...... 28 A2
Providence La **5**
  IP1................ 28 A3
Providence Stree
  IP1................ 66 B3
Pump St IP6......... 11 B2
Punchard Way IP11.. 58 C4
Purcell Rd IP1........ 6 B4
Purdis Ave IP3....... 39 C2

Purdis Farm La
  Foxhall IP10........ 40 C2
  Ipswich IP3......... 39 C2
  Purdis Farm IP10... 40 B2
Purdis Rd IP10....... 41 A2
Purplett St IP2....... 27 C1
Pykenham Way IP7... 51 A3
Pytches Cl **2** IP12.... 13 A2
Pytches Rd IP12...... 12 C2

Q

Quadling St IP1...... 67 B2
Quail Cl IP14......... 7 C3
Quantock Cl IP5..... 31 C3
Quantrill Terr IP5..... 33 A2
Quay Ctyd **2** CO11... 56 C3
Quay Side IP12....... 15 B4
Quay St
  1 Manningtree
  CO11............... 56 C3
Quebec Dr IP5....... 32 B4
Queech The IP9...... 52 C4
Queens Ave **5** IP12.. 14 C4
Queensberry Rd **1**
  IP3................ 46 B4
Queens Cl IP14....... 8 A1
Queenscliffe Rd IP2.. 36 A3
Queensdale Cl IP1... 20 B1
Queensdale Rd IP1... 20 B1
Queensgate Dr **4** IP9.. 29 C4
Queen's Head La
  IP12............... 12 B1
Queen's Rd IP11..... 64 A3
Queen St
  Felixstowe IP11..... 59 B1
  6 Hadleigh IP7..... 51 A3
  Ipswich IP1......... 67 B2
Queensway CO11..... 56 B3
Queen's Way IP3..... 38 B2
Quentin Cl IP1....... 27 B4
Quilter Dr
  Ipswich IP8......... 34 C1
  Pinewood IP8....... 42 C4
Quilter Rd IP11...... 64 B4
Quince Cl CO11...... 55 B4
Quinton Rd IP6...... 10 C2
Quintons Cnr CO7... 54 C4
Quinton's La IP11.... 60 C1
Quintons Rd CO7.... 54 C4
Quoits Field **2** IP6... 16 B4

R

RACECOURSE IP3 .... 38 B2
Radcliffe Dr IP2...... 35 A2
Raeburn Rd IP3...... 37 C1
Raeburn Rd S IP3.... 37 B1
Railway App IP1...... 60 A1
Railway St CO11...... 56 C3
Railway Terr **11**
  CO11............... 56 C3
Rampling Cl IP7...... 51 A4
Ramsey Cl IP7....... 36 A1
Ramsey Rd IP7...... 51 C4
Ramsgate Dr IP3.... 38 B3
Randall Cl IP5........ 33 B3
Randolph Cl IP4..... 30 B1
Rands Way IP3...... 38 B2
Randwell Cl IP4..... 30 B1
Ranelagh Prim Sch
  IP2................ 27 C1
Ranelagh Rd
  Felixstowe IP11..... 64 A4
  Ipswich IP2......... 67 A1
Ransome Cl IP8..... 26 A2
Ransome Cres IP3... 38 B2
Ransome Rd IP3..... 38 B2
Ransomes Europark
  IP10............... 47 C3
Ransomes Way IP3.. 39 A1
Ransom Rd IP12..... 12 A2
Ranson Rd IP6...... 10 C2
Rapier St **8** IP2...... 67 A1
Rattlesden Cl **2** IP14.. 9 A3
Raven Cl IP14........ 7 C3

Ravensfield Rd IP1... 19 B1
Ravens La IP8........ 18 A2
Ravens Way **6** IP2... 4 A4
Ravenswood Ave
  IP3................ 46 B4
Ravenswood Com Prim
  Sch IP3............ 46 C4
Raven Way IP7....... 51 A1
Raydon Croft IP14... 9 C3
Rayleigh Rd IP1...... 19 B1
Rayment Drift **5**
  IP5................ 32 C3
Reading Rd IP4...... 30 B3
Recreation La IP11... 59 C2
Recreation Rd IP14... 6 C2
Recreation Way IP3.. 38 C2
Rectory Hill CO7..... 54 B1
Rectory La
  Brantham CO11..... 55 C4
  Kirton IP10......... 5 B3
Rectory Rd IP2...... 67 B1
Redan St IP1......... 66 A4
Rede La IP6.......... 17 B4
Rede Wood Nature
  Reserve* IP3....... 3 B3
Redgate La IP9....... 45 A1
Red Hall Ct IP11..... 64 C4
Red House Cl **3** IP1.. 5 B1
Red La IP9........... 52 B2
Red Sleeve IP5....... 52 A3
Redwing Cl IP2...... 35 A3
Redwold Cl IP12..... 14 A1
Reedland Way **4**
  IP11............... 59 A1
Reeve Gdns IP5..... 32 C4
Regent St
  9 Manningtree
  CO11............... 56 C3
  Stowmarket IP14.... 7 A3
Regent Theatre*
  IP4................ 66 C3
Regina Cl IP4........ 30 B1
Reigate Cl IP3........ 38 B3
Rembrow Rd IP9..... 52 B3
Remercie Rd IP14.... 6 C2
Rendlesham Rd
  15 Felixstowe IP11.. 59 A1
  9 Ipswich IP1...... 28 A3
Renfrew Rd IP4...... 22 B1
Reynolds Ave **2** IP3.. 46 A4
Reynolds Ct **10** IP11.. 59 A1
Reynolds Rd IP3..... 38 A4
Riby Rd IP11......... 63 C3
Richardson Rd CO7.. 54 C3
Richmond Rd IP1.... 27 C3
Ridgeway IP14....... 6 B2
Rigby Ave CO11...... 57 C2
Riley Cl IP1.......... 18 C1
Ringham Rd IP4...... 30 A2
Risby Cl IP4.......... 30 B2
Ritabrook Rd IP2..... 35 B1
River Gdns IP14...... 9 B4
River Hill IP8......... 26 C4
Riverside Ave E
  CO11............... 56 B4
Riverside Ave W
  CO11............... 56 B4
Riverside Cotts
  CO11............... 55 A2
Riverside Ind Est
  IP13............... 53 B4
Riverside Ind Pk IP3.. 37 A3
Riverside Ind Est IP12.. 27 C3
Riverside Theatre The*
  IP12............... 15 B4
Rivers St IP4......... 29 C3
Riverview IP12....... 13 B3
River View CO11...... 56 B3
Robeck Rd IP3....... 37 B1
Robin Dr IP2......... 35 A3
Rodney Ct IP12...... 12 B3
Rogers Cl IP11....... 59 C2
Rogue's La IP13...... 53 B2
Roman Way IP11..... 61 A2

Romney Rd IP3. . . . . .38 A1
Rookery The CO11 . . . . 56 B3
Ropes Dr IP5. . . . . .28 B4
Rope Wlk IP4 . . . . .67 C2
Rosebery Rd
  Felixstowe IP11 . . . . . . .64 B4
  Ipswich IP4 . . . . .29 C1
Rosecroft Rd IP1 . . . . . .20 A2
ROSE HILL IP3 . . . . .37 C4
Rosehill Cres IP3 . . . . . .37 C4
Rose Hill Prim Sch
  IP3 . . . . .38 A4
Rosehill Rd IP3. . . . . . . .37 C4
Rose La IP4 . . . . 67 B2
Rosemary Ave IP11 . . . . 60 B1
Rosemary La IP4 . . . . . . 67 B2
Rose Wlk IP6. . . . . .11 A1
Ross Rd IP4 . . . . 22 B1
Roundridge Rd IP9 . . 52 C4
Roundwood Rd IP4. . . 30 A3
Rousies Cl **6** IP7. . . . . 51 B3
Routh Ave **4** IP3 . . . . . .39 C1
Rowan Cl IP3. . . . . .39 A2
Rowanhayes Cl IP2. . . 36 B3
Rowarth Ave IP5 . . . . . 32 C3
Rowley Cl CO11. . . . . . . 55 B3
Row The IP8. . . . . .18 A2
Roxburgh Rd IP4 . . . . . 22 B1
Roy Ave IP4 . . . . 30 B1
Roy Cl IP5. . . . . 32 B3
Royston Dr IP2 . . . . . . 35 A2
Rubens Rd IP3 . . . . 38 A1
Rudlands IP8. . . . . .34 C1
Rue's La IP11. . . . . .60 C4
Runnacles Way IP11. .59 A1
Rushbury Cl IP4 . . . . . 30 B4
Rush Cl IP4 . . . . 39 B4
Rushmeadow Way **1**
  IP11 . . . . .61 A3
Rushmere Hall Prim
  Sch IP4 . . . . .22 A1
Rushmere Rd IP4. . . . . 30 A3
RUSHMERE ST
  ANDREW IP5. . . . . . . .23 B1
Rushmere St IP5 . . . . . . 23 B1
RUSHMERE STREET
  IP5 . . . . .23 B2
Ruskin Cl **3** IP4. . . . . . 6 B4
Ruskin Rd IP4 . . . . 29 C1
Russell Cl IP12 . . . . 12 A2
Russell Rd
  Felixstowe IP11 . . . . . . .63 C2
  Ipswich IP1 . . . . .67 A2
Rydal Ave IP11 . . . . 61 A3
Rydal Cl IP14. . . . . .6 B2
Rydal Wlk IP3 . . . . 38 C2
Rye Cl IP3. . . . . 39 A4
Ryes Sch The IP5. . . . 25 B1
Rylands IP9 . . . . 52 B4

S

Saddlemakers La
  IP12 . . . . .13 B4
Saddlers Pl **15** IP5. . . . 4 A3
Sagehayes Cl IP2. . . . . 36 B3
St Agnes Way IP5. . . . . 31 C2
St Alban's Cath High
  Sch IP4 . . . . .31 A3
St Andrew's Church Ct
  IP5 . . . . .23 A1
St Andrews Cl IP4 . . . . 31 A1
St Andrew's Cl IP12. . 13 C4
St Andrew's Pl IP12. . 13 C4
St Andrew's Rd IP11. . 60 A1
St Annes Cl IP12. . . . . 14 B3
St Anthonys Cres
  IP4 . . . . .29 C2
St Aubyns Rd IP4 . . . . 30 A1
St Augustine Rd IP3. . 39 A4
St Augustine's Gdns
  IP3 . . . . .38 C3
St Austell Cl IP5. . . . . 32 A2

St Catherine's Ct
  IP2 . . . . .35 B1
St Clements Church La
  IP4 . . . . .67 C2
St Clement's Hospl
  IP3 . . . . .38 C4
St David's Rd **7** IP3 . .38 B3
St Edmunds Cl
  Stowmarket IP14 . . . . . . .6 C4
  3 Woodbridge IP12 . . .14 C4
St Edmund's Pl IP1. . . 28 C4
St Edmunds Rd IP14. . .6 C4
St Edmund's Rd
  Felixstowe IP11 . . . . . . .63 B2
  Ipswich IP1 . . . . .28 B4
St George's Rd IP11 . . 60 C2
St George's St IP1. . . 66 B3
St Gotthards Ave
  IP12 . . . . .4 B3
St Helens Prim Sch
  IP4 . . . . .29 B2
St Helen's St IP4 . . . . 66 C3
St Isidores IP5 . . . . . . 33 B3
St Ives Cl IP5. . . . . 32 A2
St Johns CE Prim Sch
  IP4 . . . . .30 A3
St Johns Ct IP11. . . . . 64 A4
St John's Hill **4**
  IP12 . . . . .12 C1
St John's Rd IP4. . . . . 30 A2
St John's St IP12 . . . . 12 C1
St John's Terr **5**
  IP12 . . . . .12 C1
St Josephs Coll IP2 . .36 A3
St Lawrence Gn IP5 . .32 A3
St Lawrence St IP1 . . 66 B3
St Lawrence Way
  IP5 . . . . .32 B4
St Leonards Rd **2**
  IP3 . . . . .38 B3
St Margarets CE VA
  Prim Sch IP4 . . . . .66 C3
St Margaret's Gn
  IP4 . . . . .66 C3
St Margarets Plain
  IP4 . . . . .66 B3
St Margaret's St IP4 . .66 C3
St Marks RC Prim Sch
  IP2 . . . . .35 C3
St Martins Ct IP5. . . . 33 B3
St Martins Gn **14** IP11. . 5 B1
St Marys Cath Prim Sch
  IP4 . . . . .29 C3
St Marys CE Aided Prim
  Sch IP12 . . . . .12 A1
St Mary's Cl
  Bramford IP8 . . . . .18 B1
  Felixstowe IP11 . . . . . . .58 B3
St Mary's Cres IP11. . .59 C2
St Mary's Gdns IP6 . . 11 B4
St Marys Prim Sch
  IP7 . . . . .51 B3
St Marys Rd IP4 . . . . . 29 C2
St Mary's Rd
  Creeting St Mary
    IP6 . . . . .11 B3
  Stowmarket IP14 . . . . . . .6 B3
St Marys Way IP6. . . . 21 C4
St Mathew's St Service
  Rd IP1 . . . . .66 A3
St Matthew's CE VA
  Prim Sch IP1 . . . . .66 A3
St Matthew's St IP1 . .66 A3
St Michael's Cl IP5 . . 32 A2
St Michaels Ct **6**
  CO11. . . . . .56 C3
St Nicholas Ct IP1 . . 67 B2
St Nicholas St IP1 . . 67 B2
St Olaves Rd IP5. . . . . 32 C4
St Osyth Cl IP2 . . . . . 43 C4
St Pancras Cath Prim
  Sch IP1 . . . . .19 C2
St Peter's Ave **1**
  IP6 . . . . .16 B4
St Peter's Cl
  8 Claydon IP6 . . . . . .2 B3
  Stowmarket IP14 . . . . . . .6 B2

St Peter's Cl continued
  Woodbridge IP12 . . . . . . .14 B4
St Peter's Rd IP14 . . . .6 B2
St Peter's St IP4. . . . . 67 B2
St Stephens La IP1 . . 67 B2
Salehurst Rd IP3 . . . . 39 B3
Salisbury Rd IP3. . . . . 38 A3
Sallows Cl IP1. . . . . . . 27 C3
Sally Wood's La IP6 . .11 C4
Salmet Cl IP2 . . . . 36 A3
Salthouse La IP4 . . . . 67 C2
Samford Pl IP8 . . . . . . 26 B2
Samuel Ct IP4. . . . . . . 67 C2
Sandhurst Ave IP3. . . 37 C4
Sandling Cres IP4 . . . 31 B1
Sandlings The IP3 . . . 39 A1
Sandown Cl **3** IP1 . . . 20 A3
Sandown Rd IP1. . . . . 20 A3
Sandpiper Rd
  Ipswich IP2 . . . . .35 B2
  1 Stowmarket IP14 . . . .7 C3
Sandpit Cl IP1. . . . . . . 19 A1
Sandringham Cl IP2 . .35 C2
Sandy Cl **5** IP11. . . . . 5 B1
Sandyhill La IP3 . . . . . 37 B1
Sandy La
  Barham IP6 . . . . .2 B4
  Little Bealings IP13 . . . . .25 A4
  Wickham Market
    IP13 . . . . .53 C2
  Woodbridge IP12. . . . . . .14 B2
Sapling Pl IP4 . . . . 31 B1
Saracens House Bsns
  Ctr IP4 . . . . .66 C3
Sawmill La IP10 . . . . . 48 B2
Sawston Cl **10** IP2 . . . 36 A2
Sawyers Cl IP9. . . . . . 52 B2
Saxon Cl **11** IP11. . . . . 61 A2
Saxon Way IP12 . . . . . 12 C3
Schneider Rd **3**
  IP11 . . . . .65 B4
School Cl
  1 Capel St Mary
    IP9 . . . . .52 B3
  Hadleigh IP7. . . . . .51 B2
School La
  Brantham CO11 . . . . .55 B4
  East Bergholt CO7 . . . . .54 A3
  Martlesham IP12. . . . . . .14 A1
  Mistley CO11 . . . . .57 B3
School Meadow **1**
  IP14 . . . . .9 B3
School St IP6. . . . . 11 A2
Schreiber Rd IP4 . . . . 30 B3
Scopes Rd IP5. . . . . . . 32 C4
Scott Rd IP3 . . . . 38 B1
Scrivener Dr IP8 . . . . 34 B2
Seabreeze Rd IP14 . . .7 A1
Sea Rd IP11. . . . . .63 C2
Seaton Cl CO11. . . . . . 56 A2
Seaton Rd IP11. . . . . . 59 B1
Seckford Almshouses
  IP12 . . . . .12 C3
Seckford Cl **1** IP11. . 31 C1
Seckford Hall Rd
  IP12 . . . . .14 B3
Second Ave IP11 . . . . 58 B3
Sedan Wlk IP1 . . . . . . 67 A2
Selkirk Rd IP4 . . . . . . 22 C1
Selvale Way IP11 . . . . 63 B4
Selwyn Cl IP2 . . . . 67 B1
Semer Cl IP14. . . . . . . 9 B3
Serpentine Rd IP3 . . 39 B3
Seven Cotts La IP5 . . 22 C1
Severn Rd IP3 . . . . 37 C3
Sewell Wontner Cl
  IP5 . . . . .32 C4
Seymour Rd IP2 . . . . . 67 B1
Shackleton Rd IP3. . . 38 B3
Shackleton Sq **8**
  IP3 . . . . .38 B3
Shaftesbury Sq IP4. . 67 C2
Shafto Rd IP1 . . . . 19 B1
Shakespeare Rd
  Ipswich IP1 . . . . .19 B3
  Stowmarket IP14 . . . . . . .6 B4

Shamrock Ave IP2. . . .35 B4
Shannon Rd **4** IP3 . . 46 A4
Shaw Valley Rd **7**
  IP12 . . . . .4 A4
Shearman Rd IP7. . . . 51 C2
Shelbourne Cl **7**
  IP5 . . . . .33 A3
Sheldrake Dr IP2 . . . . 35 B1
Shelley Cl IP14 . . . . . . 9 C3
Shelley St IP1 . . . . 67 B1
Shenley Rd IP3. . . . . . 38 B1
Shenstone Dr IP1 . . . 20 A3
Shepherd Dr IP8 . . . . 34 C2
Shepherds La IP14 . . . 6 A4
Sheppards Way **6**
  IP5 . . . . .33 A3
Sherborne Ave IP4 . . 22 A2
Sheridan Cl IP14 . . . . 6 A4
Sherrington Rd IP1. . 28 A4
Sherwood Fields **4**
  IP5 . . . . .33 C2
Shetland Cl
  5 Ipswich IP4. . . . . . 22 A1
  Ipswich IP4 . . . . .30 A4
Shimpling Cl **7** IP14 . . 9 B3
Ship La IP8. . . . . .18 B1
Ship Launch Rd IP3. . 37 B3
Shire Hall Yd IP4 . . . . 67 C2
Shirley Cl **9** IP1. . . . . 20 A3
Shortlands IP2 . . . . . . 35 A1
Shotley Cl
  Felixstowe IP11 . . . . . . .63 A4
  Ipswich IP8 . . . . .34 C2
Shrubbery Cl IP11. . . . 63 C4
Shrubland Ave IP5 . . 19 B1
Shrubland Dr IP4. . . . 31 C1
Shrubland Pk Gdns*
  IP6 . . . . .2 B4
Shrubland Rd CO11. . 57 C2
Sidegate Ave IP4 . . . . 30 A4
Sidegate La IP4 . . . . . 22 A1
Sidegate La W IP4. . . 21 C1
Sidegate Prim Sch
  IP4 . . . . .30 A4
Silent St IP4 . . . . 67 B2
Silk Mill Cl **2** IP7. . . . 51 A2
Silverdale Ave IP14 . . 6 C3
Silverdale Cl IP1 . . . . 20 A1
Simon's Cross IP13. . 53 A4
Simons Rd IP2 . . . . . . 12 C3
Simpson Cl IP3. . . . . . 37 C1
Sinclair Dr IP2 . . . . . . 36 C3
Sir Alf Ramsey Way
  IP4 . . . . .67 A2
Sirdar Rd IP1. . . . . 28 A2
Sitwell Cl CO11. . . . . . 56 A3
Skelton Cl CO11 . . . . 56 B3
Skipper Cl **3** IP8. . . . 43 B4
Skipper Rd **4** IP2 . . . 35 A1
Skylark La IP8. . . . . . . 34 C2
Slade St IP4. . . . . 67 C2
Slade The IP6 . . . . 16 C4
Sleaford Cl IP2. . . . . . 36 A3
Slip La IP12 . . . . 12 B3
Smart St IP4 . . . . 67 C2
Smithers Cl **9** IP9. . . .52 B3
Smithfield IP12. . . . . . 13 A2
Smiths Pl **9** IP5. . . . . 33 A3
Snowcroft IP9. . . . . . . 52 B3
Snowdon Hill IP13. . . 53 B4
Snowdon Rd IP2 . . . . 36 B2
Snows Way CO11 . . . . 55 B3
Soames Cl IP14 . . . . . 6 C3
Soane St IP4 . . . . 66 C3
Somerset Rd IP4 . . . . 29 C4
Sorrel Cl IP2 . . . . 35 C3
Sorrell Wlk IP5. . . . . . 33 C3
South Cl IP4 . . . . 29 B4
Southgate Rd IP8 . . . 34 B1
South Hill IP11 . . . . . . 63 C3
South St
  Ipswich IP1 . . . . .66 A4
  Manningtree CO11 . . . . . .56 A4
South Strand CO11 . . 56 B4
Speckled Wood Cl
  IP8 . . . . .43 A4
Speedwell Rd IP2 . . . 35 C4
Spencer Way IP14. . . . 6 B3

Spenser Rd IP1. . . . . . 19 B3
Spindler Cl IP5. . . . . . 33 A3
Spinner Cl IP1. . . . . . . 27 A4
Spinney The IP14 . . . . 9 C4
Spitfire Cl IP3 . . . . . . 38 B1
Spooners La **5** IP7. . 51 A3
Springbank Ave
  CO11. . . . . .56 A2
Springfield Ave
  IP11 . . . . .60 A1
Springfield Inf Sch
  IP1 . . . . .27 C4
Springfield Jun Sch
  IP1 . . . . .27 C4
Springfield La IP1. . . . 27 C4
Springhurst Cl IP4. . . 29 C2
Spring La IP13 . . . . . . 53 C4
Springland Cl IP4 . . . 29 C2
Spring Meadow IP6 . . 24 B4
Spring Rd IP4 . . . . 29 C2
Spring Row IP14 . . . . . 7 A3
Springtail Rd IP8 . . . . 43 B4
Spring Wood Nature
  Reserve* IP9 . . . . .43 B3
Sprites End IP11 . . . . 59 A3
Spriteshall La IP11 . . 59 A3
Sprites La IP8 . . . . 34 C1
Sprites Prim Sch
  IP2 . . . . .34 C2
SPROUGHTON IP8. . . 26 A3
Sproughton Bsns Pk
  IP1 . . . . .26 C4
Sproughton CE Prim
  Sch IP8 . . . . .26 A2
Sproughton Ct IP8 . . 26 A2
Sproughton Rd IP1. . 26 C3
Spur End IP12. . . . . . . 13 B3
Square The IP14. . . . . 9 B4
Squires La **4** IP5. . . . 4 A3
Squirrels The IP9 . . . 52 B4
Stamford Cl IP2 . . . . . 43 C4
Stammers Pl IP5 . . . . 33 B4
Stanley Ave IP3. . . . . . 38 A4
Stanley Rd IP11 . . . . . 64 A3
Starfield Cl IP4. . . . . . 30 B2
Star La IP4 . . . . 67 C2
Station Rd
  Claydon IP6 . . . . .16 A4
  Felixstowe IP11 . . . . . . .58 C3
  Hadleigh IP7. . . . . .51 B2
  Manningtree CO11 . . . . . .56 B4
  Woodbridge IP12. . . . . . .15 B4
Station Rd E IP11 . . . . 7 B2
Station Rd W IP14 . . . 7 A2
Station St IP2 . . . . 36 C3
Station Yd
  Hadleigh IP7. . . . . .51 B2
  Needham Market IP6. . . .11 B2
Steggall Cl IP6 . . . . . . 10 C4
Stella Maris IP2 . . . . . 27 A1
Stennetts Cl IP11. . . . 58 B4
Stephen Rd IP5 . . . . . 33 B4
Stephen's Ct IP4 . . . . 30 B2
Stevenson Rd IP1 . . . 66 A3
Stewart Young Gr
  IP5 . . . . .33 A3
Stockmers End **8**
  IP9 . . . . .52 B3
Stockton Cl IP7 . . . . . 51 C1
STOKE IP2 . . . . 67 B1
Stoke Hall* IP2. . . . . . 67 B1
Stoke Hall Rd IP2. . . . 67 B1
STOKE PARK IP2 . . . . 35 C1
Stoke High Sch IP2. . 36 C3
STOKE PARK IP2 . . . . 35 C1
Stoke Pk Dr IP2 . . . . . 36 A1
Stoke Quay IP2 . . . . . 67 C1
Stoke St IP2. . . . . 67 B1
Stollery Cl IP5. . . . . . . 32 B3
Stonechat Rd IP2. . . . 34 C3
Stonegrove Rd IP11 . . 63 A1
Stonehouse Rd IP2. . 36 A3
Stone Lodge La IP2. . 36 A3
Stone Lodge La W
  IP2 . . . . .35 C2
Stone Lodge Wlk
  IP2 . . . . .36 B3
Stone Pl **12** IP12. . . . . 12 C1

Stopford Ct 8 IP1....28 A3
Stour Ave IP11 ......63 B3
Stour St CO11 ......56 C3
Stourview Ave CO11 ..57 C3
STOWMARKET IP14 .. 7 B2
Stowmarket High Sch
 IP14 .... 6 B3
Stowmarket Mid Sch
 IP14 .... 6 C2
Stowmarket Rd IP6... 2 A4
Stowmarket Sta IP14 .. 7 B2
Stowupland IP14 ... 7 C3
Stowupland St IP14... 7 A2
Stradbroke Rd IP4... 30 A3
Straight Rd IP10.....40 C1
Strand The IP2 ......44 C4
Stratford Rd IP1......19 C2
Street The
 Belstead IP8.........42 C2
 Bramford IP8.........18 A2
 Capel St Mary IP9 ....52 A3
 East Bergholt CO7 ...54 A2
 Little Bealings IP13 ...25 A4
 Martlesham IP12 .....14 A1
 Nacton IP10 ....48 C1
 Pettistree IP13.......53 B1
 Wherstead IP9........44 A2
 Woodbridge IP12.....13 B3
Stricklands Rd 1
 IP14 .... 7 B1
Stuart Cl
 5 Felixstowe IP11 ....61 A3
 Ipswich IP4 ....29 C3
Stubbs Cl
 Ipswich IP3 ....38 A1
 Lawford CO11.........56 A3
Sturdee Ave IP3 .....38 B3
Sub-station Rd IP11..63 A2
Sudbourne Rd 14
 IP11 ....59 A1
Sudbury Rd 3 IP11...62 C4
Suffolk Coll IP4 .....29 B1
Suffolk Horse Mus*
 IP12 ....12 C1
Suffolk Nuffield Hospl
 The IP10 ....40 B4
Suffolk Pl IP12 ......13 A1
Suffolk Rd IP4.......66 C4
Suffolk Ret Pk IP1...28 A2
Suffolk Ski Ctr* IP2 .44 B3
Summerfield Cl IP4...31 A4
Summit Bsns Pk
 IP11 ....63 B1
Sunderland Rd 2
 IP11 ....65 B4
Sunfield Cl IP4 ......30 B2
Sun La IP12 ....12 C1
Sunningdale Ave
 IP4 ....31 A1
Sunningdale Dr
 IP11 ....60 B2
Sunray Ave IP11......60 B2
Surbiton Rd IP1......27 C3
Surrey Rd
 Felixstowe IP11 ......63 C4
 Ipswich IP1 ....28 A2
Sutton Cl IP12........13 A1
Sutton Hoo* IP12....13 C1
Swallow Cl IP11......60 C3
Swallow Rd IP2 ......34 C3
Swallowtail Cl 1
 IP8 ....43 B4
Swan Cl
 20 Martlesham Heath
 IP5 .... 4 A3
 Stowmarket IP14 ..... 6 A2
Swan Ct CO11 ....57 C2
Swan Hill IP8.........34 A2
Swan La IP6..........21 B4
Swansea Ave IP2 .....36 B1
Swatchway Cl 3
 IP3 ....46 B4
Swinburne Rd IP1....19 B3
Swinton Cl IP2 ....35 A1
Sycamore Cl IP8......34 C1
Sycamore Way CO11 ..55 B4

T
Tacket St IP4.........67 C2
Tacon Rd IP11........63 B1
Takers La IP14........ 9 B4
Tallboys Cl IP5 ......32 C4
Talmash Gdns IP2 ....36 A4
Tanners View IP1 ....27 C3
Tannery Rd IP14...... 8 C1
Tarn Hows Cl 1
 IP11 ....61 A2
Tasmania Rd IP4 .....31 A2
Taunton Cl IP1 ....20 B4
Taunton Rd IP11......59 C1
Tavern St
 Ipswich IP1 ....66 B3
 Stowmarket IP14...... 7 A2
Tayberry Pl IP3......46 C3
Tayler Cl 4 IP7......51 A2
Tayler Rd IP7........51 B2
Taylor Dr CO11 ......56 B3
Teal Cl IP2 ....35 A3
Temple Pattle CO11...55 A2
Temple Rd
 Ipswich IP3 ....38 C4
 Stowmarket IP14...... 7 A1
Tenby Rd IP2 ....36 B1
Tennyson Cl IP12.....12 A2
Tern Rd
 Ipswich IP2 ....35 B2
 Stowmarket IP14...... 7 C2
Terry Gdns IP5 ......33 B3
Thackeray Gr IP14....16 B4
Thackeray Rd IP1.....19 B3
Thanet Rd IP4 ....30 B2
Thatchers Wlk 4
 IP14 .... 9 A3
Theatre St IP12....... 12 B1
Theberton Rd IP11...63 A3
THE COMMON IP8..... 2 A1
Theobald Cl 5 IP6 ...11 A3
THE PORT OF
 FELIXSTOWE IP11 ...62 C1
Thetford Rd 2 IP1 ...28 A3
Thirlmere Ct IP11 ...61 A2
Thirlmere Dr IP14 .... 6 B2
Thistle Cl IP2.........35 C4
Thomas Arne Cl IP14 .. 6 C4
Thomas Ave IP11.....58 C4
Thomas Wolsey Specl
 Sch IP1 ....19 B3
Thomas Young Cl 3
 IP14 .... 9 A3
Thompson Rd IP1 ....27 C4
Thornbush La IP8 ....26 A4
Thorney Hall Cl IP14... 7 B2
Thorney Rd IP9.......52 B4
Thornhayes Cl IP2....36 A3
Thornhill Rd IP6...... 2 C2
Thornley Dr IP4 .....30 C4
Thornley Rd IP11.....64 C4
Thorn Way IP11 ......63 B4
Thoroughfare The 10
 IP12 ....12 C1
THORPE COMMON
 IP11 .... 5 A1
Thorpe La IP11....... 5 A1
Threadneedle St 1
 IP7 ....51 A3
Through Duncans
 IP12 ....14 C3
Through Jollys IP5 ...33 A3
Thurleston High Sch
 IP1 ....20 A4
Thurleston La IP1....17 B1
Thurlow Cl 3 IP14....15 C4
Thurmans La IP11....58 B4
Thurston Ct 6 IP11 ..62 C4
Tide Mill* IP12.......15 C4
Tide Mill Way IP12....15 B4
Timperley Cl IP7 .....51 A4
Timperley Rd IP7.....51 B4
Tinabrook Cl IP2 .....35 B1
Tinker's La IP7 ....51 A2
Tintern Cl 5 IP2 .....36 A2
Tippet Ave IP14 ...... 6 C4
Titchwell Dr 2 IP3 ...47 A4

Tokio Rd IP4 ....30 A2
Toller Rd IP3 ....37 B3
Toll Gate Rd 6 IP9 ...52 B3
Tolworth Rd IP4......30 A2
Tomline Ct IP10 .....48 C1
Tomline Rd
 Felixstowe IP11 ......64 A3
 Ipswich IP3 ....30 A1
Tommy Flowers Dr
 IP5 ....33 A3
Tomo Bsns Pk IP14.... 7 C2
Tomo Ind Est IP14.... 7 B2
Toppesfield Cl 3
 IP7 ....51 A2
Toppesfield Gdns
 IP7 ....51 A2
Top St IP12...........14 A2
Tortoiseshell Cl 5
 IP9 ....43 B4
Tovell's Rd IP4 ....29 C2
Tower Mill La IP7.....51 B3
Tower Mill Rd IP1 ....27 C3
Tower Ramparts
 IP1 ....66 B3
Tower Ramparts Sh Ctr
 IP1 ....66 B3
Tower Rd IP11........63 C4
Tower St IP1 ....66 B3
Town Gn IP14 .... 6 C2
Town Hall Galleries*
 IP1 ....66 B3
Trafalgar Cl IP4 ......29 C2
Tranmere Gr IP1 .....19 C2
Treetops IP11 ....59 B3
Treeview IP14 .... 6 B2
Trefoil Cl IP2.........35 C4
Tremlett La IP5 ......33 C3
Trent Rd IP3..........37 C2
Trimley Rd IP10 ...... 5 B3
TRIMLEY ST MARTIN
 IP11 .... 5 B1
Trimley St Martin Prim
 Sch IP11 .... 5 B2
TRIMLEY ST MARY
 IP11 ....58 C4
Trimley St Mary Prim
 Sch IP11 ....58 C4
Trinity Ave IP11......62 B3
Trinity Cl
 Ipswich IP5 ....31 C3
 Manningtree CO11....56 C2
 Woodbridge IP12.....14 B3
Trinity Distribution Pk
 IP11 ....62 B4
Trinity Farm Ct 12
 CO11 ....56 C3
Trinity Rd CO11 ......56 C2
Trinity St IP3 ....37 B4
Troon Gdns 3 IP4....22 B1
Truswell Terr CO11...55 B2
Tuddenham Ave IP4 ..29 B3
Tuddenham La IP5 ...22 B2
Tuddenham Rd
 Ipswich IP4 ....66 C4
 Westerfield IP4 ......22 A3
Tudor Ct IP4 ....66 C3
Turino Ave IP12 ...... 4 B3
Turin St IP2 ....67 B1
Turnbull Cl IP5 ....33 B3
Turner Ave CO11......56 A4
Turner Gdns IP12.....14 B3
Turner Gr IP5 ....33 A4
Turner Rd
 Ipswich IP3 ....46 A4
 Stowmarket IP14...... 6 B3
Turn La IP12 ....15 B4
Turnpike Rd IP12.....13 A2
Turret La IP4 ....67 B1
Twelve Acre App
 IP5 ....32 B3
Twinnings The IP14.... 8 C3
Two Acres IP9........52 C4
Two House Cl IP13....53 B4
Tydemans Ct 1 IP14.. 7 A2
Tylers Gn IP11........58 C3
Tyler St IP2 ....67 B1

Tylers Way 1 IP14... 9 A3
Tyrone Cl IP1.........19 A2

U
Ullswater Ave 4
 IP11 ....61 A3
Ulster Ave IP1........19 A1
Undercliff Rd E IP11 ..64 C4
Undercliff Rd W
 IP11 ....64 A3
Underhill IP14........ 6 C1
Union Rd IP14........ 6 A3
Union St E IP11 ...... 7 A2
Union St W IP14...... 7 A2
Union St IP4 ....66 C3
Unitarian Meeting
 House* IP1.........67 B2
Unity Rd IP14........ 7 A1
Unity St IP3 ....37 B4
Upland Rd IP4........30 A2
Upper Barclay St
 IP4 ....67 B2
Upper Brook St IP4...66 B3
Upper Cavendish St
 IP3 ....30 A1
Upperfield Dr IP11 ...60 C2
Upper High St IP1....66 B4
Upper Moorfield Rd
 IP12 ....60 B2
Upper Orwell St IP4 ..67 C2
Upsons Way IP5......33 B4
Upton Cl IP4 ....29 B2
Uvedale Gdns IP6 ....11 B2
Uxbridge Cres IP3....38 C1

V
Valley Cl
 Brantham CO11 ......55 B4
 Ipswich IP1 ....20 C1
Valley Farm Rd IP12 ..13 A4
Valley Rd IP1.........20 B1
Valleyview Dr IP4.....39 C4
Valley Wlk IP11.......59 C1
Vandyck Rd 7 IP3....46 A4
Vaughan St IP1.......67 B1
Ventris Cl IP2 ....27 A1
Vere Gdns IP1........20 C2
Vermont Cres IP4 ....66 C4
Vermont Rd IP4 ......66 C4
Verneuil Ave IP14.... 9 A3
Vernon St IP2 ....67 B1
Vicarage Hill 7
 IP12 ....12 C1
Vicarage La
 Bramford IP8.........18 B1
 Wherstead IP9........44 B1
Vicarage Rd IP11.....63 A4
Victoria Cres CO11...56 B3
Victoria Rd
 Felixstowe IP11 ......63 C3
 Stowmarket IP14...... 7 B3
 Woodbridge IP12.....12 C1
Victoria St
 Felixstowe IP11 ......64 A4
 Ipswich IP1 ....28 A2
Victory Ct IP14 ...... 9 A4
Victory Rd IP4........30 A3
View Point Rd IP11 ..65 B3
Viking Cl IP12........ 4 B4
Viking Hts IP12....... 4 B4
Viking Rd IP14 .... 6 C1
Vincent Cl IP1........27 B4
Vincent Drift IP5 .....33 C3
Vinery Cl IP13 ....53 B3
Vine Wlk IP9 ....52 B3
Violet Cl IP2..........35 C4
Violet Hill Rd IP14 ...26 C3

W
Wades Gr IP5.........33 B3
Wadgate Rd IP11.....63 B4
Wadhurst Rd IP3 .....39 A3
Waggoners Ct IP12 ..12 B1
Wainwright Gdns IP6.. 2 A3

Wainwright Way
 IP5 ....33 A4
Waldegrave Cl CO11 ..56 A2
Waldegrave Rd
 CO11 ....56 B2
Waldegrave Way
 CO11 ....56 A2
WALDRINGFIELD
 HEATH IP12 .... 4 C2
Waldringfield Rd
 IP12 .... 4 C4
Walker Chase IP5 ....32 C2
Walker Cl IP4 ....30 C1
Walk The
 Ipswich IP1 ....66 B3
 Walton IP11 ....59 B2
Wallace Rd IP1........27 B4
Waller's Gr IP2 ....35 C4
Walls The CO11 ......57 A3
Walnut Cl IP11 ....61 A3
Walnuts La IP13 .....53 A2
Walnut Tree Cl 4
 IP8 ....18 A2
Walnut Tree Wlk
 IP14 .... 6 C2
Waltham Cl IP2.......36 A2
WALTON IP11 ....59 C2
Walton Ave IP11......62 C3
Walton Cl 1 IP14....16 B4
Wardley Cl IP2 ....35 A1
Ward Rd IP8 ....34 B2
Ward's View IP5 ......33 B4
Wareham Ave IP3 ....39 A3
Warren Chase IP5 ....33 B3
WARREN HEATH
 IP3 ....39 C1
Warren Heath Ave
 IP3 ....39 A2
Warren Heath Rd
 IP3 ....39 A2
Warren Hill Rd IP12...14 C4
Warren La 27 IP5..... 4 A3
Warrington Rd IP1 ...66 A4
Warwick Ave IP12 ....12 B2
Warwick Rd IP4 ......29 B2
Wash La IP14......... 6 A1
Waterford Rd IP1.....19 A2
Waterhead La IP12 ...13 C4
Waterloo Rd 4 IP1...28 A3
Waterworks St IP4 ...67 C2
Waveney Rd
 Felixstowe IP11 ......63 B3
 Ipswich IP1 ....27 B4
Wayside Cl IP14 ...... 9 A3
Weaver Cl IP1 ....27 A4
Weavers Cl
 2 Hadleigh IP7......51 A3
 Stowmarket IP14...... 8 C3
Weavers Way 2 IP6... 2 B3
Webb Rd IP14 .... 9 A3
Webb's Cl IP14 .... 8 C1
Webbs Ct IP5.........32 C3
Webb St 1 IP2 ....36 C3
Weir Pl IP10........... 5 B3
Welbeck Cl IP11......58 C3
Welhams Way CO11...55 B3
Wellesley Rd IP3 .....29 C1
Wellington Cl IP7.....51 A4
Wellington St 7
 IP1 ....28 A3
Wells Cl IP4 ....29 B3
Wentworth Cl IP7 ....51 C2
Wentworth Dr
 Felixstowe IP11 ......60 C2
 7 Ipswich IP8.......34 C2
Wesel Ave IP11.......63 A3
Wesley Way IP1 ......27 C4
WESTBOURNE IP1 ...27 C3
Westbourne High Sch
 IP1 ....19 B1
Westbourne Rd IP1...19 C1
Westbury Rd IP4 .....30 B4
West End Rd IP1......67 A2
WESTERFIELD IP6....21 B4

Westerfield Rd
Ipswich IP1 . . . . .66 C4
Westerfield IP6 . . . . . . .21 B4
Westerfield Sta IP6. . .21 B3
Western Ave IP11. . . . .61 A2
Western Cl IP4 . . . . . . .39 C4
Western's End CO11 . .55 B3
Westgate St Service Rd
IP1 . . . . .66 B3
Westgate St IP1 . . . . . .66 B3
Westholme Cl IP12 . . .15 A4
Westholme Rd IP1. . . .20 A1
Westland **26** IP5 . . . . . . .4 A3
West Lawn IP4 . . . . . . .30 C4
Westleton Way **17**
IP11 . . . . .59 A1
West Meadows IP1 . .18 C4
Westminster Cl IP4. . .30 B1
Westmorland Rd
IP11 . . . . .61 A3
West Rd IP3. . . . . .39 B1
West View IP14. . . . . . . .6 B2
Westwood Ave IP1. . .28 A4
Wetherby Cl IP1 . . . . .20 B3
Wexford Rd IP1 . . . . . .19 A2
Wharfedale Rd IP1 . . .20 A1
Whatfield Way IP14. . . .9 B3
Wheelwrights The
IP11 . . . . .58 C4
Wherry La IP4. . . . . . . .67 C2
Wherry Quay IP4 . . . . .67 C2
WHERSTEAD IP9 . . . . .44 B2
Wherstead Rd IP2. . . .67 B1
Whights Cnr IP8. . . . . .34 A1
Whinchat Cl IP2. . . . . .35 A3
Whinfield **13** IP5 . . . . . .4 A3
Whinfield Ct **16** IP5. . . .4 A3
Whinneys The IP5 . . .33 A4
Whinyard Way **8**
IP11 . . . . .61 A3
Whitby Rd IP4. . . . . . . .29 C4
White Elm St IP3 . . . . .37 B4

White Horse Cl **4**
IP11 . . . . .60 C2
White Horse Rd IP9 . .52 C3
Whitehouse Com Inf
Sch IP1 . . . . .19 B1
Whitehouse Ind Est
IP1 . . . . .18 C3
Whitehouse Jun Sch
IP1 . . . . .19 A3
White House Rd IP1 . .19 A2
White Lion Ct IP7. . . . .51 A2
Whites Field CO7 . . . .54 A3
Whitethorn Rd **2**
IP3 . . . . .39 C1
Whitland Cl IP2 . . . . . .44 A4
Whittle Rd IP2 . . . . . . .27 C2
WHITTON IP1 . . . . .19 C3
Whitton Church La
IP1 . . . . .19 C4
Whitton Com Prim Sch
IP1 . . . . .19 B3
Whitton La IP1 . . . . . . .19 A4
Whitton Leyer IP8 . . . .18 C2
Whitton Sports Ctr
IP1 . . . . .19 B4
Whitworth Cl IP2. . . . .35 A2
Wickhambrook Ct **2**
IP11 . . . . .62 C4
Wickham Com Prim
Sch IP13 . . . . .53 A3
WICKHAM MARKET
IP13 . . . . .53 A3
Wicklow Rd IP1 . . . . . .19 A2
Widgeon Cl IP2 . . . . . .35 C3
Wigmore Cl
Ipswich IP2 . . . . .35 C1
Stoke Park IP2 . . . . . . .36 A1
Wilberforce St IP1. . . .28 A2
Wilderness La IP12 . . .12 C2
Wilding Dr IP5 . . . . . . .33 A3
Wilding Rd IP8 . . . . . . .34 C1
Wilford Bridge Rd
IP12 . . . . .13 C3
Wilford Bridge Spur
IP12 . . . . .13 B3
Wilfred Hurry Cl IP8 . .18 A1

Wilkes Ct IP5. . . . . .33 B3
Wilkes Way IP14. . . . . . .6 C2
Wilkinson Dr IP5 . . . . .32 C2
Wilkinson Way IP12 . .12 C2
William Booth Way **11**
IP11 . . . . .59 A1
Williamsport Way
IP6 . . . . .11 C1
William St IP1. . . . . . . .66 B3
Willoughby Rd IP2 . . .67 A1
Willow Cl **6** IP6. . . . . . .16 B4
Willowcroft Rd IP1 . . .20 A2
Willow Tree Cl IP13 . . .53 A3
Willow Wlk IP6. . . . . . .11 A4
Wilmslow Ave IP12 . . .12 A1
Wilmslow Dr IP8 . . . . .34 C2
Wilson Rd
Hadleigh IP7. . . . . .51 B2
Ipswich IP8 . . . . .34 B1
Wimborne Ave IP3 . . .39 A4
Wimpole Cl IP5 . . . . . .31 C2
Wincanton Cl IP4. . . . .22 A1
Winchester Cl IP14 . . . .6 B2
Winchester Gdns **4**
IP6 . . . . .2 C3
Winchester Way IP2 . .43 C4
Windermere Cl IP3 . . .46 B4
Windermere Rd
IP6 Felixstowe IP11 . . . . .61 A3
Stowmarket IP14 . . . . . .6 C2
Winding Piece **5**
IP9 . . . . .52 B3
Windrush Rd IP5 . . . . .32 C4
Windsor Rd
Felixstowe IP11 . . . . . .63 B3
Ipswich IP1 . . . . .27 C3
Winfrith Rd IP3. . . . . . .39 A4
Wingfield St IP4 . . . . . .67 C2
Winston Ave IP4. . . . . .30 C4
Winston Cl **5** IP11 . . . .59 A1
Withipoll St IP4 . . . . . .66 C3
Wolsey Art Gall★
IP1 . . . . .66 C4
Wolsey Gdns IP11 . . . .64 A3
Wolsey Rd **4** IP14. . . . .6 C3
Wolsey St IP1 . . . . .67 B2

Wolton Rd IP5. . . . . . . .32 C3
WOODBRIDGE IP12. . .12 B2
Woodbridge Gall★
IP12 . . . . .12 B1
Woodbridge Mus The★
IP12 . . . . .12 C1
Woodbridge Prim Sch
15 IP12. . . . . .12 C1
Woodbridge Rd IP4. . .66 C3
Woodbridge Rd E
IP4 . . . . .30 C3
Woodbridge Sch
IP12 . . . . .12 B1
Woodbridge Sta 15 C4
Woodcock Rd IP2 . . . .35 B2
Woodcote IP14. . . . . . . .6 B2
Woodfield Dr IP14. . . . .7 B1
Woodfield La IP14 . . . . .9 A4
Woodhouse La IP10 . .40 C2
Woodhouse Sq IP4 . . .67 C2
Woodlands IP7. . . . . . .50 B4
Woodlands Way IP8 . .18 C4
Woodlark Cl IP2. . . . . .35 B1
Woodlark Dr **4** IP14. . .7 C3
Woodley Com Sch
IP14 . . . . .6 B3
Woodpecker Rd IP2 . .35 A3
Woodrush Rd IP3. . . . .39 B2
Woodside IP5 . . . . .4 B3
Wood Side IP14 . . . . . . .6 B1
Woods La IP12 . . . . . . .13 A3
Woodspring Cl **12**
IP2 . . . . .36 A2
Woodstone Ave IP1. . .20 C1
Woodthorpe Cl IP7 . . .51 C2
Woodthorpe Rd IP7 . .51 B2
Woodville Rd IP4. . . . .29 C1
Woodward Cl IP2. . . . .27 A1
Woollards Cl IP1 . . . . .28 A2
Woolmers Cl IP14 . . . . .9 A4
Woolner Cl
7 Claydon IP6. . . . . . . .2 B3
5 Hadleigh IP7. . . . . . .51 B3
Woolnough Rd IP12 . .12 B2
Woolnoughs The **2**
IP5 . . . . .33 A3

Woolverstone Cl
IP2 . . . . .35 A1
Worcester Rd IP3 . . . . .46 A4
Wordsworth Cres
IP1 . . . . .19 B3
Wordsworth Rd **2**
IP14 . . . . .6 B4
Workshop La IP10 . . . .48 C1
Wren Ave IP2 . . . . .35 A3
Wrens Pk **2** IP11. . . . . .61 A3
Wright Cl IP14 . . . . .9 A3
Wright La IP5 . . . . .33 A4
Wright Rd IP3. . . . . . . .38 C2
Wroxham Rd IP3 . . . . .37 C3
Wye Rd IP3 . . . . .38 A2
Wykes Bishop St
IP3 . . . . .37 B4
Wynterton Cl IP3. . . . .38 B1
Wynton Rise IP14. . . . . .9 B4
Wyseman Pl CO11 . . . .55 A2
Wyvern Rd IP3 . . . . . . .38 C1

Y

Yale Bsns Pk IP3 . . . . .47 C4
Yarmouth Rd
Ipswich IP1 . . . . .28 A2
Woodbridge IP12 . . . . .13 B4
Yeoman Cres IP7 . . . . .51 B2
Yeoman Rd IP11. . . . . .63 A3
Yeoman Way IP7 . . . . .51 B2
Yew Ct IP2 . . . . .36 A3
Yewtree Gr IP5 . . . . . . .31 C3
Yewtree Rise IP8 . . . . .34 A3
Yew Tree Rise IP13. . . .53 B4
York Cres
12 Claydon IP6. . . . . . .2 C3
Claydon IP6 . . . . .16 B4
York Rd
Felixstowe IP11 . . . . . .64 A4
Foxhall IP5 . . . . .4 A2
Ipswich IP3 . . . . .38 A4
York St **7** CO11. . . . . . .56 C3

List of numbered locations

In some busy areas of the maps it is not always possible to show the name of every place.

Where not all names will fit, some smaller places are shown by a number. If you wish to find out the name associated with a number, use this listing.

The places in this list are also listed normally in the Index.

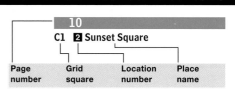

2

B3 1 Mason Ct
2 Weavers Way
3 Fletcher Cl
4 Coopers Way
5 Millers Ct
6 Foresters Wlk
7 Woolner Cl
8 St Peter's Cl
9 Mill La
10 Plummers Dell
11 Mulberry Gdns
13 Laurel Dr
C3 1 Glebe Way
2 Old Rectory Cl
3 Phillipps Rd
4 Winchester Gdns
5 Ely Rd
6 Eddowes Rd
7 Bacon Rd
8 Lincoln Gdns
9 Exeter Rd
10 Lancaster Way
11 Jubilee Cl
12 York Cres
14 Hereford Dr

3

B4 1 Church Meadows
2 Old Hall Cl
3 Gascoigne Dr
4 Freeman Ave

4

A2 1 Lingside
2 Harvesters Way
3 Forest La
5 Digby Cl
6 Mayfields
7 Mayfield La
8 Lancaster Dr
A3 1 Parkers Pl
2 Peel Yd
3 Paddocks The
4 Squires La
5 Park Cl
6 Demesne Gdns
7 Anson Rd
8 Felixstowe Rd
9 Martinsyde
10 Beardmore Pk
11 Manor Rd
12 Grove The
13 Whinfield
14 Carlford Cl
15 Farriers Cl
16 Whinfield Ct
17 Broomfield
18 Broomfield Mews
19 Saddlers Pl
20 Chase The
21 Hunters Ride
22 Burgess Pl
23 Lark Rise
24 Drift The
25 Bader Ct
26 Westland
27 Warren La
28 Avocet La
29 Swan Cl
30 Coopers Rd
31 Martlesham Heath Control Twr Mus
A4 1 Nunn Cl
2 Alban Sq
3 Green La
4 Buckingham Cl
5 Chandos Dr
6 Ravens Way
7 Shaw Valley Rd
8 Chandos Ct
9 Carol Ave
10 Crown Cl

5

B1 2 High Hall Cl
3 Red House Cl
4 Capel Cl
5 Sandy Cl
6 Crowswell Ct
7 Craig Cl
8 Meadow Cl
9 Jasmine Cl
10 Ash Gd Cl
11 Jubilee Cl
12 Heath Ct
13 Blue Barn Cl
14 St Martins Gn
15 Brick Kiln Cl

6

B4 1 Walton Cl
2 Wordsworth Rd
3 Ruskin Cl
4 Eliot Way
C3 1 Delius Cl
2 Margaret Rd
3 Kingsmead Cl
4 Wolsey Rd

7

A2 1 Tydemans Ct
2 Thurlow Ct
3 Bury St
4 Milton Rd N
5 Marriott's Wlk
B1 1 Stricklands Rd
2 Chestnut Gr
3 Hollingsworth Rd
4 Lockington Cl
C3 1 Sandpiper Rd
2 Firecrest Dr
4 Woodlark Dr

9

A3 1 Tylers Way
2 Rattlesden Cl
3 Thomas Young Cl
4 Thatchers Wlk
5 Hugh Ager Cl
B3 1 School Meadow
2 Boxford Cl
3 Hintlesham Cl
4 Lavenham Way
5 Hoxne Cl
6 Milden Cl
7 Shimpling Cl
8 Naughton Gdns

11

A3 1 Orchard Gate
2 Constitution Hill
3 King William St
4 Pightle The
5 Theobald Cl

12

C1 1 Lockwood Cl
2 Angel La
3 Beaconsfield Rd
4 St John's Hill
5 St John's Terr
6 Gladstone Rd
7 Vicarage Hill
8 Little St John's St
9 New St
10 Thoroughfare The
11 Jacob Way
12 Stone Pl
13 Carlow Mews
14 Carmelite Pl
15 Woodbridge Prim Sch

13

A2 1 Jenners Cl
2 Pytches Cl
3 Aspen Cl
4 Melton Meadow Rd
5 Grove The

14

C4 1 Gonville Cl
2 Downing Cl
3 St Edmunds Cl
4 Portland Cres
5 Queens Ave
6 Fitzwilliam Cl
7 Churchill Cl
8 Anderson's Way

15

B4 1 Bakers La

16

B4 1 St Peter's Ave
2 Quoits Field
3 Morgan Ct
4 Poplar Cl
5 Laurel Way
6 Willow Cl
7 Limekiln Cl
8 Old Paper Mill La
9 Alasdair Pl

18

A2 1 Acton Gdns
2 Lacon Rd
3 Bushman Gdns
4 Walnut Tree Cl
5 Bullen La
6 Orchard Rd

19

A1 1 Opal Ave
2 Agate Cl
C1 1 Highfield App
2 Mornington Ave

20

A3 1 Limecroft Cl
2 Maycroft Cl
3 Sandown Cl
4 Kempton Cl
5 Hollycroft Cl
6 Hazlitt Rd
7 Burke Rd
8 Kingsley Cl
9 Shirley Cl
10 Palmcroft Cl

21

A1 1 Borrowdale Ave
2 Bildeston Gdns
3 Kettlebaston Way
4 Brettenham Cres
5 Picton Ave

22

A1 1 Cranborne Chase
2 Fairlight Cl
3 Alma Cl
4 Orkney Rd
5 Shetland Cl
B1 1 Gretna Gdns
2 Forfar Cl
3 Troon Gdns
C1 1 Aberfoyle Cl
2 Dumfries Rd
3 Dumbarton Rd

28

A3 1 Lambeth Cl
2 Thetford Rd
3 Blenheim Rd
4 Waterloo Rd
5 Providence La
6 Bramford La
7 Wellington St
8 Stopford Ct
9 Rendlesham Rd

31

C1 1 Seckford Cl
2 Parnham Pl
3 Mannington Cl
4 Fordham Pl
5 Houghton Pl
6 Hintesham Cl
7 Holkham Cl
8 Melford Cl

32

C3 1 Cranwell Gr
2 Crawford La
3 Dawson Drift
4 Sherwood Fields
5 Rayment Drift
6 Butler Smith Gdns
7 Bartrum La
8 Llewellyn Drift

33

A3 1 Fairbairn Ave
2 Woolnoughs The
3 Godbold Cl
4 Banyard Cl
5 Knights La
6 Sheppards Way
7 Shelbourne Cl
8 Dickinson Terr
9 Smiths Pl

34

C2 1 Bramblewood
2 Broad Meadow
3 Laburnum Cl
4 Innes End
5 Peacock Cl
6 Halford Ct
7 Wentworth Dr
8 Magpie Cl
9 Acorn Cl
10 Milnrow
11 Chestnuts The
12 Merrion Cl
13 Matlock Cl
14 Mottram Cl

35

A1 4 Skipper Rd

36

A2 1 Crowland Cl
2 Kirkham Cl
3 Hexham Cl
4 Buckfast Cl
5 Tintern Cl
6 Byland Cl
7 Evesham Cl
8 Oaksmere Gdns
9 Prince of Wales Dr
10 Sawston Cl
11 Hengrave Cl
12 Woodspring Cl
13 Headingham Cl
14 Burghley Cl
C3 1 Webb St
2 Peppercorn Way
3 Gresley Gdns
4 Bromley Cl
5 Johnson Cl
6 Rapier St

38

B3 **1** Locarno Rd
2 St Leonards Rd
3 Shackleton Sq
4 Badshah Ave
5 Hillside Cres
6 Collingwood Ave
7 St David's Rd

39

C1 **1** Blackthorn Cl
2 Whitethorn Rd
3 Porter Rd
4 Routh Ave
5 Penny La
6 Foxburrow Rd

43

B4 **1** Swallowtail Cl
2 Admiral Rd
3 Skipper Cl
5 Tortoiseshell Cl
6 Brookview
7 Grayling Rd
8 Fritillary Cl
9 Forester Cl
10 Holly Blue Cl
11 Cinnabar Cl
12 Mayfly Cl
13 Lacewing Cl
14 Copper Gr
15 Clearwing Cl
16 Boatman Cl

46

A4 **1** Morland Rd
2 Reynolds Ave

3 Chesapeake Rd
4 Shannon Rd
5 Nightingale Sq
6 Lowry Gdns
7 Vandyck Rd
8 Leighton Sq
9 Fishbane Cl
B4 **1** Queensberry Rd
2 Nash Gdns
3 Swatchway Cl
C3 **2** Cranberry Sq
3 Mulberry Rd
4 Loganberry Rd
5 Mansbrook Bvd
C4 **1** Firefly Way
2 Hunter Rd
3 Lysander Dr
4 Darter Cl
5 Damselfly Rd
7 Pashford Pl
7 Lackford Pl
8 Chaser Cl

47

A4 **1** Alnesbourn Cres
2 Titchwell Dr
3 Havergate Rd

51

A2 **1** Church St
2 Silk Mill Cl
3 Toppesfield Cl
4 Tayler Cl
5 Gaell Cres
A3 **1** Threadneedle St
2 Weavers Cl
3 Inkerman Terr
4 Inkerman Cl
5 Spooners La

6 Queen St
B3 **1** Drapers Cl
2 Fullers Cl
3 Barnes Cl
4 Muriel Cl
5 Woolner Cl
6 Rousies Cl
7 Bourchier Cl
8 Alabaster Cl

52

B3 **1** School Cl
2 Crotchets Cl
3 Penny Meadow
4 Peter's Gr
5 Winding Piece
6 Toll Gate Rd
7 Chalkners Cl
8 Stockmers End
9 Smithers Cl

56

C3 **1** Quay St
2 Quay Ctyd
3 Brooks Malting
4 Alma Sq
5 Central Maltings The
6 St Michaels Ct
7 York St
8 Falklands Dr
9 Regent St
10 Parsons Yd
11 Railway Terr
12 Trinity Farm Ct
13 Bendalls Ct
14 Gasfield
15 Old Library The
16 Compass Ct

59

A1 **1** Kiln Field
2 Childers Field
3 Feathers Field
4 Reedland Way
5 Winston Cl
6 Otley Ct
7 Bredfield Cl
8 Brackley Cl
9 Larkhill Way
10 Reynolds Ct
11 William Booth Way
12 Generals Mews
13 Aldringham Mews
14 Sudbourne Rd
15 Rendlesham Rd
16 Mickfield Mews
17 Westleton Way
18 Mellis Ct
19 Darsham Cl
B1 **1** Hall Field
2 Garden Field
3 Crossgate Field
4 Beacon Field
5 Broom Field
6 Hamilton St
7 James Boden Cl

60

C2 **1** Gleneagles Cl
2 Prestwick Ave
3 Ferndown Rd
4 White Horse Cl

61

A2 **1** Tarn Hows Cl
2 Ennerdale Cl
3 Langdale Cl

4 Cumberland Cl
5 Grasmere Ave
6 Bishops Cl
7 Friars Cl
8 Deacon Ct
9 Barons Cl
10 Knights Cl
11 Saxon Cl
A3 **1** Rushmeadow Way
2 Wrens Pk
3 Whinyard Way
4 Ullswater Ave
5 Stuart Cl
6 Windermere Rd

62

C3 **1** Nayland Rd
2 Ickworth Ct
C4 **1** Lidgate Ct
2 Wickhambrook Ct
3 Sudbury Rd
4 Euston Ct
5 Kentford Rd
6 Thurston Ct
7 Boxford Ct

65

B4 **1** Darrell Rd
2 Sunderland Rd
3 Schneider Rd